Sparks Will Fly

SUNY series in Contemporary Continental Philosophy
Dennis J. Schmidt, editor

Sparks Will Fly

Benjamin and Heidegger

Edited by
Andrew Benjamin
and
Dimitris Vardoulakis

Published by State University of New York Press, Albany

© 2015 State University of New York

All rights reserved

Printed in the United States of America

No part of this book may be used or reproduced in any manner whatsoever without written permission. No part of this book may be stored in a retrieval system or transmitted in any form or by any means including electronic, electrostatic, magnetic tape, mechanical, photocopying, recording, or otherwise without the prior permission in writing of the publisher.

For information, contact State University of New York Press, Albany, NY
www.sunypress.edu

Production, Jenn Bennett
Marketing, Kate Seburyamo

Library of Congress Cataloging-in-Publication Data

Sparks will fly : Benjamin and Heidegger / edited by Andrew Benjamin and Dimitris Vardoulakis.
    pages cm. — (SUNY series in contemporary continental philosophy)
   Includes bibliographical references and index.
   ISBN 978-1-4384-5505-1 (hardcover : alk. paper) — EISBN 978-1-4384-5506-8 (ebook)
   ISBN 978-1-4384-5504-4 (paperback : alk. paper)
   1. Benjamin, Walter, 1892–1940. 2. Heidegger, Martin, 1889–1976. I. Benjamin, Andrew E. II. Vardoulakis, Dimitris.
   B3209.B584S635 2015
   193—dc23
                        2014012475

10 9 8 7 6 5 4 3 2 1

CONTENTS

Abbreviations	vii
Introduction: "Sparks Will Fly" *Andrew Benjamin and Dimitris Vardoulakis*	xi

Part I. Knowledge

ONE	Entanglement—Of Benjamin with Heidegger *Peter Fenves*	3
TWO	Critique and the Thing: Benjamin and Heidegger *Gerhard Richter*	27

Part II. Experience

THREE	*Stimmung*: Heidegger and Benjamin *Ilit Ferber*	67
FOUR	Commodity Fetishism and the Gaze *A. Kiarina Kordela*	95

Part III. Time

FIVE	Monad and Time: Reading Leibniz with Heidegger and Benjamin *Paula Schwebel*	123

SIX Time and Task: Benjamin and Heidegger Showing
the Present
Andrew Benjamin   145

Part IV. Hölderlin

SEVEN Who Was Friedrich Hölderlin? Walter Benjamin,
Martin Heidegger, and the Poet
Antonia Egel   177

EIGHT Sobriety, Intoxication, Hyperbology: Benjamin and
Heidegger Reading Hölderlin
Joanna Hodge   189

Part V. Politics

NINE Beyond Revolution: Benjamin and Heidegger on Violence
and Power
Krzysztof Ziarek   219

TEN A Matter of Immediacy: The Political Ontology of the
Artwork in Benjamin and Heidegger
Dimitris Vardoulakis   237

ELEVEN Politics of the Useless: The Work of Art in Benjamin
and Heidegger
David Ferris   259

Biographical Notes   283

Index   287

ABBREVIATIONS

Walter Benjamin:

AP   *The Arcades Project*, trans. Howard Eiland and Kevin McLaughlin (Cambridge, MA: Belknap, 1999). All references to the Convolutes of *The Arcades Project* are given parenthetically according Convolute number without further specification.
BA   *Briefwechsel 1938-1940: Theodor W. Adorno, Walter Benjamin*, ed. Gershom Scholem (Frankfurt am Main: Suhrkamp, 1994).
BS   *Briefwechsel 1933-1940: Walter Benjamin, Gerschom Scholem*, ed. Gershom Scholem (Frankfurt am Main: Suhrkamp, 1985).
C   *The Correspondence of Walter Benjamin 1910-1940*, ed. Gershom Scholem and Theodor W. Adorno, trans. Manfred R. Jakobson and Evelyn M. Jakobson (Chicago: University of Chicago Press, 1994).
CA   Theodor W. Adorno and Walter Benjamin, *The Complete Correspondence 1920-1940*, ed. Henri Lonitz, trans. Nicholas Walker (Cambridge, MA: Harvard University Press, 1999).
CS   *The Correspondence of Walter Benjamin and Gershom Scholem*, ed. Gershom Scholem, trans. Gary Smith and André Lefevere (Cambridge, MA: Harvard University Press, 1992).
GB   *Gesammelte Briefe*, ed. Christoph Gödde and Henri Lonitz (Frankfurt am Main: Suhrkamp, 1995-2000).
GS   *Gesammelte Schriften*, eds. Rolf Tiedemann and Hermann Schweppenhäuser (Frankfurt am Main: Suhrkamp, 1974 ff.).
OT   *The Origin of the German Tragic Drama*, trans. John Osborne (London: Verso, 1998).

SW   *Selected Writings*, ed. Michael W. Jennings (Cambridge, MA: Belknap, 1997–2003).

Martin Heidegger:

BPP   *The Basic Problems of Phenomenology*, trans. Albert Hofstadter (Bloomington: Indiana University Press, 1982).
BQP   *Basic Questions of Philosophy, Selected "Problems" of "Logic,"* trans. R. Rojcewicz and A. Schuwer (Bloomington: Indiana University Press, 1994).
BT   *Being and Time*, trans. John Macquarrie and Edward Robinson (New York: Harper, 2008).
BW   *Basic Writings*, ed. David Farrell Krell (New York: Routledge, 1993).
CP   *Contributions to Philosophy (From Enowning)*, trans. Parvis Emad and Kenneth Maly (Bloomington and Indianapolis: Indiana University Press, 1999).
FCM   *Fundamental Concepts of Metaphysics: World, Finitude, Solitude*, trans. W. McNeill and N. Walker (Bloomington: Indiana University Press, 1995).
GA   *Gesamtausgabe* (Frankfurt am Main: Vittorio Klosterman, 1974 ff.). All German references to this edition.
HH   *Hölderlin's Hymn "The Isther,"* trans. William McNeil and Julia Davis (Bloomington: Indiana University Press, 1996).
HP   *Elucidations of Hölderlin's Poetry*, trans. Keith Höller (Amherst, NY: Humanity Books, 2000).
IM   *Introduction to Metaphysics*, ed. and trans. Gregory Fried and Richard Polt (New Haven, CT: Yale University Press, 2000).
M   *Mindfulness*, trans. Parvis Emad and Thomas Kalary (London and New York: Continuum, 2006).
ML   *The Metaphysical Foundations of Logic*, trans. Michael Heim (Bloomington: Indiana University Press, 1984).
N   *Nietzsche*, vol. 4, *Nihilism*, trans. Frank A. Capuzzi (San Francisco: HarperCollins, 1991).
P   *Pathmarks*, ed. William McNeill (Cambridge: Cambridge University Press, 1998).
PLT   *Poetry, Language, Thought*, trans. Albert Hofstadter (New York: HarperCollins, 1971).
QTC   *The Question Concerning Technology and Other Essays* (New York: Harper & Row, 1977).

TB	*On Time and Being*, trans. Joan Stambaugh (New York: Harper & Row, 1972).
WT	*What Is a Thing?*, trans. W.B. Barton Jr. and Vera Deutsch (Chicago: Regnery, 1968).
ZS	*Zollikon Seminars: Protocols—Conversations—Letters*, ed. Medard Boss, trans. F. Mayr and R. Askay (Evanston, IL: Northwestern University Press, 2001).

INTRODUCTION

"Sparks Will Fly"

*Andrew Benjamin and
Dimitris Vardoulakis*

Walter Benjamin and Martin Heidegger were almost contemporaries, born in the last decade of the nineteenth century. But their life trajectories were very different. Benjamin failed in his attempt to obtain a position at a university and subsequently concentrated on essay writing, initially in the form of reviews. When that became impossible in 1933 and Benjamin was forced to exile in Paris, he started writing for academic journals published outside Germany. Heidegger became an academic star in Germany with the publication of *Being and Time* (1927). The following year, he succeeded his former teacher, Edmund Husserl, as professor at Freiburg University and five years later—at the same time that Benjamin was ostracized because of his Jewish background—Heidegger was joining the Nazi Party in order to be elected Rector. The troubled years of exile ended in Benjamin's death under unclear circumstances at the Spanish borders in 1940. Heidegger was "denazified" after World War II and allowed to return to teaching. Given their life histories, then, Benjamin, the cosmopolitan Jew, and Heidegger, who preferred his peasant hut in remote Todtnauberg to city life, seem hardly to have anything in common.

And yet, the two figures have gradually been brought closer together since the 1960s. The first move was the rediscovery of the work of Benjamin when his old friend, Theodor Adorno, started republishing his work. But the decisive move that brought Heidegger and Benjamin into contact was Hannah Arendt's introduction to *Illuminations*. Arendt, who knew both men, suggested that Benjamin's concept of truth is similar to Heidegger's concept of *aletheia*. Arendt also pointed out that they both shared a concern with the destruction of tradition, and concluded that "without realizing it," Benjamin had a lot in common with Heidegger.[1] According to Arendt, then, the two contemporary thinkers, who were quite revolutionary on their own—Benjamin as a reformer of a "crude" Marxist tradition and Heidegger as precipitating in the renewal of phenomenology and hermeneutics—and who seemed to be unaware of each others' work, were nevertheless working on philosophical platforms that can be aligned.

Arendt's interpretation is, however, problematized if we turn to Benjamin's correspondence. In a letter to Gershom Scholem, dated January 20, 1930, Benjamin intimates that he has been reading Heidegger and that when the confrontation of the thinking of the two ultimately takes places "sparks will fly." It appears then that Benjamin was aware of Heidegger's work, and moreover he was agonistically disposed toward it.

The premise of this book is that both Hannah Arendt's verdict and Walter Benjamin's remark in his letter to Scholem contain an element of truth. In other words, there are indeed certain affinities between Benjamin and Heidegger. These affinities, however, not only do not obliterate their differences, but rather they highlight the points where their thought diverges. The "wager" of all the papers contained in this book is to affirm both the continuities and the discontinuities in the thought of the two thinkers.

There are a number of sites that provide fertile ground for such a confrontation to take place. Arendt was correct to recognize that the most obvious similarity between Heidegger and Benjamin was their distancing from a certain philosophical tradition that relied on a metaphysics of presence and an epistemology of representation. The first crucial site is the theory of knowledge. Peter Fenves approaches this site through Heinrich Rickert, the neo-Kantian philosopher who was the teacher of both Benjamin and Heidegger; and Gerhard Richter shows what is at stake when the theory of knowledge privileges either critique or an investigation of the various modalities of the cognition of the thing. The theory of knowledge leads back to a reconceptualization of the subject through Benjamin and Heidegger's attempt to rethink the concept of experience. Ilit Ferber examines how emotions figure differently in the two thinkers; and Kiarina Kordela uses the Lacanian concept of the gaze to adumbrate a comparison between their distinct conceptualizations of experience.

Benjamin never wrote in a published or finished work on Heidegger. But we know from his notes that were eventually collected under the title *The Arcades Project* that he was particularly concerned to engage with Heidegger's notion of temporality. For instance, in the crucial *Konvolut N*, titled "On the Theory of Knowledge, Theory of Progress," Benjamin explicitly states that "Heidegger seeks in vain to rescue history for phenomenology abstractly through 'historicity'" (*N*3,1). Paula Schwebel shows how Benjamin and Heidegger's theories of time diverge by going to one of the sources of their respective theories, the philosophy of Leibniz; and, Andrew Benjamin argues that it is in their respective conceptions of the present that the real difference on the philosophies of time can be discerned.

Another major site of confrontation is Benjamin and Heidegger's appropriation of the Romantic heritage. Benjamin was interested in the Romantics from early on, writing his doctoral dissertation on the concept of criticism in Jena Romanticism. Heidegger was also indebted to Romanticism as we know from a series of lecture courses he offered, such as the lectures on Schelling. But there is perhaps no better place to stage the confrontation on this issue than the figure of Hölderlin. Benjamin wrote a significant essay on the Romantic poet in which his whole reception of Romanticism can be gleaned. Heidegger on his part turned to Hölderlin at a difficult time, when he resigned his Rectorship and as the clouds of war were gathering around Europe. Antonia Egel and Joanna Hodge stage the confrontation between Benjamin and Heidegger through Hölderlin, providing not only incisive readings of their essays on Hölderlin, but also highlighting the philosophical implications of these divergent readings.

There is, perhaps, no more contentious site of comparison between Heidegger and Benjamin than the question of the political commitments in their work. This is not simply because one initially embraced National Socialism while the other, by virtue of his Jewishness, was excluded from it. In addition, Heidegger is usually portrayed as a conservative thinker who can, some have argued, offer valuable insights to a politically committed position, even promote a renewal of Marxism. Conversely, Benjamin wanted to make his friends at the Frankfurt School and Bertolt Brecht believe that he was a Marxist, but did not manage to convince either that he was Marxist enough. Krzysztof Ziarek approaches this complex set up by showing that when it comes to the concept of revolution, the thoughts of Heidegger and Benjamin have certain important similarities. David Ferris and Dimitris Vardoulakis both note that Heidegger and Benjamin offered significant insights into their political commitments when they wrote about art. Thus, Ferris shows how the "uselessness" of art is in fact determinative of the politics of both Benjamin and Heidegger; and, Vardoulakis shows how the figure of Carl Schmitt can provide a cipher for their divergent politics.

The different contributions to this volume do not seek to side with one or the other thinker. Rather, they seek to realize Benjamin's prediction to Scholem—that the confrontation of their thought will make "sparks fly." Sparks, unlike a fire, do not burn out into cinders. Rather, sparks can continue to be generated whenever the two thinkers are set agonistically against each other. Thus, this book seeks to indicate that the sparks can keep on flying in productive and illuminating ways by exploring the convergences and divergences of Benjamin and Heidegger's thinking.

Notes

The editors would like to thank Liesel Senn for her assistance in the final stages of the preparation of the manuscript.

1. Hannah Arendt, "Introduction: Walter Benjamin 1892–1940" in Walter Benjamin, *Illuminations*, ed. Hannah Arendt, trans. Harry Zohn (New York: Schocken, 1969), 46.

PART ONE

Knowledge

ONE

ENTANGLEMENT—
OF BENJAMIN WITH HEIDEGGER

Peter Fenves

The Thesis

This chapter seeks to establish a single thesis: Heidegger and Benjamin became entangled with each other in the summer of 1913, when they both attended the lectures and seminars of the neo-Kantian philosopher, Heinrich Rickert, who framed his newly introduced system of value philosophy around two cardinal concepts: "bare life" (*bloßes Leben*), which is indifferent to values, and "completed life" (*vollendetes Leben*), in which all the regions of value are fulfilled. Because Benjamin and Heidegger, each in his own way, reject the notion of "completed life," there can be only bare life, and the sphere in which the term *completion* is applicable must be sought elsewhere—where life, as it were, is on the hither side of all values.

The Experiment

The concept of entanglement is different from that of influence. The latter derives from images of fluent and "local" communicability that ancient astrology, Aristotelian physics, and classical mechanics all share in common; by contrast, the former is one of the basic concepts of quantum theory, perhaps even its defining concept. In brief terms, the difference between classical and quantum theory is that the former presupposes continuous motion in space and time, whereas the latter recognizes only discrete quanta of mass-energy in space-time. Just as the use of the astrological-Aristotelian and classical-mechanical concepts of influence for the purpose of representing the relation among utterances (from poems to advertisements) emphasizes certain of its characteristics while suppressing others, so, in this study, only a few characteristics of the quantum-mechanical concept of entanglement are applied to the relation between two thinkers, namely Heidegger and Benjamin. This is not to say that entanglement here is "only a metaphor," above all because the quantum-mechanical concept, first articulated in the correspondence between Einstein and Erwin Schrödinger, is itself the result of a transference of usage from the original fields of its application to a completely new one, in which some characteristics of the older usage are emphasized, others suppressed. This study is experimental: it aims to discover in what way, and how far, the concept of entanglement can supplement and even under certain conditions replace that of influence.[1]

Image and Method

The image Benjamin uses to describe the relation between his mode of envisaging history and Heidegger's is drawn from physics. Writing to Gershom Scholem in January 1930, Benjamin describes the potential encounter as a "scintillement de l'entre-choc" (*GB*, 503). A preliminary rationale for the use of the term *entanglement* emerges out of this image. Just as physics is the field of study from which Benjamin presents his potential interaction with Heidegger, so it can be the source of the term from which the analysis of their relation can proceed. And at no time does Benjamin offer a competing image of their relation. In his view, circa 1930, their concepts of history are similar to charged particles, which explode on contact with each other. In accordance with this image, the aim of this chapter is to discover the source and course of their charge. It begins with the place and time where they may have actually encountered each other, if only obliquely, and proceeds to describe the complementary character of their initial differences. The body of the chapter then consists in a delineation of five discrete moments in which the lines of their thought are correlated despite their distance and in the absence of any common "influence" that could be responsible for these correlations.

To maintain the experimental character of this method, the correlations are not explored in detail but, rather, described so as to emphasize the proximity of their lines of thought and the divergence of their sense and direction.

Complementary Differences

Two of the basic characteristics of the quantum-mechanical concept of entanglement are emphasized here. For entanglement to take place, two "bodies" must interact with each other at a certain moment and form a single "system," but—this is the second characteristic—the condition with which they initially interact cannot be so influential that it determines the subsequent correlations. The correlations remain surprising, as though the two bodies, separate though they may be, somehow kept in contact with each other in the absence of any viable means or medium of communication. In the case of Heidegger and Benjamin, the moment can be broadly described in terms of a place and a time: Freiburg during the summer of 1913. In a letter Heidegger wrote to Heinrich Rickert soon after the publication of *Sein und Zeit* he describes this summer as a "Glanzzeit" (bright and shining time).[2] In letters of the period Benjamin says something similar: "The [summer] semester [of 1913] thus ends beautifully. I know of no other like it—I will under no condition lose sight of this time, which will be fruitful in the years to come" (*GB* 1: 160). During this "bright and shining time" Heidegger and Benjamin begin to form a single system because of the very differences that distinguish them. Among these differences, the following are particularly important: one is Catholic, the other Jewish; one is from an obscure town in Baden, the other from a wealthy district of Berlin; one remains close to his hometown during his academic studies, except when he willingly serves in the German military, whereas the other matriculates at the universities of Berlin, Freiburg, and Munich, before crossing the border to Bern, where he waits out the War; one completes his doctorate in July of 1913, while the other is only at the beginning of academic studies. Finally, whereas Heidegger in 1913 is beginning to distance himself from a staunchly antimodern version of Catholicism that had hitherto determined his relation to academic life, Benjamin is solidifying his association with the radical wing of the Freien Studentenschaft led by Gustav Wyneken, whom he describes as his "first teacher" (*GB* 1: 108). These differences can be called *complementary* because they span the extremes of the academic environment in which the two found themselves. It is even possible to identify a figure in which the complementary character of their differences coalesces: Anton Müller, co-editor of the *Freiburger Bote*, which was the Catholic newspaper for the Breisgrau area and published articles by Heidegger's mentors at the university. Coming from Heidegger's "cultural milieu," Müller becomes, for Benjamin, the "third" who solidified his friendship with the poet Friedrich Heinle, whom he first met at a bar in Freiburg and whose suicide a year after their joint departure from Freiburg produced an irrevocable break in Benjamin's life, comparable to Heidegger's break with Catholicism.

And the precise moment in which Heidegger and Benjamin became entangled can be identified with the two places where they may actually have interacted with each other: the lecture hall and seminar room where Heinrich Rickert taught in the newly constructed philosophy building during the summer semester of 1913. The complementary character of the differences between Heidegger and Benjamin extends to their relation to Rickert: Heidegger found in the foremost representative of southwest neo-Kantianism a guide to the "spiritual" power of modern philosophy, which he had dismissed as "ungodly," and Benjamin probably decided to study in far-off Freiburg primarily because of Rickert, who was more closely associated with the "free student-body" movement than any other prominent professor of philosophy.[3] Rickert, in short, showed Heidegger a possible way out of his Aristotelian-scholastic "orientation," while promising Benjamin a plausible way into the philosophical foundation of the "spiritual" movement with which he identified himself. In neither case, however, did Rickert's thought indelibly impress itself upon their subsequent work. Even among representatives of neo-Kantianism—to say nothing of phenomenology, which both of them intensely studied in subsequent years—Rickert was of secondary importance. The work of Emil Lask played a far more decisive role in the path that led Heidegger to *Sein und Zeit*, and much of Benjamin's early work can be understood as a "critical altercation" with the Marburg School in general and Hermann Cohen in particular.[4] Rickert did not so much influence their subsequent lines of thought as crystallize the "system," in which his erstwhile students became entangled.

Lectures Toward a New System

Heidegger and Benjamin became entangled elements of a single "system" on encountering the outlines of Rickert's "system of philosophy," which he first revealed in the summer of 1913. In brief terms, Rickert's system has the following characteristics: it is "value philosophy," which is not concerned with the nature of the subject or the object but with the articulation of the sphere in which meaning resides, a sphere divided into separate "regions of value"; it is "open," which means that the system not only does not foreclose future changes in "cultural life" but, on the contrary, presupposes its endless development; and its cardinal concept is that of "perfection," "consummation," or "completion" (*Vollendung*), which Rickert generally hyphenates so as to emphasize the equal significance of its two elements, "fullness" and "ending." To delineate the regions of values, he distinguishes social values from asocial ones and then identifies three independent levels of "com-pletion" (*Voll-Endung*): "in-finite totality," "com-pleted particularity," and "com-pleted totality." Multiplying two by three, Rickert thus arrives at six possible "regions of value." Whereas the first level of "com-pletion" defines the spheres of both moral action and scientific knowledge, philosophy straddles the latter two, insofar as every philosophical system is doubtless particular, while nevertheless claiming and perhaps even attaining totality. The "peculiar situation" of the philosopher, as Rickert presents it in the summer of 1913, is that of holding onto the system under construction against the "current of development"—an act of resistance to the flow of cultural history that can be justified only under the condition that the philosopher is fully convinced that he is "more comprehensive and more unified than his predecessors."[5]

The proximate purpose of Rickert's lectures and seminars in the summer of 1913 is twofold. On the one hand, he seeks to defend and develop the idea of a philosophical system against those, like Nietzsche, who accuse system-builders of intellectual mendacity, and on the other, he wishes to dissuade his students from mistaking the *Lebensphilosophie* of Nietzsche and Bergson for genuine philosophy.[6] Whereas the lecture series is largely concerned with the first aim, the accompanying seminar on Bergson's metaphysics is primarily focused on the second. The polemical direction of Rickert's courses has a constructive purpose, for he seeks to replace Nietzschean and Bergsonian *Lebensphilosophie* with his own *Philosophie des Lebens* (philosophy of life). Whereas the former is a matter of "intuition" (Bergson) or "poetic invention" (Nietzsche), the latter is fully systematic and purely conceptual. The openness of the system, moreover, makes it immune to the commonly voiced complaint that philosophy cannot capture the infinite richness of historical life. The fundamental error of contemporaneous vitalism, according to Rickert, lies in its indiscriminate promotion of "bare life" (*bloßes Leben*), which "is value-neutral [*wertindifferent*]."[7] The aim of the "philosophy of life," by contrast, lies in constructing the concept of "voll-endetes Leben" (completed, consummated, or perfected life), in which all six regions of values are fulfilled.

There is no record of what was said during the seminar; but the University of Heidelberg Library Archive has in its possession a largely complete typescript of the lecture, which begins with a discussion of both the difficulty and the necessity of constructing a "new discipline" of "completed life." The earlier sections of the lecture are concerned with social life, particularly as they relate to eros and sexual difference, while the final sections outline the lineaments of the "religion of fullness" (*Religion der Fülle*), which culminates in a demonstration of the superiority of Protestant Christianity. In a retrospective summary, Rickert then concerns himself with the traditional problem of theodicy, which he summarizes in the term *world misery* (*Weltelend*). How, he asks, can we seek to complete our life in an incomplete, imperfect world? His system of value philosophy does not provide an answer to this question but is nevertheless capable of constructing a coherent justification for an "affirmation" of life and is therefore in a position to overcome the unhappy alternative of either "theoretical or practical nihilism," each of which is paradoxically committed to the affirmation of "absolute nihilism," that is, death. "We must learn to think entirely differently," he declares, "if we want to philosophize at all. We take this as our point of departure: we are, and we want to be. Furthermore, we want freely to complete ourselves, and we want to understand how completion is possible." At end of the lecture, Rickert discloses the "final riddle": there is an absolute and ineluctable distinction between "timelessly valid values," equivalent to the "eternity of the divinity," and the temporality of humanity, "in which values must gradually be realized." Far from being a hindrance to philosophy, however, this riddle is its source and the ultimate rational for the philosophy of "completed life."

Letters in Relation to Rickert's Lectures

The complementary differences between Heidegger and Benjamin can be seen in their respective responses to the lectures and seminar they attended together. For Benjamin, the lecture series is "interesting, though problematic," whereas the seminar scarcely sustains his interest. Heidegger, by contrast, expresses greater interest in the seminar than the lecture. Nevertheless, he retains something of the lecture, and this "something" is precisely what draws Benjamin's interest: Rickert's discussion of eros and sexual difference. The middle section of the lecture—after the methodological introduction and before the sketch of a "religion of fullness"— Rickert devotes copious amounts of time to the analysis of the relation between the sexes and *inter alia* seeks to demonstrate the "advantages of the second level of com-pletion," which he identifies with femininity, on the one hand, and philosophy, on the other. Writing to both Carla Seligson and Gustav Wyneken, Benjamin expresses his astonishment that a distinguished professor of philosophy would construct his system of value philosophy with the assistance of erotic principles. And in a number of sketches and essays of the period, especially "Metaphysics of Youth" and "Socrates," both of which identify multiple levels of "completion," Rickert's conception of eros and sexual difference can be seen as the background for Benjamin's exposition.[8] Similarly, Heidegger, who discusses Rickert's work much more thoroughly than Benjamin (which is hardly surprising, given their respective academic positions), does not explicitly engage his professor's discussions of eroticism or sexual difference; but the effect of the lecture is legible in certain letters of the period, particularly ones written to female friends.

Here are Benjamin's descriptions of Rickert's lectures in letters of the period, one from early June of 1913 to a friend, Carla Seligson, the other from July of the same year to his "first teacher" (Gustav Wyneken):

> All of literary Freiburg now attends [Rickert's] public lecture; for the moment, he reads a sketch of his system as an introduction to his logic, a system that grounds a completely new philosophical discipline: the philosophy of perfect life [die Philosophie des volkommenen Lebens]. (Woman as its representative) As interesting as it is problematic. (*GB* 1: 112)

> [The lecture series] is value philosophy. [Rickert] grounds an entirely new discipline, "value-region of completed life [Wertgebiet des vollendeten Lebens]" (alongside logic, aesthetics, ethics, the philosophy of religion). Only in connection to "completed life" does the principle of femininity retain its meaning. Here, then, is a German professor, holding a chair in philosophy, who has now spoken upwards of five hours about women and the relation of the sexes. Do not presume that the term "completed life" makes the whole thing into a matter of sterile aestheticism! This, it certainly is not—but what it is, that's also not clear. For me, what he says is unacceptable, for he declares that women are in principle incapable of the highest moral accomplishment—they receive their asylum in "completed life." The women students are beside (!) themselves with joy (as far as they understand him). (*GB* 1: 117)

And here is the only comment Heidegger makes about the lecture series, which appears in a letter he wrote to Rickert in the fall of 1913, followed by the first letter to his friend, Elisabeth Blochmann, written in June 1918, where Heidegger uses the terminology of Rickert's 1913 lectures for his own purposes:

> Unfortunately I can only now express my heartfelt thanks for the strong philosophical incitement and instruction that I was able to acquire from your lectures and above all from your seminar. To be sure, my philosophical basic intuitions [philosophischen Grundanschauungen] are different; but nevertheless I would be the last one to participate in the squalid method that sees in modern philosophy only a string of "errors," the spawn of "godlessness" and the like.⁹

Because spirit as life is alone real, vital being-for-another can work such wonders. But it places the greatest demand on the existence of the ownmost personality and its value completion [eigensten Persönlichkeit u. ihrer Wertvollendung], the demand of the most inward power of acting and of being grounded in oneself. . . . And where a life of personality with inner truthfulness is on the *way* to completion [auf dem Wege der Vollendung]—and we are nevertheless *essentially underway*—there necessarily belongs to this life the acerbity of being split, the relapses and new attempts, the unbearable suffering from the problematic and questionable: these are essential parts; they belong to the ethos of truly scientific and spiritual human beings.[10]

"Idea of Completion" and "State of Perfection"

The first expression of the entanglement between Heidegger and Benjamin can be found in their initial adaptations of the term *Vollendung* viz. *Vollkommenheit* in their respective "inaugural lectures" in 1915.[11] At the beginning of his "inaugural lecture" on the concept of time in historical scholarship or "science" Heidegger takes over the term *Vollendung* but alters the field of its application. For Rickert, the concept of philosophy is defined by *completion*, whereas, for Heidegger, this term characterizes the idea of any given science, including history. None of the sciences can be effectively completed, to be sure; but there can be no science in the strict sense without the idea of its completion. This thesis, which seems to represent a straightforward acquiescence to Rickert's system, actually runs counter to its underlying intention, for it aligns science rather than philosophy with *Vollendung*. At the same time, it silently poses a question that the system was meant to answer: what, after all, is the idea of philosophy? With regard to Benjamin, the "inaugural lecture" that he held in conjunction with his election to the presidency of the "free student-body" organization to which he belonged was transformed into the essay published in 1915 under the title "The Life of Students." About student life, one thing is clear: it is not completed; otherwise, there would be no sense to the word *study*. As with Heidegger's "inaugural lecture," Benjamin's essay is concerned with nothing so much as the concept of historical time. In its opening paragraph he proposes a slight yet revealing replacement for the middle level of *Voll-Endung* in Rickert's schema. Instead of "com-pleted particularity," Benjamin introduces the concept of an "immanent state of perfection," in which fullness is already at its end and therefore appears, if it can appear, only in the most finite—or, to use Benjamin's later terms, *transient*—things and thoughts. In both cases the adaptation of Rickert's terms, whether it be *Vollendung* or *Vollkommenheit*, makes systematic value-philosophy questionable.

Here is the relevant passage from the opening of Heidegger's "Concept of Time in Historical Scholarship [*Wissenschaft*]" (1915):

> Science is a complex of theoretical modes of knowledge, ordered and justified by means of principles. Modes of knowledge are recorded in judgments; these judgments are true, that is, they are valid. And indeed, strictly speaking, the act of judgment that the researcher does during the acquisition of knowledge is not valid; rather, it is the *sense* of the judgment—its content. Every science, thought in the idea of its completion [*Vollendung*], is a complex of validating sense that stands on its own. The particular, concrete sciences as temporally conditioned cultural facts are never completed [*vollendet*] but are always underway in their search for truth.[12]

And here is the opening of Benjamin's "Life of Students" (1915):

> There is a conception of history that, confident in the infinitude of time, distinguishes only the tempo ... with which human beings and epochs advance along the path of progress. This accords with the incoherence, lack precision, and laxity of demand such a conception imposes on the present. The following meditation, by contrast, concerns a particular state [*Zustand*] in which history rests concentrated as a point of combustion-focus [*Brennpunkt*], which it has been in the images of thinkers from time immemorial. The elements of the final state [*Endzustand*] do not appear as formless progressive tendencies but are deeply embedded into every present moment as the most endangered, scandalous, and ridiculed creations and thoughts. The historical task consists in purely forming this immanent state of perfection [*den immanenten Zustand der Vollkommenheit*], making it visible and dominant in the present. This state cannot be circumscribed with pragmatic descriptions of details ... but can be grasped only in its metaphysical structure, like the messianic kingdom or the French-revolutionary idea. (*GS* 2: 75)[13]

Scholastic Theories of Meaning

The second expression of the entanglement of Heidegger and Benjamin can be found in their completely independent decisions to write *Habilitionsschriften* on a rather arcane topic: the theory of meaning in Duns Scotus. The impetus for Heidegger's decision was apparently Rickert, who suggested the topic and to whom the resulting study is dedicated.[14] The primary rationale for this decision lies in the original "orientation" of Heidegger's early thought and the corresponding expectation that a *Habilitationsschrift* on a scholastic thinker would help him obtain an academic position in Catholic philosophy. A degree of dissatisfaction with his Catholic-scholastic orientation can be discerned, however, not only in the argumentative structure of *Duns Scotus' Doctrine of Meaning and Categories*, where the writings of Rickert and Husserl are of greater importance than any Catholic authority, but also in its very title. In June 1914, as Heidegger was making his decision, Pope Pius X issued a *motu proprio summorum pontificum* in which he declared that Thomas Aquinas would henceforth be the sole authority in matters of doctrine—which means, in effect, that any doctrine derived from Duns Scotus (who, as it happens, probably did not write the primary text under consideration in Heidegger's qualifying dissertation) is potentially heretical.

Since the orientation of Benjamin's early thought was anything but Catholic-scholastic, the basis of his decision to write on Scotian theories of language and meaning around 1920 cannot be so readily identified. It could be imagined, for instance, that a discussion of scholastic thought would allow him to combine his earlier work in the theory of language with speculative theology, on the one hand, and phenomenology, on the other. But none of this is evident from the available writings. The name "Duns Scotus" first appears in his correspondence in response to Scholem's query whether he had read Heidegger's *Habilitationsschrift*—which he had not (*GB* 2: 76). Regardless of its rationale, however, the thoroughness with which Benjamin pursued the topic can be judged by the extensive list of textual material he collected in three separate files under the title "Word and Concept." Near the top of the list is *Duns Scotus' Doctrine of Meaning and Categories*, and near the bottom is another item written by Heidegger, a little-known 1912 article entitled "Recent Research into Logic," which appeared in *Literarische Rundschau für das katholische Deutschland*, edited by Joseph Sauer, who also contributed to the aforementioned *Freiburger Bote*.[15] There is only one plausible explanation for the appearance of Heidegger's youthful work in the space of Benjamin's notes—beyond the infinitesimal possibility that the two discussed the article in the summer of 1913: Benjamin read *Duns Scotus' Doctrine of Meaning and Categories* with such attention that he noticed the title of the article in the last of its footnotes, whereupon he placed it in his own notes. And presumably around the same time he abandoned the idea of writing on scholastic theories of meaning and turned to the German *Trauerspiel*. As he writes to Scholem, rescinding his earlier view, "the text of Heidegger perhaps does reproduce that which is most essential in scholastic thought for my problem" (*GB* 2: 127).

"Bare Life" and "Being-at-Death"

The third expression of their entanglement also takes shape in the early 1920s, when both Heidegger and Benjamin dismantle the concept of "completed life" in complementary fashion. In brief, while Heidegger replaces *Vollendung* with *Vollzug* (carrying out, accomplishment, or, literally, "full draft") in conjunction with the "de-structuration" or "deconstruction" (*Destruktion*) of the problem of life, Benjamin advances the counter concept of "bare life" in the context of a critique of "power" or "violence" (*Gewalt*). In slightly more expansive terms, first with regard to Benjamin: while remaining silent about Rickert, he makes "bare life" into the nucleus of a "philosophy of life" that is decidedly neutral with regard to value. The critical character of this philosophy consists in the identification of "the law" (*das Recht*) as the value-creating and therefore life-destroying force; the end of the law thus becomes the paradoxical "purpose" of life. And with regard to Heidegger: after undertaking a thorough analysis of Rickert's work in his lectures on "the destination of philosophy" for the summer semester of 1919, in the following summer semester he adopts the Rickertian problem of "concept construction" so as to accomplish the deconstruction of value philosophy in general. Instead of discussing the character of completed life, Heidegger isolates the "genuine *Vollzug*" in which "self-worldly *Dasein*" carries itself out in the absence of an "end" external to the motility of the *Vollzug* itself. This is possible only if the *Vollzug* consists in sheer "renewal," where the end is always already there, not something newly or "freely" posited, as Heidegger says in *Phänomenologie der Anschauung und des Ausdrucks* (*GA* 59: 75). As Heidegger notes in parentheses, presumably referring to Rickert's seminar in 1913, only the analysis of the *Vollzug*-character of "self-worldly *Dasein*" prepares the way for a "genuinely decisive critique of Bergson" (*GA* 59: 82). The outcome of Heidegger's double-edged critique of Rickert's system of completed life expresses itself most sharply at the beginning of the second part of *Sein und Zeit*, where Heidegger returns to the concept of *Vollendung*, making the acerbic comment that it is more appropriate for a description of a piece of fruit than an analysis of the totality of *Dasein*. He thus goes even further than his former teacher in splitting *Voll-endung* into its component parts. In the space that Rickert reserves for "vollendetes Leben" Heidegger first emphasizes the *Voll*, then the *Endung*—but never the two together. In order words, he first identifies the mode of *Voll-zug* in which *Dasein* is genuinely "self-worldly" and then, in his *magnum opus*, describes the structure of "being-at-the-end" (*Sein-zum-Ende*), which is to say, "being-at-death" (*Sein-zum-Tode*).

One dimension of the entanglement of Heidegger with Benjamin can thus be expressed in the following equation, each side of which is on the hither side of completed life: bare life = being-at-death. The equation indicates that in a certain situation, yet to be determined, life and death are themselves entangled.

Here is the crucial sentence from Benjamin's "Toward the Critique of Power-Violence [Gewalt]," where he sketches the lineaments of a philosophy of life that is neither *Lebensphilosophie* nor value philosophy:

> The triggering of legal power, which cannot be more precisely presented here, goes back to the indebtedness [Verschuldung] of bare, natural life, which innocently and unhappily delivers over the living to the atonement [Sühne] that its indebtedness "atones for" ["sühnt"]—and indeed also expiates the culprit [Schuldigen], not however from culpability [Schuld] but from the law. For with bare life the dominance of law [Herrschaft des Rechts] over the living stops. (*GS* 2: 200)

And here is the passage from *Being and Time* that prepares the way for an analysis of the situation in which an original concept of *Schuld* (guilt, culpability) can be constructed in the absence of any consideration of the legal powers that would determine guilt and innocence:

> With its ripeness the fruit *completes* itself [vollendet *sich*]. But is the death attained by *Dasein* a completion in this sense? Indeed, *Dasein* has with its death 'completed its course.' Has it thereby also necessarily exhausted its specific possibilities? Are they not, rather, taken from it? 'Incomplete' *Dasein* also ends. Then again, it is so little necessary that *Dasein* come to fruition with its death that it can have already overstepped fruition before its end. For the most part, it ends in incompleteness [*Unvollendung*], broken down and exhausted ... *Vollendung* is a derivative mode of "finishedness" [*Fertigkeit*, viz. skill or proficiency]. This is only possible as a determination of an object [*Vorhandenen*] or useful thing [*Zuhandenen*].[16]

Two Entanglements in 1935

As the fourth expression of their entanglement, Heidegger and Benjamin speak of *entanglement* around the same time but in very different places: Heidegger uses the term in a lecture series at the University of Freiburg in the summer semester of 1935, soon after he returns to the lowly position of professor, having relinquished his rectorship under ambiguous circumstances. The importance of this lecture series, "Introduction to Metaphysics," can be gauged by the fact it was the first one Heidegger decided to publish after World War II, presumably because it would demonstrate that by 1935 he had broken with the Nazi-inflected language that was audible in his writings and speeches from the previous two years. A single passage, with a parenthetical remark that was subsequently added—when precisely it was added, no one knows—indicates the underlying rationale for his acceptance of the rectorship. In short, he wanted to save Nazism from Rickertism:

> In 1928, there appeared a complete bibliography of the concept of value, part 1. Here 661 texts on the concept of value are listed. Presumably the number has in the meantime grown to the thousands. One calls all of this "philosophy." What today is completely [*vollends*] identified with the philosophy of National Socialism, but which does not have the slightest to do with the inner truth and greatness of this movement (specifically, the encounter of planetarily destined technology with modern humanity), this makes its hauls of fish in the cloudy waters of "value" and "totalities."[17]

Whatever else may be said about this passage, it identifies the basis for Heidegger's association with the Nazi movement, namely its "inner truth," and further indicates what he sought to establish by virtue of being rector: purify Nazism of value philosophy, so that its inner truth could be recognized as such. And as for the passage in which Heidegger, for the one and only time, so far as I know, weaves the term *entanglement* into his carefully introduced lexicon, this, too, is related to his rectorship. The term *rector* derives from the same word as *correct*: whoever occupies the position of rector has the ability to correct whatever goes wrong in his sphere. In the decisive sphere, however, the sphere of truth as the event-space of unconcealment, there is no place for either correct or incorrect, hence no rector position, properly speaking. Just as the voice of "ein Führer" can be heard in the title of the lecture series, "Einführung in die Metaphysik," so does the resignation from the rectorship resonate in the space disclosed by the entanglement that captures Heidegger's attention in the summer of 1935.

Benjamin, for his part, uses the term *entanglement* in a crucial section of a major essay he wrote in the final months of 1935, while living in France, having been exiled from Germany because of the very regime whose "essence" Heidegger identifies in the "Introduction to Metaphysics." When Heidegger speaks of entanglement in 1935, it is with reference to spatiality; when Benjamin does so, it is for the purpose of describing the character of temporality. And Benjamin's political engagement runs directly contrary to Heidegger's. It is as though all of the differences between the two students of Rickert are sharpened to a single point, which revolves around the question that Heidegger poses in the parenthetical addition to his "Introduction to Metaphysics": how is the confrontation between modern humanity and modern technology to be understood? For Heidegger, according to his own self-assessment, or perhaps his own self-promotion, the confrontation with essence of technology requires, or retrospectively excuses, an engagement with Nazism, which is itself to be freed from all value-philosophizing; for the other, it requires that the Marxist concept of history be so revised that the analysis of the social whole include a counterpart in the superstructure to the basic category of productive forces. This counterpart consists in the forces of technical reproduction, which are the matrix of alterations in the relatively independent sphere of culture. And the scale of these changes is expressed in the entanglement of opposing temporal modes.

Here is Heidegger's use of *Verschränkung* in a section of *Introduction to Metaphysics* whose very title, "Limitation of Being [Beschränkung des Seins]," is implicated in the problematic "space, as it were" that is therein designated:

> The space, as it were, in which the entanglement of being, unconcealment, and appearance opens up I understand as errancy [Den Raum gleichsam, der sich in der Verschränkung von Sein, Unverborgenheit und Schein eröffnet, verstehe ich als die Irre]. Appearance, illusion, deception, confusion, errancy stand in determinate relations with respect to their essence and occurrence, relations that have so long been misinterpreted for us by psychology and the theory of knowledge that in our everyday existence [Dasein] we scarcely experience and recognize them as powers in their appropriate transparency.
>
> The task, then, is to gain insight into how, on the basis of the Greek interpretation of being as *physis*, and *only from this interpretation*, both truth in the sense of unconcealment and appearance [Schein] as a determinate mode of emergent self-showing necessarily belongs to being.[18]

And here is Benjamin's use of the same term in the original version of the "Artwork in the Age of its Technical Reproducibility," which was probably written in the fall of 1935:

> What actually is an aura? A strange web of space and time: the singular appearance of a distance, regardless of how near it may be. . . . Day after day, a need asserts itself more irrefutably, the need to get hold of an object at close range in an image [Bild], or, rather, in a copy [Abbild], a reproduction. And the reproduction, as done in illustrated newspapers and newsreels, differs unmistakably from the image. Temporal uniqueness and duration are as narrowly entangled in the latter as fleetingness and repeatability are in the former [Einmaligkeit und Dauer sind in diesem so eng verschränkt, wie Flüchtigkeit und Wiederholbarkeit in jenem]. The unwrapping of the object from its covering, the destruction of the aura, is the signature of a perception whose "sense for the homogeneous in the world" (Johannes Jensen) has so increased that, by means of reproduction, it extracts it [homogeneity, "das Gleichartige"] even from the temporally unique. Thus is manifest in the field of perception what in the theoretical spheres noticeable in the increasing significance of statistics.[19]

Another Entanglement in 1935

Among the "theoretical spheres" in which—to cite the previously quoted passage from Benjamin's "Artwork in the Age of its Technical Reproducibility"—statistics play an increasingly significant role, none is more notable than mathematical physics. In 1935, under the pseudonym of Detlev Holz, Benjamin writes a review of a book about Schiller in which he praises the eminent English physicist Arthur Stanley Eddington as popularizer *par excellence*, for he allows the reader "once in his lifetime" to adopt "the standpoint on which the avant-garde of contemporary science stands. That is decisive" (GS 3: 450–451). Among the claims Benjamin encountered in Eddington's *Nature of the Physical World*, which he read in its 1931 German translation, there is this: "It now seems clear that we have not yet got hold of *any* primary law—that all those laws at one time supposed to be primary are in reality statistical."[20] The fact that quantum mechanics not only has no theory of the underlying elements but positively forbids the formulation of such a theory was a source of increasing concern for Einstein, who had long been suspicious of quantum theory, even though he helped lay its foundations with his 1905 paper on the photoelectric effect. Thirty years later, in search of a demonstration of the "incompleteness" of the interpretation of quantum theory associated with Niels Bohr and his institute in Copenhagen, he devised a thought experiment that can be described as the physical correlate to the phenomenon of the aura, as Benjamin describes it in the passage above. Two bodies can form a system, in which, according to the Copenhagen interpretation, they somehow interact with each other in the absence of any medium of interaction that conforms to the special theory of relativity, for the communication between the two bodies must be faster than the speed of light. If there is something uncanny about the aura, so there is something spooky about the phenomenon Einstein identified in a paper he and two colleagues published in the spring of 1935.[21] The crux of the so-called EPR thought experiment (where "EPR" stands for Einstein-Podolsky-Rosen) lies in showing that there is a fundamental inconsistency between the assumption of a complete state of the two particles and the assignment of labels to the particles separately that would capture the correlated values for the results of both position and momentum measurements. The correlations between the particle pair are such that they cannot be attributed to a *common cause*, to use the term later proposed by Hans Reichenbach, who, as it happens, was an acquaintance of both Benjamin (because of his involvement in the school-reform movement) and Einstein (because of his interest in the philosophical implications of the theory of relativity). With this thought experiment, Einstein sought to demonstrate that quantum mechanics, as interpreted by Bohr and his colleagues, may be altogether correct but was nevertheless "incomplete."

Convinced of the importance of the EPR thought experiment, Erwin Schrödinger wrote a series of letters to Einstein in the summer of 1935 in which he began to use the term *Verschränkung* to describe character of the two bodies that somehow remain in communication with each other, no matter how far apart they may be. Convinced of both the scientific and philosophical significance of the EPR paper, Schrödinger responds in the summer and fall of 1935 with a series of letter to Einstein and publications of his own, especially a report on the "current situation in quantum mechanics," which appeared in Berlin-based journal *Naturwissenschaften* near the end of the year. In this report, which Schrödinger also calls a *general confession*, *Verschränkung* is introduced as a technical term that circumscribes the relation between the two bodies that, having once interacted, somehow remain bound to each other despite their distance. In Schrödinger's original usage of the term, however, *Verschränkung* does not refer to the relation between two bodies per se but, rather, the relation between the scientist and the two-body system—"the entanglement of our knowledge concerning the two bodies."[22] In highly schematic terms, this means that the knowledge of an identifiable system can be maximal; but after a process in which the component bodies of the system are separated, each going its own way, knowledge is not split into the sum of knowledge about the individual bodies: "What remains *of this*," Schrödinger writes, where "this" refers to the knowledge of the bodies taken individually, "can become submaximal, indeed eventually very strongly so."[23] There is, in other words, a hole in whole knowledge. To make sense of this lack of knowledge in the midst of complete knowledge, Schrödinger, who was a student of classical German philosophy, describes the epistemic situation circa 1935 in terms of a Kantian formula: "antinomies of entanglement" are inseparable from the quantum-mechanical wave equation, as it is currently interpreted. According to Kant, empirical science should be free of antinomies, which only befalls reason when it seeks to transcend spatial and temporal relations; as Schrödinger discovers, however, this is not the case. And this discovery corresponds to the quasi-space Heidegger circumscribes by means of the term *entanglement*. For just as the entanglement of knowledge is an intensification of the Kantian idea of antinomy at the outermost edges of contemporary physics, so the "entanglement of being, unconcealment, and appearance [*Verschränkung von Sein, Unverborgenheit und Schein*]" is an intensification of the same idea at the threshold of metaphysics.

One of the cases Schrödinger adduces for epistemic entanglement appears earlier in the report than the remarks cited above; but there is reason to suppose that the case in question was added at the last minute—added, perhaps, after Schrödinger had sought to withdraw the report from *Naturwissenschaften* because its founder and current editor, Arnold Berliner, had in the meantime been dismissed from his position in accordance with Nazi racial policies.[24] (He committed suicide in 1942, a day before his scheduled deportation.) Regardless of when the case entered into Schrödinger's report, it is now inextricably connected with his name. He calls it "burlesque," presumably because it stages a mockery of quantum mechanics in particular and the natural sciences in general. One of the entangled bodies is a living thing, specifically a cat, which is placed in a closed container that Schrödinger himself calls a "hell machine" (*Höllenmaschine*). The other body is a tiny portion of a radioactive substance. The decay of this substance, for which there is no law, is registered by a Geiger counter that, once activated, smashes a bottle of poison, thus killing the cat. The disturbing character of this, perhaps the most famous thought experiment in modern science, derives from a basic assumption about life, namely that it is as separate from death as are the living body is from the decaying substance: life and death do not blur into each other. Except perhaps in the case of Kafka's Hunter Gracchus, a living thing must be either alive or dead at any given instant. It is perhaps no accident that Schrödinger's example of a living thing is, like the Hunter Gracchus, a hunter that is barred from hunting. In any case, the exemplary cat not only shows that porosity of the distinction between the micro- and macroscopic worlds but is itself enmeshed in two forms of modern technology: the mechanically reproducible artwork, on the one hand, and mechanized killing, on the other. Although it is rarely discussed in this context, the question to which the burlesque case of the imprisoned cat responds—"Are the Variables Really Blurred?"—is specifically framed with reference to the ambiguous status of the photographic image: a blurry picture can be the result of a blurry thing, such as fog or clouds, in which case the variables really are blurred, or it can be the result of an unstable or poorly focused camera, in which case they may be in perfectly fine shape. And the nonhunting cat, encased in a metal chamber, lost to the world for an hour, awaits the moment in which "a little flask with hydrogen cyanide is smashed." Hydrogen cyanide, also known as *prussic acid* in English and *Blausäure* in German, as Schrödinger doubtless knew, was mass produced in 1935 under the generic name "Zyclon B."

Here are some of the first and last sentences of the four-page paper by Einstein, Podolsky, and Rosen, which appeared in 1935:

> Whatever the meaning assigned to the term *complete*, the following requirement for a complete theory seems to be a necessary one: *every element of the physical reality must have a counterpart in the physical theory.* [. . .] While we have thus shown that the wave function does not provide a complete description of the physical reality, we left open the question of whether or not such a description exists. We believe, however, that such a theory is possible.[25]

And here is the disquieting case that Schrödinger describes in response to his correspondence with Einstein:

> One can even set up entirely burlesque cases [ganz burleske Fälle]. A cat is penned up in a steel chamber, along with a hellish machine (which must be secured against the direct attack of the cat): in a Geiger counter there is a tiny bit of radioactive substance, *so* small, that *perhaps* in the course of the hour one of the atoms decays, but also, with equal probability, perhaps none; if it happens, the counter tube discharges and through a relay releases a hammer which shatters a small flask of prussic acid. If one has left this entire system to itself for an hour, one would say that the cat still lives *if* meanwhile no atom has decayed. The first atomic decay would

have poisoned it. The psi-function of the entire system would express this by having in it the living and dead cat (pardon the expression) mixed or smeared out in equal parts.[26]

Nietzsche, the Messiah

The entanglement of Heidegger with Benjamin goes beyond their correlated uses of the term *entanglement* in 1935 and culminates in fundamentally opposed deployments of the cardinal term that they heard in a lecture hall and seminar room during the summer of 1913, as the esteemed professor of value philosophy revealed for the first time his "system": *Vollendung*. No term is more important for the lecture series Heidegger developed while on leave from the university in 1938, as he reflected on what he had done in his previous lectures on Nietzsche and what ultimately the name "Nietzsche" means. The first session of his lecture series for the summer semester of 1939 is thus entitled "Nietzsche as thinker of the completion [*Vollendung*] of metaphysics" (*GA* 47: 1). And Rickert's term is equally prominent in a short text that Benjamin read to Adorno in early 1938, saying—ambiguously—that it belongs to the "newest of the new," which understandably led Adorno to believe that Benjamin had recently written it. In neither case, moreover, Rickert is simply forgotten. Yet he is remembered for the sake of renunciation. In Heidegger's subsequent lecture series on Nietzsche, the value philosophy of Windelband and Rickert is presented as a nihilistic half-measure meant to avert the unfolding of the completion that has already occurred in Nietzsche's doctrines; and in the same year, shortly before his death, Benjamin writes a letter to Adorno in which his renunciation of Rickert, evident in letters written over the span of more than twenty years, is concentrated into a single remark: "I am indeed a student of Rickert (just as you are of Cornelius [who rejected Adorno's first *Habilitationsschrift*, forcing him to change directors and write a second])" (*GB* 6: 455).

Both the extensive lecture series Heidegger delivered to a group of students in 1939 and the fragment that Benjamin read to a single student in 1938 turn into reflections on the same phenomenon: the advent of nihilism. Heidegger undertakes an extensive reflection on "European nihilism" as the last of his Nietzsche lectures; Benjamin concludes his fragment with a highly abbreviated exposition of nihilism as the "method" of "world politics." And for both of them, despite the fundamentally divergent direction of their thought (signaled by the differences between "Nietzsche" and "the messiah," on the one hand, and "Europe" and "world," on the other), the *nihil* of nihilism can be succinctly described as the condition that at once accomplishes and thwarts *Voll-Endung*—a Janus-faced condition of absolutely empty beginning, which is equivalent to the strangely incomplete state of completion without end.

Here are passages from the beginning and the end of the lecture series Heidegger delivered in the summer semester of 1939 under the title "Nietzsche's Doctrine of the Will to Power as Knowledge":

> In the thought of the will to power Nietzsche thinks in advance the metaphysical ground of the completion of modernity. In the thought of the will to power, however, metaphysical thought completes itself [sich vollendet]. Nietzsche, the thinker of the thought of the will to power, is the *last metaphysician* of the West. The age whose completion unfolds in his thought, modernity, is an end-time [Endzeit], which means: an age in which there arises some day and somehow the historical decision whether this end-time is the closing time of Western history or the counter-play [Gegenspiel] to another inception. To run through the train of thought that led Nietzsche to the will to power means: to open one's eyes to this historical decision. [. . .] In the completion of Western metaphysics through Nietzsche the question of truth, which bears all thinking and in which being still persists [west], despite its metaphysical interpretation, not only up until now unasked; it is entirely blocked, for the dignity of being is secured as the value of the highest will to power and therefore the absence of questioning itself. For this reason, this completion of metaphysics comes to its end. This end, however, is for the other thinking the distress [Not] of the other beginning. It lies to us and those to come whether we experience its necessity [Notwendigkeit]. Such experience demands that the end be thought as completion. (*GA* 47: 22 and 272)

And here are the beginning and end of the brief text that Adorno dubbed "Theological-Political Fragment," where the repeated use of *vollenden* is striking, not least because in its second instance, the expected theological term would be something like "revelation" or "expiation," *offenbaren* or *entsühnen*, as the latter was used in the passage from "Toward the Critique of Power-Violence" cited earlier. Benjamin goes so far as to define *vollenden* by means of *vollenden*, thus making it the self-defining term *par excellence*:

> The messiah first completes [vollendet] all historical occurrence, and indeed in the sense that he first redeems, completes [vollendet], creates the relation of historical occurrence to the messianic itself. For this

reason, nothing historical can of itself and from itself want to be related to the messianic. [. . .] To strive for this [the eternal and total transience of messianic nature], even for those levels of the human being which are nature, is the task of world politics, whose method is nihilism. (*GS* 2: 204)

Entangled Relations

The idea of influence is advantageous for a description of relations among utterances for at least two reasons. As the word suggests, influence is the function of a fluid medium, and yet both those who influence and those who undergo influence are discrete bodies that remain intact despite their immersion in the flow around them. "Influencers," in other words, can be isolated from the medium in which they exert their influence and considered solely in their own terms. And the same is true of the "influenced": they can be regarded in their own terms, fully abstracted from the fluxions in which they are localizable. Regardless of whether influence is understood along astrological-Aristotelian lines, in which case there is an essential difference between supra- and sub-lunar spheres, or along the lines of classical mechanics, where there is no such difference, the continuity of the in-flow and out-flow assumes that time itself flows in a unidirectional manner: either forward, as in most "influence studies," or backward, as in Borges's "Kafka's Precursors" or its parody in the form of a theory of the anxiety of influence. None of this is true of entanglement. The term was adopted by Schrödinger to emphasize the eerie inseparability of certain bodies that, having momentarily come into contact with each other, form a single system. Instead of unidirectional flow, there are nonlocal correlations—which in the case of this study are the correlated construction of certain questions and use of certain words, including *entanglement*. As separability vanishes, so, too, does the idea of flow—or the lack thereof, which would take the form of a mystical *nunc stans*.

Entanglement is the name of a relation that departs from the two basic interpretations of relationality: the classical one, in which the *relata* are the concrete items, while the relation is an *abstractum*; and the Hegelian critique of this interpretation, which presents the relation alone as concrete and recognizes the abstract character of the *relata*. In the relation of entanglement, by contrast, the relation between the relation and the *relata* is itself entangled, such that none can be seen as a derivative from the other. This makes the use of the term *entanglement* slippery, if not altogether spooky, for it can be grounded neither in the reality of the separable *relata* nor in the reality of the relation of the whole. And unlike a "crossed" or "hybrid" relation, there is no univocal line of descent through which the deviations can be mapped. It is in view of this spooky relation that Einstein insisted on the incompleteness of any theory where it could be found. And it is because both Benjamin and Heidegger reject the application of the term *complete* to life that they become entangled, each reflecting in ever more exacting terms on what there is of life in the absence of its supposed—which is to say, mendaciously posited—completion. Because the entangled relations are slippery and perhaps even spooky, the identification of where one occurs outside the sphere of the exact sciences is similarly slippery and inclined toward spookiness; but the mere possibility of such a relation allows for a connection among utterances that transcends the endlessly recycled alternatives of both monologue and dialogue, on the one hand, and speech act and discourse, on the other.

Notes

1. See especially the collection of essays edited by Wolf Lepenies, *Entangled Histories and Negotiated Universals: Centers and Peripheries in a Changing World* (Frankfurt am Main: Campus, 2003); see also Michael Werner and Bénédicte Zimmermann, "Beyond Comparison: Histoire Croisée and the Challenge of Reflexivity," *History and Theory* 45 (2006): 30–50.
2. Martin Heidegger and Heinrich Rickert, *Briefe 1912 bis 1933 und andere Dokumente*, ed. Alfred Denker (Franfurt am Main, 2002), 61–62.
3. Heidegger's relation to Rickert is well documented in *Briefe*, passim; on Rickert's relation to the Freien Studentenschaft, see Imtraud and Albrecht Götz von Olenhausen, "Walter Benjamin, Gustav Wyneken und die Freistudenten vor dem Ersten Weltkrieg," *Jahrbuch des Archivs der deutschen Jugendbewegung* 13 (1981): 99–128, esp. 106–108.
4. A thorough treatment of Emil Lask's importance for Heidegger can be found in Theodore Kiesel, *The Genesis of Heidegger's "Being and Time"* (Berkeley: University of California Press, 1993), esp. 33–39 (concerning Lask's role in his *Habilitationsschrift*). Kiesel is less assiduous in tracing the import of Rickert's work in Heidegger's early philosophical itinerary, yet he makes a compelling case that Lask's interrupted work (he was killed in the War) impressed a fundamental trait on Heidegger's developing thought. Benjamin, for his part, emphasizes the importance of the Marburg School in numerous places, including his *Lebensläufe* (for instance, *GS* 6: 218) and in letters to Scholem (for instance, *GB* 1: 441, where the term *critical altercation* is drawn).
5. Heinrich Rickert, "Von System der Werte," *Logos* 4 (1913), 295–327; here, 325. This is the first published version of Rickert's system, which, as he indicates in

the preface to its first (and, as it turns out, only) full treatment, was first elaborated in the summer of 1913; see Rickert, *System der Philosophie: Erster Teil, Allgemeine Grundlegung der Philosophie* (Tübingen: Mohr, 1921), vii;
6. An incomplete typescript of Rickert's lectures is preserved in the University Archive at the Heidelberg University under the title Heid. Hs. 2740. I thank the University Library and Clemens Rohfleisch in particular for giving me access to this typescript.
7. Rickert, "Vom System der Werte," 316: "Even as we speak of 'life value' here more than anywhere else, in order to characterize this com-pleted particularity [voll-endliche Partikularität], we must not forget that life as bare life [bloßes Leben] is value-neutral [wertindifferent]; the expression 'life value' is therefore better avoided." Other uses of *bloßes Leben* (bare life) can be found, for instance, in *System der Philosophie*, 45–46; and *Die Philosophie des Lebens: Darstellung und Kritik der philosophischen der Modeströmungen unserer Zeit* (Tübingen: Mohr, 1920), iv, xi, and 181: "[we stand] at the end of the philosophy of bare life" (iv).
8. See especially Walter Benjamin, *GS* 2: 97 (for "Metaphysics of Youth") and *GS* 2: 130 (for "Socrates").
9. Heidegger and Rickert, *Briefe*, 11–12.
10. Martin Heidegger and Elisabeth Blochmann, *Briefwechsel, 1918–1969*, ed. Joachim Storck (Marbach: Deutsche Schillergesellschaft, 1989), 7.
11. In the letter to Carla Seligson quoted earlier, Benjamin describes Rickert's lectures in 1913 as a "Philosophie der Vollkommenheit" (philosophy of perfection). There is no doubt that Rickert's primary term is *Vollendung*; but Benjamin may not have simply misheard the professor when writing to Seligson, for Rickert, who was only beginning to outline his system, may have first introduced it in terms of *Vollkommenheit* and then decided that *Vollendung* was ultimately more appropriate. This question cannot be answered by reference to the relevant typescript because the first pages are missing. As an aside, Robert Musil, who had been trained in a different though related philosophical context, published a volume under the title *Vereinigungen* (Unities) in 1911; the second of its two stories is entitled "Vollendung der Liebe," often translated as "Perfection of a Love."
12. Martin Heidegger, "Der Zeitbegriff in der Geschichtswissenschaft," *Zeitschrift für Philosophie und philosophische Kritik* 161 (1916); reprinted in *GA* 1: 416.
13. For a further discussion of the image of the *Brennpunkt* (as both "point of combustion" and "focal point"), see my essay "'Combustion-Focal Point': Studying the Image in Benjamin's 'Life of Students,'" *Yearbook of Comparative Literature* 56 (2012): 185–191.

14. For evidence of Rickert as the source of Heidegger's decision to write about Scotian speculative philosophy, see *Briefe*, 17.
15. See Walter Benjamin Archive, Akademie der Künste, Berlin, MS 1851–1853; Joseph Sauer, "Der Feldberg: Ein Nachwort," *Breisgauer Chronik: Beilage zum Freiburger Bote* 4 (1912), Nr. 1.
16. Martin Heidegger, *Sein und Zeit* (= *Gesamtausgabe*, Bd. 2), ed. Friedrich Wilhelm von Hermann (Frankfurt am Main: Klostermann, 1977), 244. In his "System der Werte" Rickert had already suggests this point, for he concludes with a discussion of the "com-pleted fruit [voll-endete Frucht] of our individual and particular efforts" (326). In addition, he asserts the following, which bears comparison with Heidegger's analysis of "being-at-the-end": "[Systematic philosophers] were *capable* of making an end—that was their greatness" (326). In one of Heidegger's last letters to Rickert, who was angered by comments that he reportedly made about him in his dispute with Cassirer, he claims that they indeed have common ground with regard to "finitude" (*Briefe*, 63).
17. Martin Heidegger, *Einführung in die Metaphysik* (= *Gesamtausgabe*, Bd. 40), ed. Petra Jaeger (Frankfurt am Main: Klostermann, 1983), 207–208.
18. Heidegger, *Einführung in die Metaphysik*, 116–117.
19. Benjamin, *GS* 1: 440; cf. *GS* 1: 479 and *GS* 7:355; the same terms are used in Benjamin's earlier essay, "Eine kleine Geschichte der Photographie," *GS* 2: 379.
20. Arthur Stanley Eddington, *The Nature of the Physical World* (New York: Macmillan, 1928), 98.
21. Albert Einstein, Boris Podolsky, and Nathan Rosen, "Can Quantum-Mechanical Description of Physical Reality Be Considered Complete?" *Physical Review* 47 (1935); reprinted in *Quantum Theory and Measurement*, ed. John Archibald Wheeler and Wojciech Hubert Zurek (Princeton: Princeton University Press, 1983), 138–141.
22. Erwin Schrödinger, "Die gegenwärtige Situation in Quantummechanik," 23 *Naturwissenschaften* (1935): 827; reprinted in Schrödinger, *Gesammelte Abhandlungen*, ed. Austrian Academy of Science (Vienna: Verlag der Österreichischen Akademie der Wissenschaften, 1984), 3: 494.
23. Schrödinger, *Gesammelte Abhandlungen*, 3: 494.
24. See Arthur Fine, *The Shaky Game: Einstein, Realism, and the Quantum Theory*, 2nd ed. (Chicago: University of Chicago Press, 1996), 80–82.
25. Einstein, Podolsky, and Rosen, "Can Quantum-Mechanical Description," in *Quantum Theory and Measurement*, 138 and 141.
26. Schrödinger, "Die gegenwärtige Situation in Quantummechanik," in *Gesammelte Abhandlungen*, 3: 489.

TWO

CRITIQUE AND THE THING

Benjamin and Heidegger

Gerhard Richter

In memoriam
Marc Eli Blanchard (1942–2009)
scholar and resistance fighter
in the belly of the beast

I.

Few mobilizations of the modern concept of critique are as memorable as Kant's in the *Critique of Pure Reason*, which became decisive for all philosophical engagements with critique that followed it. In his Preface to the 1781 edition, Kant argues that "our age is the genuine age of *critique*, to which everything must submit." He then goes on to explain the role that critique ought to play from that point forward. Critique is to respond to the demand "that reason should take on anew the most difficult of all its tasks, namely, that of self-knowledge, and institute a court of justice [*einen Gerichtshof einzusetzen*], by which reason may secure its rightful claims while dismissing its groundless pretensions . . . and this court is none other than the *critique of pure reason* itself." Kant elaborates: "Yet by this I do not understand a critique of books and systems, but a critique of the faculty of reason in general, in respect of all the cognitions after which reason might strive *independently of all experience*, and hence the decision about the possibility or impossibility of a metaphysics in general."[1] If the task of critique as a form of knowledge and self-knowledge is to function as a court of law, a *Gerichtshof* for thought itself, then critique is charged not merely with criticizing existing structures and practices from a perspective external to them but also, first and foremost, with formalizing the general laws and principles that establish the conditions and frameworks whereby possibilities of meaning are created by consciousness prior to its encounter with an object of sense perception. In other words, the form of critique envisioned by Kant inquires into the fundamental conditions of possibility for judgment and experience. But Kant's *Gerichtshof*, as a court of law constituted by the rigors of critique itself rather than by the requirements of some external agency, must constantly work to establish the protocols of reading and interpreting according to which it could pass judgment (*richten*). In order to get it right (*richtig*), those who preside over this court as critics or judges (*Richter*) are called upon perpetually to question the assumptions and procedures that orient (*ausrichten*) their thinking in light of the need for a critique that is the self-critique of reason. We might say, therefore, that post-Kantian critique unfolds under the sign of a triple demand: to advance a critical perspective on the object; to delimit the parameters that establish critique as a self-critique of the principles of reason; and to conceive of critique as a self-constitutive praxis that takes itself as its object in a self-reflexive examination of its own presuppositions and processes.

Central among those in the twentieth century who took up the variegated questions of the Kantian *Gerichtshof* of critique were Walter Benjamin and Martin Heidegger, thinkers who, while contemporary to each other (Benjamin was three years younger than Heidegger), are seldom read together in a sustained manner.[2] And perhaps, it could be argued, it is better that way. For what would it mean to "compare" two philosophers whose idiomatic and unmistakably singular signatures sponsor radically different perspectives and truth claims? Will anything ever be gained, one might ask, by comparing a great philosophical work, literary text, painting, or piece of music to something else? After all, comparison is vulnerable to arbitrariness, exhaustion, and boredom, because anything can always be compared with anything else. Even the habitual, and perhaps too thoughtless, statement, "You cannot compare the two," is implicitly based on a prior (and likely unspoken) comparison that has led the speaker to the conclusion that two things cannot be compared; but even here, the demand for noncomparison is based on a prior comparison. Is, therefore, that which is most valuable not lodged precisely in the endeavor to compare something not with something else but *with itself*? This mode of self-comparison requires a form of radically engaged reading and interpreting, a commitment actually to enter the inner world and logic of this particular artwork or this particular text and to do justice to what is most distinctive and idiosyncratic about it.

But it is also in comparison to something else that what is most specific about a work or a thought is cast into rigorous relief. Only by understanding how *this* work differs from *that* work, regardless of the modes of self-differentiation that may be operative within the individual works, can the singularity of something fully emerge. There is, hence, a form of comparison that *singularizes*. Yet even this singularization, meant to make specificity visible, can, through excessive comparison, also make specificity disappear. As the philosopher Berel Lang once aptly put it in relation to Heidegger's later silence with respect to his political commitments during the Third Reich, "one way to make something disappear is to place it, like a grain of sand in the desert, in a mass of supposed likeness."[3] While one's initial impetus for comparing a grain of sand with other grains may well have been to bring to the fore precisely what makes the initial grain of sand singular and specific, in fact different from all other grains of sand, there comes a point—and it is not at all certain that this point is merely a numerical one—when the act of comparison begins to move from the specification of difference to its eradication.

And yet, as Friedrich Hölderlin, the poet to whom both Benjamin and Heidegger dedicated some of their most important texts, knew, "it is lovely to compare." When we set out to compare two writers as idiosyncratic and as influential as Benjamin and Heidegger, a few basic facts should be borne in mind. Benjamin, an antifascist, dialectically oriented, academically marginalized German-Jewish writer who committed suicide while attempting to escape Nazi persecution, often was highly skeptical of Heidegger's ontological project, writing to Gershom Scholem on January 20, 1930, that "I will find Heidegger on my path, and I expect sparks will fly from the shock of the confrontation" (*CS* 359f./ *GB* 3: 503). And Heidegger, a securely installed university professor, and later rector, with sympathies during the 1930s for the National Socialist movement, provides no evidence of ever having seriously engaged, or even read, a single text by Benjamin. We do know, however, that after World War II when Benjamin's and Heidegger's mutual close friend Hannah Arendt—a former student of Heidegger's whose first husband also was Benjamin's cousin—returned to Freiburg to present a lecture on Benjamin on July 26, 1967, Heidegger, whose infamous meeting with the poet Paul Celan had occurred in his Todtnauberg hut the day before, was present in the audience, and he discussed Arendt's Benjamin lecture with her the following day.[4] In the extended published version of her text on Benjamin, Arendt states: "Without realizing it, Benjamin actually had more in common with Heidegger's remarkable sense for living eyes and living bones that had sea-changed into pearls and coral, and as such could be saved and lifted into the present only by doing violence to their context in interpreting them with 'the deadly impact' of new thoughts, than he did with the dialectical subtleties of his Marxist friends."⁵ And recently it has been suggested, based on evidence found in a little-known text by Heidegger on Rafael's Sistine Madonna that was first published in 1955 under the title "Über die Sixtina," that he had read Benjamin's "The Work of Art in the Age of Its Technical Reproducibility," whose third version includes an extensive footnote to Hubert Grimme's work on Rafael's Madonna, a work Benjamin also had emphasized in his earlier review essay "The Rigorous Study of Art."⁶

On the systematic level of their respective ways of thinking and writing, we might say that, for all that separates them, Benjamin and Heidegger also are connected in important and often unacknowledged ways that directly concern the content and implications of some of their core concepts. These include their shared interest in the complex relationship between construction and destruction (Benjamin's *Destruktion* and Heidegger's *Abbau*); the fate of the work of art and the aesthetic under conditions of modernity (Benjamin's *Reproduzierbarkeit* and Heidegger's *Ur-sprung*); the question of technology in relation to consciousness and thinking (Benjamin's *Zerstreuung* and Heidegger's *Gestell*); the poetry of Hölderlin; the question of what constitutes an image (Benjamin's *dialektisches Bild* and Heidegger's *eidos*); the theory and practice of translation (Benjamin's *Übersetzbarkeit* and Heidegger's *Über-setzen*); the significance of thinking forms of historicity (Benjamin's *Jetzt-Zeit* and Heidegger's *Geschichtlichkeit*) rather than conventional history; their perpetual return to and transformation of Kant; and, perhaps above all, their common effort to approach phenomena rigorously through a textually and linguistically mediated model. One might call this model a *Sprachdenken*, a sustained, caring, and careful approach that emphasizes the role played by *language* in the formation of thought and culture. This shared emphasis regards language not primarily as an instrument of communication or as the cognitive attestation of an extra-linguistic reality that waits to be referenced by a speaker but rather as an elusively self-referential condition of possibility in living, thinking, and acting that never can be reduced to the recording, transmission, and reception of a stable meaning.⁷ The image of Benjamin and Heidegger as absolute opposites, even antipodes, legitimate as it often may be, should not, as the British critic Howard Caygill once elegantly put it, become "a sentimental idyll, a 'left melancholic' alibi for not examining the possible complicity between their ... views," which only would serve to "sacrifice the light ... cast upon prevailing assumptions about the relationship between history, politics, and art under modernity."⁸

Bearing this context in mind, I wish to suggest that in spite of the many undeniable, and often unbridgeable, differences between the two with respect to philosophical, political, historical, and personal matters, Benjamin and Heidegger share a fundamental set of concerns. Both thinkers' projects can be read as sustained engagements with the Kantian inheritance of critique in a way that deviates markedly from the neo-Kantianisms that were prevalent in German-speaking countries during Benjamin's and Heidegger's years of intellectual formation. Both Benjamin and Heidegger recognize that critique derives from the Greek *krinein*, which means to separate, to choose, and to decide, but also is the climax or turning point in the course of an illness. The two writers, albeit from differing perspectives, each mobilize the concept of *Kritik* in relation to Kant's canonical account of critique as transcendental philosophy in the terms initially outlined in the First Critique. While Benjamin seeks to stage critique as a mode of thought distinct from the operations of commentary (for instance, in his seminal essay on "Goethe's Elective Affinities"), Heidegger relates his reading of Kant's concept to the question of what constitutes a "thing," *ein Ding*. Of particular interest are the ways in which each thinker surprisingly establishes a relationship between critique and the question of the thing or "thingness"—as a cultural object and also as formal mode of intellectual intuition—giving rise to new and deeper understandings of the striking similarities and differences between textually mediated forms of dialectical materialism and fundamental ontology. While Benjamin works his way through Kantian *Kritik* dialectically in order to fashion himself as belonging to the critics whom he characterizes as *Physiognomen der Dingwelt* or physiognomists of the world of things, Heidegger recasts the Kantian problematic of *Kritik* in terms of an unexpected and far-reaching positivity, especially in such works as "Das Ding" and in his lecture course on Kant, entitled *Die Frage nach dem Ding*. It is perhaps no accident at all, then, that Arendt in her conjunction of Benjamin and Heidegger mobilizes the trope of *things*—eyes, bones, pearls, coral—to concretize the thinkers' strange common orbit. But this shared orbit is determined not primarily by concerns of classic phenomenology, the call by Heidegger's teacher Edmund Husserl to return "to the things themselves" and to read the phenomena of one's *Lebenswelt* accordingly, but rather by a commitment to rethinking, in relation to the thing, a possible practice of critique in a transformative post-Kantian vein.

II.

Let us backtrack, turning first to Benjamin. It is well known that a perpetual confrontation with the concept and the praxis of *Kritik* occupies a central role throughout his entire corpus. For instance, the young Benjamin of "The Life of Students" (1915) already understood the "sole task of critique" as being to "liberate what is to come from its deformation in the present by an act of cognition" (*SW* 1: 38/ *GS* 2: 75). Subsequent to that Benjamin wished to become the "most significant critic" of German literature, and, later, in 1931, he began to compose a text to be entitled "Die Aufgabe des Kritikers" ("The Task of the Critic")—an essay that was to give a general theoretical account on the model of his earlier "Die Aufgabe des Übersetzers" ("The Task of the Translator"), but which survives today only in the form of notes (*SW* 2: 548f./ *GS* 6: 171f.).⁹ Later still, Benjamin made plans with his friend Bertolt Brecht jointly to establish a new journal entitled *Krise und Kritik*, a project that never came to fruition. What is perhaps less well appreciated, however, is the extent to which the Kantian concept of critique inflected Benjamin's understanding of his own engagement with critique. As early as 1917, Benjamin writes to Scholem that "no matter how great the number of Kantian minutiae that may have to fade away," he is capable of envisioning his own critical project only "by means of the revision and further development of Kant" and "the only thing I see clearly is the task . . . that what is *essential* in Kant's thought must be preserved" (*CS*: 97/ *GB* 1: 389). The first sustained Benjaminian text to emerge from this simultaneous appropriation and development of Kantian critique is "Program for a Coming Philosophy" (1917–1918) and its articulation of the critical possibility of creating a form of Kantian critique oriented toward a thinking yet to come. But it is not until Benjamin's essay on Goethe's *Elective Affinities*, begun shortly after his Kant essay and eventually published in 1924–1925, that Benjamin finds a critical mode that he considers, as he indicates in a letter to Scholem, both a piece of "exemplary critique [*exemplarische Kritik*]" and a decisive "prolegomenon to certain purely philosophical expositions [*Vorarbeit zu gewissen rein philosophischen Darlegungen*]" (*CS*: 194/ *GB* 2: 208). The exemplarity of Benjamin's Goethe essay could be said to be operative on at least three levels: it constitutes a prime example of Benjamin's mode of self-reflexive critique; it takes as its object one of the exemplary novels of *the* exemplary classical German writer; and it indirectly unfolds in the orbit of Friedrich Schlegel's critique of another novel by Goethe, *Wilhelm Meister's Apprenticeship*, a piece of critique taken to be exemplary of Early German Romantic literary theory.¹⁰

What, for Benjamin, distinguishes critique from the related form of commentary is, among other things, the fact that it always is oriented towards the truth content of the artwork: "Critique seeks the truth content [*Wahrheitsgehalt*] of a work of art; commentary, its material content [*Sachgehalt*]. The relation between the two is determined by that basic law of literature according to which the more significant the work, the more inconspicuously and intimately its truth content is bound up with its material content" (*SW* 1: 297/ *GS* 1: 125). In this sense, critique, as the praxis of *krinein*, draws on the shifting and inconstant figures of separation that characterize truth content and material content. "If," Benjamin writes, "to use a simile, one views the growing work as a burning funeral pyre, then the commentator stands before it like a chemist, the critic like an alchemist. Whereas, for the former, wood and ash remain the sole objects of his analysis, for the latter only the flame itself preserves an enigma: that of what is alive. Thus, the critic inquires into the truth, whose living flame continues to burn over the heavy logs of what is past and the light ashes of what has been experienced" (*SW* 1: 298/ *GS* 1: 126). According to this image, critique has its source in a flickering, dangerous flame in whose light what is to be separated is both seen for the first time and burned to ash. These cinders and ashen traces continue to testify to what was separated by critique, even if what has been separated in this way only can be thought as absence, or as a presence that has fled into a vast, unapproachable distance.

The concept of critique that Benjamin wishes to think toward is indebted both to the fundamental Kantian articulation and to the Early Romantic development of the concept, especially that of Friedrich Schlegel. Schlegel's theory of critique made a more profound impression on Benjamin than other historical attempts at furthering and reorienting Kant's concept of critique, including even Fichte's concept of critique as abstract negation and Herder's attempted system of a so-called meta-critique.[11] In his programmatic 1804 essay "On the Essence of Critique," Schlegel gives shape to the German Romantics' notion of critique as the progressive mediator between philosophy and history. He writes:

> We should think of critique as a middle term between history and philosophy, one that shall join them both, and in which both are to be united to form a new, third term. Without philosophical spirit, such a critique cannot thrive—everyone agrees on this—nor without historical knowledge. The philosophical elaboration and examination of history and of traditions is unquestionably critique. But any historical view of philosophy is, just as unquestionably, critique as well. It is apparent that the compilation of opinions and systems that is usually called philosophy cannot be meant here. . . . We may bring together the most solid results of a historical mass under a concept, or else we may specify a concept not merely in order to allow distinctions, but rather to construct the concept in its becoming, from its earliest origins to its final completion, giving this, together with the concept, its own inner history. Both of these are characterizations, the highest task of critique and the most intimate union of history and philosophy.[12]

If it is true, as one reader aptly puts it, that the general orientation of Benjamin's project is to invent a "thinking which attempts to utter in critique the truth that denies itself to any philosophical system,"[13] then Schlegel's definition of critique as the mediator between philosophy and history provides us with a clue as to Benjamin's path. Conventional forms of philosophy and historiography are not sufficient to perform their own work while also taking into account the important insights generated by the other. It is in critique that the dialogue between them takes place. At the same time, critique is neither a system nor a method, neither a task to be fulfilled nor a predetermined intervention to be executed upon the world of things. Rather, critique is a perpetual engagement with itself, not in the sense of an endlessly narcissistic self-reflection but rather in the sense of a self-conscious commitment to reinvestigating, even reinventing, on the most rigorous level imaginable, its assumptions and procedures with each new object.

It is no accident, therefore, that critique—pushed to the extreme position of a perpetual self-definition—comes to play a significant role in Benjamin's 1920 doctoral dissertation on the theory of art criticism in German Romanticism. There, in the course of providing a brief genealogy of the modern term "critique," Benjamin writes that of "all the technical terms of philosophy and aesthetics in the works of the early Romantics, the words 'critique' and 'critical' are easily the most often encountered." He continues: "Through Kant's philosophical work, the concept of critique had acquired for the younger generation an almost magical meaning." For Romantics such as Novalis and Schlegel as well as "for speculative philosophy, the term 'critical' meant objectively productive, creative out of thoughtful deliberation. To be critical meant to elevate thinking so far beyond all restrictive conditions that the knowledge of truth sprang forth . . . from insight into the falsehood of these restrictions" (*SW* 1: 142/ *GS* 1: 52). If to practice critique means to push thinking beyond its presumed limits and to submit to scrutiny the very idea of a delimited thinking, the critical stance that Benjamin envisions starts with the restlessness of a negativity rather than with the assured imposition of external critical standards onto an object or idea. To practice critique in this way is to remain open to its difficulties, its others, even the perpetual threat of its impossibility, an uncontainable threat which makes it a form of critical potentiality in the first place.

While Benjamin's concept of critique and its practice is heavily inflected by Kant's and the Romantics', what distinguishes it, among other things, is the insistence on articulating the relationship not only between philosophy and history, critique and reason, or critique and forms of consciousness, but also between critique and the thing (*das Ding*). It is that in the *Arcades Project* he evokes the image of collectors and, by extension, himself as an obsessive collector of things, as "physiognomists of the world of things [*Physiognomen der Dingwelt*]" (*AP* H2,7; H2a,1). To practice the kind of philosophical, literary, aesthetic, and cultural critique that Benjamin has in mind, the critic must learn how to read *die Dinge*, the things that, at times inexplicably, inhabit his world. As one of Benjamin's German editors, Rolf Tiedemann, reminds us in his introduction to the first publication of the *Arcades Project* in 1982, the "prolegomena to a materialist physiognomics that can be gleaned from the *Passagen-Werk* counts among Benjamin's most prodigious conceptions."[14] Learning to practice critique by way of a consideration of, and perpetual reengagement with, the thing-world means learning to read the thing as though it were a text, to be read and reinterpreted again and again, until "the real can be read like a text [*das Wirkliche wie einen Text lesen*]" (*AP* N4,2).

It is this thing-orientation of critique that Benjamin's essay on Goethe's novel makes vivid. There, we are told that "because what is eternal in the work stands out only against the ground of those realities, every contemporary critique, however eminent, comprehends in the work more the moving truth than the resting truth, more the temporal effect than the eternal being." Benjamin continues by suggesting that "the most essential contents of being-in-the-world [*wesentlichsten Inhalte des Daseins*] are capable of stamping their imprint on the world of things [*Dingwelt*], indeed that without such imprinting they are incapable of fulfilling themselves" (*SW* 1: 298/ *GS* 1: 126). To interrogate modes of being in the world, critique in the Benjaminian sense fastens upon those things that not only represent what they themselves are—this chair, this desk, this toy—but also bear the inscription of existence that the *Dingwelt* to which they belong has bestowed upon them. The thing is that which presents the material manifestation of existence to itself as a system of signs to be interpreted by the physiognomist of the world of things.

We have known for a while that Benjamin's own obsession with the *Dingwelt* compelled him to collect myriad things, including children's books and snow globes, and to comment on the appearance, for instance, of small marzipan figurines. Likewise, we have been reminded by Benjamin scholarship of the general fact that many of his literary and philosophical reflections, whether they concern such matters as history, memory, art, or technology, turn on his evocations of concrete objects, "old and used, neglected and buried, dusty and hidden, broken and repaired."[15] Such things in Benjamin's texts include, among many others, "objects of daily use, commodities, garbage, children's toys, socks, telephones, glass shards, bottle openers, [and] antiques."[16] By the same token, the omnipresence of objects among Benjamin's own words also leads him to become a reader of literature who is especially sensitive to the abiding presence of objects among the words of authors such as Kafka, Proust, Robert Walser, Franz Hessel, and Louis Aragon.[17] It is therefore no accident that the children rummaging through the debris in the thought-image "Construction Site" from *One-Way Street* emerge as secret revolutionaries of a politically saturated modernist montage, subjects for whom it is precisely in their relation to the discarded objects of modernity ("they feel irresistibly drawn to debris") that they come to encounter "the face that the world of things turns especially to them and them alone [*das Gesicht, das die Dingwelt gerade ihnen, ihnen allein, zukehrt*]" (*SW* 1: 449/ *GS* 4: 93).[18] And when it comes to a thing such as the telephone, an object that Benjamin in the *Berlin Chronicle* strategically calls his "twin," the textual imbrication of thingliness, thinking, selfhood, and critique even functions as one of the primal scenes of his entire autobiographical corpus.[19]

But it is in the *Arcades Project* that he provides a number of sustained conceptual insights into the material and theoretical relation to things first broached in the Goethe essay. While the figure that Benjamin emphasizes in the *Arcades Project* is often that of the collector—especially in Convolutes H and I—the general points he advances also can be said to apply to the critic and to the relation between critique and thing. It is in the context of a massive theoretical and historiographic effort that critique and thing are made to speak to each other. As in so many other regards, Baudelaire is enlisted as Benjamin's crown witness: "One must make one's way through *Les Fleurs du mal* with a sense for how things are raised to allegory [*wie die Dinge zur Allegorie erhoben werden*]. The use of the uppercase lettering should be followed carefully" (*AP* H1a,3). The thing emerges as thoroughly allegorical, even when it consists of the materiality of the letter in Baudelaire. If the thing is elevated to the level of allegory, it is made to speak *otherwise*, representing not only itself, its appearance as and in form, but also that which within it remains unspoken and unthought.

If critique is to confront the double nature of the thing, it is called upon to fashion perspectives that would do justice to the requirements of the critical act in relation to the position and presentation of the thing. As Benjamin argues:

> The true method of making things present to oneself [*die Dinge sich gegenwärtig zu machen*] is to present them in our space (not to present ourselves in their space). . . . Thus presented, the things allow no mediating construction from out of "larger contexts." The same applies to the viewing of great things from the past—the cathedral of Chartres, the temple of Peastum—when, that is, a favorable prospect presents itself: to receive the things in our space. We do not put ourselves into their place; they step into our life [*Nicht wir versetzen uns in sie, sie treten in unser Leben*]. (*AP* H2,3)

To relate to a thing on the rigorous level of critique requires that one tear it of its "own" context, shunning all the surrounding elements that are assumed to provide meaning. This method is not one of empathy, in which the critic enters the space and context of the thing in order to comment upon the ways in which it looks like, or does not look like, the other things inhabiting its orbit. On the contrary, to relate to a thing in this Benjaminian way is to perform a certain kind of violence, in which the provenance of a thing is robbed of the aura of its naturalness and in which the rightful positionality—and therefore assumed meaning—of a thing is displaced with an eye toward recontextualizing it in a critical constellation that is quite alien to it. The moment in which the thing enters the space of Being-in-the-world, when it encroaches and even intrudes, it no longer can be held at a safe distance. It is only now, in this unsettling moment of having been encroached upon, that a critique of the thing is moved to question its own methodological procedures and to reinvent itself in accordance with the strange singularity and incommensurate idiomaticity of the thing that has arrived. Benjamin's passage, finally, also reverberates with an earlier one from "The Return of the Flaneur," a review of Hessel, in which he quotes Hessel's remarkable words "We see only what looks at us [*Nur was uns anschaut sehen wir*]" in a gesture that implies a complex reversal of the directionality of looking conventionally believed to obtain between humans and things (*SW* 2: 265/ *GS* 3: 198). Here, it is precisely the thing staring at us that causes it to step into our field of vision.[20]

We might say that it is according to this particular logic of a thing looking at us and stepping toward us that one of the dimensions of what Benjamin, in the section of his dissertation on German Romanticism that investigates the relation between the Early Romantic theory of art and Goethe, calls "criticizability" (*Kritisierbarkeit*) is cast into exacting relief. He writes: "The concept of a critique of art . . . itself bespeaks an unambiguous dependence on the center of the philosophy of art. This dependence is most acutely formulated in the problem of the criticizability of the artwork. . . . The entire art-philosophical project of the early Romantics therefore can be summarized by saying that they sought to demonstrate in principle the criticizability of the work of art" (*SW* 1: 178f./ *GS* 1: 110). While the specific thing that Benjamin here connects to criticizability is the aesthetically mediated realm of the artwork, the speculative investment in criticizability also can be extended to a larger, more encompassing *Dingwelt*. That is to say, if his concern is with articulating a rigorous concept of criticizability, it must unfold in relation to something, to some thing, that allows the act of critique to become not simply the execution of a preestablished agenda or a methodological doctrine but rather the manifestation of the idea of a potentiality, an as yet unpredictable, future-oriented critical attitude. This potentiality of the act of critique is encoded in the suffix "-ability" (*-ierbarkeit*). As Samuel Weber has shown in his recent study of the numerous terms ending in "-ability" that traverse Benjamin's entire corpus (including criticizability, reproducibility, translatability, citability, legibility, and impartibility, among many others), Benjamin is concerned with a certain *virtuality* of writing and thinking, one that emphasizes radical *possibility* over achieved actuality.[21] We can now add that the criticizability of a thing depends on the ways in which it presents itself to the critic—rather than the critic entering the orbit of the thing—in a way that works to keep possibility alive even in a thing, that is, even in the realm of something whose meaning and function already appear to have been decided upon by virtue of its having assumed a particular shape and determined position in the *Dingwelt*.

If Benjamin emphasizes the moments of potentiality and possibility in relation to a critique of the thing, his critical gesture also implies that the thing cannot simply be assumed to remain self-identical and fully transparent to the linguistically mediated consciousness with which it interacts. We could say that Benjamin here provides a reinterpretation and actualization of Hegel's discussion of the thing in the section on consciousness entitled "Sense-Certainty: Or the 'This' and 'Meaning' [*Meinen*]" from *The Phenomenology of Spirit*. There, Hegel writes:

> They speak of the existence [*Dasein*] of *external* objects [*Gegenstände*], which can be more precisely defined as *actual*, absolutely *singular, wholly personal, individual* things [*Dinge*], each of them absolutely unlike anything else; this existence, they say, has absolute certainty and truth. They mean *this* bit of paper on which I am writing—or rather have written—*this*; but what they mean is not what they say. If they actually wanted to *say* 'this' bit of paper which they mean, if they wanted to *say* it, then this is impossible, because the sensuous This that is meant *cannot be reached* by language [*der Sprache . . . unerreichbar ist*], which belongs to consciousness, i.e. to that which is inherently universal. . . . If nothing more is said of something than that it is an *actual thing* [*ein wirkliches Ding*], an *external object*, its description is only the most general and in fact expresses its sameness with everything rather than its difference.[22]

To confront the *Dinge* and *Gegenstände* upon which it fastens, consciousness, along with the language that mediates it, is called upon to show itself responsible to the ways in which its inscription in the perpetual dialectic of particularity and universality inflects the manner in which a thing can be thought and spoken about in the first place. While in his lecture course on aesthetics Hegel emphasizes that the concept, as something universal and intangible, needs the manifestation of the particular in order to make it concrete, here his argumentation proceeds in the other direction, as it were: because consciousness by virtue of language is always already indebted to a sign system of universal signification, it cannot ever quite account for the singularity and idiomaticity of *this thing*, which shares its designation with so many other things like it.

In the section of the *Phenomenology* entitled "Perception: Or the Thing and Deception [*Die Wahrnehmung oder das Ding und die Täuschung*]," Hegel therefore proposes the following dialectical account of the thing: "The Thing is a *One* [*Das Ding ist Eins*], reflected into itself; it is *for itself*, but it is also *for an other*; that is to say, it is an other on its own account, just because it is for an other. Accordingly, the Thing is for itself and *also* for an other, a being that is doubly differentiated but also a One."[23] Training the focus of his general discussion of the for-oneself and the for-another on the particular question of thing, Hegel opens up a dialectical space in which to consider the thing as something that is at once unified enough to be recognizable as a thing—as *this* thing or as *that* thing—and traversed by a certain nonself-identity in which it vacillates between a self-referential determinant (being for itself) and an other-directed entity (being for another). One of the questions posed by this dialectical self-differentiation of the thing concerns its availability to a critical consciousness, which also must, in the critical act, take into account this radically dialectical movement. If Benjamin wishes to develop a concept of critique that travels through an engagement with the thing, it is in part because of the Hegelian inheritance that complicates any interrogation of the thing, and even the thingness of the thing. What a Benjaminian criticizability of the thing therefore also would have to entail is a consideration of how a thing can become an object of critique when it no longer merely is an object, that is, when it no longer will remain an effect of the subject-object split and of a perspective that assumes it to be transparently available to critical consciousness. This, too, is why for Benjamin the things inhabiting the *Dingwelt* "step toward us," as he puts it, *treten in unser Leben*, as unfinished business.

For Benjamin's idea of critique, in which the critic becomes a physiognomist of the *Dingwelt*, the thing's hermeneutic instability embodies simultaneously the predicament of postlapsarian, secularized modernity itself. It is no accident that in his *Trauerspiel* book, *The Origin of the German Mourning Play*, Benjamin provocatively suggests that on the Baroque stage, which, for him, can be read as an allegory of modernity as such, "any person, any thing [*jedwedes Ding*], any relation can mean absolutely anything else [*kann ein beliebiges anderes bedeuten*]" (*OT*: 175/ *GS* 1: 350). This separation of sign and signification is not simply a liberation from the strictures of a prematurely imposed stable meaning, it also is a cause for mourning. This mourning, for Benjamin, is anchored in the world of things. The fidelity or faithfulness that traverses this particular form of mourning cannot be thought in isolation from the ways in which it is directed not to a person or an idea but rather to a thing. Speaking of the figure of the courtier in the mourning play, Benjamin states:

> His infidelity [*Untreue*] to the human being corresponds to a fidelity [*Treue*] to these things to the point of being absorbed in contemplative devotion to them. Only in this hopeless fidelity to the creaturely . . . does the concept of this behavior stand in the location of its adequate fulfilment. For, all essential decisions before human beings can violate fidelity; in them, higher laws obtain. Fidelity is fully appropriate only to the relation between the human being and the world of things [*Dingwelt*]. The latter knows no higher law, and fidelity knows no object to which it might belong more exclusively than the world of things. . . . Melancholy betrays the world for the sake of knowledge. But in its tenacious sunkenness [*ausdauernde Versunkenheit*] it admits dead things into its contemplation [*nimmt die toten Dinge in ihre Kontemplation auf*] in order to redeem them. . . . The persistence that takes shape in the intention of mourning is born of its fidelity to the world of things. (*OT*: 156f./ *GS* 1:333f.)

To the extent that the critical act—especially the one involving an *allegorical* reading, which, for Benjamin, is the preferred mode in the *Trauerspiel* book and in his theory of reading more generally—is capable of being informed by a certain fidelity, it can only be a fidelity that pertains to an interpretation of the perpetually shifting relations between human and thing. Even the cardinal sin of melancholia—betraying the world in exchange for the fruits of *Wissen*—is reconfigured when seen from this perspective. Like the winged figure dispassionately staring at the manifold things that surround it in Albrecht Dürer's famous allegorical woodcut "Melancholia," the melancholic critic opens the space of reflection to the dead things, displaying a certain hospitality toward them, and even making them the focus of his reflections.[24] In this act of critique, the thing in a certain sense appears as both dead and alive: dead, because it belongs merely to the dead *Dingwelt* as an inanimate, mute entity; alive, because it enters into critical contemplation ("*nimmt die toten Dinge . . . auf*") in yet another act of what Benjamin calls the thing's "stepping toward us." We might say that this movement of the thing is one of Benjamin's responses to the Hegelian challenge of having to regard *das Ding* both as something self-referential and as something other-directed, as an object readily available to critique and as a dialectical phenomenon that works to elude its critic's gaze. The thing becomes, we might say, part of the realm of what Benjamin terms *das Ausdruckslose*, the expressionless, a moment or realm that is cognizable as something but that refuses to provide a hermeneutic key to itself.[25]

III.

Let us now turn to Heidegger. It is an open question to what extent Heidegger's project, which is concerned with the end of metaphysics and the exhaustion of traditional—especially institutional—modes of philosophy, can be said to participate in the work of critique at all. It is perhaps telling that one looks in vain for entries on "critique" in today's standard reference works of Heidegger scholarship.[26] And from the perspective of critique understood as a form of historical materialism, it is as though many readers and scholars had accepted the logic of Heidegger's former student Herbert Marcuse, who had completed his doctoral thesis on Hegel's theory of historicity under Heidegger's direction, and who, after an initial attempt to bring Heideggerian thought and Marxian critique together, abandoned the project of a "Heideggerian Marxism" as impossible.[27] And yet, especially the relation between critique and the materiality of a thing—a relation that concerns Heidegger as much as it does Benjamin—would still deserve to be analyzed with comparative reference to a Marxian notion of materialism. After all, in the "Letter on 'Humanism,'" Heidegger, in a rare reference to Marx, suggests a certain link between his concern with submitting to critique the ways in which the question of Being has been occluded and the Marxian critique of estrangement:

> What Marx, coming from Hegel, recognized in an essential and significant sense as the alienation of the human being has its roots in the homelessness of the modern human being. This homelessness is specifically evoked from the destiny of Being in the form of metaphysics, and through metaphysics is simultaneously fortified and covered up as such. Because Marx, by experiencing alienation, reaches into an essential dimension of history, the Marxist view of history is superior [*überlegen*] to that of other historical accounts. But since neither Husserl nor—so far as I have seen until now—Sartre recognizes the essential importance of the historical in Being, neither phenomenology nor existentialism enters that dimension within which a productive dialogue with Marxism first becomes possible. (*P* 258f./ *GA* 9: 339f.)

The implication of these lines is not only that there may be much stronger affinities than is commonly assumed between, on the one hand, Heideggerian concepts of ontological historicity in which the commemorative thinking of modes of Being have been repressed, and, on the other hand, the repression that is given voice in Marxian materialism, but they also suggest that questions concerning Marx's critique of the reified thing in terms of its embodiment of commodity fetishism would here join concerns over the ontological assumption that human beings and the being of things has been occluded in favor of a superficial rationalism. By the same token, these lines also cast the project of rehabilitating the thinking of Being as, *among other things*, a critical and material intervention into ossified ways of thinking and acting, that is, as a form of critique.

To be sure, if post-Kantian critique, even in its transformations through Hegel and Marx, can, from a certain perspective, be considered to be one of the primary preoccupations of metaphysical speculation, then it would appear problematic to ascribe a *critical* component to a project that is more concerned with the truth of *aletheia*, or unconcealment, than with any truth-content of critique. And yet, careful readers of Heideggerian ontology and of the post-Kantian tradition of critique have begun to intuit that there is more of a relation between the existentialist path of thinking and the post-Kantian concept of critique than may at first be obvious. It has been convincingly argued, for instance, that the basic orientation of *Being and Time* is precisely to conjoin a properly critical attitude in the area of epistemology to a fundamental reconsideration of *Dasein* as an unthought mode of Being-in-the-world. "Construing *Dasein* as being-in-the-world (marked by care for being)," the political theorist Fred Dallmayr reminds us, "did not signal a return to a pre-critical or substantive metaphysics," but revealed, in "its basic anti-objectivism," that "fundamental ontology was not alien to, but rather a precondition of possible critique—though a critique cognizant of its underpinnings and limitations."[28] From this vantage, "Heidegger's work can be seen as a primary exemplar of a perspective combining ontological reflection with post-Kantian (not subject-centered) critique."[29] According to the demands of this critique, even a reflection on *Dasein* must be a form of critical *self-reflection*, even when it takes certain elements of post-Kantian rationalism to task for its occlusion of what Heidegger regards as the more primordial question—the question of Being.

It is Heidegger himself, for instance in his 1964 lecture "The End of Philosophy and the Task of Thinking"—one of his most significant statements regarding his vision for a rigorous thinking yet to come—who explicitly relates this thinking to the critical act. Whereas philosophy in its classical, metaphysical sense is concerned with providing answers to questions, what is needed is a different kind of thinking, one that emphasizes the importance of the path (*der Weg*) and that takes into account what has remained unthought. Heidegger writes: "Questions are paths toward an answer. If the answer could be given it would consist in a transformation of thinking, not in a propositional statement about a matter at stake." Suggesting that his text belongs to a larger attempt at articulating the question of Being in an even "more primordial fashion" than that of *Being and Time*, the task can be outlined as follows:

> This means to subject the point of departure of the question in *Being and Time* to an immanent critique [*Kritik*]. Thus it must become clear to what extent the *critical* question [*die* kritische *Frage*] as to what the matter of thinking is necessarily and continually belongs to thinking. Accordingly, the name of the task of *Being and Time* will change. (BW 431/ GA 14: 69)

Whereas *Being and Time* had articulated its tasks in terms of an anthropologically mediated ontology rather than of critique, Heidegger now regards the future of actual thinking, rather than merely "doing" philosophy, as being tied to the question of critique, even italicizing the adjective "*kritisch*" to make his point. The work of critique here is conceptualized not primarily as a mode of external intervention, that is, as a movement of separation between entities that are assumed already to exist as a form of presence and self-identity. Rather, critique is a mode of thinking about the very acts of questioning, even of the idea of the question itself. Therefore, Heidegger speaks not simply of critique but rather of a "kritische *Frage*."

What this questioning pursued by the kritische *Frage* entails cannot be thought in isolation from a consideration of the ways in which it differs from classical metaphysics. Heidegger explains: "All metaphysics, including its opponent, positivism, speaks the language of Plato. The basic word of its thinking, that is, of its presentation of the Being of beings [*das Sein des Seienden*], is *eidos*, idea: the outward appearance in which beings as such show themselves." He adds: "Outward appearance, however, is a matter of presence" (BW 444/ GA 14: 82). What is needed to cognize any presence, even the presence of the *eidos*, is the light provided by a sudden clearing (*Lichtung*) that traverses Being but nevertheless has tended to remain "unthought" (*ungedacht*) in Western philosophy. To approach the unthought by means of the kritische *Frage* means above all to break with the convention of translating the Greek *aletheia* as truth, carrying it into the realm of the critical question by rendering it as unconcealment. As Heidegger argues:

> *Aletheia*, unconcealment thought as the clearing of presence, is not yet truth. Is *aletheia* less than truth? Or is it more, because it first grants truth as *adaequatio* and *certitudo*, because there can be no presence and presenting outside the realm of the clearing?

> This question we leave to thinking as a task. Thinking must consider [*muß sich darauf besinnen*] whether it can even pose this question at all as long as it thinks philosophically, that is, in the strict sense of metaphysics, which questions what is present only with regard to its presence. (*BW* 446/ GA 14: 86)

What is disclosed in the critical question is that we still do not know how to think, are still in need of an understanding of thinking. The unconcealment that facilitates our cognition of the changed status of truth in the task of thinking is itself the commencement of an education in thinking, a thinking that perpetually questions its own assumptions. The thinking (*das Denken*) yet to come pursues previously untrodden paths and fosters forms of contemplative vigilance and attentiveness with regard to what had hitherto remained unthought in metaphysics. "The task of thinking," in Heidegger's view, "would then be the surrender of previous thinking to the determination of the matter of thinking" (*BW* 449/ GA 14: 90). This determination is inseparable from certain modes of interpreting the status of the kritische *Frage*.

As in the case of Benjamin's development of critique, it is through constant dialogue, explicit or implicit, with the Kantian formulation of critique that Heidegger's own engagement with the kritische *Frage* unfolds. The question and the questioning of critique in Kant's enterprise have not settled a priori on an assumed negativity of critique. In the *Critique of Pure Reason*, Kant writes:

> What sort of treasure is it that we intend to leave to posterity, in the form of a metaphysics that has been purified through critique but therefore also brought into a changeless state? On a cursory overview... one might believe that one perceives it to be only of *negative* utility, teaching us never to venture with speculative reason beyond the boundaries of experience; and in fact that is its first usefulness. But this utility becomes *positive* when we become aware that the principles with which speculative reason ventures beyond its boundaries do not in fact result in *extending* our use of reason.... Hence a critique that limits the speculative use of reason is, to be sure, to that extent *negative*, but because it simultaneously removes an obstacle that limits or even threatens to wipe out the practical use of reason, this critique is also in fact of *positive* and very important utility. ... To deny that this service of critique is of any *positive* utility would be as much as to say that the police are of no positive utility because their chief business is to put a stop to the violence that citizens have to fear from other citizens, so that each can carry on his own affairs in peace and safety.[30]

The question regarding the negativity or positivity of critique strikes at the core of the concept of a transcendental, critical philosophy. Here, the radicality of Kant's concept of critique does not just lie in the fact that his transcendental method accords it a functional value that was without precedent in what Kant himself had already referred to as an age of critique.[31] The true radicality of his concept of critique lies instead in its extension to the self-critique of reason on the far side of critique as posited negativity. Reason here must also submit itself to the demands of critique if it is to arrive at self-knowledge. It must learn, as Rodolphe Gasché reminds us, not only to think its criteria and boundaries through the aspect of critique, but to establish critique as the gold standard of its own chief enterprise.[32] We recall, therefore, that post-Kantian critique is at the same time to be a critical theory of itself, a type of contemplation that turns away from all dogmas and forms of mere skepticism to make the radicality of self-reflection the principle of every critical movement of thought.

In paragraph 21 of the second chapter of *Die Frage nach dem Ding* (literally, "The Question Concerning the Thing" or "The [Status of the] Question After the Thing" and published in English under the title *What Is a Thing?*), a text based on a lecture course on Kant held in Freiburg during the winter semester of 1935–1936, Heidegger pursues the question: "What does 'Critique' mean in Kant?" He writes: "We are accustomed to hearing something overwhelmingly negative whenever this word is mentioned. For us, to criticize means to find fault, to tally mistakes, to point out shortcomings, and to dismiss what is thereby found wanting. We must try to distance ourselves from this customary and misleading meaning when faced with the title *Critique of Pure Reason*."[33] Heidegger continues:

> "Critique" comes from the Greek *krinein*, which means "to sort" [*sondern*], "to sort out," and thus "to lift out that special sort" [*das Besondere herausheben*]. . . ."Critique," far from being something negative, designates the most positive positivity, the positing of what must be put in place before everything else as the determining and decisive agency. Critique is thus decision in this pre-positional sense. Only in consequence of this, because to criticize means to select and to bring out what is special, uncommon, and at the same time measure-giving, is it also to reject what is commonplace and unsuitable. (*WT* 119f./ *GA* 41: 121f.)

We should note that if Heidegger associates with critique nothing negative but rather "the most positive positivity," we cannot but hear echoes of Benjamin's understanding of critique along positive rather than negative lines: "Thus, critique, in complete opposition to the present-day conception of its essence, is, in its central intention, not judgment but, on the one hand, the completion, supplementation, and systematization of the work and, on the other hand, its dissolution in the absolute" (*SW* 1: 159/ *GS* 1: 78). Critique, for both Benjamin and Heidegger, is not primarily the negation of something but its radical affirmation, a way of accentuating what is distinct and singular in an argument, a mode of discourse, or a work.

Heidegger proceeds to provide historical texture to this systematic view of the workings of critique by arguing that the general meaning of the word "critique" gradually takes shape in the second half of the eighteenth century in discussions of art, the analysis of artistic forms, and the promulgation of rules and decrees. "But the word," Heidegger adds, "receives a fuller sense through Kant's work" (*WT* 120/ *GA* 41: 122). It is incumbent on thought, according to this view, to understand this fuller meaning. "If critique has this positive meaning," he remarks, "then the *Critique of Pure Reason* will not simply dismiss and rebuke pure reason, 'criticize' it, but will instead first set out to circumscribe its decisive, peculiar, and hence proper being. This act of circumscription is not primarily one of preventative foreclosure [*Abgrenzung gegen*], but rather one of enclosure [*Eingrenzung*], in the sense that it demonstrates the inner articulation of pure reason" (*WT* 120/ *GA* 41: 122). From this situation, the conclusion could be drawn that critique is not simply "censorship." Referring to Leibniz and Baumgarten, Heidegger adds that one would be equally mistaken to regard "the architectonics, the architectural plan of the essential structure of pure reason," as "mere 'display'" (*WT* 122/ *GA* 41: 123). From the perspective of fundamental ontology, a concept of critique interpreted in this way would help to determine the essence of reason itself.

This determination would need to be thought in relation to the opposing figures of foreclosure and enclosure, *Ab-grenzung* and *Ein-grenzung*. If the self-reflexive gesture of critique is one of *Eingrenzung* rather than of *Abgrenzung*, as Heidegger claims almost in passing, then *Abgrenzung* could be seen as a defensive ploy, a self-defensive measure directed by critical thought against another that threatens to hinder its movement from outside, as it were. The *Eingrenzung* performed by critique, by contrast, remains in principle open to the influence of that other, whether that influence be friendly or hostile, since unlike *Abgrenzung* it does not seek to expel it as a persistent danger. The *Eingrenzung* of critique is far more preoccupied with its own procedures, cognitive schemata, and unexpressed assumptions; indeed, it seeks its most radical fulfilment in the interminable determination of its own assumptions and in their critique. In this sense, critique wants nothing more than to criticize itself; that is to say, it would first come to itself by interrogating and hence potentially taking leave of itself. Such *Eingrenzung*, in contrast to *Abgrenzung*, would at the same time also have to be conceived as a potentiality, a state in which agreement on its own assumptions and inferential models remains still to come.

It is now time to take seriously Heidegger's statement that "even this understanding is only in the service of an insight into the question 'What is a thing?' [*dient nur der Einsicht in die Frage: 'Was ist ein Ding?*']" by turning toward the speculative field in which this Heideggerian engagement with the movement of Kantian critique finds expression, namely, in his thinking about the thing (*WT* 123/ *GA* 41: 125). In the First Critique Kant speaks of "the distinction between things [*Dinge*] as objects of experience and very same things as things in themselves, which our critique has made necessary," linking the concept of critique to a consideration of the thing in a manner that will not elude Heidegger.[34] Yet what are the relays between critique and the question concerning the thing in Heidegger's project? As Heidegger's student Walter Biemel reminds us, Heidegger's task as outlined already in *Being and Time* is to inquire into the essence of the beings that surround us in our quotidian life-world. But even when Heidegger addresses such everyday things as chairs and hammers, his aim is not to provide any kind of "picture-book phenomenology" of things that already are familiar but rather to think toward the ways in which our relation to things inflects how we inhabit the world in and as our *Dasein* via particular and often unthought modes of being.[35] While Heidegger's interest in the question of the thing in the aftermath of Kantian critique traverses much of his thought, it receives some of its most explicit treatments in certain passages of *Being and Time* (1927, especially paragraphs 15 and 16), in the Kant book *Die Frage nach dem Ding* (based on a 1935–1936 Freiburg lecture course and first published in 1962), in the 1936 essay "The Origin of the Work of Art," and in the later essays "Das Ding" ("The Thing") and "Building Dwelling Thinking" (1950–1951).

We might say, first of all, that it is not a mere contingency of discursive organization that Heidegger's analysis of critique as the most positive positivity is embedded in a consideration of the logic of transcendental principles as they relate to the question of the thing in Kant. In Section B of *Die Frage nach dem Ding*, entitled "Kant's Manner of Asking About the Thing," we read that what is essential in "the philosophical determination of the thingness of the thing which Kant has created" is "not an accidental by-product"; rather, "the determination of the thingness of the thing is its metaphysical center. By means of an interpretation [*Auslegung*] of Kant's work we put ourselves on the path of the inherently historical question concerning the thing" (*WT* 55/ *GA* 41: 55). It is interesting to note that Heidegger here uses the word *Auslegung* instead of the word derived from Latin, *interpretation*, which also is commonly used in German. *Auslegung* literally is a laying-out, a placing before oneself, of the elements that comprise the matter calling for understanding. As such, an *Auslegung* as a laying-out retains, at least to a German ear, the imagery of actual things being presented in a concrete, almost haptic sense.

For Heidegger, approaching the question of Kantian critique through an investigation of the thingness of the thing is a way of inhabiting Kant's thought from the inside, as it were. He writes: "We turn our question 'What is a thing?' into Kant's and, vice versa, Kant's question into ours. . . . We need not report in broad surveys and general phrases 'about' the philosophy of Kant. We put ourselves within it" (*WT* 56/ *GA* 41: 56). This mode of dwelling in Kant's thought, in his way of inventing the modern concept of critique, is what also should give rise to a questioning of the thing. For Heidegger, this becomes evident already in a consideration of the title of Kant's First Critique:

> *Critique of Pure Reason*—everyone knows what "critique" and "to criticize" mean; "reason" and what a "reasonable" man or a "reasonable" suggestion is, are also understood by everyone. What "pure" signifies in distinction to impure (e.g., impure water) is clear also. Yet we cannot think anything appropriate to the title, *Critique of Pure Reason*. Above all, one would expect a critique to reject something unsatisfactory, insufficient, and negative; one would expect criticism of something like impure reason. Finally, it is quite incomprehensible what the *Critique of Pure Reason* can have to do with the question concerning the thing. And yet we are completely justified in asserting that this title expresses nothing else but the question concerning the thing—but as a question. The question is, as we know, historical. The title means this history in a decisive era of its movement. The title means this question, and it is a thoroughly historical one. In an external sense this means that Kant, who was thoroughly clear about his work, gave it a title demanded by his age and, at the same time, led beyond it. What history of the question concerning the thing is expressed in this title? (*WT* 61f./ *GA* 41: 61f.)

To pursue the question of the thing that emerged from a consideration of critique, Heidegger interrogates the logic of categories as modes of assertion, such as quality, relation, time, and place. This interrogation leads him to assert that the thinking about the thingness of the thing and its truth are to be found not simply in the material there-ness of the object, but in certain principles of pure reason. According to the Kantian scheme as interpreted by Heidegger, "the pure inner lawfulness of reason, from out of its fundamental principles and concepts, decides about the being of what is, the thingness of things" based on a series of principles (including the principle of contradiction and the principle of sufficient reason, among others) that can be schematized and formalized through an act of reason's self-constitution. It is here that pure reason becomes "the authoritative court of appeal for the determination of the thingness of all things as such—it is this pure reason which Kant places into 'critique'" (*WT* 118f./ *GA* 41: 119f.). In short, we could say that Heidegger's argument is that if critique for Kant is the self-knowledge of pure reason, then it is the question of the thing, even the thingness of the thing, that determines the principles according to which an act of understanding is grounded in a mode of reflective judgment.

While Heidegger lays out the general relation between critique and the thing in his engagement with Kant, a more detailed interrogation of the vexing question of the thingness of the thing is carried out in "The Origin of the Work of Art." There, distancing himself from conventional views of the thing—as substance characterized by determinable characteristics, as the unifying term with which mind organizes the multiplicity of its sensory data, and as the form of matter that is shaped into cognizable form—he advances a notion of the thing that unfolds on the far side of its tool-likeness or its mere equipment-character. To choose this path is, for Heidegger, to be invited to the table of "the feast of thinking [*das Fest des Denkens*], assuming that thinking is a craft [*das Denken ein Handwerk ist*]" (*BW* 144/ *GA* 5: 3). Reminding us of the thingliness of even the most rarefied work of art, Heidegger writes: "The picture hangs on the wall like a hunting rifle or a hat. A painting, e.g., the one by Van Gogh that represents a pair of peasant shoes, travels from one exhibition to the other. Works are shipped like coal from the Ruhr and logs from the Black Forest." He continues: "During the war Hölderlin's hymns were packed in the soldier's knapsack together with cleaning gear. Beethoven's quartets lie in the storerooms of the publishing house like potatoes in a cellar" (*BW* 145/ *GA* 5: 3). But Heidegger's point is not to reduce the work of art to its thingness, however conceptualized, if by the thing's thingness is meant only its conventional interpretations. Rather, the point is not to perpetuate the concept of the thing as all that appears, as all that is and that is *as such*—Heidegger mentions such things as the stone in the road, the thistle in the field, the cloud in the sky, the leaf in the autumn breeze, the jug, the airplane, and the radio—but rather to differentiate the general realm of beings (*das Seiende*) from the mode of Being proper to a thing.

In order to understand this Heideggerean argument, we might say that a careful approach to this dimension of the thing as *Ding* also would entail its differentiation from contiguous determinations, including other German words for "thing" such as *Gegenstand* (literally, a "standing-against"), *das Objekt*, and *die Sache*. In the area of psychoanalysis, for instance, Jacques Lacan in his seminars reminds us to distinguish between *das Ding* and *die Sache* when we approach the far-reaching consequences of the relation that Freud posits between the pleasure principle and the gestures of sublimation.[36] But the particular kind of distinction that Heidegger wishes to make here is that between *Ding* and *Zeug*, understood as the shaped material used as a kind of equipment. "The equipmental being of equipment [*Zeugsein des Zeuges*]," Heidegger argues, "reliability, keeps gathered within itself all things according to their manner and extent. The usefulness of equipment is nevertheless only the essential consequence of reliability. The former vibrates in the latter and would be nothing without it. A single piece of equipment is worn out and used up; but at the same time the use itself also falls into disuse, wears away, and becomes usual" (*BW* 160/ *GA* 5: 20). But precisely this predominance of the equipment-character of beings is what needs to be called into question in order to appreciate more fully the essence of the thingness of the thing. The space of the work of art is delimited by its contiguity with both the realm of the *Zeug* and the realm of the *Ding*. The crux of Heidegger's reflections here is that what "matters is a first opening of our field of vision to the fact that what is workly in the work, equipmental in equipment, and thingly in the thing comes closer to us only when we think the Being of beings [*das Sein des Seienden denken*]." Yet this opening up does not mean that a consideration of the thingness of the work of art leads us to a determination of that work, as if the thinking of the thingness of the thing could be instrumentalized, and then presumably discarded, in the service of ascertaining the alleged meaning of a work. For Heidegger, if unconcealment takes shape in the work of art, "then the road toward the determination of the thingly reality of the work leads not from thing to work but from work to thing" (*BW* 165/ *GA* 5: 25).[37] The question concerning the thing therefore remains uncannily open, resistant to being instrumentalized in the service of this or that regime wishing to dominate the world of beings.

Heidegger's 1950 talk "The Thing" inflects his concern with the thingness of the thing found in the Kant lecture and in the artwork essay in new ways. Specifically, the text situates the question concerning the thing in relation to his other speculative preoccupations at the time: the uncanny fulfilment and closure of Western metaphysics through modern technics ("The Question Concerning Technology," 1953), the meaning of thinking under such conditions ("What Is Called Thinking," 1952), and the problem regarding the relationship between how one dwells and how one thinks ("Building Dwelling Thinking" as well as "Poetically Man Dwells . . . ," 1951). It pursues intricate questions concerning the thing's relation to the disappearance of the experience of distance and proximity in the age of global travel and telecommunication; to the scientific view of the thing as a matter of physical describability; to the experience of a gathering; and, perhaps most mystifying, to the fourfold (*das Geviert*), the name that Heidegger bestows on his ontological constellation of mortals, Gods, heaven, and earth. Unlike Plato's view of all that is present as a matter of prior manufacture and of its mode of appearance,

Heidegger focuses on the ways in which a thing exists as a such-and-such, that is, on the as-ness of the thing as it discloses itself as a form of presence. Asking about the particular thingliness of the thing, he provides the example of a jug (*der Krug*) and the manifold ways of looking at its being-as-a-thing, submitting to scrutiny the numerous ways of looking at a jug, none of which ultimately satisfy. The crux of the difficulties in ascertaining the thingness of the jug for Heidegger is lodged at the core of the insight that "no presentation of what is present [*Vorstellung des Anwesenden*], in the sense of what stands forth and of what stands over against as an object [*im Sinne des Herständigen und Gegenständlichen*], ever reaches to the thing *qua* thing [*gelangt jedoch nie zum Ding als Ding*]. The jug's thingness resides in its being *qua* vessel." Heidegger continues in "The Thing":

> We become aware of the vessel's holding nature [*das Fassende des Gefäßes*] when we fill the jug. The jug's bottom and sides obviously take on the task of holding. But not so fast! When we fill the jug with wine, do we pour the wine into the sides and bottom? At most, we pour the wine between the sides and over the bottom. Sides and bottom are, to be sure, what is impermeable in the vessel. But what is impermeable is not yet what does the holding. When we fill the jug, the pouring that fills it flows into the empty jug. The emptiness, the void, is what does the vessel's holding. The empty space, this nothing of the jug, is what the jug is as the holding vessel. . . . But if the holding is done by the jug's void, then the potter who forms sides and bottom on his wheel does not, strictly speaking, make the jug. He only shapes the clay. No—he shapes the void [*er gestaltet die Leere*]. . . . The vessel's thingness does not lie at all in the material of which it consists, but in the void that holds [*Das Dinghafte des Gefäßes beruht keineswegs im Stoff, daraus es besteht, sondern in der Leere, die faßt*]. (PLT 166f./ GA 79: 7f.)

Heidegger's point is neither to challenge the laws of physics nor to assert the metaphysical nature of the thing. Rather, he wishes to question the narrowly conceived notion of scientific rationality that would reduce the thingness of the thing either to its physical qualities or to its mere existence as substance to be calculated according to predetermined measuring sticks. This scientific view ultimately leads to the erasure of thing as thing, that is, as a provocation to our received and proscribed modes of *Dasein*. For Heidegger, by contrast, once the questioning of the thingness of thing commences, thinking the thing will not lead us to a stable determination of its essence but ever more deeply into a certain void, an obscurity of the unthought that perpetually calls for thinking.

This call for thinking cannot but engage the etymology of the very word and concept that are at stake here. Therefore, Heidegger clarifies the word-historical imbrications of the thing, summarizing his thoughts as follows:

> The Roman word *res* names that which concerns somebody, an affair, a contested matter, a case at law. The Romans also use for it the word *causa*. In its authentic and original sense, this word in a way signifies "cause [*Ursache*]"; *causa* means the case [*den Fall*] and hence also that which is the case [*was der Fall ist*], in the sense that something comes to pass and becomes due. Only because *causa*, almost synonymously with *res*, means the case, can the word *causa* later come to mean cause, in the sense of the causality of an effect. The Old High German word *thing* or *dinc*, with its meaning of a gathering specifically for the purpose of dealing with a case or matter, is suited as no other word to translate the Roman word *res*, that which is pertinent, which has a bearing. From that word of the Roman language, which corresponds to the word *res*—from the word *causa* in the sense of case, affair, matter of pertinence—there develop in turn the Romance *la cosa* and the French *la chose*; we say *das Ding*. In English *thing* has still preserved the full semantic power of the Roman word: 'He knows his things," he understands the matters that have a bearing on him; "he knows how to handle things," he knows how to go about dealing with affairs, that is, with what matters from case to case; "that's a great thing," that is something grand (fine, tremendous, splendid), something that comes of itself bears upon the human being. (*PLT* 173/ *GA* 79: 14)

But crucially, for Heidegger, the Romans left important features of the thing and its essential or primordial aspects unthought, bestowing upon the history of Western metaphysics a reductive perspective on the thingness of the thing that even the German mystic Meister Eckhart and, later, Kant and his engagement with the thing-in-itself (*Ding-an-sich*), could not fully overcome. Ultimately, according to this account, the task that presents itself to thinking is inflected by the view that the thing "things," "*das Ding dingt*," and that the very thing that the thing things is world. This world is a matter of disclosure and unconcealment vis-à-vis the human *Dasein* that always already finds itself having been thrown into it, what in *Being and Time* is termed our human experience of existential *Geworfenheit*, or thrownness.

This kind of thinking of the thing that things world is also a question of coming and of vigilance. "When and in what way do things come as things?" Heidegger asks, adding: "They do not come *by means of* human making [*kommen nicht durch die Machenschaften des Menschen*]. But neither do they appear *without* the vigilance [*Wachsamkeit*] of mortals. The first step toward such vigilance is the step back from the thinking that merely represents—that is, explains—to the thinking that responds and recalls [*Der erste Schritt zu solcher Wachsamkeit ist der Schritt zurück aus dem nur vorstellenden, d.h. erklärenden Denken in das andenkende Denken*]" (PLT 179/ GA 79: 20).

Heidegger here conjoins his reflections on the thing with the most salient concerns of his later work. Rather than viewing philosophy as a metaphysical activity to be pursued by the mere machinations or obscure dealings (equally valid translations of *Machenschaften*) of human activity, thinking—both the thinking that considers the thing, and thinking more generally—no longer is to be tied to mere explanation, a scientific gesture that often explains away the unthought, rather than attempting to learn to think it.[38] Silently alluding to Hölderlin's poem "Andenken," Heidegger's *andenkendes Denken* is a thinking that unfolds on the far side of mere calculation and rationalization. Rather, the vigilance that it performs—and *Wachsamkeit* will be a key operative concept for all of the later Heidegger—is both commemorative (*an etwas denken*) and constantly on the way somewhere else, somewhere that has not yet been reached as a destination (*andenken* as *denken an*). Like in his lecture "Who Is Nietzsche's Zarathustra?"—presented in 1953, only a couple of years following "The Thing"—Heidegger casts doubt on the claims made by both science (empiricism) and theology (belief) regarding what can be understood and experienced, instead focusing on facing a thinking kind of questioning that turns on what remains *fragwürdig*, questionable, or *frag-würdig*, worthy of being questioned. This thinking is, among other things, not a mere change in attitude, the adoption of a new method or recalibrated system. It is, rather, a tentative, probing, provisional questioning, even as it mediates upon the most obscure and fundamental issues of the unthought (*andenken* as an-denken, as a kind of initial thinking in the direction or according to the eventual possibility of something, as when one says in modern German, "Wir haben es schon einmal angedacht," but still must concretize our plans and paths further). Uncompromising vigilance—at once haptic (like the jug) and speculative, commemorative and critical, inscribed in what has come to pass and persistently oriented toward a thinking yet to come—is the thinking that the thingness of the thing calls for.

IV.

Rainer Maria Rilke, a poet of significance to both Benjamin and Heidegger, and the author of what he famously called *Dinggedichte*, or "thing-poems"—poems that allegorize particular things, such as a flower, while they themselves assumed the shape of language-as-thing—once confessed to Lou Andreas-Salomé that "*nur die Dinge reden zu mir* (only things speak to me)."[39] Rilke makes this statement in the context of what one might call his "thing letter," a missive that pivots on an analysis of Rodin's artistic way of dealing with the world of things. But in what ways can the thing in the world of things, artistic or otherwise, be made to speak? This question of making something speak, making it tell us something that we did not already know, has provided the impetus for a broad span of artistic and scholarly experiments, from contemporary British artist Willard Wigan's exquisite microsculptures that fit in the eye of a needle and often are made from dust fibers or tiny plastic slivers, via John Sallis' remarkable meditation on the concept and experience of stone, including mountains, writing tablets, towers, cathedrals, temples, and tombstones, all the way to Alphonso Lingis' poetically inflected departures from conventional philosophies of mind toward an understanding of our experience of the thingness of things in terms of the specific kind of response that a thing elicits from an embedded and bodily consciousness.[40]

How does the thing speak in and for Benjamin and Heidegger? If the two writers, as the ones who are related in their nonrelation, can be thought together as each having worked toward a rearticulation of the Kantian project of critique not by reverting to any form of Neokantianism but rather by interlacing the concept of critique with a consideration of the thingness of the thing, their methodological perspectives emerge in a dual vision. For both thinkers, the form of critique that is mobilized *in relation to* the thing—even when it is not directed *at* the thing—proceeds by denaturalizing the contextual determination that is conventionally reserved for a reading of things. Both Benjamin and Heidegger require that the thing be torn out of its assumed context—in Benjamin's case, the ossified constellation of its historical embeddedness, and in Heidegger's case, the hidden metaphysical assumptions about the things that present themselves as beings—in order to become thinkable in a new way. While for Benjamin a certain criticizabilty of the thing that encroaches upon the allegedly familiar territory delimited by the critic's purview names its status as a form of potentiality and futurity, for Heidegger the thing qua thing refuses itself to the received standards according to which Western thought relates our *Dasein* to our experiences of a thing while it leaves the more difficult questions concerning the thingness of the thing largely untouched. What calls for critique in Benjamin's model is the very moment when the thing withdraws from the transparency of its *Dingwelt* in order to step into our field of vision and consciousness as an unanchored object, a piece of debris that asks to be reinterpreted along with the cultural framework from which it emerged. What calls for critique in the Heideggerian sense is that moment when our uncompromising vigilance of thought no longer can be reduced to the certainties of a philosophical tradition in which the thing figures merely as an object exhibiting the laws of physics or a certain set of scientifically describable qualities. We might say that for both Benjamin and Heidegger, there remains something *unthought* in both critique and the thing—unthought not in the sense of an unfinished project that is as yet incomplete but in principle, and with sufficient time and appropriate progress, is completable, but rather in the sense that this unthought has remained obscure even to the critic and therefore to the very ways in which questions about an issue such as critique and the thing have been posed in the first place. The thinking of critique via the thingness of the thing therefore requires, in both the Benjaminian and Heideggerian models, a recalibration of the *question* that is meant to guide the unpredictable path of our vigilant thinking.

While both Benjamin's and Heidegger's rearticulations of critique via the question of the thing entertain certain parallels with powerful contemporary revisions of critique such as Max Horkheimer's 1937 "Traditional and Critical Theory"—the first essay in Western thought in which the term Critical Theory is used and discussed—their projects do not fasten, like Horkheimer's, upon a revision of the subject-object split that was inherited by bourgeois philosophy from an overly narrow interpretation of Descartes' scientific method, which is in turn extended to all forms of knowing to disastrous effect.[41] Similarly, while both Benjamin and Heidegger, for all their differences from each other and from Theodor W. Adorno, would share the sentiment the latter expresses in his late essay entitled "Critique" that the "damaged German relationship to critique is most comprehensible in its lack of consequence," their transformation of critique in relation to the elusive behavior of the thing does not seem to provide an immediate political framework for the mobilization of critique as a mode of intervention.[42] And finally, although both Benjamin and Heidegger see the need for a transformation of Kantian critique in nontranscendentalist terms and although both their projects would find common ground with the discussion of a "critical attitude" in the Michel Foucault of "What is Critique?", their projects are not primarily designed as archaeologically oriented tools with which to excavate a history of mentalities.[43]

What then, one might finally ask, are the ethico-political stakes of Benjamin's and Heidegger's theoretical reinscriptions of Kantian critique in terms of the thing? Is not the apparent lack of a consistent perspectival basis in their rereadings of critique evidence of a certain political lack of consequences, given that in the long and variegated history of critique, critique typically is marshalled as a form of specified resistance? Did not Marx, who famously called for a "ruthless critique of everything that is" name his most important work on political economy a *critique*? And is not critique tied first and foremost to the political concern identified by

Foucault when he lends voice to critique's "perpetual question which would be: 'how not to be governed like that, by that, in the names of those principles, with such and such an objective in mind and by means of such procedures, not like that, not for that, not by them?'"[44]

To be sure. Yet this political question, in relation to the reworkings of critique that we have encountered in Benjamin and Heidegger, is provided with a richer texture when we turn to a rather different source, Jacques Derrida. Derrida, a perspicacious and perpetual reader of both Benjamin and Heidegger, once articulated the difference between his form of deconstruction and conventional models of critique as follows:

> The *critical* idea, which I believe must never be renounced, has a history and presuppositions whose deconstructive analysis is also necessary. In the style of the Enlightenment, of Kant, or of Marx, but also in the sense of evaluation (aesthetic or literary), *critique* supposes judgement, voluntary judgement between two terms; it attaches to the idea of *krinein* or *krisis* a certain negativity. To say that all this is deconstructible does not amount to disqualifying, negating, disavowing, or surpassing it, of doing the *critique of critique* (the way people wrote critiques of the Kantian critique as soon as it appeared), but of thinking its possibility from another border, from the genealogy of judgment, will, consciousness or activity, the binary structure, and so forth. This thinking perhaps transforms the space and, through aporias, allows the (non-positive) affirmation to appear, the one that is presupposed by every critique and every negativity.[45]

The idea of critique that emerges here both affirms critique and unsettles it, as if it were engaged in a Heideggerian *Ab-bau*, a simultaneous destruction and construction, and in a Benjaminian mode in which construction is presupposed by destruction, as the *Arcades Project* has it. While the critical idea is not to be renounced, not even by its radical transformation, it is to travel through a series of impossibilities and forms of self-resistance that open critique to its unacknowledged presuppositions.

Certainly, Derrida's project is not Benjamin's, nor is it Heidegger's. And yet, when seen from the vantage point of Derrida's reformulation of critique, Benjamin's and Heidegger's reworking of Kantian critique in the course of their engagements with the thing assume the ethico-political urgency of a true question. To adopt this perspective is not the same as arguing that conventional political categories of left and right are displaced when they are exposed to the revolutionary thought of Benjamin and Heidegger.[46] Rather, we might say that once critique has freed itself from its origin in the primordial acts of separation and decision as well as from the metaphysics of binary thinking, its radical potentiality can begin to unfold as a non-normative dynamic, a mode of thinking and being that does not take its self-identity and self-presence, even in ethico-political terms, for granted. After all, if transformed and transformative modes of Kantian critique are to have a future, as the heterogenous and yet subtly imbricated projects of Benjamin and Heidegger—and, for that matter, of Derrida—suggest, this future is to be thought as a politics of the question. And this politics of the question, as a form of critique, would have to begin here, with the things that surround us.

Notes

On occasion, I have modified existing translations in my text in order to enhance their fidelity to the original.

1. Immanuel Kant, *Kritik der reinen Vernunft*, *Werkausgabe*, ed. Wilhelm Weischedel (Frankfurt am Main: Suhrkamp, 1974), vol. 3, 13; *Critique of Pure Reason*, trans. Paul Guyer and Allen W. Wood (Cambridge: Cambridge University Press, 1999), 100.
2. One of the more notable exceptions is, perhaps, the work of Italian philosopher Giorgio Agamben, whose texts often draw on both the Benjaminian and the Heideggerian traditions.
3. Berel Lang, *Heidegger's Silence* (Ithaca, NY: Cornell University Press, 1996), 22.
4. See Heidegger's letter to Arendt dated August 10, 1967, in which he refers to their previous meeting in July, during which they must have discussed Arendt's lecture on Benjamin. After all, Heidegger writes that on "the day after our meeting, on Friday, July 28th, I found the passage that goes with the Mallarmé quotation in Benjamin." In the same letter, Heidegger also registers his concern over the possibility that Arendt may have created trouble for herself by having prefaced her Freiburg lecture on Benjamin with an explicit greeting of Heidegger. Hannah Arendt and Martin Heidegger, *Briefe 1925–1975*, 3rd, expanded edition (Frankfurt am Main: Klostermann, 2002), 155f. See also the remarks by the volume's editor, Ursula Ludz, with respect to the timing of Heidegger's attendance at Arendt's Benjamin lecture following his visit with Celan and regarding the fact that Heidegger, on the day after her lecture, presented her with an inscribed copy of the Reclam version of his *The Origin of the Work of Art*. Annotations to *Briefe 1925–1975*, 322.

5. Hannah Arendt, "Walter Benjamin: 1892–1940." Introduction to Walter Benjamin, *Illuminations: Essays and Reflections*, trans. Harry Zohn (New York: Schocken, 1985), 1–51, here 46.
6. Burkhardt Lindner, entry on "Das Kunstwerk im Zeitalter seiner technischen Reproduzierbarkeit." *Benjamin-Handbuch: Leben—Werk—Wirkung*, ed. Burkhardt Lindner (Stuttgart: Metzler, 2006), 229–251, here 240.
7. For a concise differentiation of Benjamin's and Heidegger's shared non-instrumentalist view of language from theories of language following from the premises of Carnap, Quine, and others in the Anglo-Saxon analytic tradition, see Martin Seel, "Sprache bei Benjamin und Heidegger," *Merkur* 46: 4 (April 1992): 333–340.
8. Howard Caygill, "Benjamin, Heidegger, and the Destruction of Tradition," *Walter Benjamin's Philosophy*, eds. Andrew Benjamin and Peter Osborne (London: Routledge, 1994), 1–31, here 1.
9. For a philological contextualization of this fragment in the early Benjamin's work, see Uwe Steiner, *Die Geburt der Kritik aus dem Geiste der Kunst: Untersuchungen zum Begriff der Kritik in den frühen Schriften Walter Benjamins* (Würzburg: Königshausen & Neumann, 1989), 263.
10. Uwe Steiner makes this observation in "Kritik," *Benjamins Begriffe*, eds. Michael Opitz and Erdmut Wizisla (Frankfurt am Main: Suhrkamp, 2000), 479–523, here 498.
11. For a sustained discussion of Fichte's and Herder's transformations of the Kantian system of critique, see Kurt Röttgers, *Kritik und Praxis: Zur Geschichte des Kritikbegriffs von Kant bis Marx* (Berlin: de Gruyter, 1975).
12. Friedrich Schlegel, "Concerning the Essence of Critique," trans. Andreas Michel and Assenka Oksiloff. *Theory as Practice: A Critical Anthology of Early German Romantic Writings*, eds. Jochen Schulte-Sasse et al. (Minneapolis: University of Minnesota Press, 1997), 268–277, here 276f.;"Vom Wesen der Kritik," *Schriften zur Literatur*, ed. Wolfdietrich Rasch (Munich: Deutscher Taschenbuch Verlag, 1985), 250–259, here 259.
13. Bernd Witte, *Walter Benjamin: Der Intellektuelle als Kritiker—Untersuchungen zu seinem Frühwerk* (Stuttgart: Metzler, 1976), 5.
14. Rolf Tiedemann, "Dialectics at a Standstill: Approaches to the Passagen-Werk," trans. Gary Smith and André Lefevere. *On Walter Benjamin: Critical Essays and Reflections*, ed. Gary Smith (Cambridge, MA: MIT Press, 1988), 260–291, here 281.
15. Dorothea Kimmich, *Lebendige Dinge in der Moderne* (Konstanz: Konstanz University Press, 2011), 55. Kimmich's study as a whole provides a sensitive reading of literary modernity and the thing.

16. Kimmich, *Lebendige Dinge in der Moderne*, 55. For a reading of Benjamin's image of the sock in relation to his preferred literary and philosophical genre of the *Denkbild*, see my discussion of the "The Sock" from the *Berlin Childhood around 1900* in *Thought-Images: Frankfurt School Writers' Reflections from Damaged Life* (Stanford, CA: Stanford University Press, 2007), 9–11.
17. Kimmich, *Lebendige Dinge in der Moderne*, 58.
18. For a reading of "Construction Site" in the context of Benjamin's political montage, see Michael W. Jennings, "Trugbild der Stabilität. Weimarer Politik und Montage-Theorie in Benjamins *Einbahnstraße*," trans. Gerhard Richter and Michael W. Jennings, *Gobal Benjamin*, vol. 1, eds. Klaus Garber and Ludger Rehm (Munich: Fink, 1999), 517–528.
19. I analyze this imbrication in detail in "Benjamin's Ear: Noise, Mnemonics, and the Berlin Chronicle," *Walter Benjamin and the Corpus of Autobiography* (Detroit, MI: Wayne State University Press, 2000), 163–197.
20. A sustained reading of the gaze in relation to its objects can be found in my "Benjamin's Eye/I: Vision and the Scene of Writing in the Berlin Chronicle around 1900," *Walter Benjamin and the Corpus of Autobiography*, 199–229.
21. Samuel Weber, *Benjamin's -abilities* (Cambridge, MA: Harvard University Press, 2008).
22. G. W. F. Hegel, *Phänomenologie des Geistes*, Werke, vol. 3 (Frankfurt am Main: Suhrkamp, 1986), 91f.; *Phenomenology of Spirit*, trans. A. V. Miller (Oxford: Oxford University Press, 1979), 66; *Phänomenologie des Geistes*, Werke, vol. 3 (Frankfurt am Main: Suhrkamp, 1986), 91f.
23. Hegel, *Phenomenology*, 74; *Phänomenologie*, 101f.
24. For a fuller reading of Dürer's woodcut in the context of Benjamin's and the artist Anselm Kiefer's angelology, see my "History's Flight, Anselm Kiefer's Angels." *Connecticut Review* 24:1 (Spring 2002): 113–136.
25. A general discussion of "the expressionless" in Benjamin is offered by Winfried Menninghaus, "Das Ausdruckslose: Walter Benjamins Kritik des Schönen durch das Erhabene," *Walter Benjamin 1892–1940*, ed. Uwe Steiner (Bern: Lang, 1992), 33–76.
26. See, for instance, the comprehensive and learned volumes *Heidegger-Handbuch: Leben—Werk—Wirkung*, ed. Dieter Thomä (Stuttgart: Metzler, 2003); *The Cambridge Companion to Heidegger*, 2nd edition, ed. Charles Guignon (Cambridge: Cambridge University Press, 2006); and *A Companion to Heidegger*, eds. Hubert Dreyfus and Mark Wrathall (Oxford: Blackwell, 2005).
27. See the essays and statements collected in Herbert Marcuse, *Heideggerean Marxism* (Lincoln: University of Nebraska Press, 2005).

28. Fred Dallmayr, *Between Freiburg and Frankfurt: Toward a Critical Ontology* (Amherst: University of Massachusetts Press, 1991), 27.
29. Dallmayr, *Between Freiburg and Frankfurt*, 31.
30. Kant, *Critique of Pure Reason*, 114f.; *Kritik der reinen Vernunft*, 29f.
31. I borrow the remaining lines of this paragraph along with the following two paragraphs from my *Afterness: Figures of Following in Modern Thought and Aesthetics* (New York: Columbia University Press, 2011), where they appear in a slightly different version.
32. Rodolphe Gasché, *The Honor of Thinking: Critique, Theory, Philosophy* (Stanford, CA: Stanford University Press, 2007), 13. See also Klaus Düsing, "Immanuel Kant. Aufklärung und Kritik," *Philosophen des 18. Jahrhunderts. Eine Einführung*, ed. Lothar Kreimendahl (Darmstadt: WBG, 2000).
33. My understanding here is indebted to Gasché's insightful interpretation of this Heideggerian passage in *The Honor of Thinking*, 14.
34. Kant, *Critique of Pure Reason*, 115; *Kritik der Urteilskraft*, 31.
35. Walter Biemel, "Die Entfaltung von Heideggers Ding-Begriff," *Gesammelte Schriften* (Stuttgart-Bad Cannstatt: Frommann-Holzboog, 1996), vol. 1, 353–378, here 356.
36. See the reflections collected in Jacques Lacan, *The Seminar of Jacques Lacan, Book VII: The Ethics of Psychoanalysis 1959–1960*, ed. Jacques-Alain Miller, trans. Dennis Porter (New York: Norton, 1992), especially the section entitled "Introduction to the Thing" (17–84). It will be necessary, in another context, to trace the similarities and differences between Heidegger and Lacan as they converge on *das Ding*. In his seminar, Lacan leaves much interpretive work for his readers to accomplish when he contents himself with a passing reference to Heidegger's *Ding* in general:

> To have confirmation of the appropriation of the vase for this purpose, look up what Heidegger affirms when he writes about *das Ding*. He's the last in a long line to have meditated on the subject of creation; and he develops his dialectic around a vase. I will not be concerned here with the function of *das Ding* in Heidegger's approach to the contemporary revelation of what he calls Being and that is linked to the end of metaphysics. . . . You will see the function Heidegger assigns it [*das Ding*] of uniting celestial and terrestrial powers around it in an essential human process. (120)

37. In another discussion, it would be illuminating to consider Heidegger's emphasis on the movement of the work leading to the thing—rather than vice

versa—also in relation to the framework of his more general understanding of physicality. A suggestive start has been made by the philosopher Charles E. Scott, *The Lives of Things* (Bloomington: Indiana University Press, 2002), 57–67, who locates Heidegger's general idea of physicality in the context of his post-Husserlian understanding of the phenomenological concept of *Lebenswelt*.

38. By contrast, a Heideggerean thinking of thingliness always also involves a rigorous reconsideration of what it is that causes us to speak of someone as human or of something as an object endowed with this or that meaning. The thing cannot but be inscribed in the attitudes through which we relate to objects, and by extension, to being-in-the-world itself. As Hubert Dreyfus eloquently observes in his engagement with Heidegger:

> Our everyday know-how involves an understanding of what it is to be a person, a thing, a natural object, a plant, an animal, and so on. Our understanding of animals these days, for example, is in part embodied in our skill in buying pieces of them, taking off their plastic wrapping, and cooking them in microwave ovens. In general, we deal with things as resources to be used and then disposed of when no longer needed. A Styrofoam cup is a perfect example. When we want a hot or cold drink it does its job, and when we are through with it we throw it away. This understanding of an object is very different from what we can suppose to be the Japanese understanding of a delicate, painted teacup, which does not do as good a job of maintaining temperature and which has to be washed and protected, but which is preserved from generation to generation for its beauty and social meaning. Or, to take another example, an old earthenware bowl, admired for its simplicity and its ability to evoke memories of ancient crafts, such as is used in a Japanese tea ceremony, embodies a unique understanding of things. It is hard to picture a tea ceremony around a Styrofoam cup.

"Heidegger on the Connection between Nihilism, Art, Technology, and Politics," *The Cambridge Companion to Heidegger*, 2nd ed., ed. Charles Guignon (Cambridge: Cambridge University Press, 2006), 345–372, here 351. One might add that this also would be one of the conceptual conjunctions between late Heidegger's reading of the thing and his critique of the *Ge-stell*, the technical enframement through which objects, and the world as such, become mere entities of an omnipresent *Be-stand*, a standing reserve or stockpile, in which

everything, having lost the capacity for distance, absence, and singularity, can simply be placed on order—becomes, that is, with every placed order a treacherous affirmation of the modern world's principle orderability.
39. Rainer Maria Rilke, *Briefe* (Frankfurt am Main: Insel, 1987), vol. 1, 61.
40. See John Sallis, *Stone* (Bloomington: Indiana University Press, 1994) and Alphonso Lingis, *The Imperative* (Bloomington: Indiana University Press, 1998), especially the remarkable sections on the intimate and alien nature of things and on their production, pageantry, and purpose (73–102).
41. Max Horkheimer, "Traditional and Critical Theory," trans. Matthew J. O'Connell, *Critical Theory: Selected Essays* (New York: Continuum, 1999), 188–243.
42. Theodor W. Adorno, "Critique," *Critical Models: Interventions and Catchwords*, ed. and trans. Henry Pickford (New York: Columbia University Press, 1998), 281–288, here 286; "Kritik," *Gesammelte Schriften*, ed. Rolf Tiedemann (Frankfurt am Main: Suhrkamp, 1997), vol. 10, 785–793, here 791.
43. Michel Foucault, "What Is Critique?" *The Essential Foucault*, eds. Paul Rabinow and Nikolas Rose (New York: New Press, 2003), 263–278.
44. Ibid., 265.
45. Jacques Derrida, "'A "Madness" Must Watch Over Thinking,'" trans. Peggy Kamuf, *Points . . . Interviews, 1974–1994*, ed. Elizabeth Weber (Stanford, CA: Stanford University Press, 1995), 338–364, here 357. In an investigation that exceeds the boundaries of the current project, it also will be fruitful to engage at length with the few pages that Derrida devotes to Heidegger's thinking of the thing in relation to the constellation of the animal, mortality, death, and sovereignty, the topics of Derrida's last seminars. See specifically the opening "detour" of Derrida's seminar on February 5, 2003, in *The Beast and the Sovereign*, vol. 2, ed. Michel Lisse, Marie-Louise Mallet, and Ginette Michaud, trans. Geoffrey Bennington (Chicago: University of Chicago Press, 2011), 119–126.
46. This is the argument made throughout Willem van Reijen, *Der Schwarzwald und Paris: Heidegger und Benjamin* (Munich: Fink, 1998). It is plausible, however, to redraw the political divisions between Benjamin and Heidegger along the interpretative lines of specific conceptions of philosophical issues in their work, such as their divergent views of time and historicity. For an extended analysis of Benjamin's and Heidegger's perspectives on the conjunction of art and historicity, see Stefan Knoche, *Benjamin—Heidegger: Über Gewalt – Die Politisierung der Kunst* (Vienna: Turia & Kant, 2000). Cf. Andrew Benjamin's suggestive observation that their differing concepts of what constitutes the present allow us to appreciate the extent to which "the ineliminable presence of a different politics . . . can be reworked as the primordial conflict over the

nature of the present.... What is proposed is a conflict that cannot be resolved by a simple deferral to the instant. The conflict between Benjamin and Heidegger is political for precisely this reason." "Time and Task: Benjamin and Heidegger Showing the Present," *Present Hope: Philosophy, Architecture, Judaism* (London: Routledge, 1997), 26–55, here 28.

PART TWO

Experience

THREE

STIMMUNG

Heidegger and Benjamin

Ilit Ferber

A Critical Junction

The question of the philosophical encounter between Heidegger and Benjamin can be tackled in various ways. It can be approached through specific references of one to the other's writings or ideas, such as Benjamin's letters to Scholem and Brecht in which he proposes establishing a reading group that would "demolish Heidegger." We might also consider Benjamin's blunt disregard of Heidegger in his own work despite the clear evidence that he was in fact knowledgeable about Heidegger's writings and even influenced by them.[1] It can be addressed by means of a comparison of the themes with which both philosophers dealt almost simultaneously—modernity, structures of temporality and history, tradition and the work of art. Or, it can be examined by constructing an imaginary encounter of ideas so as to reveal their hidden ties regarding the promotion of similar philosophical agendas, whether the fundamental changes in subjectivity produced by modernity[2] or the relatedness between the work of art and the discussion of its origin.[3] Anyone taking any of these approaches is bound to find some compelling and productive points of conjunction that not only suggest a profound similarity between both thinkers but also evoke thought-provoking ways in which each illuminates the other's ideas. The productivity of these confluences inevitably intimates that when Benjamin wrote to Scholem that he expects "sparks will fly" from the shock of his confrontation with Heidegger (*CA*: 359–360), he was referring to more than heated disputes about their diverse ideas on history (on this occasion) but also to the consequent outbursts of the productive sparks that their encounter might yield.

As Hamacher points out, however, the vulgar idea of an "*influxus physicus*" would not do justice to the complexity of both thinkers' "trains of thought."[4] My interest in examining the philosophical encounter between Benjamin and Heidegger, therefore lies less in tracing the similarities in the themes that preoccupied the two or in pointing to the reasonable possibility that both preferred to ostensibly ignore the other's work for their own reasons. My interest is, instead, to reconstruct the objects of their mutual philosophical criticism and draw the implications these criticisms yield. More specifically, both Benjamin and Heidegger were attracted by the possibility of proposing an alternative to a structure they took to be one of philosophy's deepest and darkest myths—the subjective formation of knowledge and experience. Each from his own unique perspective was most vehemently convinced that the problem of subjectivity was one of the most profound and primary distortion to mislead philosophical thinking, a distortion to be disclosed, explicated, and overcome by means of an alternative philosophical premise that would redefine human experience and knowledge. The problem of subjectivity and its dismantling, therefore, was not only a common theme in Benjamin's and Heidegger's oeuvre; it was also a strong philosophical *determination* they concurrently shared. What the structure of the subject (and its inherent correspondence with an independent object) conceals can be disclosed, according to Benjamin and Heidegger, only by means of an alternative philosophical structure in which the relationship between man and world is completely overturned. This alternative structure, I suggest, can be conceived in terms of *Stimmung* (attunement) or mood. I therefore take *Stimmung* to be a subject both thinkers shared but, more profoundly, an organizing principle underlying the philosophical alternative they both offer to the structure of subjectivity and the subject-object divide.

Heidegger's criticism of subjectivity is directed first and foremost at the weight of its authority and extensive ramifications. He describes the distinction between subject and object as a "cancerous evil" and an "erroneous opinion"; however, he is more fiercely concerned with the grip this distinction holds over philosophical thinking (*ZS*: 192/ *GA* 89: 240).[5] Heidegger holds that the relationship between subject and object is presupposed, not established, and it is this presupposition, "unimpeachable in its facticity," that renders the distinction so baleful. The strength of this presumed relationship has thus left all questions of ontological meaning, one of the core issues Heidegger seeks to consider, in complete darkness (*BT*: 86/ *GA* 2: 59). Heidegger therefore acknowledges that the reigning subject-objects structure is in fact a powerful expression of a fundamentally epistemological configuration, that of a knowing subject confronting the objects of his consciousness (found most strikingly in Kant but also in Descartes, two thinkers Heidegger critiques), that has come to prevail the very structure of philosophy, clouding philosophy's scrutiny and precluding the disclosure of the structure of Being. Heidegger's criticism of this model is couched in terms of the fundamental separation between the subject and the object, a separation most evident in the German word *Gegen-Stand*, that is, object as what is stood against by the subject who experiences it.

To Heidegger, the accepted model contains a misconception of the subject as inherently independent from the world, the latter being a space containing free-standing objects to which the subject's intentional consciousness is directed: "In interpretation, we do not, so to speak, throw a 'signification' over some naked thing which is present-at-hand, we do not stick a value on it" (*BT*: 190/ *GA* 2: 150). Such a configuration would obstruct the possibility of undertaking an ontological rather than a merely epistemological inquiry. In other words, Heidegger does not wish to focus on relations between subjects and what he calls the present-at-hand object; instead, he is concerned with an ontological inquiry of Dasein focusing on the question of being. Instead of the philosophical "trend toward the 'subject,'" Heidegger seeks to convey "that philosophical inquiry somehow understood that the basis for every substantial philosophical problem could and had to be procured from an adequate elucidation of the 'subject.'" (*BPP*: 312). As Jean-Luc Marion points out, what exists in the world in the form of the object does not do so as a result of an objectivization performed by the subject, nor does the subject exist independently of those objects. Marion continues by arguing that Dasein determines the world as much as the world determines it; Dasein is therefore "handled, as it were, by that which it handles."[6]

Strikingly similar formulations appear in Benjamin's 1918 "On the Program of the Coming Philosophy." In an ambitious attempt to present his criticism of the Kantian system, Benjamin attacks what he takes to be Kant's "naked, primitive and self-evident" structure of experience, an experience that is "virtually reduced to a nadir, to a minimum of significance" (*SW* 1: 101). He locates the crux of the problematic primarily in the fact that "Kant's conception of knowledge is as a relation between some sort of subjects and objects or subject and object—a conception that he was unable, ultimately, to overcome, despite all his attempts to do so; and second, the relation of knowledge and experience to human empirical consciousness, likewise only very tentatively overcome. These two problems are closely interconnected" (*SW* 1: 103). What Benjamin is troubled by, and what would become the main task of his "coming philosophy," is that Kant constitutes experience solely on the basis of a scientific, empirical model and, accordingly, on an insubstantial, poor, and flimsy structure of experience. In formulations similar to those of Heidegger, Benjamin claims that a structure in which a subject is defined by means of its "cognizing consciousness" can only lead to a structure of experience in which objects confront it, an experience whose "sad significance" is limited to the criteria of certainty (*SW* 1: 101). An alternative structure, he states, would begin with the fundamental separation between knowledge and experience so that the latter would cease to be limited to constraints of Kantian understanding and categorization and would thus be able to open experience to richer and deeper contents.

What this "higher form of experience" would introduce into philosophy is the possibility of metaphysics—a possibility that, in Kant's eyes (as largely determined by enlightenment views)—is "a disease that expresses itself in the separation of knowledge from the realm of experience" (*SW* 1: 102). Benjamin's task is, therefore, to open up the Kantian system to metaphysics, that is, to locate the meaning of experience beyond the borders of mere epistemology. This task involves the search for an autonomous, innate sphere "of total neutrality in regard to the concepts of both subject and object" (*SW* 1: 104). It is not Benjamin's intent to cancel any form of subjectivity or objectivity altogether; it is rather, to redefine these forms' ability to relate to one another neutrally, that is, to establish relationships free of the oppressive power of subjective consciousness and knowledge and in the absence of an isolated, independent object. Benjamin's alternative would consequently articulate a "sphere" in which a different structure of experience is at stake, one dominated, in contrast to Kant, by its metaphysical and speculative weight.[7]

Deeply related to the problem of the subject-object divide with which the two thinkers are preoccupied is another crucial concept: intentionality. Both Heidegger and Benjamin are indebted to Husserl's discussion of intentionality and seem to draw (directly in Heidegger's case, indirectly in Benjamin's) much from his rigorous account of the role of intentionality in the structure of consciousness. Responding to Brentano's use of *intentionality*,[8] Husserl employs the term to describe what he takes to be the phenomenological structure of experience. Intentionality, as distinguished from mere intention, refers to the structure of human awareness of the world, which Husserl first characterizes in *Logical Investigations* as an immediate and united structure of consciousness comprised of acts, contents, and objects, and later in *Ideas I* as a pure experience of consciousness drawing on the necessary distinctions "between the *components proper* of intentive mental processes and their *intentional correlates* and their components . . . the distinction served us to make clear the own peculiar being of the phenomenological sphere."[9]

Intentionality embodies the conceptual structure that Husserl applies to explain awareness of the world as inherently object-oriented, although not necessarily in the form of a thematic structure of attention. Nonetheless, intentionality is not a property of objects and is therefore not an ontological quality; rather, it distinguishes the structure of consciousness itself. For Husserl, the notion of intentionality strengthened his account of another key phenomenological term: *epoché* (or methodical "bracketing"). By focusing on the intentional structure of consciousness, Husserl was able to confine or "bracket" the ontological state of reality, thereby inhibiting reality's acceptance in favor of the process of consciousness itself, viewed as independent from the object of intention.

The criticism offered by both Heidegger and Benjamin thus stems from one and the same philosophical impetus: not only is the dominance of the structure of subjectivity at stake, but also, and more importantly, subjectivity's authority is disputed and challenged. For Heidegger like Benjamin, this model is insufficient in its account of human experience; more crucially, it precludes the possibility of understanding the very heart of the human experience of the world, which stretches far beyond the narrow configuration of subjects versus objects. Heidegger famously formulates his alternative in the notion of "Being-in-the-world," which relays an entirely different way of considering the fundamental structure of Dasein: "While the traditional doctrine of the subject is based on a subject-object-*split*, the view of being-in-the-world . . . allows a removal of this split in the sense of immediacy bridging over the split" (*ZS*: 190/ *GA* 89: 237). It is not that Dasein replaces the subject, nor that transcendence replaces that structure of subjectivity. What Heidegger seeks to show is that it "eliminates" the question of subjectivity altogether (*ZS*: 192/ *GA* 89: 240).

Dasein in this sense is not constituted as a subject confronting a world that serves as an object of its knowledge but as what Heidegger calls the *commercium* of the subject with the world. This unity is not created as a result of knowledge, nor is it derived from the way the world acts upon the knowing subject; instead, it conditions the possibility of knowledge in the first place (*BT*: 90/ *GA* 2: 62). What Heidegger desires is to challenge an epistemology limited to what is present-at-hand and expressed only in a specific form of encounter between a knowing subject and the objects cognized. He seeks a much richer notion of Being whose relationship with its world does not stem from any fundamental separateness but from Dasein's being always-already embedded in the world.

Benjamin suggests something similar when he describes the coming philosophy's task as that of finding an autonomous sphere for knowledge, one in which relations between subjects and objects are neutral (*SW* 1: 104). This structure gives rise to Benjamin's conception of a higher, transcendental experience, one that retains some of Kant's formal structures and terminology but overturns them in order to encompass the rich realms of experience left outside the Kantian system.[10]

At stake for Benjamin is the search for an alternative way to approach the conundrum of human experience without falling into the problematic structure of the subject-object fissure, or renouncing "experience" itself, that is, the way in which the world affects or comes to be meaningful for man.

I would argue that Heidegger and Benjamin attend to this problem, most notably in their consideration of the term *Stimmung*, a concept whose translation has always been problematic but that can be provisionally rendered as attunement or mood.[11] More specifically, they both develop the idea of *Stimmung*, albeit in different ways, while establishing it as a fundamental structural element of their philosophical alternatives to subjectivity and the relations it maintains with the world. By bringing the two accounts of *Stimmung* together, I hope to show that this term is not so much a "theme" that preoccupied both Heidegger and Benjamin but, rather, an essential constituent at the heart of their philosophical alternatives to the structure of subjectivity.

For Heidegger, the case is simpler. He clearly spells out how the structure of Dasein serves as an alternative for a subject facing an object; he accordingly presents *Stimmung* as what constitutes and conditions Dasein's Being-in-the-world. In Benjamin's case, however, things are not so precisely drawn, let alone given a discursive philosophical account. However, by utilizing the idea of *Stimmung* as part of his own philosophical method, Benjamin goes further in revealing the term's philosophical implications. What is given a scrupulous and deliberate account in Heidegger turns into a powerful operative principle in Benjamin. That principle does not, however, consistently govern Benjamin's philosophical thinking. It is here that the implications of the meeting between the two thinkers become evident: it lies in the unique form in which they contribute to each other's consideration and employment of *Stimmung*. I begin with Heidegger's theory of moods and then go into Benjamin's own postulations. But first, a few words on *Stimmung*.

Stimmung, a word described by Leo Spitzer as virtually untranslatable,[12] fluctuates between two ostensibly polar facets of mood or attunement: the internal and the external. These may also be characterized as descriptions of the internal ambience of the subject's feelings, endowed with a psychological dint, as opposed to an account of "atmosphere" or objective attributes of the subject's environment. *Stimmung* also vacillates between its musical connotations, located in its *concentus* and *temperamentum*, what can also be described by the Greek word *harmonia*, meaning attunement, accord, harmony, and its later provenance as a psychological term.[13] In line with these sonic connotations, the concept *Stimmung* is also closely connected to the word *Stimme* (voice), and thus to expression and its mark of individuality. But what English renderings of the word specifically shun is the posited connection between the musical and the psychological, the external and the internal—all of which appear, separately, in the different translations of the word into mood, attunement, or accord. Not only do the English translations fail to encompass all these denotations, they do not capture the unique interconnectedness found in the German *Stimmung*. As Agamben shows in his subtle discussion of *Stimmung*, which he also describes as "emotional tonality,"[14] the term expresses a unity between a subjective feeling and a human being's accord with his or her surroundings (a landscape, for instance). *Stimmung*, in German, thus transmits a conceptual integration—or a harmonious unity[15]—of the objective or factual with the subjective and psychological.

The importance of this term for Heidegger's and Benjamin's criticisms of the subject-object fissure and their concern with the possibility of positing a different form of connection between a human being and his world now begins to come clear. *Stimmung* cannot be located on either side of the threshold that Heidegger and Benjamin wish to transcend—it lies precisely *on* that threshold, at its verge. It is therefore never merely subjective nor objective, nor is it limited to an individual's internal psychological state or any reference to his world. But, more important than its unrestricted relationship to these categories is *Stimmung*'s crucial relevance to the primacy of their interconnection. Hence, by giving *Stimmung* a constitutive role in their philosophical theories, Heidegger and Benjamin are able to address the problematic inherent in the division between man and the world without eliminating any of its components.

Heidegger and the Importance of *Stimmung*

Stimmung makes its first appearance in Heidegger's early *Being and Time*. Despite the term's considerable shifts in Heidegger's subsequent thought, it remains central to his understanding of philosophy as well as his celebrated account of Being. Heidegger's discussion of anxiety as a fundamental mood (*Grundstimmung*) in *Being and Time* and of boredom in *The Fundamental Concepts of Metaphysics* are two renowned and thoroughly discussed examples, one might even say exemplars of his analysis of *Stimmung*. However, a more analytical and systematic account of the structure of *Stimmung* appears in *Being and Time*, prior to his phenomenological explication of anxiety. It is at this preliminary stage that Heidegger summons the structure of *Stimmung* to challenge notions of a psychological "inner" and an objective "outer" configuration. By doing so he suggests an alternative structure of meaning that evinces an ontological rather than a psychological or subjective structure.

In this discussion, *Stimmung* emerges first and foremost as a distinctive dimension of the structure of Dasein itself, with which Heidegger wishes to fundamentally challenge the subject-object antithesis. *Stimmung*, accordingly, appears prior to any cognitive engagement or epistemological attitude to the world. When approaching them, objects necessarily appear as independent entities whose meaning "objectively" exists for the subject to reveal. Such a discursive structure of knowledge obstructs the fundamental Da of Dasein, treating the two as independent entities. In arguing that *Stimmung* is neither internal nor external (*BT*: 176/ GA 2: 136) but operating precisely at the threshold between the two, Heidegger establishes *Stimmung* as an intersection between man and the world: to use Heideggerian terms, *Stimmung* is what determines Dasein's Being-in-the-world. Insofar as it can never be located inside the subject, or outside in the world, *Stimmung* marks the distinct configuration in which Dasein finds itself always-already within the world. This structure conveys the challenge Heidegger poses to Husserlian intentionality, namely, that the subject, contrary to constituting his world by objectifying it, now aims to do so by opening it up, subsequent to realizing that his being is always-already within the world. In this way, as Marion puts it, by abandoning "objectivization of the object," Heidegger renounces the title of "subject" in favor of Dasein.[16] Dasein thus does not merely confront but rather constitutes the world of objects, determining it by its moods and the unique way of opening up rather than simply representing or conceptualizing the world.

It is important to note that Heidegger uses the related term *Grundstimmung*, a fundamental mood, in two principal senses. In *Being and Time*, the term appears as describing anxiety, and denotes an individualizing, nonhistorically determined mood. Yet, in *The Fundamental Concepts of Metaphysics*, Heidegger refers to boredom as a *Grundstimmung* of an age rather than of an individual. *Grundstimmung* is a fundamental attunement preceding any subjective or intentional determination. It is a fundamental attunement as it opens Dasein to the world prior to any determination of "who" opens "what";[17] furthermore, it has the power to reveal the fundamental structure of *Stimmung* per se, a structure not distinctly divulged in other moods. But even more crucially, Heidegger directly links between fundamental attunements and the foundation of philosophy itself, arguing that our "being gripped philosophically and our philosophical comprehension necessarily arise from Dasein's fundamental attunements [*Grundstimmungen*]" (*FCM*: 7/ GA 29/30: 9–10).

In this sense, Dasein does not create the world, nor does it bring about its own attunements; it verily finds itself simultaneously in attunement to and in the world. The fundamental quality of *Stimmung* is therefore, a presupposition for maintaining any epistemological approach; that is, it is ontologically anterior to the realm of epistemology. Dasein's relation to the world is determined only by the various modes in which *Stimmung* attunes Dasein to the world and synchronizes it within it. The discovery of the world as what is meaningful to us becomes possible only through *Stimmung*. In consequence, *Stimmung* has the power to open the world for us and in us, to transform the world into something that matters to us. Focusing on the explicit structure of Being thus allows Heidegger to treat *Stimmung* ontologically, that is, as a constitutive element of Being—a concept that does not fall prey to the subject-object divide; instead, it provides the primary conditions for conceptualizing it in the first place.

Heidegger continues to expand on this interconnection between Dasein and the world, which he terms *Befindlichkeit*, translated as attunement or affectedness[18]—both stressing the term's ontic rather than psychological veins.[19] But this finding oneself, manifested in the use of *finden* in *Befindlichkeit*, is not to be understood as a spatial description of a situation or position within the world but, in accordance with the dual structure of *Stimmung*, as what lies neither inside nor outside, but what constitutes their inherent interconnectedness. Hence, "having a mood is not related to the psychical in the first instance, and is not itself an inner condition which then reaches forth in an enigmatical way and puts its mark on things and persons" (*BT*: 176/ *GA* 2: 137). The best way to grasp the significance of this statement is to think about *Stimmung* as a "disposition" or "disposedness" that brings the word closer to the equiprimordial "present perfect" of states such as disclosedness or thrownness.[20]

More importantly, *Befindlichkeit* refers to the way that Dasein finds itself affected (*Betroffenwerdens*) by the world and always-already situated in the world as what matters to it. Being in a certain mood (*Stimmung*) determines the ways that the world affects Dasein, what carries specific import for us and binds us to the world: "The fact that this sort of thing can 'matter' to it is grounded in one's affectedness. . . . Dasein's openness to the world is constituted existentially by the attunement of affectedness" (*BT*: 176/ *GA* 2: 137, revised translation). Put differently, *Stimmung* (mood or attunement) is the way in which the world discloses and unfolds itself—how we find ourselves in the world, and how it matters to us. *Stimmung* thus has the power to make the world into something meaningful. Yet, this meaningfulness does not have a structure resembling that of desire, an emotive experience in which a certain object grabs our attention. *Stimmung* is less constrained; it reveals itself in an all-encompassing mode, in totality. In that sense, *Stimmung* is necessary for the disclosure and appearance of the world, in its entirety, as hopeful, boring, or anxious. And so, the world is not "colored" or veiled by a certain mood but is constituted *of* and made intelligible *by Stimmung*.

Heidegger vividly unravels this structure in his description of sadness:

> When I am in a mood of sadness, then things address me quite differently or not at all. Here we do not mean feeling in the subjective sense that I have a feeling for something. Feeling [as existential mood] concerns my whole being-in-the-world as my being a Self. Attunement [*Gestimmtheit*] is not something standing for itself but belongs to being-in-the-world as being addressed by things. Attunement and being related [*Bezogensein*] are one and the same. (*ZS*: 202–203/ *GA* 89: 251)

Quite conspicuous here is Heidegger's insistence on maintaining the reciprocal structure of relations between man and world, that is, it is not only that Dasein attends the world differently from within the openness of moods, but it is also the world that addresses Dasein. It is in this sense that moods do not belong to a subject or even to his peculiar perspective. What Heidegger indicates in this passage is precisely that *Stimmung* pertains to the significance of the threshold between being and world, to the hyphens of Being-in-the-world.

The position of *Stimmung* at the threshold returns us to the feature of totality. That is, *Stimmung* does not disclose separate objects in the world but the totality of the world itself, in a structure completely dissimilar from the intentionality of cognitive comprehension. Instead, it functions as the substratum for any intentional act. Heidegger adds that no thought exists without *Stimmung* initially setting the conditions of its possibility; hence, "understanding always has its mood" (*BT*: 182/ *GA* 2: 143). What Heidegger offers here is a novel perspective from which to account for the relationship between *Stimmung* and philosophy or, more precisely, the only possible structure in which, according to his view, the relationship of philosophy to the world can be conceived.[21]

Heidegger consequently points to the disclosive nature of *Stimmung*; he writes that "mood is a primordial kind of Being for Dasein, in which Dasein is disclosed to itself prior to all cognition and volition, and beyond their range of disclosure" (*BT*: 175/ *GA* 2: 136). Elsewhere he states: "The possibilities of disclosure that belong to cognition reach far too short a way compared with the primordial disclosure belonging to moods, in which Dasein is brought before its Being as 'there'" (*BT*: 173/ *GA* 2: 134). With these claims, Heidegger departs from the traditional conception of affect and sensuous states as secondary to the "higher" cognitive faculties of reason and will.[22] He perceives *Stimmung* as revealing the fundamental qualities of our Being-in-the-world, preceding and thus conditioning any "cognitive" disclosure undertaken with the faculty of reason.[23] *Stimmung*, as mood or attunement, thus cannot be thought of as mere emotional responses or experiences; it is rather "the fundamental ways in which we *find* ourselves disposed in such and such a way.

Attunements are the '*how*' [*Wie*] according to which one is in such and such a way. . . . And yet this . . . is never—simply a consequence or side-effect of our thinking, doing, and acting. It is—to put it crudely—the presupposition for such things, the 'medium' within which they first happen" (*FCM*: 67–68/ *GA* 29/30: 100–101). With this Heidegger lays claim to much more than some additional characterization of moods: they not only determine the way or mode of Being-in-the-world, they condition it. This is formulated at one point in Heidegger as an act of "displacement," meaning the power of *Stimmung* to place Dasein into a relation with the world that conditions the latter's understanding and disclosure (*BQP*: 161/ *GA* 45: 186–187). Any account of cognition or emotion is therefore always-already determined and conditioned by moods. Hence, "Dasein always has some mood" and is "never free of moods" (*BT*: 173, 175/ *GA* 2: 134, 136).

In addressing the problem of the subject-object divide, Heidegger confronts the Husserlian phenomenological project and transforms it by assigning to *Stimmung* an underlying structure parallel to intentionality. This revision is a necessary outcome of Heidegger's refutation of the structure entailing a subject intentionally facing an object. Heidegger's reflections on moods cannot, therefore, be object-oriented, as Husserl suggests, but are instead, object-less and intention-less.[24] Heidegger's most lucid account of the difference between intention and lack of intention is his comparison of fear and anxiety (*BT*/ *GA* 2: §28 and §40).[25] He describes fear as a state of mind constituted by the threat posed by a specific and identifiable object; in other words, we are afraid of those objects or situations that we feel threaten us. Fear thus evinces an intentional structure because it is always directed toward discrete phenomena. Anxiety, however, is an exemplar of a fundamental mood. In *Being and Time*, Heidegger approaches this mood from the opposite direction: anxiety is primordial precisely because nothing specific acts as its cause. In states of anxiety, nothingness itself is disclosed, a structure epitomizing Heidegger's Being-in-the-world. Unlike our response to fear, we experience anxiety in a way that is not object-oriented but unintentional. No subject-object relation emerges because one's Being-in the world is itself conditioned by mood. Due to its inherent evasion of the subject-object structure, anxiety therefore discloses "the *world as world*" (*BT*: 232/ *GA* 2: 187), that is, the world in its totality rather than any object given in it. In other words, it is the fundamental indeterminacy inherent in anxiety that differentiates this mood from fear. There is no "in the face of" to which anxiety is directed—and this indeterminacy is precisely what makes us anxious (*BW*: 100–101). At the same time, it defines what this state is really about: "*Being-in-the-world itself is that in the face of which anxiety is anxious*" (*BT*: 232/ *GA* 2: 187).

It is important to note here the dialectical nature of anxiety's negative characterization. According to Heidegger, anxiety is revelatory precisely because it cannot disclose anything specific in the world, any object of intention. Anxiety is the state in which entities in the world lose their meaningful structure; and it is only from within this fundamental negativity, the "nothing and nowhere," that Dasein can disclose the innermost possibilities of its being (*BT*: 231/ *GA* 2: 186–187). This "nothing and nowhere" is what allows anxiety to disclose something about the world as such, as totality, as what conditions and constitutes the very possibility of encountering anything specific. Unlike fear, for example, which faces a specific entity, what Dasein faces in anxiety is Being-in-the-world itself. In "What is Metaphysics," Heidegger elaborates on this negative characteristic of anxiety; he explains that it is precisely in the "clear night of the nothing of anxiety"—that Dasein confronts the nothing and, consequently, its own Being (*BW*: 103).[26]

Anxiety is not only a fundamental mood according to *Being and Time*; it exemplifies Heidegger's approach to the structure of *Stimmung* in general. Distancing moods from cognitive divulgence of the world as well as from its subjective, psychological understanding as emotion or pathology, Heidegger stresses the disclosive power of *Stimmung*. However, this power can actualize itself (and this, according to Heidegger, only in rare moments [*BW*: 100]), exclusively from within the depth of nothingness. The potential disclosure integral to *Stimmung* extends from within the fundamental inability to locate its origin (being neither external nor internal) and from its essentially nonintentional structure (*Stimmung* does not originate from an object or event, nor does it refer to any). Most crucially, Dasein is faced with nothingness itself, with the slipping away of everything but Being-in-the-world (*BW*: 100–103; *BT*: 229–232/ *GA* 2: 185–188)—the burden of nothingness is therefore the key to the revelatory power of *Stimmung*.

Benjamin and the Death of Intention

The movement from *Stimmung* in Heidegger to Benjamin's account of the same term, deserves some preliminary remarks. The weight of the philosophical encounter between the two does not rest, to my mind, so much on an analytical comparison between their treatments of *Stimmung*, nor on any wish to stake a claim regarding its elusive albeit striking similarity. It does revolve, however, around the force motivating the two thinker's philosophical work as couched in their mutual criticism of the subject-object divide and its implications for our understanding of human experience.

It can hardly be said that Heidegger's scrupulous account of *Stimmung* is perfectly reflected in Benjamin. We find no orderly focused account of *Stimmung* in the latter, especially not a straightforward description of its structure and purpose. As is usually the case in Benjamin, we can trace his elaboration of *Stimmung* only as it emerges from within a specific historical and conceptual context—the German baroque—and in only one manifestation of *Stimmung*—melancholy.[27] And so, despite Benjamin's specificity and overly concrete account of melancholy in German baroque theater, we eventually discover that all the characteristics of *Stimmung* so rigorously articulated by Heidegger are ultimately found in Benjamin's discussion. That being said, Benjamin does not serve as a "test case" or variation of Heidegger's presentation of moods. It is in Benjamin's concrete, historical, and philosophical use of melancholy that we find the more profound penetration into the philosophical nature of *Stimmung*, especially regarding its ontological qualities.

Benjamin is keen on distancing himself from a psychological or pathological understanding of melancholy but also from a discussion of *Stimmung*'s disclosive nature. While retaining the prominent features Heidegger finds in moods, Benjamin shifts his consideration of the term to the context of philosophy's approach to the world as well as to truth (formulated through an array of Platonic notions such as Ideas and their relations to phenomena) (*OT*: 33–38). It is therefore not Dasein that is endowed with the revelatory power ascribed to melancholy, nor is it the world itself that is melancholic in the eyes of its beholder. In Benjamin's account, melancholy captures the fundamental structure of the philosophical exploration itself, particularly in how it reveals the world to the individual.[28] But here again Benjamin, like Heidegger, is not thinking of the world as "given" to the melancholic subject, on the contrary. The melancholy gaze has the power to change not only the subject's view of the world by way of perspective (i.e., the gaze on a separate and independent entity); it can, moreover, change the ontological nature of the world itself. To establish this claim, I now turn to various sections from *The Origin of German Tragic Drama* to delineate the different ways in which Benjamin develops this melancholic structure. This will not result in an orderly, argumentative presentation of Benjamin's theory of *Stimmung* but will uncover the philosophical foundations of Benjamin's book, in which *Stimmung* serves as a key concept.[29]

Although Benjamin devotes the conclusion of the book's first part, "*Trauerspiel* and Tragedy," to a discussion of melancholy (*OT*: 138–158), it is important to note that in his discussion of *Trauer*, he moves rather freely between two different synonyms of the term—mourning and melancholy—while referring to them as by and large interchangeably.³⁰ Benjamin richly characterizes melancholy by means of a detailed description of its fecund history, including medical, astrological, cultural, religious, literary, and aesthetic accounts. At the same time, he disdains to include the psychological and pathological narratives so dominant at the time, especially Freud's authoritative description of melancholia and its deviation from mourning.³¹ Melancholy has always been marked by acute contradictions in its depiction, ranging from its positive, creative facets—such as depth, creativity, and bursts of genius—to its negative qualities, including gloominess, despondency, and isolation. The concept's history is saturated with different and at times conflicting articulations that, paradoxically, seem to consistently point to more or less the same set of features, notions of closure, contemplation, loss, passivity, sloth, and genius. These have always been connected to melancholy, whether in reference to the body or the soul, and vice versa.³² Benjamin refers to this plethora of interpretations, emphasizing their tentative complementarity rather than their overt opposition, while using them as the historical and theoretical backdrop against which he can develop his own discussion of melancholy as a baroque state of mind on the one hand, and as a principle of mood governing thought on the other.

Benjamin stays in tune with the diversity of historical descriptions of melancholy yet structures his account around the special way in which mood determines the subject's encounter with the world. Benjamin's account therefore portrays the different ways in which melancholy ontologically establishes and constitutes the subject as well as the world itself. Benjamin confronts the problem of this encounter by employing the dialectic inherent in melancholy, which brings together the power of creativity, contemplation, and bursts of genius together with profound suffering, gloominess and despondency (*OT*: 138–158). He writes that "the history of the problem of melancholy unfolds within the perimeter of this dialectic" (*OT*: 150). He summons the medical as well as the philosophical accounts given by Aristotle, Albertinus, and Ficino, to name just a few, and draws a complex picture in which melancholy serves as an exemplary mood within which the world is disclosed. The affinity of the melancholic to Saturn, considering another example, is brought to demonstrate that the planet's great distance from earth as well as the long durations of its orbits intimate the melancholic's unique ability for introspection, abstract thought, and contemplation (*OT*: 149).³³

But the wisdom of the melancholic, accompanied by his or her profound contemplative abilities, does not simply open up possibilities for revealing the world; it does so in a distinctive way. This is most evident in two correlated arguments made in the *Trauerspiel* book, both directly resonating Heidegger's characterization of mood. First, *Stimmung* is not intentionally structured; it thus offers an alternative structure to the relationship between man and the world that challenges the subject-object fissure. Second, the nature of the disclosure initiated is not only different from the discovery knowledge can offer, it is also articulated as the essential preconceptual stratum constituting any subsequent knowledge.

Inasmuch as a theoretical and critical rather than pathological, or therapeutic, conception of melancholy is necessary to understand the philosophical context of *Stimmung*'s structure, I set aside those parts in the book in which Benjamin describes the allegorical, baroque state of mind or remains restricted to the description of the structures of the plays themselves. Instead, I focus on a more methodological understanding of mood.[34] This shift is necessary in order to fathom Benjamin's formulation of the relationship between truth and intention as it appears in the book's prologue: "The object of knowledge, determined as it is by the intention inherent in the concept, is not the truth. Truth is an intentionless state of being, made up of ideas. The proper approach to it is not therefore one of intention and knowledge, but rather a total immersion and absorption in it. Truth is the death of intention" (*OT*: 36).[35]

Benjamin's reference to intention reflects a strong philosophical framework that can be viewed as a direct response to Duns Scotus's scholastic discussion of the notion as well as to the philosophical dominance that Husserl attributed to intentionality.[36] The negative allusion to "intentionality" conveys Benjamin's criticism of two of the main presuppositions inherent to Husserl's intentional structure: first, the separation between the subject and the object of his consciousness; and second, the separation between the object and the intentional act of establishing the subject's awareness of that object. The core of both of these presuppositions is the fundamental chasm Husserl introduces into the structure of his phenomenological method—that between the subject and the object. Benjamin's criticism of this stance is molded in the special form of subjectivity he promotes, which is not determined by subjective confrontation with an object but, rather, by immersion in it. This idea is already pronounced in Benjamin's aforementioned critique of the Kantian system. A common nucleus is, therefore, evident in Benjamin's criticism of Kant's concept of experience as well as in his rebuke of Husserl's structure of intentionality, namely, the potentially vexing emphasis that both thinkers (despite their polar positions) impose on the subject.

In his discussion of intentionality, Benjamin focuses on a philosophical scheme that, while not avoiding the division between the thinking subject and the objects of his consciousness, challenges the intentional structure that such a division begets. This is most clearly demonstrated in the Benjamin's aphoristic declaration that truth is the death of intention. Apart from the negative allusion to Husserl, this obscure statement intimates Benjamin's distinction between truth and knowledge—a distinction that can be understood as reflecting the conundrum of intentionality, the same issue around which Benjamin establishes an alternative formulation questioning epistemological models based on the subject's primacy. Benjamin proposes that the object and the subject's immersion in it dominate the acquisition of knowledge. That is, when abiding to an intentional structure, knowledge is possessed by the knowing subject and "its every object is determined by the fact that it must be taken possession of—even if in a transcendental sense—in the consciousness. The quality of possession remains" (*OT*: 29).

Understanding its task as the acquisition of knowledge and establishment of a coherent system built on those foundations, philosophy treats its objects as if they "came flying in from outside," directly into the spider's web woven for that purpose. The unity of truth, Benjamin continues, does not lie in its coherence but in its inner law of essences, which can never be possessed or approached intentionally. This form of existence is peculiar to truth, Benjamin explains, in being "devoid of all intention, and certainly does not itself appear as intention. Truth does not enter into relationships, particularly not intentional ones. The object of knowledge, determined as it is by the intention inherent in the concept, is not the truth" (*OT*: 35–36).

These passages provide the main outlines of Benjamin's fundamental distinction between knowledge (pertaining to concepts) and truth (pertaining to ideas) reinforced by his use of the notion of intentionality. Knowledge is always about a relationship between the subject and the object of consciousness, conceived principally in terms of judgment; it is thus an intentionality-structured rather than a truth-structured relationship. Renouncing the judgmental structure of knowledge thus entails repudiation of any form of intentional relations. Ideas replace concepts, and totality substitutes for judgment. Instead of the intentional structure of subjective awareness that Benjamin assigns to knowledge, truth operates within an entirely different order, where immersion and absorption provide the conditions of possibility for truth's presentation (*Darstellung*) rather than its possession. This distinctive disposition bears deep affinities to the melancholic, fathomless attachment to an object that is not in fact there; or, put differently, a bond to an object with which it is impossible to maintain an intentional relationship. What we can discern here is an endeavor to think of melancholy as a *truth-relation*. This statement requires a careful explication.

The nonintentional nature of melancholic loss positions that relationship within the world rather than within a specific object (as in mourning), a feature crucial to Benjamin's application of nonintentionality to truth. Being "the death of intention," truth—Benjamin proclaims—precludes the possibility of intention but also of desire. Weber describes this as the disconnection between pointing-at (the movement of mind or language) and that at which it is pointed, or an opposition to the union of form and content that Benjamin associates with poetic work.[37] Moreover, the structure of an intention-less relationship undermines the classic subject-object duality, placing the discussion of truth and ideas outside the subjective-psychological realm and the emotional attachment to objects.

Benjamin's discussion of the functions of feeling and emotions in the baroque plays and their special connection with objects provides a constructive basis from which to explore this intention-less object-relation, based on immersion. Benjamin himself provides an abstruse account of this structure: "Whereas in the realm of emotions it is not unusual for the relation between an intention and its object to alternate between attraction and repulsion, mourning is capable of a special intensification, a progressive deepening of its intention" (*OT*: 139). Benjamin suggests here a structure of emotion that is constituted by incessant movement between attraction and repulsion. Such fluctuation, so inherent to emotion, is always given in reference to the object of its desire, which indicates just how intrinsic such movement is to referential structures. Within this framework, the question of whether an object is present or absent becomes decisive—and the anatomy of desire is precisely this, namely, it flares when its object is absent, when it refers to what is not at hand. In that sense, desire is constituted as an intentional gesture toward what is missing. Emotions, as Benjamin describes them here, are similarly dependent on the object, its presence or absence and on the repetitive rhythm of oscillation between want and satisfaction. Such movement prevents disclosure of anything but the subject's fluctuation between yearning and fulfillment vis-à-vis his object of desire. This shift from emotion to knowledge provides Benjamin with the opportunity for associating the intentional structure of desire with the flatness of knowledge—both being object-oriented and possessive.

He continues:

> For feelings, however vague they may seem when perceived by the self, respond like a motorial reaction to a concretely structured world. If the laws which govern the *Trauerspiel* are to be found, partly explicit, partly implicit, at the heart of mourning, the representation of these laws does not concern itself with the emotional condition of the poet or his public, but with a feeling [*Fühlen*] which is released from any empirical subject and is intimately bound to the fullness [*Fülle*] of an object. This is a motorial attitude which has its appointed place in the hierarchy of intentions and is only called a feeling because it does not occupy the highest place. It is determined by an astounding tenacity [*Beharrlichkeit*] of intention. (*OT*: 139)

The constitution of the *Trauerspiel* inheres in mourning; however, not in its subjective, personal meaning (that of the poet or his public) but in mourning's structure. That is, the connection between subject and object is determined by a "motorial" or automatic reaction—or attitude—to a "concretely structured world." This world itself functions as the object of intention rather than merely some "thing" located within it, a "target" toward which the act of consciousness is directed. Such an attitude, because it operates in a world of objects, neutralizes the desire felt in the attachment to a single object. This "motorial" mechanism begets the immediacy inherent in intention but without being causally related to the specific object. The intending subject is, therefore, situated *within* the world, and not simply positioned opposite the object of desire. The neutralization of desire consequently revokes the inherent distinction—and ensuing relationship—between subject and object. What Benjamin offers here is intention that is immediate without being directed. This configuration exhibits what Benjamin takes to be the melancholic structure of relations, namely, relations that are intensive as much as they are nonintentionally structured.[38]

In Benjamin's differentiation between intention and emotion, the latter perpetually oscillates between attraction and repulsion (a structure in close affinity to Freud's description of the melancholic's ambivalence).[39] Mourning, on the contrary, is an intentional, gripping feeling, alien to ambivalence and fixed on its object. Benjamin clearly states that the condition he is describing involves immersion bereft of interest, desire or intention: "On the road to the object—no: within the object itself [*auf der Straße zum Gegenstande—nein: auf der Bahn im Gegenstande selbst*]—this intention progresses as slowly and solemnly as the processions of the rulers advance" (*OT*: 140). This path, winding within the object, can be mistaken for empathy, a stance enabling entry into a separate entity, but it is emphatically not so. The unique lack of intention in Benjamin's proposed structure echoes the utterly different approach that knowledge and truth each demands (*OT*: 28–38). The continuous alternation between attraction and repulsion, so characteristic of emotions, resembles the flatness of knowledge, which is rendered superficial by its intrinsic lack of totality.

The aforementioned road's redefinition from an approach *to* the object to an approach *into* the object reflects Benjamin's interest in the alternative to intention. The kind of intention negated with respect to its association to truth is, therefore, the straightforward type of intention that relates a subject with the object of its interest. From the perspective of the object's interiority, however, this kind of intention appears quite differently; it resembles the aforementioned immersion in the material. Truth's persistence and alienation from the world does not, therefore, contradict its own nature. Truth, according to Benjamin, being complete and inclusive, thus echoes the melancholic's tenacious grappling with the object, and the attachment to the object's fullness, namely, melancholy's opposition to the polarity and flatness of emotions and knowledge, respectively. The characterization of truth as totality, reinforced by truth's nonintentional nature, is demonstrated by the tenacity of its attachments, which know neither external conflict nor inner struggle. Hence, totality proves to be the only appropriate approach for achieving complete immersion in the Idea. The quality of scission distinctive to knowledge parallels the aforementioned emotions of attraction and repulsion, which are unstable and hesitant in their connection to the object at hand. Their stammering is as far from truth as can be, with the fluctuation between the two emotions resembling the flatness of knowledge, which is rendered superficial by its intrinsic lack of totality. The difference between truth and knowledge is also related to the distinction between possession and immersion—or, to the external and the internal attitude, respectively. The presentation (*Darstellung*)[40] of truth also alludes to its quality of fullness. Furthermore, because the Idea expresses truth, it abstains from judging knowledge, which remains forever doomed to suffering from the duality between the true and the false.

In a short piece on Calderon and Hebbel, Benjamin dwells on the relationship between sadness and intention. He writes that "sadness . . . would be boundless, were it not for the presence of that intentionality . . . which manifests itself with an assertiveness that fends off mourning. A mourning-game [*Trauer-Spiel*], in short" (*SW* 1: 373). Benjamin positions sadness and mourning here as antithetical to intention, thereby ascribing to intention the power to defend itself against the two states. Intentionality thus has the power to encapsulate sorrow, to set it within the threshold of the intended object and prevent it from expanding endlessly and curelessly. This explication parallels the characterization of the melancholic, whose loss is undefined and thus boundless. Since there is no tangible object at which the melancholic can direct his sorrow, his gaze can only turn inward in a Nietzschean gesture, toward a place where it can find only the boundlessness of his own loss. Benjamin's distinction between truth and knowledge as it appeared in the preface to the Trauerspiel book, can now be reread in light of the distinction between intention and lack-of-intention toward the object.

Stimmung between Heidegger and Benjamin

The philosophical approach from which Benjamin examines the notion of Stimmung and his attempt to bind it together with philosophy's quintessential concerns (truth, subjectivity and epistemology) is echoed in Heidegger's response to the question "what is metaphysics," elaborated in a text bearing the same title. There, Heidegger develops an answer within the context of anxiety, specifically, the fundamental emptiness and nothingness it occasions. *Stimmung* must be awakened, to use a formulation found elsewhere (*FCM*: 59–60/ *GA* 29/30: 90–91),[41] so as to reveal the structure of Being before Dasein. This structure, however, also strongly bears on questions essential to metaphysics, namely, the questions of world, finitude and solitude. It is in this sense that anxiety or boredom, have the power to open those issues and provide conditions conducive to yielding their answers. Importantly, it is the very structure of *Stimmung* that enables this opening: its being medial, neither subjective nor objective, and nonintentional, makes it possible for *Stimmung* to bridge between a subjective or psychological configuration and mood's ability to transform and thus redefine Dasein's relation to the world. All these characteristics are disclosed from within "the clear night of the nothing" (*BW*: 103); nothingness is what brings Dasein to confront itself and being as such: "Our inquiry concerning the nothing is to bring us face to face with metaphysics itself" (*BW*: 106).

However, as an alternative to a subjective-objective epistemological model, *Stimmung* raises the question of its potential philosophical contribution to Heidegger's as well as Benjamin's writings. What does such a *Stimmung*-determined encounter between an individual or Dasein and the world demonstrate or offer? Is it really the case that with the introduction of *Stimmung*, something about the relationship between subjects and objects is effectively undermined? Or, rather, is that relationship itself transformed, thereby pinning down the unavoidable divide still lurking between them? At this point, the debate regarding the junction between Heidegger and Benjamin becomes instructive.

Heidegger's painstaking account of moods and how they affect Dasein's Being-in-the-world leaves us with the sense of a latent philosophical offering. I prefer to conceive of this offering as a "bequest" because although Heidegger's intent may appear to emphasize the disclosive nature of *Stimmung* with reference to Dasein, he repeatedly stresses the ability of moods to disclose the world itself, ontologically. When we are sad or wondrous, we not only reveal ourselves anew (not the least regarding our psychological state) but we also, and more decisively, find ourselves in a transformed world. Moods therefore have the power to ontologically affect the world precisely because it is disclosed to us only within in the clearing of our moods, never independently of them. It is nonetheless questionable as to whether Heidegger indeed succeeds in establishing the purely ontological implications of Dasein and *Stimmung*. This doubt arises chiefly because we can still debate whether the structure of Being-in-the-world indeed challenges the subject and the limited form of his epistemological confrontation with the world or whether it provides a mere substitute for the idea of a subject, now renamed, while leaving at its wake a residual subjectivism. In this sense Heidegger bequeaths a promise for an ontology of *Stimmung*, but the question whether such a promise can be fulfilled or utilized remains undetermined. It is here Benjamin becomes decisive to *Stimmung*'s ontological explication.

When reflecting on Benjamin's critique of Kant, one conundrum remains to be tackled, namely, Benjamin's use of "neutrality." To reiterate, Benjamin seeks to find a sphere of "total neutrality in regard to the concepts of both subject and object" (*SW* 1: 104) in his critique of the meager, inadequate Kantian conception of experience. He thereby challenges the predominance of the subject in Kant's epistemological model. Benjamin's summoning of neutrality here can be explained using his theory of *Stimmung* since *Stimmung* is precisely what can be taken to be neutral in regard to subject and object. Not only does *Stimmung* not belong or stem from either subject or object; it is an undifferentiated stratum that precedes the existence of both. In consequently, more than the world can only be revealed in a certain mood, it is the subject itself, or the mere possibility of subjectiveness, that is disclosed in mood. In being "neutral," *Stimmung* not only challenges the structure of intentionality, it constitutes and determines the very subject who finds himself disclosed through it. Such an interpretation of neutrality and the role it plays for Benjamin is bivalent: first, it provides a direct link between Benjamin's critique of Kant as well as his overall philosophical motivation to the question of *Stimmung*; second, it utilizes *Stimmung* as a term having profound ontological implications, beyond its being merely psychological or descriptive.

Benjamin's often diffused discourse on the subject of *Stimmung*, especially melancholy, can benefit from Heidegger's strict conceptualizations but it also suggests a reciprocal explanation of Heidegger through his deep discussion of mood's strong ontological implications. This Benjamin does by remaining committed to a nonpsychological, nonsubjective understanding that precludes genuine access to those implications. For instance, Benjamin distinctly states that the nonintentional structure at stake is *not* that of a conscious subject, a position that cannot be reduced to mere criticism of Husserl. Rather, the nonintentional structure he proposes describes truth itself. Placing truth—but not the knowing subject—at the center of his scrutiny of melancholy and thus of mood allows Benjamin to situate his discussion directly in the heart of philosophical activity per se. It is therefore not the philosopher who is melancholic (as in Aristotle's famous contention regarding the melancholy of "great men" or Ficino's account of the melancholy of scholars) but the structure of truth itself, as disclosed by *Stimmung*. The intense immersion that Benjamin develops not only defines how *Stimmung* can determine the individual's presence in the world (or in Heidegger's terms, its

Being-in-the-world), but fuses its own being with that of the world itself. In this way, *Stimmung* becomes truly and fundamentally ontological.

Agamben notes that we can identify a characteristic *Stimmung* in every thinker.[42] In the case of Heidegger and Benjamin, there is not only a determining *Stimmung* to be traced in their thought, but more profoundly, the very *question* of *Stimmung*. It follows that the case of anxiety, boredom or melancholy is less important here than the mere fact of *Stimmung*, qua *Stimmung*, as always present not as the philosopher's state of mind but as determining the task of philosophy itself.

Notes

1. Caygill offers a concise account of such remarks and discusses the points of thematic intersections between the two. See Howard Caygill, "Benjamin, Heidegger and the Destruction of Tradition," in eds. Andrew Benjamin and Peter Osborne, *Walter Benjamin's Philosophy: Destruction and Experience* (New York: Routledge, 1994), 1–3. Weber notes that Benjamin abandoned his initial idea to write his Habilitation on the scholastic treatise and Duns Scotus when he discovered that Heidegger has written his own Habilitation on the topic. See Samuel Weber, "'Streets, Squares, Theaters': A City on the Move—Walter Benjamin's Paris," *Benjamin Now: Critical Encounters with the Arcades Project*, Boundary 2, Spring 2003, 18, note 2.
2. See Howard Caygill, "Benjamin, Heidegger and the Destruction of Tradition," in *Destruction and Experience*, 30.
3. See Alexander García Düttmann, "Tradition and Destruction: Walter Benjamin's Politics of Language," in *Walter Benjamin's Philosophy: Destruction and Experience*, 48ff.
4. See Werner Hamacher, "Now: Walter Benjamin on Historical Time," in ed. Andrew Benjamin, *Walter Benjamin and History* (New York: Continuum, 2005), 235–236, note 7.
5. In this case, Heidegger directs his attack of Binswanger apropos his *Über Sprache und Denken*, where he finds a discussion of the subject-object division. He returns to his criticism of Binswanger in a lecture from 1969, where he argues that Binswanger's solution to the problem, through the possibility of allowing subjectivity to "transcend" out of itself into the external world, is far from acceptable. To this Heidegger asks, "How a subjectivity, primarily represented as immanence, could ever get even the faintest idea of an external world," and summons his own solution in the form of Being-in-the-world,

which "is never a property of a subjectivity no matter how it is represented, but from the beginning it is the human being's way of existing" (*ZS*: 227/ *GA 89*: 286).

6. Jean-Luc Marion, "L'Interloqué," in eds. Eduardo Cadava, Peter Connor, and Jean-Luc Nancy, *Who Comes After the Subject?* (New York: Routledge, 1991), 237.
7. On Benjamin's "Program of the Coming Philosophy," see Howard Caygill, *Walter Benjamin: The Colour of Experience* (London: Routledge, 1998), 1–13; Peter Fenves, *The Messianic Reduction: Walter Benjamin and the Shape of Time* (Stanford: Stanford University Press, 2011), 152–186.
8. Brentano follows medieval scholastic terminology in his development of the structure of intentionality while emphasizing its roots in Aristotle, Augustine, and Aquinas. He refers to intentionality as "a content, direction toward an object . . . or immanent objectivity," and adds that "every mental phenomena includes something as object within itself." Franz Brentano, *Psychology from an Empirical Standpoint* (New York: Routledge, 1995), 68.
9. Edmund Husserl, *Ideas Pertaining to a Pure Phenomenology and to a Phenomenological Philosophy*, trans. F. Kersten, in *Collected Works*, vol. II (Hague: Martinus Nijhoff, 1983), 213. Husserl develops here two terms important for his account of the intentional act of consciousness: noesis and noema, see ibid., chapter 3.
10. Despite his fierce criticism of the Kantian system, Benjamin is very keen on underscoring his deep philosophical commitment to Kant, repeatedly proclaiming his debt to that work. Manifestations of this commitment appear on virtually every page of the text. See for instance: "The central task of the coming philosophy will be to take the deepest intimations it draws from our times and our expectations of a great future, and turn them into knowledge by relating them to the Kantian system. The historical continuity that is ensured by following the Kantian system is also the only such continuity of decisive and systematic consequences" (*SW* 1: 100).
11. On the translation of *Stimmung* into English, see Michael Inwood, *A Heidegger Dictionary* (Oxford: Blackwell, 1999), 15–16, 130–131.
12. Leo Spitzer, "Classical and Christian Ideas of World Harmony: Prolegomena to an Interpretation of the Word 'Stimmung,'" cited in David E. Wellbery's entry, "*Stimmung*," in *Ästhetische Grundbegriffe: Historische Wörterbuch in sieben Bänden*, Band 5, ed. Karlheinz Barck (Stuttgart: Verlag J. B. Metzler, 2003), 703.
13. Giorgio Agamben, "Vocation and Voice," *Qui Parle*, vol. 10, no. 2 (1997), 89–90. On the meaning of "*Stimmung*" see also Wellbery, "*Stimmung*," 703–733;

Giorgio Agamben, *Language and Death: The Place of Negativity*, trans. K. E. Pinkus and M. Hardt (Minneapolis: University of Minnesota Press, 1999), 55, where Agamben links *Stimmung* and *Stimme*, arguing that *Stimme* is more originary than *Stimmung*, while pointing to the structure of the voice as the most original and negative of metaphysical foundations (59).
14. Giorgio Agamben, *The Open: Man and Animal*, trans. K. Attel (Stanford, CA: Stanford University Press, 2004), 49.
15. Agamben, "Vocation and Voice," 89–90.
16. Marion, "L'Interloqué," 237.
17. Bret W. Davis, *Heidegger and the Will: On the Way to Gelassenheit* (Evanston, IL: Northwestern University Press, 2007), 7–8. For a detailed history of the term *Grundstimmung* in Heidegger, see ibid., 306–307, note 8.
18. *Befindlichkeit* was translated by Macquarrie and Robinson as "state of mind," a misleading term in the context of Heidegger's argument. On the problematic translation of *Befindlichkeit*, see Hubert L. Dreyfus, *Being-in-the-World: A Commentary on Heidegger's Being and Time, Division I* (Cambridge, MA: MIT Press, 1991), 168; see also William Large, *Heidegger's Being and Time* (Bloomington: Indiana University Press), 2008, 123–134.
19. See Theodore Kisiel, *Heidegger's Way of Thought: Critical and Interpretative Signposts*, eds. A. Denker and M. Heinz (New York: Continuum, 2002), 67.
20. Kisiel, *Heidegger's Way of Thought*, 67–68.
21. For a discussion of the inherent relationship between moods and philosophy, see Hagi Kenaan and Ilit Ferber, "Moods and Philosophy," in eds. Kenann and Ferber, *Philosophy's Moods: The Affective Grounds of Thinking* (Dordrecht: Springer, 2011), 3–10.
22. In his *Fundamental Concepts of Metaphysics*, Heidegger declares that what he calls "profound boredom'" is a "fundamental attunement" of *Dasein* (*FCM*: 80/ GA 29/30: 119–120). This is not the first time that he deals with this concept; his description of anxiety (*Angst*) in *Being and Time* can be viewed as an important treatment of the subject.
23. See Quentin Smith, "On Heidegger's Theory of Moods," *The Modern Schoolman*, 58 (1981), 211–235.
24. A discussion of the complexity of Heidegger's relation to Husserl, his teacher and main philosophical rival (Heidegger dedicates *Being and Time* to his mentor "in friendship and admiration"), is well beyond the scope of this essay. For the major texts comprising their debate about phenomenology, dated 1927–1931, see Edmund Husserl, *Psychological and Transcendental Phenomenology and the Confrontation with Heidegger (1927–1931)*, in *Collected Works*, ed. R. Bernet (Springer, 1997). On this relationship see also, Theodore Kisiel, "From

Intuition to Understanding: On Heidegger's Transposition of Husserl's Phenomenology," in Kisiel, *Heidegger's Way of Thought*, 174–186.
25. See also "What is Metaphysics," (*BW*: 100–101).
26. In this text, Heidegger makes a direct connection between the nothingness at stake in anxiety, and the question of metaphysics: "Our inquiry concerning the nothing is to bring us face to face with metaphysics itself" (*BW*: 106), and "The question of the nothing puts us, the questioners, in question. It is a metaphysical question. . . . This implies that metaphysics belongs to the 'nature of man.' It is neither a division of academic philosophy not a field of arbitrary notions. Metaphysics is the basic occurrence of Dasein. It is Dasein itself" (*BW*: 109).
27. Benjamin's discussion of melancholy is not the only case of *Stimmung* to be found in his writings. Another notable case is clearly that of boredom. For more on Benjamin's idea of boredom see, for example, Andrew Benjamin, "Boredom and Distraction: The Moods of Modernity," in ed. Andrew Benjamin, *Walter Benjamin and History* (New York: Continuum, 2005), 156–171; Carlo Salzani, "The Atrophy of Experience: Walter Benjamin and Boredom," in eds. B. Dalle Pezze and C. Salzani, *Essays on Boredom and Modernity* (Rodopi: Amsterdam, 2009), 127–154.
28. Benjamin no doubt continues Heidegger's attempt to challenge the subject-object divide; however, his discussion of *Stimmung* is more focused on the question of intentionality's relation to truth. There is much to say about Heidegger's conception of truth and the bearing its structure has on *Stimmung* but such a discussion lies far beyond the scope of this paper. What is nevertheless interesting is that both Heidegger and Benjamin remain faithful to truth (as well as to disclosure or unconcealedness, to use Heidegger's terms) as the primary foundation of their philosophical motivations.
29. I have elaborated on the ideas that follow in Ilit Ferber, *Philosophy and Melancholy: Benjamin's Early Reflections on Theater and Language* (Stanford University Press, 2013), see esp. 1–10, 44–56.
30. This point was also made by Hanssen who argues that Benjamin seemingly remains "oblivious" to the distinctions between mourning and melancholia. Hanssen thus insinuates that Benjamin was acquainted with the distinction but chose to ignore it, or merely forgot it. See Beatrice Hanssen, "Portrait of Melancholy (Benjamin, Warburg, Panofsky)," *MLN* 114.5 (1999), 1003. A typical example of Benjamin's integration of mourning and melancholy are statements like "the theory of mourning . . . can only be developed in the description of that world which is revealed under the gaze of the melancholic man (*OT*: 139; emphasis added).
31. See Sigmund Freud, "Mourning and Melancholia," in ed. and trans. James

Strachey, *The Standard Edition of the Complete Psychological Works of Sigmund Freud*, vol. 14, (London: Hogarth Press, 1957), 243–258.

32. In the fluctuating movement of its internal history, melancholy has been described as a somatic condition (a humeral imbalance resulting in the excess of black bile), brought on by the melancholic's sins (sloth or acedia in the religious context of the Middle Ages); the consequence of demonic undertakings or witchcraft (in the seventeenth century); an inclination or mood (in the Renaissance); a desirable state inducing productivity and genius; and finally, a pathology (in the nineteenth century). For some illuminating genealogies of this type, see the canonical text by R. Klibansky, E. Panofsky, and F. Saxl, *Saturn and Melancholy: Studies in the History of Natural Philosophy, Religion and Art* (London: Nelson, 1964); Max Pensky, *Melancholy Dialectics: Walter Benjamin and the Play of Mourning* (Amherst: University of Massachusetts Press, 2001); Julia Kristeva, *Black Sun: Depression and Melancholia*, trans. L. S. Roudiez (New York: Columbia University Press, 1992). For a useful anthology containing an illuminating introduction to the different approaches to melancholy, see ed. Jennifer Radden, *The Nature of Melancholy: From Aristotle to Kristeva* (Oxford: Oxford University Press, 2000). For a description of the surprising continuity in the accounts of melancholy up to Freud, see Giorgio Agamben, *Stanzas: Word and Phantasm in Western Culture*, trans. L. Martinez (Minneapolis: University of Minnesota Press, 1992), esp. 3–19.

33. Saturn and melancholy are further compared as bearing the spirit of contradiction that endows the soul "with sloth and dullness" on the one hand, and with "the power of intelligence and contemplation" on the other. For this comparison and the connection between Saturn and Cronos, see *OT*: 149–150.

34. On the distinction between "intention" with reference to allegory and to truth, see *OT*: 229.

35. Another interesting place in which Benjamin discusses intentionality and its absence is found in his account of the Mediaeval treatise, which serves him as a model for philosophical thinking. See *OT*: 28.

36. Benjamin read Husserl around 1913, and wrote a fragment on Scotus in 1920. See "According to the Theory of Duns Scotus" (*SW* 1: 228). Another relevant fragment from 1922–1923 is "Stages of Intention" (*SW* 2: 391–392). Hamacher points out the importance of Benjamin's engagement with Heidegger's doctoral thesis on Duns Scotus; see, Werner Hamacher, "'Now': Walter Benjamin on Historical Time," 236, note 7. For a discussion of Benjamin's relation to Husserl, especially in regard to Husserl's notion of *epoché*, see Peter Fenves, "The Genesis of Judgment: Spatiality, Analogy, and Metaphor in Benjamin's 'On Language as Such and on Human Language,'" in ed. David S. Ferris, *Walter*

Benjamin: Theoretical Questions (Stanford, CA: Stanford University Press, 1996); and Peter Fenves, *The Messianic Reduction: Walter Benjamin and the Shape of Time* (Stanford, CA: Stanford University Press, 2011), 44–78.

37. Samuel Weber, *Benjamin's -abilities* (Cambridge, MA: Harvard University Press, 2008), 71.
38. In his rigorous interpretation of this special form of melancholic subjectivity, Pensky argues that the relation between subject and object encompasses what Benjamin views as the crucial polarity inherent in *Trauer*: its enclosure of subjective as well as objective moments. The objective, real state of affairs thus resonates with feelings that remain locked within the subject. Pensky characterizes this object of feeling as the empty world, a world devoid of meaning, which stands as an empirical object, continually taking upon itself a multiplicity of historically contingent forms. This abundance of meaning constitutes the "real insight into the ontological status of the world of human experience" (see Pensky, *Melancholy Dialectics*, 92).
39. Another example of this movement can be found in Lohenstein's *Sophonisbe*, where the oscillation between desire and hate control the scene. See *OT*: 83.
40. Mistakenly translated as "representation" and thus ignoring its differentiation from the quality of representation in knowledge.
41. The idea of awakening is also significant to Benjamin and appears, to take one important example, in his oft-quoted Convolute N of the *Arcades Project*, which includes numerous dispersed comments on the subject. On Benjamin's use of the term, see also Weber, *Benjamin's -abilities*, 164–175.
42. Agamben, *The Open*, 65.

FOUR

COMMODITY FETISHISM AND THE GAZE

A. Kiarina Kordela

I approach the works of Benjamin and Heidegger through the mediation of two engaging commentaries on their work, which I intertwine and develop further, particularly in relation to Karl Marx's theory of commodity fetishism and Jacques Lacan's theory of the gaze. These commentaries are offered by Rebecca Comay, in her "Framing Redemption: Aura, Origin, Technology in Benjamin and Heidegger," and Howard Caygill, in his "Benjamin, Heidegger and the Destruction of Tradition." In doing so I intend: (a) to show that Benjamin's concept of the gaze reflects the epistemology entailed in Marx's theory of commodity fetishism; by overcoming the dominant oppositions between both object and subject and thing-in-itself and representation, as well as their entailed anthropomorphism, Benjamin's epistemology poses an alternative to the Kantian paradigm, as the proper ground of knowledge in secular capitalist modernity; (b) to examine the possible ramifications of Benjamin's theories of the gaze and of allegory, particularly for our era; and (c) to foreground certain central differences between Benjamin and Heidegger that are entailed in their respective approaches to the gaze and history.

The Gaze in Benjamin and (Not in) Heidegger

At first sight, the concept of the gaze figures centrally in both Heidegger and Benjamin. As Rebecca Comay succinctly puts it in her insightful essay, "Heidegger distinguishes the ontic seeing (*Sehen*), which passes transitively from subject to object, from a prior ontological glancing (*Blicken, Erblicken*)." "To glance at something (*erblicken*)" is, in Heidegger's words, "to glance at that which in the thing seen turns its glance to us [*anblickt*]."¹ Thus, for Heidegger, true "'insight [*Einblick*] into that which is' . . . is not that transitive or unilinear 'inspection' that habitually determines our relation to the ontic . . . but is rather the intransitive 'in-flashing' (*Einblitz*) in which man, seeing, is seen."² The primordial "forgetfulness" of Being concerns this ontological intransitive or self-reflective glance, whose oblivion allows for the ontic experience of transitive seeing. Conversely, Heidegger's "forgetfulness of forgetfulness" is the process in which one forgets to forget, that is, one becomes conscious of that which has been forgotten, so that, for instance, "what had been passively suffered in unconscious complicity becomes explicitly grasped just *as* complicity," or, just as "what is most dangerous about the danger . . . is that 'it is not experienced *as* the danger.' . . . *Ereignis* is the danger that comes to mark itself reflexively 'as danger.'"³ Accordingly, in his assessment of technology, Heidegger maintains that the shift from "a prereflective submission to technology to" what Rodolphe Gasché has called "the 'quasi-transcendental' grasp of its 'essence,'" which involves an "epistemological turn . . . from a contemplative or eidetic [ontic] 'looking' to a radically insecure 'glancing': from the representational grasp of the world as *Weltbild* to the glimpse of a prior 'lighting.'"⁴

Turning now to Benjamin, Comay rightly warns us "against taking . . . his essay ["Das Kunstwerk im Zeitalter seiner Reproduzierbarkeit"] to be in any sense an unmodulated celebration of the media" alongside an unambiguous condemnation of the pretechnological aura. First of all, one must not overlook the fact that "the post-auratic, post-cultic product is described by Benjamin in the very language of the commodity," which is characterized by a "universal equality of things" and a "distracted public," which Benjamin depicts "in essentially consumerist terms," as capable of "'absorbing' the product rather than being 'absorbed' by it."⁵ One must also not forget, Comay reminds us, that in several of his publications "Benjamin had voiced a repeated elegy for the deteriorated aura," indexing at least an ambivalence regarding the function of aura, insofar as, on the one hand, "in its institutionalized or 'cultic' form, [aura] would seem to be guilty of just that authoritarianism which makes all culture . . . a place of barbarism," but, on the other hand, "it had also promised the utopia of a reconciliation beyond every domination and all control."⁶ In other words, Comay argues, "a 'Marxist' defense of aura is thus both plausible and suggested" by Benjamin's work.⁷

Benjamin's most widely known definition of aura from "Das Kunstwerk im Zeitalter seiner technischen Reproduzierbarkeit" ("The Work of Art in the Age of Technological Reproducibility") concerns "the here and now of the work of art— its unique existence in a particular place," which "withers in the age of mechanical reproduction," as "the technology of reproduction detaches the reproduced object from the sphere of tradition" and "substitutes a mass existence for a unique existence" (*SW* 4: 253–254). But, a "'Marxist' defense of aura," Comay suggests, "is no doubt the point of Benjamin's alternative definition of aura . . . as the perception of the object's ability to 'return the gaze.'"[8] In Benjamin's words from "On Some Motifs in Baudelaire" ("Über einige Motive bei Baudelaire"):

> Inherent in the gaze, however, is the expectation that it will be returned by that on which it is bestowed. Where this expectation is met (which, in the case of thought processes, can apply equally to an intentional gaze of awareness and to a glance pure and simple), there is an experience [*Erfahrung*] of the aura in all its fullness. . . . Experience of the aura thus arises from the fact that a response characteristic of human relationships is transposed to the relationship between humans and inanimate or natural objects. The person we look at, or who feels he is being looked at, looks at us in turn. To experience the aura of an object we look at means to invest it with the ability to look back at us. (*SW* 4: 338/ *GS* 1.2: 646–647)

Comay perspicaciously foregrounds the radical nonreducibility of Benjamin's line of thought to yet another anthropomorphic "expression of the metaphysics of the subject," characterized by "the ego consolidating itself through a movement of reflexive totalization or mediated return-to-self through the Other." This is equally true of "the Romantic *topos* of nature's self-reflexive *Wiederspiegelung*," which "Benjamin had . . . invoked . . . in order to describe the mimetic doubling of every gaze."[9] When Schlegel argues that "everything that is thinkable, thinks itself," or when Novalis writes that "in all the attributes with which we see the fossil, it sees us," and when later Benjamin infers from such statements, in Comay's words, "that every object is itself a subject, and thus that all cognition is already self-recognition"—in all these instances, a thought is formulated that, far from committing an anthropomorphic projection onto the inanimate world, manages to "exceed the closure of subjective (and indeed intersubjective) space" and enters the space of subject-object indeterminacy.[10]

I would maintain that it is, above all, this subject-object indeterminacy—and not merely the alienation of human labor in the process of commodification—that Marx endeavors to point to in his theory of commodity fetishism. As Marx writes, commodity fetishism is the process in which "the products of labour become commodities" with "socio-natural properties," that is, "*sensuous* things which are at the same time *supra-sensible* or *social*."[11] If Ferdinand de Saussure's linguistics had preceded him, Marx would have been able to formulate his discovery by stating that in capitalism commodities become signs: those sensuous material sound waves or written characters (signifiers), which are also supra-sensible and socially (i.e., differentially) determinable concepts (signifieds). Even without this terminological repertory, Marx was able to grasp that in capitalism, "[v]alue ... transforms every product of labour into a social *hieroglyphic* ... for the characteristic which objects of utility have of being values is as much men's social product as it is their *language*."[12] This means, Marx continues, that,

> [T]he commodity form, and the value-relation of the products of labour within which it appears, have absolutely no connection with the physical nature of the commodity and the material [*dinglich*] relations arising out of it. It is nothing but the definite social relation between men themselves which assumes here, for them, the fantastic form of a relation between things.[13]

In other words, the distortion that confers a "fantastic form" on this process lies exclusively on the fact that men mistake "their language" as expressing not their own "definite social relation" but "a relation between things." It is this point that leads Marx to the conclusion that "in order, therefore, to find an analogy we must take flight into the misty realm of religion"; just as "there the products of the human brain appear as autonomous figures endowed with a life of their own ... so [too] ... in the world of the commodities ... the products of men's hands" are endowed with a life of their own and appear as if they were expressing exclusively their own relations, when, in truth, they also express the relations between their producers.[14] The "fantastic form" of commodity fetishism lies in this projection of men's own relations onto what will retroactively constitute itself as external reality—be it a transcendent divine world or the material world of commodities, and ultimately nature. In truth, however, (commodified) nature, like divinity, is nothing other than the hieroglyphic that keeps the secret of men's own relations and has "absolutely no connection with the physical nature" of the things in which it manifests itself. What men mistake for the relations of so-called external objects is at the same time the network of their own relations, the subjects' relations. The primary point of commodity fetishism is this coincidence between subject and object relations—combined with the corollary illusion that makes subjects disavow the truth about their own relations as a truth concerning exclusively the relations of objects. This double mechanism, Marx concludes, "I call ... the fetishism which attaches itself to the products of labour as soon as they are produced as commodities, and is therefore inseparable from the production of commodities" in secular capitalist modernity.[15] This is arguably Marx's most significant contribution to understanding the specifically modern concept of "subjectivity," whose legacy is continued in Benjamin's work. In secular capitalist modernity, anthropomorphism is the illusion that necessarily accompanies the objective constitution of subjectivity, as the very defense mechanism of the subject against becoming conscious of precisely its own objective constitution.

Note that, as the earlier remarks indicate, the subject-object indeterminacy at the root of both commodity fetishism and Benjamin's gaze entails a radical reconceptualization of secular epistemology, which, ever since Kant, has severed nature, or the thing-in-itself, from representation. This dominant (Neo-)Kantian epistemological paradigm finds its epitome in de Manian deconstruction insofar as, according to de Man, "the paradigmatic structure of language is rhetorical rather than representational or expressive of a referential, proper meaning."[16] To be sure, de Man does not deny the referentiality of language altogether, but deprives it from all "extralinguistic referent or meaning," to reduce the referent to "the intralinguistic resources of figures"—a distinction equally predicated on the dualism between a presumed extralinguistic essence (thing-in-itself) and language, as on the dualism between object and subject.[17] Jim Hansen keenly juxtaposes de Man's epistemology to Benjamin's, insofar as "nature is never a first principle in itself for Benjamin because it is always involved in a dialectic with history and, thus, is only open to us through history and language," so that "history and the historicity of understanding are subject to nature, and nature is acknowledged as a category subject to historical thought."[18] Hansen elaborates further the difference between de Man and Benjamin by writing that, for de Man, "the linguistic context or constructedness of an allegory, its situatedness, always collapses that allegory's pretension to be transcendentally or transhistorically true," and this should serve as a lesson for the "critic" that "the trick is to be aware of this aporia, to see allegory . . . as the ironic 'pseudoknowledge' of its own impossibility."[19] Whereas for Benjamin, "allegorical form itself . . . is produced by certain kinds of historical crises," so that "allegory reflect[s] some historical failure of or crisis in human perception en masse, in de Man it reflects a deconstructive move on the part of either a piece of writing or an individual writer."[20] For de Man, "'The Truth' gets replaced by contextual and discursive truths of various hermeneutic circles," and "discursive historicity acts as the negative ontological principle of de Manian critique."[21] By contrast, "Benjamin extrapolates from allegorical form a theory of human finitude," in which, "allegory's apparently arbitrary linking of an unrepresentable idea to a material emblem indicates that the idea itself was dialectically enfolded into a material history strewn with similarly transient ideas"; for "history . . . is written on transient nature, and, subsequently, allegory represents the irrecoverable loss of the object's originary sense." In this way, "allegory historicizes itself, and immanent critique, then, becomes an allegorical method for discussing and meditating on lost forms," whereby "formalism itself becomes allegorical."[22] Through Benjamin's "maneuver," which "almost seems more like a Mobius strip, an immanent critique actually transforms into a sophisticated, negative form of transcendent criticism."[23] Thus, in Hansen's concise conclusion, although both "in de Man and in Benjamin, formalism" and the question of the allegorical form "become . . . the way for modern thought to negotiate the problem of historicity," Benjamin "enfolds the transcendent into the immanent while de Man's approach deconstructs the transcendent via the immanent."[24] Benjamin's quest, therefore, is not one "for a historicism that practices 'strategic essentialism,' but rather [one] for a politically and historically inflected formalism that practices 'strategic deconstruction,'" that is, "a formalism capable of doubting its own truth-claims without giving up on the object's *Warheit-Gehalt* (truth-content) wholesale."[25] To renounce this content is to fall prey to precisely the ideological fantasy of commodity fetishism and to forget that the "truth-content" of the object is intimately accessible because it coincides with the truth-content of the subject.

Just as Marx's commodity fetishism radically undermines the closeness or autonomy of the subject, Benjamin's gaze or, as Comay writes (explicitly echoing Emmanuel Levinas), "eying the other as eye, or facing the other's face as a face" would "break the appropriate circle of identification of every ego and thus dislodge the very economy of the Same."[26] Rather than a "*Projektion* or *Übertragung* from man to nature . . . it is ultimately uncertain from which direction the alleged transfer comes."[27] More specifically,

> [I]f the auratic perception of nature's gaze involves a humanization, or perhaps, still better, a socialization of the natural, Benjamin carefully resists the obvious inference. That is, that a massive anthropocentric subsumption is at work. . . . Closer scrutiny suggests that we should not take for granted just what either *man* or *nature* have come to mean.[28]

For "the auratic experience of a 'humanized' nature involves simply the recognition of the 'forgotten human residue in things.'"[29] Importantly, this primary "forgotten human residue" consists not of the notorious capitalist alienation with its "reified traces of human labor that have been obscured by commodity fetishism," but a "forgetting even prior to the reification of labor through the occultation of its social form."[30] As Benjamin writes, "there must be something human about things which is not the result of labour," and it is the forgetfulness of this "something" that constitutes the primal Fall and underlies, in Comay's words, "the Fall as the alienation of labor" (*OT*: 93).³¹ This is "the Fall from the [prelapsarian] Adamic naming of the animals to the 'prattle' of signs" or, in Benjamin's idiom, allegories, which amounts to "the Fall from noncoercive cohabitation to 'the arbitrary rule over things'" that is imposed the moment things are no longer just objects of utility but also exchange-values, and, hence, to recall Marx's words, they have "absolutely no connection with [their] physical nature . . . and [their] material [*dinglich*] relations."³² It is not that, as Comay writes, "the reification of labor in commodity fetishism would be already a second-order decline, the Fall of a Fall, the reification of reification," if by this is meant either a chronological or a causal hierarchy.³³ Rather, the two Falls (the one from the prelapsarian Adamic naming to allegory—that is, to the arbitrary sign—and the other from a nature that is both usable and spiritual to a nature whose objects of utility are also signs) are immanent in one another, presuppose one another, and are the two manifestations, on the intertwined levels of signification and economy, of the simultaneous advent of secular thought and the capitalist mode of production. The arbitrariness of the exchange-value of commodities—the fact that the value of each commodity is determined through purely differential relations to the values of all other commodities, independently of the commodities' physical properties—is coupled with what Irving Wohlfarth distils in Benjamin's allegory as, in Comay's words, the "linguistic arbitrariness in the semiotic conception of language."³⁴ In Wohlfarth's own words, what Benjamin calls in *Einbahnstraße* (One-Way Street) the "fall of language" "into the abyss of the mediateness of all communication [*den Abgrund der Mittelbarkeit aller Mitteilung*]" (*SW* 1: 120/ *GS* 2.1: 154) is

> immediately identified with the curse of labour. With the expulsion from Paradise, man is condemned to till the fields (*Acker*) by the sweat of his brow. Nature is now an object of technical manipulation, something to belabour, no longer the object of auratic contemplation, a silent language to be listened to. Proper names therewith degenerate into the inappropriate babble of Babel. This latter consequence of the Fall, Benjamin notes, comes about only "later." In his reading of Genesis, however, such consequences seem almost contemporaneous, if not indeed synonymous, with the Fall. It is therefore difficult to distinguish cause from effect.³⁵

The Fall into "labour" coincides with the semiotic Fall or "shift from names to signs," that is, "from ideas that have a *fundamentum in re*" to arbitrary "concepts that are mere *flatus vocis*," insofar as, in Benjamin's pathbreaking reading of the German baroque tragic drama or *Trauerspiel*, the sign is allegory, that is, in his words, "it means precisely the non-existence of what it presents" (*OT*: 233).³⁶ And both Falls are ultimately contemporaneous, if not indeed synonymous, with the "brutal transition from a self-sufficient, 'feudal' economy to a restless dynamic that seems recognizably 'bourgeois.'"[37] The Fall from Paradise launches "technical manipulation" and is, therefore, "the Fall . . . that inaugurated the 'age of mechanical reproduction'"; in other words, "the 'loss of aura' that Benjamin will later associate with the advent of mechanical reproduction would date back as far as the Fall."[38] We can accept Comay's reading of Benjamin's conception of the "'original sin,'" in "Über Sprache überhaupt und über die Sprache des Menschen" ("On Language as Such and on the Language of Man"), as "a loss of the primal affinity between the speechless 'language of things' and the [postlapsarian] Adamic language of naming," whereby "the reification of labor in commodity fetishism would be simply a doubling or compounding of that sin," but only insofar as by this we also mean that the "original sin" itself is a doubling or compounding of the (ostensibly) subsequent sin, the reification of labor.[39] The original is itself no less a copy than its copy, for the advent of the secular-capital couplet—as the full meaning of commodity fetishism allows us to understand—amounts to precisely this obliteration of transitive causality between the two modalities of human exchange (economy and communication/ representation), as well as among the temporal modes of past, present, and future.[40] It is in the same move that the "speechless 'language of things'" yields to the arbitrary babble of the allegoric sign and that the speechless materiality of pure use-values yields to the differential 'language' of exchange-values. In short, there can be no other allegory but, to borrow an essay's title "allegory in the world of the commodity."[41]

This secular-capitalist transformation of materiality and immateriality (commodities and thought) into arbitrary differential systems, that is, into autonomous and machinic *structures*, entails the end of anthropomorphic or humanist thought—something toward which Benjamin's work strives, perhaps ironically, through its mystic, even hyperhumanist, style.[42] Invoking the Heideggerian "forgetfulness of a forgetfulness" required to experience the aura in the era of mechanical reproduction, Comay remarks that:

> [T]he layered reminiscence at work in the (re)experience of the aura thus exceeds the egocentric grasp of a humanistic self-consciousness and indeed points to a humanity beyond human self-production and control. If, indeed, humanity is still the word for it.[43]

What takes place in Benjamin—as well as, according to Benjamin, in Baudelaire—is a reversal of the direction of auratic "projection" . . . culminating in the "more real humanism," which Benjamin sees announced by [Karl] Kraus. This new humanism heralds not a "new man" (*neuer Mensch*) but rather a "nonhuman," a "monster" (*Unmensch*). Such an "inhuman" humanism would displace the "cosmopolitan rectitude" projected by bourgeois idealism, with its inherent spiritualization of the natural and its essentialization of *homo sapiens*. "Humanity" would receive its materialist determination.[44]

To this Comay appropriately adds that "such an anti-humanist determination of *das Menschliche* would not involve a naturalism along biologistic or organicist lines"; rather, Benjamin aims at "an allegorical 'destruction of the organic.'"[45]

We can grasp the logic of this allegorical destruction by analogy to Benjamin's conceptualization of history. As Howard Caygill notes, in Benjamin, "history becomes an allegory, withholding its meaning just as it seems to offer it"; similarly, the allegorical destruction of the organic or, for that matter, of the human, involves a withholding of organicist or humanistic meaning, just as it seems to offer it—a fact that, to repeat, relates to Benjamin's style.[46] Of course, beyond referencing it through his style, Benjamin does not shun also explicit treatment of this issue, such as in his statement in "Die Aufgabe des Übersetzers" ("The Task of the Translator") that "certain correlative concepts retain their meaning, and possibly their foremost significance, if they are not from the outset used exclusively with reference to man" (*SW* 1: 254/ *GS* 4.1: 10). In either mode (style or theme), Benjamin's antihumanism entails "a movement beyond facticity," and both modes "exemplify the radically nonempiricist materialism or the antiphenomenological phenomenology of Benjamin's auratic vision." [47]

Benjamin's allegorical anti-humanism entails, as we shall eventually see, an anti-subjectivist history, which, along with its concomitant conception of the gaze, constitutes one of the central points of difference between Benjamin and Heidegger. To grasp this difference we must approach more closely Benjamin's and Heidegger's respective approaches to history. As Caygill notes, "although couched in the numbing idiom of academic Neo-Kantianism, Heidegger's analysis of historical time is already far beyond it," for "it points to a radical understanding of time as *tradition*, that is, as a passing on of the past to the present which," at the same time, "is also the present's constitution of its past."[48] This conception of historical time, along with Heidegger's notorious attack against the opposition subject-object, may at first give the appearance of a close affinity between his and Benjamin's work. I would grant that this is true as far as the questions go that the two thinkers raise, but not their answers. A decisive point of deviation between them lies in the fact that, as Caygill stresses, Heidegger's primary agenda throughout his work remains the search "for the basis of authentic experience in time," something which radically differs from Benjamin's quest.[49] This difference is already reflected methodologically in the fact that, as Caygill remarks, while Heidegger restricts "the analysis of historical time to the contrast of natural and historical science, Benjamin introduces the function of time in aesthetics," and "specifically in the distinction between the dramatic forms of tragedy and *Trauerspiel*." By analogy to the distinction between pre- and postlapsarian languages—that is, pre- and secular-capitalist language and economy—Benjamin's "tragic time is authentic, and marks a present which is redeemed and completed by gathering its past to itself, while time for *Trauerspiel* is inauthentic: the past ruining the present and making it entirely in vain."[50] For Benjamin, "tragic time" is precisely the Heideggerian conception of historical time, to which Benjamin persistently juxtaposes, as in "Tragedy and *Trauerspiel*," a history that is "infinite in every direction and unfulfilled in every moment" (*SW* 1: 55). This means, as Caygill writes, that "redeemed time for [Benjamin] is not a continuous substance underlying past, present and future, but the Messianic interruption of the temporal order itself."[51] Crucially, as is the case with all of Benjamin's mystic or religious references, this "Messianic interruption" is to be understood allegorically, that is, as representing that which does not exist, and hence, in this case, as something that cannot occur within historical time and ontic experience but only as "the end of history." As Caygill's succinctly concludes: "it is the distinction between fulfillment *in* historical time and the fulfillment *of* historical time which marks the difference between Heidegger and Benjamin."[52] Again in Caygill's words:

> Benjamin insists on the complete exteriority of Messianic time, one whose advent brings with it the "cessation of happening." In the absence of the Messianic fulfillment of time there can be none in time: all events in time are not only inauthentic, but they can never attain authenticity.[53]

Benjamin stages the difference between Heidegger and himself as the distinction of "the authenticity of the tragic death from the inauthentic death of *Trauerspiel*"; while "tragic death marks a moment of fulfillment," whereby "all the events of a life gather significance from the anticipation of this moment . . . death in *Trauerspiel* does not fulfill a life," but is instead "one of a series of insignificant moments" in a game in which "each moment is a fraud, a repetition of a repetition," or, in Benjamin's words, again from "Tragedy and *Trauerspiel*," every moment is "all play, until death puts an end to the game, so as to repeat the same game, albeit on a grander scale, in another world"[54] (*SW* 1: 57). This means that, while "for Heidegger, origin and tradition are equivocal," so that "they can be either authentic or inauthentic, fulfilling or destructive," for "Benjamin there is no such equivocation: origin and tradition are unequivocally destructive"; in short, "the difference hinges around the possibility of an authentic site where tradition can be gathered."[55]

This site, as Caygill notes, "is described topologically" by "Heidegger in 1916 and later in *Being and Time*" "in terms of 'the subject' or 'that which lies under.'" And while Heidegger "grants the possibility of gathering tradition on the ground of the subject . . . Benjamin refuses it."⁵⁶ Thus, for Heidegger, "the site of tradition is surrendered to the subject of tradition, be it the hero, the poet, the leader or the people."⁵⁷ While Heidegger "very rapidly translated the handing over of tradition into the agonal, or dialectical, logic of subjectivity," Benjamin "insisted upon the destruction of tradition" and "avoided any temptation to transform the site of tradition into the place of the subject."⁵⁸ For Benjamin, "the site of tradition is not a place where past, present and future are gathered together for resolute action, but one where the present is haunted not only by its past but also by its future of becoming past." For this reason, tradition "is a place of *mourning*," in which "origin and its objects can never attain authenticity, but are always indebted to something which does not disclose itself."⁵⁹ Unlike in Heidegger, in Benjamin there is no place in the ontic or factual domain, in which the original or tradition could manifest itself as such, in its complete or fulfilled form, so that "the world handed down to us by tradition is uncanny, undecipherable, always other," and "characterized by confusion and indecision," just as "in the act of 'handing over' there is no community or subject to give or receive," for "the subject is . . . ruined by tradition."⁶⁰ This starkly contrasts with Heidegger, for whom, "the moment of origin is potentially a moment of clarity and resolute decision," it is a moment "of historical decision, enabling Dasein to choose as a subject its own destiny," as in Benjamin's tragedy, "while *Trauerspiel* ends with indecision and uncathartic catastrophe."⁶¹

Now we can see clearly the difference between Heidegger's and Benjamin's conceptions of the gaze. For Benjamin, the "original" gaze cannot be given on the ontic level and cannot be realized within historical time. As Benjamin writes, "that which is original is never revealed in the naked and manifest existence of the factual," for "on the one hand it needs to be recognized as a process of restoration and re-establishment, but, on the other hand, and precisely because of this, as something imperfect and incomplete" (*OT*: 45). This is why, as Jacques Lacan put it, "there is no Other of the Other," which is to say, there is no gaze of the Other, and precisely for this reason, "the gaze I encounter . . . is not a seen gaze, but a gaze imagined by me in the field of the Other."⁶² For, if the gaze needs to be imagined by the subject in the field of the Other in order for it to be restored or reestablished, it is precisely because it is imperfect and incomplete in the first place. By contrast, for Heidegger historical time is the very promise of the ontic, factual manifestation of the gaze as the precondition of historical decision.

I see as a crucial function of passages like the above in Benjamin's work, as well as in Caygill's reading of Benjamin, the attempt to prevent interpreting Benjamin's thought as a movement that posits incompleteness against the background of a presupposed, and longed for, totality—an interpretation all the more tempting as the logic of the syntagmas expressing Benjamin's thesis can lend itself to such an interpretation. For, as Andrew Benjamin writes, "consistent with . . . the present as loss and the resolution or overcoming of loss as futural, is a conception of the subject of experience as that which while modern (secular) . . . can at the same time see itself as a divided unity, and hence will be able to see itself as no longer alienated and therefore as reunited."[63] Such an interpretation would have not only philosophical but political consequences, insofar as, "while the subject of experience may be divided, the nature of what may be antagonistic . . . none the less gestures towards its own unity, in the same way as the idea is revealed as fulfilled 'in the totality of its history.'"[64] Benjamin's extensive construction of both origin and death (in the *Trauerspiel*) as moments of indecision and absence of meaning aim at precisely preempting the hypothesis of, in Andrew Benjamin's words, "the future [as] a possibility of resolution," the latter being conceived "of course . . . as totality," even if by this is not meant "necessarily a return to the totality that was, but rather to a future totality," for "the consequence of this" hypothesis, "is that it both demands, as well as gives rise to, a conception of the future as a synthesized totality, where identity must always precede and ground difference."[65] If Benjamin and, for that matter, Baudelaire allow us to infer "that inherent in each is a futural dimension that necessarily depends upon a conception of the present either as incomplete or as the locus of loss"—which, to repeat Benjamin's words, demands "restoration and re-establishment"—they do so only insofar as they simultaneously recognize, returning to Benjamin's words, that, "precisely because of this," this futural moment is "something imperfect and incomplete."[66] According to Benjamin, neither identity and completeness nor difference and incompleteness can be the ground, insofar as each idea entails and presupposes the other as its supplement.

To recapitulate, the difference between Heidegger and Benjamin lies in the possibility or impossibility of the Real (be it the moment of origin, in the context of historical time, or the gaze, in the context of perception and interpretation/ knowledge) to manifests itself ontically as such. On the one hand, there is Heidegger's invocation of the "subject" at the "moment of clarity," in which "the moment of origin" and that of "resolute decision" can potentially be realized in history. On the other hand, Benjamin opposes this position by arguing that it is impossible for the moment of "origin" to occur in the "manifest existence of the factual," and that its reestablishment remains by necessity a pure desire that only reconfirms its "imperfect and incomplete" character. In other words, for Heidegger there is the possibility that a moment can occur at which history becomes fully conscious of itself (not unlike Hegel), whereas for Benjamin an unconscious surplus always exceeds any historical consciousness (not unlike Lacan).[67]

Let us recall that Lacan defined "the unconscious of the subject" as the "irreducible, *non-sensical*—composed of no meanings—signifying chain."[68] This explains why for Benjamin, as Caygill rightly discerns, "there is no final decision which would give meaning to the events which preceded [death], simply indecision and accident in the face of catastrophe."[69] Bringing together Benjamin's and Caygill's words, "whereas tragedy ends with a decision—however uncertain this may be—there resides in the essence of *Trauerspiel*, and especially in the death scene," the inalienable fact that "this death did not complete a life, give it meaning, but cut it off and left it in question" (*OT*: 137).[70] By contrast, the fact that, for Heidegger, meaning can be completed in history—through the decision made by a "subject"—or that truth can reveal itself ontically—amounts to presupposing both a complete and perfect gaze in the Other and a fully conscious historical subject, which, as such, is immune to ideological imaginary constructions.

These Heideggerian presuppositions are expressed quite subtly. Recurrently Heidegger stresses in *Being and Time* that, even as "falling [*Verfallen*]," that is, the "basic kind of Being which belongs to everydayness," "has mostly the character of Being-lost in the publicness of the 'they'"—whereby "Dasein has . . . fallen away [abgefallen] from itself as an authentic potentiality for Being its Self"—nevertheless, "falling is a definite existential characteristic of Dasein itself" and "reveals an *essential* ontological structure of Dasein itself" (*BT*: 219–220 and 224/ *GA* 2: 233–234 and 238). Such statements seem to indicate that, for Heidegger, the imaginary is integral to the ontological structure of Dasein. He categorically declares that Dasein is always "fallen" and, hence, always prey to the untruths and illusions of the "they," and cautions us not to "take the fallenness of Dasein as a 'fall' from a purer and higher 'primal status,'" for "not only do we lack any experience of this [primal status] ontically, but ontologically we lack any possibilities or clues for Interpreting it" (*BT*: 220/ *GA* 2: 233–234). There is no pre- or nonfallen state of Dasein, yet, crucially, there is instead the difference between Dasein's "inauthenticity" and "authenticity." This difference Heidegger defines as one between, on the one hand, "a quite distinctive kind of Being-in-the-world—the kind which is completely fascinated by the 'world' and by the Dasein-with of Others in the 'they,'" and, on the other hand, "*authentic* existence," as "not something which floats above falling everydayness," but as "only a modified way in which such everydayness is seized upon" (*BT*: 220 and 224/ *GA* 2: 233 and 238). What is more—for herein lies the crucial Heideggerian leap—Dasein's means to its authenticity is "resoluteness" (*Entschlossenheit*), a term that "signifies letting oneself be summoned out of one's own lostness in the 'they,'" and which Heidegger further defines as "*the resolution*"

[*Entschluß*] that "*is precisely the disclosive projection and determination of what is factically possible at the time* [*ist gerade erst das erschließende Entwerfen und Bestimmen der jeweiligen faktischen Möglichkeiten*]" (*BT*: 345/ *GA* 2: 395). Once again Heidegger emphasizes that even "resoluteness, as *authentic Being-one's-Self*, does not detach Dasein from its world" and its fallenness, and that, "disclosed in its 'there,' [Dasein] maintains itself both in truth and untruth with equal primordiality" (*BT*: 344–345/ *GA* 2: 395–396). And at the same moment that Heidegger adds that "this 'really' holds in particular for resoluteness as authentic truth [*Das gilt "eigentlich" gerade von der Entschlossenheit als der eigentlichen Wahrheit*]," he entirely undermines the equo-primordiality of truth and untruth by stating that in the case of "resoluteness as authentic truth . . . resoluteness appropriates untruth authentically" [*eignet sich die Unwahrheit eigentlich zu*] (*BT*: 345/ *GA* 2: 396). In other words, although the essential ontological characteristic of Dasein is to be primordially submerged in both truth and untruth, the moment that Dasein lets itself be summoned out of its lostness in the "they," it finds the resolution to determine the factical possibilities at the time, and this determination is, according to Heidegger, supposed to be unalloyed from any ideological and generally imaginary factors, because—being the disclosive projection of the factical possibilities of a world that possesses a self-understanding that coincides with consciousness—it constitutes a revelation of authentic truth.

Allegorical Gaze

Although, as we have seen, for Benjamin the fall coincides with the inception of secular thought and the capitalist mode of production, this does not mean that Benjamin does not acknowledge the historical specificities that characterize distinct eras within modernity, as well as the circular temporality in which these eras are mutually determined. If Benjamin was able to lay out the epistemological premises of secular representation on the basis of Baroque allegory, it is precisely because he approached the latter from within the discourse of late modernism, in which these premises were first made explicit. Similarly, one may retroactively be able to discern the necessity of the aura's withering throughout modernity, but this is possible only after its explicit manifestation had taken place in modernism. And today it seems imperative to address the status of the aura in the age of digital reproducibility of both the artwork and the documentation of life. Is it possible that today the withering of the aura experiences its culmination in the total absence of the gaze on the part of the object, and, if so, would this phenomenon render both Heidegger's and Benjamin's positions on the possibility or impossibility of a complete or fulfilled gaze obsolete?

Indeed, rather than attaining a forgetfulness of forgetfulness that would remind us that what we have forgotten is the gaze, the question of the gaze seems to fall itself into oblivion in the era of postmodernity, in the same movement as history is perceived as the effect of neither heroes or people, nor ideological (imaginary) calls, but of presumed inexorable and autonomous mechanisms of the market. Our era may reveal that the moment when danger becomes absolute is when history is perceived as automatic fate. At that moment, the difference between Heidegger and Benjamin may no longer matter, as heroes, people, poets, and ideology meet under the illusory haze of being themselves the sole danger.

At least, this is one possible consequence of Benjamin's position, one that seems not irrelevant to Lacan's declaration in his 1970s television broadcast that "anyway capitalism, that was its starting point: getting rid of sex."[71] For, as Comay reminds us, both "Marx had already commented in 1844 that sexual relations would always be an index of the political possibilities of the day," and "Benjamin remarks on the link between libidinal and political potency."[72] The reason for this link between these two domains of human life lies in the centrality of the gaze in both. In "Eduard Fuchs, Collector and Historian," Benjamin remarks, in Comay's succinct summary, "that the human upright posture made face-to-face—that is, auratic—orgasms for the first time possible, enabling at once both (and for the same reason) erotic fantasy and the utopian yearning for social change."[73] In *Das Passagen-Werk* (*Arcades Project*), too, Benjamin writes:

> The distance that is there in the eyes of the beloved and that draws the lover after it is the dream of a better nature. The decline of the aura and the waning of the dream of a better nature—this latter conditioned on its defensive position in the class struggle—are one and the same. It follows that the decline of the aura and the decline of sexual potency are also, at bottom, one. (*AP* J76,1)

In other words, as Comay comments, for Benjamin, "the decline of erotic/auratic eye contact would imply the dissipation of the revolutionary urge as such" and the concomitant distrust of revolutionary tendencies, whether in heroes, people, or poetry.[74]

However, we must not forget that Benjamin's approach is allegorical, which above all means governed by the principle of—and, depending on circumstances, possibly strategically aiming at—the nonexistence of whatever is presented in representation. As Comay writes in her commentary on *Das Passagen-Werk*, "in the 'frozen unrest' of its images—transfixed, as though by Medusa, by the very reifications it would reflect—allegory in its abstraction and fragmentation both repeats and apotropaically resists the devaluating movement of the commodity."[75] By definition, allegory is an approach, if not a method or strategy, in which the procedures of the dominant modes of production, representation and communication, and sexuality are replicated, but with a displacement that brings about the opposite effect: for instance, instead of the devaluation of the object (and of the subject), they would bring about their hyper-evaluation.

The devaluation of the commodity consists above all in losing its value as an object of utility—its purpose ceases to be the satisfaction of needs—while its raison-d'être becomes to be pure exchange-value in the service of a theoretically infinite accumulation of surplus-value. Love, Benjamin suggests in "Karl Krauss," is an allegory that, in replicating and displacing the devaluating mechanism of the commodity, is capable of resisting its effects, insofar as, in "seeing" the other, what we perceive is "how the beloved grows distant and lustrous, how her minuteness and her glow withdraw," in a way that, as Comay puts it, "turns love itself into the infinite 'gratitude' (*Dank*) that renounces all satisfaction and finds its promise in the pure 'name'" (Benjamin *SW* 2: 453/ *GS* 2.1: 362).[76] To stress that love involves a renunciation of satisfaction, Benjamin invokes the "Platonic love, which does not satisfy its desire in what it loves, but possesses and holds it in name"; yet, at stake is not just renunciation of satisfaction but a total "self-renunciation" that knows nothing other "than giving thanks . . . for to thank is to put feelings under a name" (*SW* 2: 453/ *GS* 2.1: 362). Just as "love is not possession, but gratitude," allegory "is the medium neither of clairvoyance nor of domination," but rather "it is the theater of a sanctification of the name" against "the theurgy of the 'word-body'" (*SW* 2: 453 and 451). Contrary to the capitalist renunciation of satisfaction, which brings about the devaluation of things and people for the sake of the accumulation of capital, love's renunciation of satisfaction restores in the other her or his unsubstitutionable uniqueness, indicated by the other's "name"—only insofar as this name, like exchange-value and unlike the "word-body," has broken all ties with any physical body. In the allegorical gaze, as in the erotic eye contact, as Benjamin writes in "Central Park," "the commodity"—and, in the case of sexuality, the commodified human subject—"wants to look itself in the face," a gesture that the does not differ from "quotation," as defined in the essay on Krauss, since only "to quote a word is to call it by its name" (Benjamin *SW* 4: 173/ *GS* 1.2: 671; and *SW* 2: 453). In capitalist exchange, a commodity sees only its reflection in the mirror of another commodity that functions as its equivalent-value and whose value is supposed to express the relative value of the first commodity, as its own exchange-value.[77] The semiotic equivalent of this procedure is the dictionary use of language, in which one term is defined by being substituted for other words; to this use of language Benjamin juxtaposes quotation, for only quoting a word calls it by name, thereby breaking the *mise-en-abîme* of imaginary reflections. Similarly, in love, by seeing in the other a unique, unsubstitutionable or nonexchangeable being, the imaginary mirror is broken, and one is left with one's own face. This is also to say that in love one can no longer be one's own distant spectator, at once present and absent, as if one were looking at someone else's life. By "being captured allegorically" in this reconfiguration of presence and absence, "the phantasmagoria of capitalism would both achieve and resist" the "final 'distortion' [*Entstellen*]," as Benjamin puts it in *Zentralpark*, of objects and subjects "in the flattened space-time of pure exchange."[78]

Sexuality, therefore, bears for Benjamin the same political potentials as technology, and he is, as Caygill writes, "by no means naïvely optimistic" about either. Just as Benjamin "is convinced that the technological reconfiguration of the site of tradition is ineluctable, and may lead either to the 'renewal' or 'destruction' of humanity'"—even as by "renewal" he cannot mean a complete or fulfilling redemption—so, too, the absence or presence of an auratic gaze in love may lead sexuality (and, by extension, politics) either to a consumerist replication of copulative acts, in which the self and the other are equally devalued, or to the erotic encounter with one's own and the other's presence.[79] Similarly, film may be, as Benjamin's essay on technologically reproducible art indicates, the best form of art for Fascist purposes, just as it can "potentially [be] a thoroughly politicized art," capable of renewing society, insofar as, in Benjamin's words, film "is piecemeal, its manifold parts being assembled according to a new law" (*SW* 4: 265).[80] Both terrains, technologically reproducible art and sexuality, constitute two-way streets, which, with Caygill, we could describe as follows:

> Through the power of technology it is possible to create giant auratic works of art—cities and entire peoples—who are simultaneously present and absent to themselves. The configuration of this presence and absence may be managed ritually or politically. In the former the people *are staged* as present and absent: they participate avidly in their own history while spectating it as someone else's history . . . they participate in their own destruction and enjoy the spectacle.[81]

Caygill's last words almost verbatim echo Benjamin's conclusion in his essay on the work of art:

> Humankind['s] . . . self-alienation has reached the point where it can experience its own annihilation as a supreme aesthetic pleasure. Such

is the aestheticizing of politics, as practiced by fascism. Communism replies by politicizing art. (*SW* 4: 270)

Caygill elaborates on this politicization by writing:

> In the politicization of art, the management of presence and absence is itself deliberative, the configuration of the site is itself at issue; it is no longer simply given as the stage upon which the play of presence and absence may be performed.[82]

Is it possible that allegory, because it postulates the nonexistence of that which is represented, and hence the possible existence of what is not represented, requires that the gaze must first eclipse from representation (artistic or otherwise) in order for the management of presence and absence to be able to become deliberative, in order for art and all fields of representation to cease to be simply given as a stage for a preset play?

If this is so, then this would be the point where Benjamin and Theodor Adorno's negative dialectic would meet. For, recalling Adorno's definition of negative dialectic in the context of art, "art is the social antithesis of society," that is, "works of art are after-images or replicas of empirical reality, inasmuch as they proffer to the latter what in the outside world is denied them."[83] This means that Benjamin's allegory, which "means precisely the non-existence of what it presents," is no different from Adorno's "works of art," which "do not lie" and "what they say is literally true," because they depict the "outside world" negatively.[84] Thus, according to Adorno's negative dialectic, "there is a grain of validity even," for instance, in the (Kantian) secular "contemplative attitude toward art, inasmuch as it underscores the important posture of art's turning away from immediate praxis and refusing to play the world game" of a "society" that is "dominated . . . by brutal self-interest."[85] By the same token, only a society dominated by a brutal gaze could produce art and modes of representation in which the gaze is absent. In the era of the panoptical quasi-universal surveillance, then, the task of allegory becomes not only not to represent the gaze but also to enable thereby negatively the existence of a gaze other than the actually existing brutal gaze of control.

Notes

1. Rebecca Comay, "Framing Redemption: Aura, Origin, Technology in Benjamin and Heidegger," in eds. Arleen B. Dallery, Charles E. Scott, and P. Holley

Roberts, *Ethics and Danger: Essays on Heidegger and Continental Thought* (Albany, NY: State University of New York Press, 1992), 139–167, here 158; referring to Heidegger's *Der Satz vom Grund*, GA 10: 68.
2. Comay, "Framing Redemption," 158; referring to Heidegger's "Die Kehre," QTC 46–47/ GA 79: 74–76.
3. Comay, "Framing Redemption," 157; Heidegger, QTC 37–41; and again, from Heidegger's "Die Kehre": "Aber die Gefahr, nämlich das in der Wahrheit seines Wesens sich gefährdende Seyn selbst, bleibt verhüllt und verstellt. Diese Verstellung ist das Gefährlichste der Gefahr. . . . Ist die Gefahr als die Gefahr, dann ereignet sich eigens ihr Wesen" (*GA* 79: 68 and 72).
4. Comay, "Framing Redemption," 157; referring to Heidegger's "Die Frage nach der Technik" ["The Question Concerning Technology"], QTC 32/ GA 7: 33; see Rodolphe Gasché, *The Tain of the Mirror: Derrida and the Philosophy of Reflection* (Cambridge, MA: Harvard University Press, 1988).
5. Comay, "Framing Redemption," 143.
6. Ibid., 144.
7. Ibid., 154.
8. Ibid., 144.
9. Ibid., 145.
10. Ibid. Note that Schelling represents the same idea, as, for instance, in his "Vom Ich als Prinzip der Philosophie oder über das Unbedingte im menschlichen Wissen": "Es [Sein] ist, indem es gedacht wird, und es wird gedacht, weil es ist; deswegen, weil es nur insofern ist und nur insofern gedacht wird, als es *sich selbst* denkt." F. W. J. Schelling, "Vom Ich als Prinzip der Philosophie oder über das Unbedingte im menschlichen Wissen," in *Sämmtliche Werke*, ed. K. F. A Schelling, Stuttgart, 1856–1861, vol. I, 13–176, here 42.
11. Karl Marx, *Capital: A Critique of Political Economy*, vol. 1., trans. Ben Fowkes (London: Penguin Books, 1990), 165; emphasis mine.
12. Ibid., 167; emphasis mine.
13. Ibid., 165.
14. Ibid.
15. Ibid., 16. Paul de Man, *Allegories of Reading. Figural Language in Rousseau, Nietzsche, Rilke, and Proust* (New Haven, CT: Yale University Press, 1979), 106.
17. Ibid., 105.
18. Jim Hansen, "Formalism and Its Malcontents: Benjamin and De Man on the Function of Allegory," *New Literary History*, 35:4 (2004): 663–683, here 678.
19. Ibid., 672.
20. Ibid.

21. Ibid., 676.
22. Ibid., 675.
23. Ibid., 676.
24. Ibid., 669.
25. Ibid., 680.
26. Comay, "Framing Redemption," 145.
27. Ibid., 147.
28. Ibid.
29. Ibid.; Benjamin's May 7, 1940, letter to Adorno, in *CA*: 326/ *GS* 1.3: 1134.
30. Ibid. In my opinion, Comay's reading of commodity fetishism does not go much further than what she herself characterizes as an "insufficiently radical" reading of Marx, but through her references to Benjamin's approach to language she nevertheless succeeds in discerning that at stake is not simply the alienation of labor.
31. Ibid.
32. Ibid., 148; citing Benjamin *OT*: 233.
33. Comay, "Framing Redemption," 148.
34. Ibid., 165, n. 25.
35. Irving Wohlfarth, "On Some Jewish Motifs in Benjamin," in ed. Andrew Benjamin, *The Problems of Modernity: Adorno and Benjamin* (London: Routledge, 1989), 157–215, here 160.
36. Ibid., 161.
37. Ibid.
38. Ibid., 160.
39. Comay, "Framing Redemption," 148; Benjamin *SW* 1: 69–70/ *GS* 2.1: 151.
40. In other words, topoi such as tragedy or the precapitalist mode of production, to which Benjamin attributes unity or completeness, are to be understood not as actual historical moments of the past, but—not unlike Freud's murder of the primal father or the witnessing of the primal scene—as imaginary constructions, that are nevertheless necessary in order to comprehend our secular, fallen, allegorical, and capitalist present. Another way of putting it would be perhaps to liken Benjamin's past and, for that matter, future, with Jacques Derrida's spectrality, which, as Berber Bevernage puts it, "cannot be *dated*—in a chain of presents, according to a calendar—but it surely is historical," insofar as, now in Warren Montag's words, it "'was never alive enough to die, never present enough to become absent,'" or, foregrounding the logico-synchronic dimension of history, insofar as "spectrality or the denial of 'full absence' is the logical other of Derrida's lifelong deconstruction of full presence." Berber Bevernage, "Time, Presence, and Historical Injustice," *History*

and Theory 47:2 (2008): 149–167, here 164; citing Warren Montag, "Spirits Armed and Unarmed: Derrida's Specters of Marx," in ed. Michael Sprinker, *Ghostly Demarcations: A Symposium on Jacques Derrida's Specters of Marx* (London: Verso, 1999), 71–74, here 74; see also Jacques Derrida, *Specters of Marx: The State of the Debt, the Work of Mourning, and the New International*, trans. Peggy Kamuf (New York: Routledge, 1994). If Benjamin's past, present, and future, are conceived not as distinct points in linear or diachronic time but synchronic logical functions, then they may prove valuable in addressing what Andrew Benjamin rightly identifies as "the philosophical challenge at the present—indeed of the present," by which he means our "postmodern" present, namely, "to map the interarticulation of the desire for unity with the necessity of differential plurality," as contemporaneous historical demands (Andrew Benjamin, "Tradition and Experience: Walter Benjamin's *Some Motifs in Baudelaire*," in ed. Benjamin, *The Problems of Modernity*, 138).

41. I am referring to Lloyd Spencer, "Allegory in the World of Commodity: The Importance of Central Park," in ed. Peter Osborne, *Walter Benjamin: Critical Evaluations in Cultural Theory*. Volume II (London: Routledge, 2005), 118–134.
42. Fred Rush subtly points to the centrality of structure in Benjamin's epistemology in his analysis of the latter's "conception of an Idea," which, according to Rush, is "the key to reconstructing and assessing Benjamin's views in the Preface" of his *Trauerspiel* book, which lays out Benjamin's epistemology. Fred Rush, "Jena Romanticism and Benjamin's Critical Epistemology," in ed. Peter Osborne, *Walter Benjamin: Critical Evaluations*, volume II, 63–81, here 73). "A constellation" (*Sternbild* or *Konstellation*), which is a "connection . . . of particulars in Ideas," can "be considered as a 'system,' so long as one varied enough the criteria for systematicity" (74–75). And just as "system" involves no meaning whatsoever, "Benjamin makes a stronger claim that Ideas have nothing at all to do with knowledge" (74; referring to Benjamin *OT*: 34/ *GS* 1.1: 214).
43. Comay, "Framing Redemption," 148.
44. Ibid., 148–149; citing from Benjamin's "Karl Krauss" (*SW* 2: 454/ *GS* 2.1: 363).
45. Comay, "Framing Redemption," 149; citing from Benjamin's "Zentralpark" ("Central Park"), *SW* 4: 173/ *GS* 1.2: 669.
46. Howard Caygill, "Benjamin, Heidegger and the Destruction of Tradition," in ed. Peter Osborne, *Walter Benjamin: Critical Evaluations in Cultural Theory*, vol. 1 (London: Routledge, 2005), 291–317, here 308.
47. Comay, "Framing Redemption," 151.
48. Caygill, "Benjamin, Heidegger and the Destruction of Tradition," 296.

49. Ibid., 297.
50. Ibid., 298.
51. Ibid., 298–299.
52. Ibid., 299.
53. Ibid.
54. Ibid.
55. Ibid., 301.
56. Ibid.
57. Ibid., 305.
58. Ibid., 305–306.
59. Ibid., 306.
60. Ibid., 308.
61. Ibid., 308–309.
62. Jacques Lacan, *Book XX. Encore, 1972–1973: On Feminine Sexuality; The Limits of Love and Knowledge*, ed. Jacques-Alain Miller, trans. Bruce Fink (New York: Norton, 1998, 81; and *The Four Fundamental Concepts of Psychoanalysis*, ed. Jacques-Alain Miller, trans. Alan Sheridan (New York: Norton, 1981), 84.
63. Andrew Benjamin, "Tradition and Experience," 136–137.
64. Ibid., 137.
65. Ibid., 138.
66. Ibid., 136.
67. It is worth noting that in an essay on Benjamin's reading of Romanticism in his dissertation (*The Concept of Criticism in German Romanticism*)—an essay that, to my understanding, is more concerned with the impact of Benjamin's dissertation on the reception of Romanticism, rather than with the relation between Romanticism and Benjamin's thought itself—Winfried Menninghaus attributes to "the total absence of Schelling" throughout Benjamin's dissertation, "including the bibliography," a "polemic quality," which he justifies as follows: "The Romantics (as Benjamin understands them) deny the unconscious in art and postulate a completely conscious context of reflection. Schelling by contrast conceives of the Absolute as 'something eternally unconscious' in which there 'is no duplicity whatsoever' and which, 'precisely because all consciousness is conditional on duplicity, may never attain consciousness.'" Winfried Menninghaus, "Walter Benjamin's Exposition of the Romantic Theory of Reflection," in ed. Osborne, *Walter Benjamin: Critical Evaluations*, vol. I, 44–45; citing F. W. J. Schelling, *System des transzendentalen Idealismus*, in *Schriften von 1799–1801* (Darmstadt: Wissenschaftliche Buchgesellschaft, 1975), 600. In other words, Menninghaus argues that, at least for the Benjamin of *The Concept of Criticism in German Romanticism*, Romanticism is

irreconcilable with the concept of the unconscious. Given that at least up until, and including de Man, the reception of Romanticism has been "see[ing] the Romantics enthroning reflection as the warrant of immediacy and the full infinity of thinking, and indeed as the (self-representational) form of the Absolute," which, according to Menninghaus, is exactly how Benjamin read them in his dissertation, Mennighaus's thesis that Benjamin's reading of the Romantics is predicated on the exclusion of the unconscious seems indeed a cogent (and also polemic) gesture (58). In his analysis of the epistemology presented in Benjamin's *Habilitationsschrift* (*Der Ursprung des Trauerspiels*) and other works of that period, Fred Rush presents a more generous thesis regarding Benjamin's indebtedness to Romanticism, arguing that Benjamin's "historical antecedents" are to be found "in the Romanticism of the so-called Jena circle that drew its philosophical sustenance from the very thinker whose views Hegel displaced: Kant," and in which Benjamin "finds . . . a general model of interpretation that he considers significant for more explicitly epistemological themes" (Rush, "Jena Romanticism and Benjamin's Critical Epistemology," 64 and 67). Nevertheless, Rush's interpretation is not incompatible with Menninghaus's regarding Benjamin's position on totality or the Absolute, and its inaccessibility. In his reading of Romanticism, Benjamin acknowledges "the claim that the Jena writers typically make: art is not just incomplete, it cannot be completed" (ibid., 68). Yet, even as the Romantics assert that art can never access the Absolute, "the idea that the Romantics may indulge in is that, though we can never get all the way there," we can come closer, whether through "feeling" or because "artworks *qua* perspectives on the Absolute tend to have a cumulative and progressively inclusive character," so that "the more perspectives one invents and inhabits, the more adequate to the Absolute one is" (ibid., 70). "What bothers Benjamin," Rush continues, "is not the concept of the Absolute *per se*; indeed, the absolute is a central concept for him"; rather, "what Benjamin objects to is the idea that entertaining or inhabiting multiple perspectives *converge* upon the Absolute, even if a point of absolute convergence is only ideal. It is the idea of increasing degrees of immediacy that offends him" (ibid., 70). For, "for Benjamin, the profane world of finitude is of an entirely other order from the Absolute," so that "an 'infinite approach' of the profane to the Absolute is an impossibility" (ibid., 70). To maintain that a certain approach can provide greater proximity to the Absolute is for Benjamin "not to take into full account the fallen status" of existence and thought, as well as to forget that "works are saved *as* ruins, not *from* ruins" (70 and 77). In short, "Benjamin thinks that this idea of progressive reflective purchase on the Absolute, through art or otherwise," maintained by "at least one

strand of thought in Romanticism" (though definitely not Schelling), "gets the transcendent nature of the Absolute wrong" (ibid., 76). More radical than the above accounts of Romanticism may be Menninghaus's interpretation, which indicates that, to refer to Klaus Peter's question, whether "'it is rather Schelling than Schlegel [whom Benjamin describes] in his interpretation of Schlegel,'" in either case it would be an incomplete world or history that should reveal itself in the writings of Romanticism, as the title of Peter's work indicates—even as I would also maintain that Schelling offers its clearest and most systematic formulation. Menninghaus, "Walter Benjamin's Exposition of the Romantic Theory of Reflection," 60, n. 75; citing Klaus Peter, *Idealismus als Kritik: Friedrich Schlegels Philosophie der unvollendeten Welt* (Stuttgart: Kohlhammer, 1973), 26; see also Jochen Schulte-Sasse, "General Introduction: Romanticism's Paradoxical Articulation of Desire," in eds. Jochen Schulte-Sasse et al., *Theory as Practice: A Critical Anthology of Early German Romantic Writings* (Minneapolis: University of Minnesota Press, 1997), 1–43.
68. Lacan, *Four Fundamental Concepts*, 250.
69. Caygill, "Benjamin, Heidegger and the Destruction of Tradition," 307.
70. Ibid.
71. Jacques Lacan, *Television: A Challenge to the Psychoanalytic Establishment*, ed. Joan Copjec, trans. Denis Holier, Rosalind Krauss, Annette Michelson, and Jeffrey Mehlman (New York: Norton, 1990), 30.
72. Comay, "Framing Redemption," 154.
73. Ibid.; referring to Benjamin *SW* 3: 279ff and 299, footnote 70/ *GS* 2.2, 497ff.
74. Comay, "Framing Redemption," 154.
75. Ibid., 159; Benjamin *GS* 5.1 410.
76. Comay, "Framing Redemption," 154.
77. See Marx's *Capital*, particularly the chapter "The Value-Form, or Exchange-Value," 138–163.
78. Comay, "Framing Redemption," 159; Benjamin *GS* 1.2: 671.
79. Caygill, "Benjamin, Heidegger and the Destruction of Tradition," 315.
80. Ibid., 314. As I argue elsewhere, this ambivalence, or absence of naive optimism, characterizes also Heidegger—for even as he may consider redemption or a moment of fulfillment possible within history, he offers nothing that guarantees its advent—and is possibly a defining characteristic of modernism (see A. Kiarina Kordela, "Value," in eds. J. D. Mininger and Jason Michael Peck, *Keywords in German Aesthetics* [Cambridge: Harvard University Press, forthcoming]). This ambivalence is further reflected in secondary literature, whether as a conscious dilemma or as an unwitnessed contradiction. For instance, commenting on Benjamin's diagnosis of "modernity as the collapse

of the aura," Gerald Moore, on the one hand, laments this phenomenon insofar as it amounts to "the disappearance of the rhythms of history that reinscribe the past within the present," so that "in modernity, the experience of art becomes" one "of isolation," as opposed to the premodern era in which "these rhythms had unconsciously permeated the subject in a way that safeguarded against collapse into the oppressive interiority of pure self-presence." Gerald Moore, "Clockwork Politics: Rhythm and the Production of Time in Mauss, Benjamin and Lefebvre," in eds. Elizabeth Lindley and Laura McMahon, *Rhythms: Essays in French Literature, Thought and Culture* (Bern: Peter Lang, 2008), 134–144, here 140. On the other hand, however, Moore also states that "our projected behaviour is conditioned by the disciplining presence of rhythm," and that, therefore, "the expectation of its [the rhythm's] continuation mitigates the threat of a revolutionary future, that is, a decisive break with the established order of tradition" (139).
81. Caygill, "Benjamin, Heidegger and the Destruction of Tradition," 315; emphasis mine.
82. Ibid.
83. Theodor Adorno, *Aesthetic Theory*, ed. Gretel Adorno and Rolf Tiedemann, trans. C. Lenhardt (London: Routledge, 1984), 11 and 6.
84. Ibid., 8.
85. Ibid., 17.

PART III

Time

FIVE

MONAD AND TIME

Reading Leibniz with Heidegger and Benjamin

Paula Schwebel

My argument takes its starting point from a narrow, even dry, observation: Heidegger and Benjamin developed parallel interpretations of the monadology—Leibniz's counterintuitive portrayal of individual substances as non-extended, metaphysical points, which mirror the universe in their intensive perceptual states.[1] At stake for both—albeit in markedly different ways—is the temporalization of Leibniz's substantial unities. A monadic structure underlies Heidegger's argument that Dasein exists as an ecstatic, temporal unity. Monads are unities of *becoming*, rather than static, objectively present beings. Heidegger's analysis of "historicity" in the second part of *Being and Time* (1927) is radicalized, and brought to a new level of clarity in his 1928 lecture course on Leibniz, *The Metaphysical Foundations of Logic*. An interpretation of the monadology is also at the core of Benjamin's philosophy of history, from the "Epistemo-Critical Prologue" to *The Origin of German Tragic Drama* (1925), to his late theses "On the Concept of History" (1940). According to Benjamin, monads are full of time; they retain a latent past, and they anticipate the future. But the temporal content in a monad is not chronological; it is rather *legible* in a prestabilized configuration of minute detail in the monad. By narrowing our focus on Heidegger and Benjamin's respective monadologies—so I propose—we gain a determinate point of access into the vast question of how each thinker conceived of historical time.

Husserl in the Background

My main sources are Benjamin's "Epistemo-Critical Prologue" (first published in 1928), and Heidegger's 1928 lecture course, *The Metaphysical Foundations of Logic*.[2] Despite the temporal proximity of these texts, it is not possible to claim that Heidegger was familiar with Benjamin's monadology, or that Benjamin was aware of Heidegger's interpretation of Leibniz. However, there is a plausible third source, common to both Heidegger and Benjamin, and that is Husserl. That Husserl informed Heidegger's reading of Leibniz cannot be surprising, given the pervasive, subcutaneous presence of Husserl in Heidegger's early work. I tread on less-established ground in suggesting that Husserl figures in the background of Benjamin's monadology, although I draw support from Peter Fenves' recent book, which interprets Benjamin's early work as critically engaged with Husserl.[3] I suggest that Benjamin's monadology reveals his proximity to a discussion that was ongoing within phenomenology. During the 1920s, when Husserl was working toward a genetic phenomenology, he took Leibniz's monad as the model for a temporally adumbrated, "living" unity of genesis.[4] In Husserl's monadology, we can trace the origin of Heidegger's ecstatic unity of temporality, as well as Benjamin's "now" of recognizability, in which a latent past can be recollected by attending to the minute interconnections between phenomena. By going back to Husserl, more importantly, we can specify where Benjamin and Heidegger diverge.

Husserl's earliest use of the term *monad* can be found in his 1911 essay, "Philosophy as a Rigorous Science," in which he refers to the unity of immanent time consciousness as monadic.[5] Above all, Husserl's *Nachlass* from 1921 to 1928 reveals the importance of the monadology for his development of a genetic phenomenology.[6] In the fifth of the *Cartesian Meditations*, first delivered as two lectures in Paris in 1929 (too late to have informed Benjamin's and Heidegger's arguments) Husserl articulated a monadological theory of intersubjectivity, in which he describes the shared world as a "community of monads," existing in harmony with each other.[7] It is plausible that Heidegger had access to Husserl's unpublished texts on the monad.[8] But how much of this material could Benjamin possibly have known? Fenves suggests that Benjamin had read Husserl's "Philosophy as a Rigorous Science," *Logical Investigations*, and perhaps *Ideas I*.[9] As I argue, Benjamin frames his monadic "theory of ideas" as a criticism of Husserl's method of "*Wesensschau*," or eidetic intuition (a method that Husserl first elaborated in the sixth of his *Logical Investigations*).[10] At the very least, then, we can regard Benjamin's monadology as a prescient echo, or anticipation, of Husserl's monadic variations toward a genetic phenomenology.

In *Logical Investigations*, Husserl sought to ground cognition in intuition. By intuition, Husserl did not mean immediate sense perception, but rather the fulfillment, or complete presentation, of the ideal structures (i.e., essences) intended by our mental states. Such an analysis is static, because it refers to essential possibilities that are fixed, or already foreseen in a completely developed absolute consciousness. In his later writings, Husserl recognized a more primordial absolute, which is temporally adumbrated, and therefore exceeds what can be rendered present in intuition. Taken as a temporal unity, such an absolute is not static, but is what Husserl referred to as a "living present."[11] Husserl's model for this living, self-temporalizing absolute is Leibniz's monad. Husserl conceives of monads as simple unities that are continuously becoming in time.[12] In their retention of a latent past, and their protention of an expected future, monads exceed what can be presented in a static now-phase of consciousness. Each monad, according to Husserl, is an individuated, concrete, "factical" unity, because it expresses its own unique history in the entirety of its temporal unfolding. As Husserl puts it, each monad is a "unity of its living becoming, a unity of its history," which includes its whole "sedimented history as a horizon."[13]

Although I cannot expand on Husserl's monadology here, I raise it as a hypothesis to explain why Benjamin and Heidegger, at roughly the same time, developed parallel, yet opposing readings of Leibniz's monadology. I say opposing, rather than simply different, because Benjamin and Heidegger were both concerned with the same question—namely, how to reconcile essences with their genesis—but they accomplished this reconciliation from opposite directions. Benjamin argues that an origin is revealed when an idea has absorbed the virtual totality of its past and subsequent history (OT 45–46/ GS 1: 226). Time is *in* ideas, according to Benjamin, but not *as* temporality. Historical content is only expressed indirectly in a configuration of minute detail in an essence. Heidegger takes up Husserl's argument that monads are self-temporalizing unities, but he conceives of genesis in terms of *original* temporalization. Temporalization is not immanent *in* consciousness, but precedes the possibility of consciousness. According to Heidegger, monads are original unities because monads *originate* time: monads are self-generating, *ecstatic* unities of temporality (ML 207/ GA 26: 268).

Heidegger's Monadology and the Temporal Ground of Being

The explicit aim of Heidegger's 1928 lectures is to "dismantle" Leibniz's logic, in order to recall its "living" philosophical source in ontology (ML 6/ GA 26: 8).

Heidegger begins with Leibniz's putatively "logical" definition of individual substances in the "Discourse on Metaphysics." Leibniz proceeds from the nature of propositional truth, or the interconnection of predicates in an underlying subject, to a definition of individual substance as that which has a notion so complete that it contains all of its possible predicates:

> Now it is certain that every true predication has some basis [*quelque fondement*] in the nature of things, and when a proposition is not an identity, that is to say, when it is not expressly contained in [*compris*] the subject, it must be included in it virtually. This is what the philosophers call *in-esse* when they say that the predicate is in [*est dans*] the subject. So the subject term must always include the predicate term in such a way that anyone who understands perfectly the concept of the subject will also know that the predicate belongs to it. (*ML* 31/ *GA* 26: 40)[14]

Heidegger argues that the principle of *in-esse* cannot be understood solely on logical grounds because it invokes a *perfect understanding*, from which all possible predications of a subject can be deduced. The "subject" term is ambivalent: it is both the logical subject of a statement, and the *preeminent* subject, an absolute consciousness, which grasps the harmonious belonging together of a manifold in the simple simultaneity of intuition (*ML* 33/ *GA* 26: 42).

According to Heidegger, Leibniz's definition of substance in the "Discourse" is rooted in the Scholastic notion of divine intuition. But Heidegger's discussion of divine intuition pertains to what Husserl means by eidetic intuition, and it does so in two respects. First, Heidegger explicates the temporal meaning of intuition, as the presentation of all of reality in an eternal presence, or *nunc stans*. Intuition is not a simple staring, or absence of mediations. Rather, it renders all of reality present [*gegenwärtig*], including what is past and what has yet to occur (*ML* 57–58/ *GA* 26: 71). Second, Heidegger shows that intuition has a constitutive character (*ML* 67/ *GA* 26: 83). What this means can be illustrated in connection with Leibniz's concept of intuitive knowledge. Intuitive knowledge is knowledge in a particular mode: it does not add any new determinations to what is known adequately, but discursively. What is peculiar to intuitive knowledge is that it presents all of the predications of a subject as belonging together in a coherent totality, or as thoroughly interconnected in a unity. By presenting the thoroughgoing interconnection of a manifold of determinations, intuition *demonstrates* that an individual essence is possible, that is, real (*ML* 68/ *GA* 26: 84). Thus, for Leibniz, truth is given in intuition, rather than in judgment as such. As Heidegger remarks, a proper understanding of this point would clarify the stakes of Husserl's eidetic intuition:

"Today phenomenology speaks of the 'vision' of essences, *Wesens-'schau.'* The purport of this frequent but misleading term can only be clarified by radicalizing this entire problematic" (*ML* 67/ *GA* 26: 83). If the truth of a judgment consists in the harmonious belonging together of a manifold of determinations on some *ground*, then the problem that needs to be radicalized is how to think of this ground, or the basis of unification.

Heidegger argues that Leibniz's monadology answers the question of how a manifold is unified in an individual substance. Whereas the basis for the unity of an essence is the presentation of all attributes simultaneously in static intuition, or a *nunc stans*, a monad *actively* unifies a temporal manifold. The key metaphysical feature of monads, according to Heidegger, is their "active force" (*vis activa*), or *drive* (*ML* 82/ *GA* 26: 96). Drive is not a static capacity, but it is essentially self-propulsive. As simple unities, monads do not *subsequently* assemble an aggregate. This would give monads the character of a composite. Rather, monads *originate* the manifold out of their own drive. The character of this manifold is *temporal succession*: "Drive submits itself to temporal succession, not as if to something alien to it, but it is this manifold itself. From drive itself arises time" (*ML* 92/ *GA* 26: 114).

Like Husserl, Heidegger interprets Leibniz's monads as self-temporalizing unities. But Heidegger's argument goes further: according to Heidegger, the drive-character of monads is not only generative, but is also primordially transcending. We have already seen that drive produces a succession of states, and is thus self-surpassing in the continuity of its changes. Heidegger now argues that drive surpasses *beings* as such, unifying the manifold from a primordial *understanding of being*. Here, Heidegger gives a transcendental interpretation of monadic unification. He argues that monads must be able to unify *any possible* manifold, which means that unification precedes any determinate relation to existing beings: "Inasmuch as drive primordially unifies, it must already anticipate every possible multiplicity, must be able to deal with every multiplicity in its possibility. That is, drive must have already surpassed and overcome multiplicity" (*ML* 91/ *GA* 26: 114). Heidegger refers to this primordial surpassing of beings as the "world character" of monads (*ML* 91/ *GA* 26: 114).

Heidegger's discussion of the world character of monads is ambiguous. On the one hand, he describes monads as surpassing beings as such, and unifying the manifold out of a primordial *understanding of being*. On the basis of this argument, Heidegger suggests that an intentional comportment to beings is made possible by Dasein's prior *Being-in-the-world*. But Heidegger also explains the world character of monads as an intentional comportment *toward* the world. According to the latter argument, each monad unifies a manifold by representing it from a "point-of-view." As such, the world is refracted by as many views as there are individuals (*ML* 95/ *GA* 26: 118). This second interpretation is more consistent with Leibniz's argument that each monad is a concentrated world, which relates to other monads only indirectly, according to a preestablished harmony (*ML* 96/ *GA* 26: 119). What can explain the ambiguity of Heidegger's argument?

Heidegger's "guiding clue" for interpreting the monadology is the being that we ourselves are, or Dasein (*ML* 85/ *GA* 26: 106). This being can be understood in an ontic way, as an *analogy* on the basis of which we can understand other beings. Or this being can be understood ontologically, insofar as Dasein has an *understanding of being*. Heidegger suggests that Leibniz was unable to recognize the ontological meaning of his argument, and that he conceived of monads as mind-like (i.e., analogically), because of their capacity for representation, or for unifying a manifold within a simple point of view (*ML* 88/ *GA* 26: 109). But, according to Heidegger, something like *Being-in-the-world* is anticipated in the monadology insofar as monads unify the manifold by surpassing beings simply and in advance. Thus, Heidegger interprets representation as *reaching out ahead* to a primordial unity from which monads relate to the manifold. Representation implies unification of the manifold in advance, or prior to any intentional comportment to beings. The argument gets lost in translation, since Heidegger draws on the forward reach implied in the German terms "*vor-stellend*" and "*re-prae-sentierend*" (*ML* 90/ *GA* 26: 112).

Heidegger conceives of temporality from the vantage point of Dasein's primordial transcendence. So far, we have understood primordial transcendence in terms of the world character of Dasein. Dasein surpasses beings in advance, unifying them from a prior understanding of being, or Being-in-the-world. The world is not a composite of beings; on the contrary, intentional comportment to beings is grounded in a prior unification that surpasses beings in advance. Heidegger's understanding of temporality is already implicit in this argument. By surpassing beings in advance, Dasein comports itself to beings from ahead of itself. Dasein comes to itself from an ecstatic future. This is also a transcendental argument of sorts: possible experience is grounded *a priori* in a unification, which constitutes the horizon of possibilities in advance. Heidegger argues that this unification is not grounded in a static "unity of apperception," but in primordial temporalization, or self-generation.

Heidegger's argument radicalizes Husserl's understanding of immanent time consciousness. Husserl conceives of immanent time consciousness as a horizonal unity of retention, protention, and making-present. The temporal horizon is not an aggregate of "nows," which must subsequently be strung together. Rather, there is a *continuum* of time, which arises from a unity that exceeds the "now," in its retention of the past and its protention of an expected future (*ML* 203/ *GA* 26:

262). Heidegger argues that time *originates* in this horizontal unity (*ML* 203/ *GA* 26: 263). By implication, there *is* no consciousness in which time unfolds. Instead of speaking of a unity of *immanent* time consciousness, Heidegger speaks of an *ecstatic* unity of temporalization.

According to Heidegger, Husserl analyzes time as "on hand" in various states of intentional consciousness. For instance, Husserl treats the phenomenon of remembrance as *intending* a past, expectation as *intending* a future. Underlying these analyses is an understanding of intentional consciousness as primary, and of time as taking place "in the subject" (*ML* 204/ *GA* 26: 264). What Husserl calls "consciousness of time," Heidegger refers to as primordial temporalization:

> We purposely call primordial time temporality in order to express the fact that time is not additionally on-hand, but that its essence is temporal. This means that time "is" not, but rather temporalizes itself. . . . Temporality in its temporalizing is the primordially self-unifying unity of expectancy, retention, and making-present. (*ML* 204/ *GA* 26: 264)

Primordial temporalization first makes possible the phenomena of intentional comportments *in* time:

> But all these comportments would not be possible, i.e., this directing oneself toward something that will somehow be "then" would have no open direction if the Dasein that hopes, fears, etc., did not, as Dasein as such, stretch itself into a then-quality, completely aside from what it might encounter in the then. What we called expecting is nothing other than getting-carried-away into the then-quality which lies at the basis of those comportments, which has previously already overleapt all possible beings about which we can and must say, they will be "then." (*ML* 205/ *GA* 26: 265)

As a temporal stretching, Dasein transcends a static ego. But this self-transcendence is not simply a continuous becoming (i.e., Husserl's "*living* present"). Rather, self-transcendence *leaps over* the manifold of time, in order to unify it from "the basis of those comportments," from a *ground* that precedes any possible comportment in time. This surpassing leap is what Heidegger refers to as the *ecstatic* character of time:

> This means Dasein does not become gradually expectant by traversing serially the beings that factually approach it as things in the future, but

this traversing goes gradually through the open path made way by the *raptus* [rapture] of temporality itself. . . . Temporality is itself the self-unifying ecstatic unity in ecstatic temporalization. (*ML* 205/ *GA* 26: 265–266)

The whole horizon of time, including the retention of what *has been*, temporalizes itself from an ecstatic future. This explains Heidegger's argument in *Being and Time* that "authentic historicity" retrieves what-has-been from Dasein's projection of the future: "this having-been-ness temporalizes itself only from out of and in the future. The having-been is not a remnant of myself that has stayed behind and has been left behind by itself" (*ML* 206/ *GA* 26: 266; cf., *BT* 353/ *GA* 2: 386). The past, which seems to be something complete, has an *open* character:

What-has-been is, of course, no longer something present, and to that extent one might arrive at the common inference that nothing can be altered; it is finished. This is not the way it is. The having-been-ness, rather, of what-has-been becomes the having-been, first of all and constantly, in the respective future. (*ML* 206/ *GA* 26: 267)

On the basis of the foregoing analysis, Heidegger argues that the unity of temporality cannot be anything like the distance *between* now and the past, or now and the future; this would suggest that time is thing-like, and measurable. Nor is time *in* something like an "I-nucleus" [*Ichkern*] (*ML* 208/ *GA* 26: 268). The unification of temporalization is bounded by a horizon of possibilities. Heidegger emphasizes that this notion of a horizonal boundary is not located in a "subject":

We must keep in mind . . . that the ecstasis surpasses every being and the horizon is not located, say, in the sphere of the subject . . . it is neither spatially nor temporally located, in the usual sense. It "is" not as such, but it temporalizes itself. (*ML* 208/ *GA* 26: 269)

According to Heidegger, this ecstatic horizon is the temporal condition for the possibility of the world. The world character of primordial transcendence is not transcendence toward a static totality (i.e., the sum total of possible conditions, or the transcendental ideal, if by this one understands something that is already completed). Heidegger refers to the possibility of world as "*worlding*," or "*world-entry*" (*ML* 209/ *GA* 26: 271).

Without elaborating what he means, Heidegger indicates that primordial world-entry is primal history [*Urgeschichte*], and should be understood as "the region of the mythic":

From this primal history a region of problems must be developed which we are today beginning to approach with greater clarity, the region of the mythic. The metaphysics of myth must come to be understood out of this primal history, and it can be done with the aid of a metaphysical construct of primal time, i.e., the time with which primal history itself begins. (*ML* 209/ *GA* 26: 270)

In the *Metaphysical Foundations of Logic*, Heidegger says nothing more about what he means by "primal history" as mythic time, hence my interpretation can only be speculative. In the first place, the origin of temporalization must be prehistorical, in the same way that Being-in-the-world is pre-ontological; that is, as the condition of possibility for an experience that is given, albeit in an ontologically unclarified way. In this vein, Heidegger argues that the *possibility* of Dasein's being in history has its *ground* in primordial temporalization (*BT* 345/ *GA* 2: 376). But what makes this temporality mythical, and not just prehistorical (where "pre" is understood as a condition of possibility) is that Dasein freely chooses which of its inherited possibilities to retrieve. Heidegger argues that "authentic" historicity consists in the resolute choice of heroes, and the loyalty to what has been retrieved:

> The authentic retrieve of a possibility of existence that has been—the possibility that Dasein may choose its heroes—is existentially grounded in anticipatory resoluteness; for in resoluteness the choice is first chosen that makes one free for the struggle to come, and the loyalty to what can be retrieved. (*BT* 352/ *GA* 2: 385)

Heidegger asks about the weight of the past for authentic historicity; alluding to Nietzsche's *Untimely Meditations* (1874), he formulates this question in terms of the "advantage" or "disadvantage" of historiography for life (*BT* 361/ *GA* 2: 396). He answers that an authentic relationship to what has been inherited consists in freely and resolutely willing its *recurrence* as a possibility of Dasein's existence (*BT* 358/ *GA* 2: 392): "Repetition first makes manifest to Dasein its own history" (*BT* 353/ *GA* 2: 386). Authentic historicity, as the comportment to what-has-been from Dasein's free projection of possibilities, leads Heidegger to an archaic, rather than a historical interpretation of historicity.

This is where Benjamin confronts Heidegger, where "sparks will fly" from the contrast between their ways of looking at history, as Benjamin writes to Scholem (1930, *C* 358/ *GB* 3: 503). As I understand it, the confrontation concerns the incompleteness of the past and what this means for the present. In the *Arcades Project*, Benjamin quotes Horkheimer, who argues that the past must be understood as complete rather than open, because past injustice cannot be elided by one's free choice: "Past injustice has occurred and is completed. The slain are really slain" (*AP* N8, I). Benjamin disagrees with Horkheimer, but not because what-has-been is retrieved from an ecstatic future. The slain *are* indeed slain, but Benjamin realizes that even the dead will not be safe from the victorious enemy (*SW* 4: 391/ *GS* 1: 695). If history is not merely a science of what is factually "determined," this is because it is also a form of remembrance [*Eingedenken*]: "What science has 'determined,' remembrance can modify. Such mindfulness can make the incomplete (happiness) into something complete, and the complete (suffering) into something incomplete" (*AP* N8, I). Remembrance can modify the past, ever so minutely, by recollecting it in a constellation with the "now," a constellation that becomes legible, without intention, in a moment of danger (*AP* N3, 1; cf., *SW* 4: 391/ *GS* 1: 695). Benjamin's conception of historical time, as the recollection of what is latent in the now, has its roots in an alternative interpretation of the monadology.

Benjamin's Monadic Theory of Ideas and Virtual History

Unlike Heidegger, Benjamin does not interpret monads as the beings that we ourselves are. As he puts it in a 1923 letter to Florens Christian Rang, the monadology constitutes, for him, "the *summa* of a theory of ideas" (*C* 225/ *GB* 2: 393). Husserl was one source, among others, for Benjamin's monadic theory of ideas. Benjamin alludes to Husserl's understanding of philosophy as an eidetic science,[15] but also to the critical idealism of the Marburg School (Hermann Cohen and Paul Natorp), which appropriated Platonic ideas as fundamental "hypotheses" that constitute the possibility of cognition (*OT* 34/ *GS* 1: 214). Benjamin also names the Jena Romantics as precursors for his "theory of ideas," because the early Romantics established the criterion for the criticism of art in the fulfillment of an idea implicit in individual artworks.[16]

In the "Epistemo-Critical Prologue," Benjamin concurs that the task of philosophy should be understood as the representation [*Darstellung/ vergegenwärtigung/ Repräsentation*] of ideas.[17] Like Husserl, Benjamin understands ideas as essences, rather than as psychological notions or linguistic abstractions.[18] But Benjamin diverges from Husserl on the question of how ideas are *given* to consciousness. According to Husserl, ideas are presented to consciousness in essential intuition [*kategoriale Anschauung, Wesensschau*]. Without mentioning Husserl by name, Benjamin emphatically rejects the view that ideas are given to intuition:

> Ideas are not among the given elements of the world of phenomena. This gives rise to the question of the manner in which they are in fact given, and whether it is necessary to hand over the task of accounting for the structure of the world of ideas to a much-cited intellectual vision [*intellektuelle Anschauung*]. . . . The being of ideas simply cannot be conceived of as the object of vision, even intellectual vision. For even in its most paradoxical periphrasis, as *intellectus archetypus*, vision does not enter into the form of existence [*Gegebensein*] which is peculiar to truth, which is devoid of all intention [*Intention*], and certainly does not itself appear as intention. Truth does not enter into relationships, particularly intentional ones. (*OT* 35/ *GS* 1: 215–216)

It is compelling to think that Benjamin has Husserl in view when he criticizes intellectual intuition and intentionality in the "Epistemo-Critical Prologue." In a 1928 copy of his *Curriculum Vitae*, Benjamin lists Husserl among the four sources for the theory of ideas in his early work (*SW* 2: 77/ *GS* 6: 218). Moreover, in the "Epistemo-Critical Prologue," Benjamin cites an essay by Husserl's student, Jean Héring, in support of his argument that ideas are not intuitable.[19] According to Héring, each individual essence "must be searched for laboriously at the appropriate place in its world, until it is found, as a *rocher de bronze*, or until the hope that it exists is shown to be illusory" (*OT* 37–38/ *GS* 1: 218). The process of ideation cannot be merely mental, but requires an exhaustive search among disparate elements of the phenomenal world. Because essences cannot be fulfilled in thought, such a search has no guarantee of discovering its object. The force of this critique is twofold: first, even though Husserl clearly distinguishes essences from empirical facts, his argument that essences are "given" to intuition endows them with a factual character, which ideas do not have. As the citation from Héring indicates, "essences . . . lead a life that differs utterly from that of objects [*Gegenständen*] and their conditions" (*OT* 37/ *GS* 1: 218). Second, it is not within the power of thinking alone to determine whether an essence will be discovered. Ideas have a *historical* fulfillment:

> In its finished form philosophy will, it is true, assume the quality of doctrine, but it does not lie within the power of mere thought to confer such form. Philosophical doctrine is based on historical codification. It cannot therefore be evoked *more geometrico*. (*OT* 27/ *GS* 1: 207)

Notice that Benjamin does not dispute the completed form [*abgeschlossenen Gestalt*] of philosophical ideas, but he argues that this completion takes place when an idea is saturated with the totality of its *history* (*OT* 47/ *GS* 1: 228).

Benjamin adheres to Leibniz's definition of individual essences in the "Discourse on Metaphysics," §8. Herein, Leibniz argues that, "the nature of an individual substance is to have a notion so complete that it is sufficient to contain and to allow us to deduce from it all the predicates of the subject to which this notion is attributed."[20] The language of deduction is misleading, because the totality of predications that are virtually contained in a subject constitutes the concrete expression of an individual's entire history. The passage from the "Discourse" continues thus:

> God, seeing Alexander's individual notion or *haecceity*, sees in it at the same time the basis and reason for all the predicates which can be said truly of him, for example, that he vanquished Darius and Porus; he even knows *a priori* (and not by experience) whether he died a natural death or whether he was poisoned, something we can know only through history. Thus when we consider carefully the connection of things, we can say that from all time in Alexander's soul there are vestiges of everything that has happened to him and marks of everything that will happen to him and traces of everything that happens in the universe, even though God alone could recognize them all.[21]

Indeed (as Heidegger recognized), this definition of individual substance has its ideal in God's intuition of all the predicates in an essence *at the same time*. But this simultaneity of presence does not mean that the content of an essence is "timeless," as Husserl's method of eidetic intuition would suggest. Rather, essences are *filled* with time. What God recognizes in Alexander's individual notion is the entirety of Alexander's past and subsequent history. Ideas are so full of time that we, finite understandings, cannot apperceive the full scope of their content. Yet, because historical becoming is preestablished in a complete essence, *our* knowledge, acquired "through history," is conceived of in figural, rather than in temporal terms, as what can be discovered when we focus our attention on the minute interconnections between phenomena. The latent past and the incipient future are discoverable when we consider, with sufficient exactitude, the nexus of detail implicit in presence.

Benjamin follows Leibniz's definition scrupulously. He argues that ideas have an inner history, which is not an open-ended temporal becoming, but is bounded by their essential being. Unlike empirical time, ideas can be virtually fulfilled. According to Benjamin, "the representation of an idea cannot be considered successful unless the whole range of possible extremes it contains has been virtually explored":

Virtually, because that which is comprehended in the idea of origin still has history, in the sense of content, but not in the sense of a set of occurrences which have befallen it. Its history is inward in character and not to be understood as something boundless, but as something related to an essential being, and it can therefore be described as the past and subsequent history of this being. (*OT* 47/ *GS* 1: 227)

Benjamin's concept of the "virtual" [*virtuell*] adheres to Leibniz's use of this term in the same passage of the "Discourse" (§8). According to Leibniz, predicates are either explicitly, or else virtually, contained in a subject. In the case of explicit containment, we are dealing with necessary, or analytic truths. In the case of virtual containment, we are dealing with contingent, or historical truths—that is, it is only *virtually* contained in Alexander's essence that he vanquished Darius and Porus. The virtual is the implicit. But we miss the meaning of this term if we think of it as merely the opposite of what can be made explicit. Virtuality refers to the complete expression of reality as it is unified in an individual point of view. The virtual is not what is generally possible; nor is it bounded by what can be presented to consciousness. Its horizon includes everything that can be said of an individual: the full scope of its past and subsequent history, and all of its interconnections to the world. As Benjamin recognizes, and as Leibniz also implies with his notion of haecceity, the horizon of an individual essence can only be captured by a proper name: "Truth is not an intent which realizes itself in empirical reality; it is the power which determines the essence of this empirical reality. The state of being, beyond all phenomenality, to which alone this power belongs, is that of the name" (*OT* 36–37/ *GS* 1: 216).

Leibniz's argument would seem to strip contingent truths of their historical character, because even future contingent states are foreseen in the prestabilization of becoming in an essence. Benjamin agrees that the history in ideas is not "pure" or "pragmatically real" (*OT* 47/ *GS* 1: 227). The content in a monad is only "virtually" historical: once contingent phenomena are redeemed in an essence, the process of fulfillment can be inferred from a state of completion and rest (*OT* 47/ *GS* 1: 227–228). This content is only privatively temporal, because whatever process was involved in an idea's fulfillment gets swallowed up in the complete expression of an essence. But this does not mean that ideas are supra-temporal *Eide*. Historical content is *legible* in the configuration of minute detail in each individual essence.

In a fragment entitled "Theory of Knowledge" (1920–1921), Benjamin describes the nexus of determinations in the truth as that which is recognizable in "logical time":

> Truth resides in the "now of knowability" ["*Jetzt der Erkennbarkeit*"]. Only in this is there a (systematic, conceptual) nexus [*Zusammenhang*] — a nexus between existing things and also with the perfected state of the world. The now of knowability is logical time, which has to replace that of timeless validity. (*SW* 1: 276/ *GS* 6: 46)

Far from being timeless, the nexus of determinations within an idea takes shape in a singular configuration of detail at a precise moment in time — the "now of knowability."[22] This time is logical, rather than chronological. It refers to the fulfillment of an idea, which exceeds empirical time. Ideas are images of the fulfilled world, in which existing things are represented in their thoroughgoing interconnection with all of reality. This virtual, thoroughgoing interconnection in "logical time" is Benjamin's interpretation of the "world character" of monads, so to speak. Rather than narrating a chronology, the task of the historian would require a search amidst the disparate, concrete elements of the phenomena for immanent structures, capable of a "virtual" fulfillment that would prove their authenticity as "original" ideas (*OT* 46/ *GS* 1: 226). This task is not projected onto an open future, but has an integral totality of detail, the world, as its virtual object: "And so the real world could well constitute a task," writes Benjamin, "in the sense that it would be a question of penetrating so deeply into everything real as to reveal thereby an objective interpretation of the world" (*OT* 48/ *GS* 1: 228).

The virtual history within a monad exceeds the bounds of what can be apperceived, or presented to consciousness. This excess within the monad explains why ideas cannot be intended. Here, I have the occasion to point out a crucial difference between Heidegger and Benjamin's interpretations of the monadology: according to Heidegger, monads exceed what can be represented in a "now" (i.e., the *nunc stans* of absolute consciousness) because monads are continuously surpassing themselves in their drive. Interpreted ontologically, monads *transcend phenomena* in advance in order to unify the manifold from out of a primordial understanding of being. For Benjamin, the excess within the monad is a *fullness of detail*, rather than a surpassing *beyond* phenomena. Accordingly, Benjamin describes the mode in which ideas are given as a deepening of attention to the minute complexity of the phenomena. This descent into micrological detail alone reveals an "objective interpretation of the world" (*OT* 48/ *GS* 1: 228). By contrast, a model of cognition in which a conscious ego *intends* objects falsifies experience by providing a merely subjective interpretation of the world.

Monads contain an infinity of *latent* detail, most of which is too minute or too invariable to be noticed.[23] Latency is another aspect of what Benjamin means by the virtuality of ideas. According to Leibniz, we have latent knowledge of everything that is implicit in our ideas, and we can recognize these implications by focusing our attention. As Leibniz writes in the "Discourse on Metaphysics," "our soul knows all these things virtually and requires only attention to recognize truths." In explaining this idea, Leibniz appeals to a notion of memory that is not oriented to the past, or what is no longer present, but that has to do with *noticing* what is latent in presence:

> Memory is needed for attention: when we are not alerted, so to speak, to pay heed to certain of our own present perceptions, we allow them to slip by unconsidered and even unnoticed. But if someone alerts us to them straight away, and makes us take note, for instance, of some noise which we have just heard, then we remember it and are aware of having had some sense of it.[24]

In the *Arcades Project*, Benjamin captures this Leibnizian notion remembrance precisely when he describes a process of awakening to a not-yet-conscious knowledge of what has been. What is at stake in this awakening is "the dissolution of 'mythology' into the space of history" (*AP* N1, 9).

Benjamin and Leibniz both take up a modified notion of Platonic anamnesis in connection with the idea of memory as recognition (*OT* 36–37/ *GS* 1: 217).[25] According to Leibniz, anamnesis is not the remembrance of something that we once *had* as an object for consciousness but have since lost. Recollection involves focusing our attention within the infinity of latent detail implicit in experience. Such focusing allows us to notice a portion of what is latent in our *petites perceptions*. Noticing does not transform the content of what is apprehended. The only transformation that occurs, and it is not a negligible one, is that attention concentrates the manifold in a particular way, illuminating a determinate configuration of detail within the infinite horizon of perceptibility.

Leibniz's notion of latency refers to a "subject" that is not limited by consciousness. But this subject is not unconscious, unless we understand this as the negation of a privation (i.e., insofar as it refers to an *idea* that transcends the limits of finite, conscious awareness). For Leibniz, it is God—a perfect understanding—who ensures that everything in nature is recognized, and hence recognizable for us. Because of God, "all the hairs on our head are numbered."[26] Benjamin does not write in an explicitly theological mode, but as he argues in the *Arcades Project*, "in remembrance we have an experience that forbids us to conceive of history as fundamentally atheological, little as it may be granted to us to try to write it with immediately theological concepts" (*AP* N8, 1). In the "Epistemo-Critical Prologue," Benjamin invokes anamnesis to the same effect: "Since philosophy may not presume to speak in tones of revelation, this can only be achieved by recalling in memory the primordial form of perception. Platonic anamnesis is, perhaps, not far removed from this kind of remembering" (*OT* 36–37/ *GS* 1: 217).

Benjamin did not sufficiently clarify the distinction between latency and the unconscious.[27] In his 1931 essay, "A Little History of Photography," he describes latency as the "optical unconscious." Unlike the human eye, a camera is able to capture a split second in time; the resulting image records the infinitesimally minute details of perception. Because a photograph exposes what is only latent in conscious experience, it expresses a nature that is "other" than what can be consciously intended: "For it is another nature which speaks to the camera rather than to the eye: 'other' above all in the sense that a space informed by human consciousness gives way to a space informed by the unconscious" (*SW* 2: 510/ *GS* 2: 371). Benjamin should rather have said that a space informed by human consciousness gives way to a space uninformed (or un-deformed) by human consciousness.

This space, uninformed by human consciousness, is what Benjamin describes as "natural history" [*natürliche Geschichte*] in the "Epistemo-Critical Prologue." Natural history is an expression of the life of works and forms that need protection from human life in order to unfold clearly (*OT* 47/ *GS* 1: 227). Natural history is precisely not determined by Dasein's projection of its own possibilities. In a parenthetical note in *Arcades Project*, Benjamin writes: "Secularization of history in Heidegger" (*AP* N8a, 4). Benjamin appeals to the virtual expression of essences, not to bring God immediately into history, but rather to open a space in which historical description is not structured in advance by the possibilities of human life.

A Leibnizian idea of expression underlies the notions of virtuality and latency that I have invoked in my interpretation of Benjamin's monadology. Whereas, for Descartes, the distinguishing feature of mental states is an accompanying awareness in consciousness, for Leibniz, mental states are primarily expressive, and need not be conscious.[28] Expression, I submit, provides the correct framework for interpreting Benjamin's argument that ideas are represented, but are neither intended by consciousness, nor apparent to intuition. As we saw, the horizon of what is virtual, or implicit, in an individual essence includes all of its past and subsequent history, as well as a view of the universe as it relates to that individual. Leibniz uses the term *expression* to characterize this manner of representing the whole universe from a point of view. Leibniz illustrates what he means by expression with the example of a single city, viewed from multiple positions.[29] Although each view of the city differs from all the others—for instance, in terms of what is in the foreground, and what fades into the background—each view preserves the same proportions and intrinsic relationships as all the others. Leibniz defines expression more generally as the "constant and ordered relation between what can be said of one and of the other."³⁰ Expression is not sensuous mimesis, but is a structural isomorphism, capable of representing the minute interconnections between details that remain undetectable to the human eye.

A Leibnizian understanding of expression underlies Benjamin's argument that ideas are to phenomena as constellations are to stars, or that ideas represent the phenomena by determining the nexus of their relations. Ideas express the phenomena by representing the relationships that obtain between disparate phenomenal elements, thus providing the phenomena with their "virtual arrangement" (*OT* 34/ *GS* 1: 214). The phenomena, in turn, represent ideas in concrete constellations. Each individual idea has a figure, or is embodied in a fragile nexus of phenomenal detail.³¹ Ideas are made manifest only insofar as they bring about configurations within the phenomena (*OT* 35/ *GS* 1: 215).

Expression is not limited by the conscious mind; yet, insofar as each monad represents the universe from a *perspective*, expression is finite, rather than perfect. Each individual monad clearly and distinctly represents what is close to it (i.e., its own body), while expressing the rest of the universe in an obscure horizon. Finitude, so conceived, has little to do with the duration and limits of human life; it is rather a matter of focus, or concentration. Each monad *abbreviates* the universe from a point of view.

In Benjamin's later work, including the *Arcades Project* and the theses "On the Concept of History," it becomes clear that the perspective from which monads concentrate the universe is the "now of recognizability" ["*Jetzt der Erkennbarkeit*"]. Just as, in the "Epistemo-Critical Prologue," Benjamin treats each idea as absolutely original, or discontinuous from all the others, so, too, is each "now" utterly unique in the way that it concentrates the temporal horizon. Because the fullness of time is concentrated in each singular "now," there can be no repetition, or recurrence in history. Memory is modification, even if it leaves all the elements intact; the modification consists in focusing the manifold from a point of view. Only by treating each "now" as an isolated totality, or monad, is it possible to represent the constellation that each present has with its "fore-history." As Benjamin writes in the *Arcades Project*:

> For the materialist historian ... there can be no appearance of repetition in history, since precisely these moments in the course of history which matter most to him, by virtue of their index as "fore-history," become moments of the present day and change their specific character according to the catastrophic or triumphant nature of that day. (*AP* N9a, 8)

The "now"—the nucleus around which historical detail is constellated—is not an eternal *nunc stans*: "The true image of the past flits by. The past can be seized only as an image that flashes up at the moment of its recognizability, and is never seen again" (*SW* 4: 390/ *GS* 1: 695). There are no grounds on which to guarantee that what has been will be recognized; the recognition of the past is bound up with the real danger of its loss. Historical knowledge is not a possibility for any subject at any time; it is not, like Heidegger's category of "historicity," a constitutive possibility for Dasein. The recognizability of the past is conditioned in all respects by the circumstances under which one endures and with which one struggles.

The prestabilization, or stasis of Leibniz's "virtual" history has its dialectical counterpart in the utter contingency of what is recognizable in the "now." Thinking cannot determine in advance which details will stand out on the horizon of *petites perceptions*. In a flash of recognition, the primordial fullness of perception [*Urvernehmen*] is concentrated in a figure. Benjamin suggests that what is genuinely historical requires such a concentration. It is only when the flow of events comes to a standstill that history takes form. Otherwise it is washed away in the indifferent flow of temporality.

The confrontation between Benjamin and Heidegger's understandings of historical time raises the question of the open character of the past. According to Heidegger, what-has-been is retrieved from an ecstatic future. Heidegger's argument follows from his interpretation of monad as a self-surpassing unity, rather than a static unity of apperception. Construed accordingly, Dasein retrieves its inheritance from beyond itself, or from a projection of its possibilities. For Benjamin too, the past cannot be understood as a *fait accompli*; but this is where the comparison with Heidegger ends. According to Benjamin, the past is awakened in remembrance of what has hitherto slipped by unnoticed. Benjamin's understanding of remembrance, as noticing what is latent in presence, has its roots in a different reading of Leibniz's monadology. Remembrance does not retrieve the past as it was; rather, it expresses the "world of all-sided and integral actuality" from the vantage point of what is recognizable *now* (*SW* 4: 404/ *GS* 1: 1238). That the past is citable in all of its moments in the fullness of time is a messianic idea; but Benjamin's messianism is oriented to the past, rather than projected onto a world to come (*SW* 4: 390, 397/ *GS* 1: 694, 704).

Notes

1. I develop the themes pursued in this article at greater length in my forthcoming monograph, *Walter Benjamin's Monadology*. In the process of writing this

article, I was fortunate to be able to discuss my ideas with Eduard Iricinschi, Sami Khatib, and Vivian Liska.
2. Heidegger's 1928 lecture course, *Metaphysische Anfangsgründe der Logik im Ausgang von Leibniz* (*GA* 26), is the earliest of his interpretations of Leibniz. In addition to these lectures, Heidegger devoted a long section of the second volume of his book on Nietzsche to Leibniz, as well as the 1956–1957 lecture course and address, *Der Satz vom Grund* (*GA* 10). The extant secondary literature has focused mostly on *Der Satz vom Grund*. See, in particular, Renato Cristin, *Heidegger and Leibniz: Reason and the Path*, trans. Gerald Parks (The Netherlands: Kluwer, 1998). I focus on Heidegger's 1928 interpretation because it enables a philosophical comparison with Benjamin's monadology in a more direct way than is afforded by the later texts, in which Heidegger does not address the monad as such.
3. See Fenves, *The Messianic Reduction: Walter Benjamin and the Shape of Time* (Stanford, CA: Stanford University Press, 2011).
4. My argument draws on Anthony Steinbock's discussion of Husserl's monad in *Home and Beyond: Generative Phenomenology after Husserl* (Evanston, IL: Northwestern University Press, 1995), 29–48.
5. "Philosophie as strenge Wissenschaft" first published in *Logos* 1 (Tübingen: 1910–11), 289–341; English translation in *Phenomenology and the Crisis of Philosophy: Philosophy as Rigorous Science, and Philosophy and the Crisis of European Man*, trans. Quentin Lauer (New York: Harper & Row, 1965), 108.
6. Several short texts on the monadology are included in Husserliana XIV, *Zur Phänomenologie der Intersubjektivität: Texte aus dem Nachlass. Zweiter Teil*: 1921–1928, ed. Iso Kern (The Hague: Martinus Nijhoff, 1973).
7. Husserliana I, *Cartesianische Meditationen und Pariser Vorträge*, ed. Stephan Strasser (The Hague: Martinus Nijhoff, 1991), §60.
8. In 1928, Heidegger was editing Husserl's *Vorlesungen zur Phänomenologie des inneren Zeitbewusstseins*, which appeared in the *Jahrbuch für Philosophie und phänomenologische Forschung*, vol. 9 (1928), and were also published in a separate volume in Halle, 1928. Reprinted in Husserliana X, *Zur Phänomenologie des inneren Zeitbewusstseins* (1893–1917), ed. R. Boehm (The Hague: Martinus Nijhoff, 1966). In *The Metaphysical Foundations of Logic*, Heidegger refers to Husserl's lectures in §12 "Transcendence and Temporality" (*ML* 196–219/ *GA* 26: 252–284).
9. Fenves traces Benjamin's "entry into the phenomenological school" to his attendance in Moritz Geiger's seminar on Kant's third *Critique*. According to Fenves (who cites Benjamin's correspondence), in addition to Husserl's "Philosophie als strenge Wissenschaft," Benjamin read "Husserl's difficult, principle

groundwork," which Fenves interprets as either *Logical Investigations*, or *Ideas* (Fenves, *The Messianic Reduction*, 8–9; cf., GB 1: 301–302).
10. Husserl, *Logische Untersuchungen. Zweiter Teil: Untersuchungen zur Phänomenologie und Theorie der Erkenntnis* (Halle: Max Niemeyer, 1901; 1968).
11. *Husserliana* XIV 36, cf., Steinbock, *Home and Beyond*, 33.
12. *Husserliana* XIV 35, cf., Steinbock, *Home and Beyond*, 33.
13. *Husserliana* XIV 36, cf., Steinbock, *Home and Beyond*, 36.
14. Heidegger cites G. W. Leibniz, *Hauptschriften zur Grundlegung der Philosophie*, ed. E. Cassirer, trans. A. Buchenau (Leipzig: Philosophische Bibliotek, vols. 107 and 108, 1904–1906). The English edition of Heidegger's *Metaphysical Foundations of Logic* uses *Gottfried Wilhelm Leibniz: Philosophical Papers and Letters*, 2nd edition, trans. Leroy Loemker (Boston: D. Reidel, 1969), 307.
15. In his 1928 *Curriculum Vitae*, Benjamin describes his method as "closer to an eidetic way of observing phenomena than to a historical one" (*SW* 2.1, 78/ *GS* 6: 219).
16. In my forthcoming book, I argue that Benjamin's monadic "theory of ideas" developed in response to the "idea of art" in Jena Romanticism. In his doctoral thesis, "The Concept of Criticism in German Romanticism" (1919), Benjamin mentions that the early Romantics precisely did not conceive of reality as "an aggregate of monads locked-up in themselves" (*SW* 1: 145–146/ *GS* 1: 56). On the contrary, they conceived of each individual work as "a relative unity," or mere *mode* in the medial unfolding of the absolute work of art. The early Romantic "idea of art" is a continuum that converges on the absolute, whereas Benjamin argues for a harmonic discontinuum of original ideas, each of which expresses the whole universe from its own windowless point of view.
17. Like Husserl, Benjamin uses the term *vergegenwärtigen* to describe the process of representation, in which ideas are fulfilled (*OT* 29/ *GS* 1: 209).
18. Essences, according to Benjamin, are simple unities that are prior to the coherence of consciousness (*OT* 30/ *GS* 1: 210). Benjamin emphasizes that ideas are "objective interpretations" of the world, rather than subjective concepts and categories (*OT* 34/ *GS* 1: 214). It is important to note that the meaning of "objectivity" [*objective*] should not be understood positivistically, but is intended only as a counterargument to the subjective constitution of reality.
19. Jean Héring, "Bemerkungen über das Wesen, die Wesenheit und die Idee" (*Jahrbuch für Philosophie und Phänomenologische Forschung*, IV: 1921), in *OT* 37–38/ *GS* 1: 218.
20. Leibniz, "Discourse on Metaphysics," in Leibniz, *Philosophical Essays*, trans. Roger Ariew and Daniel Garber (Indianapolis, IN: Hackett, 1989), §9.
21. Ibid.

22. The concept of the "Jetzt der Erkennbarkeit" appears again in the *Arcades Project*, where it is translated as the "now of recognizability." In the late work, Benjamin describes the relation [*Beziehung*] between the "now" and "what-has-been," rather than the nexus between actuality and the perfected state of the world (*AP* N3, 1).
23. In the Preface to the *New Essays on Human Understanding*, Leibniz writes: "There are hundreds of marks that force us to judge that there is at every moment an infinity of perceptions in us, unaccompanied by awareness and unaccompanied by reflection; that is, an infinity of changes in the soul itself of which we are not aware." Leibniz, *New Essays on Human Understanding*, ed. Peter Remnant and Jonathan Bennett (Cambridge: Cambridge University Press, 1997), §53.
24. Leibniz, *New Essays*, §54.
25. As Leibniz writes in "Discourse on Metaphysics," §26:

> We have all these forms in our mind; we even have forms from all time, for the mind expresses all its future thoughts and already thinks confusedly about everything it will ever think distinctly. And nothing can be taught to us whose idea we do not already have in our mind. . . . This is what Plato so excellently recognized when he proposed his doctrine of reminiscence, a very solid doctrine, provided that it is taken rightly and purged of the error of preexistence, and provided that we do not imagine that at some earlier time the soul must already have known and thought distinctly what it learns and thinks now. . . . [O]ur soul knows all these things virtually and requires only attention to recognize truths, and . . . consequently, it has, at very least, the ideas upon which these truths depend. One can even say that is already possesses these truths, if they are taken as relations of ideas.

26. Leibniz, "Discourse on Metaphysics," §37.
27. Leibniz's notion of *petites perceptions* has a marked influence on nineteenth- and twentieth-century *Lebensphilosophie*, especially insofar as it suggested a theory of the unconscious. We see this influence in Herbartian psychology, as well as in Ludwig Klages, who adopted Leibniz's notion of latency to describe a non-Freudian, or nonmechanistic, theory of unconscious life. Benjamin's own doctoral supervisor, Richard Herbertz, wrote his inaugural dissertation on Leibniz's theory of the unconscious: *Die Lehre vom Unbewussten im System des Leibniz* (Halle: Niemeyer, 1905).

28. For an exceptionally clear article on the distinction between the Cartesian notion of mental phenomena as essentially conscious, and Leibniz's notion of mental phenomena as expressive, or representational, see Allison Simmons, "Changing the Cartesian Mind: Leibniz on Sensation, Representation and Consciousness," *The Philosophical Review* 110 (2001): 31–75.
29. Leibniz, "Discourse on Metaphysics," §9.
30. Leibniz: *Die philosophischen Schriften* (ed. Gerhardt C.I.; 7 vols., Berlin, 1875–1890), II: 112. Leibniz scholars generally uphold the argument that expression is a structural isomorphism. See Robert McRae, *Leibniz: Perception, Apperception, and Thought* (Toronto: University of Toronto Press, 1976), 23 and 42; Donald Rutherford, *Leibniz and the Rational Order of Nature* (Cambridge; Cambridge University Press, 1995), 236; Simmons, "Changing the Cartesian Mind," 67–68; and Stephen Montague Puryear, *Perception and Representation in Leibniz* (PhD Dissertation, University of Pittsburgh, 2006), 12. Chris Swoyer argues against this view, because he sees structural isomorphism as requiring an exact, unequivocal relationship between expression and expressed, whereas Leibnizian expression is equivocal; see Swoyer, "Leibnizian Expression," *Journal of the History of Philosophy* 33 (1995): 65–99.
31. Leibniz understands the body of a monad as a "well-founded-phenomena," or a cluster of dependent monads that are configured around a central monad. In the "Principles of Nature and Grace," Leibniz writes: "[E]ach distinct simple substance or monad, which makes up the center of a composite substance . . . and is the principle of its unity, is surrounded by a mass composed of an infinity of other monads, which constitute the body belonging to this central monad, through whose properties the monad represents things outside of it, similarly to the way a center does." Leibniz, *Philosophical Essays*, 207.

CHAPTER 6

TIME AND TASK

Benjamin and Heidegger Showing the Present

Andrew Benjamin

Opening the Present

Writing takes place in time. There is, in addition, the time of writing. This twofold positioning of time—an ineliminable doubling of time, the recognition of which becomes the affirmation of an original difference, the truth of ontology, is, from the start, in this particular presentation, mediated by another presence. In this instance the mediation is given by the effective presence of an announced task. The task's enactment, an enactment that must maintain a link to its founding articulation within intentionality—for example, its being the result of a decision—reiterates the twofold temporality already located in the connection between writing and time. What emerges from this given relation is the interplay of writing, time, and task. What is involved in this relation is the possibility of thinking the relation between politics and time. This possibility arises because such a thinking must occur in a "now" that, in eschewing its reduction to the *nunc stans* while nonetheless maintaining a relation to it, a relation that marks a presence that takes place at the same time, demands to be thought at the present as the present. In opening this "now," what is opened up is the ontology of the present. What is proposed, therefore, with Benjamin, is furthering the possibility for a philosophical thinking of the present.

In broad terms what is involved here is a specific opening of the present. This is a task made all the more difficult by the demand that it also involve an already existent consideration, at the present, as the present, of the possibility of thinking philosophically about philosophy's history. (The problem of the relationship between history and philosophy's history is raised by having to pursue this particular path.) As the present is itself already thought within the work of Benjamin and Heidegger, to engage with their thinking is itself to take up the present and therefore to move toward a consideration of the ontology of the present by maintaining it as the site in which such movements are sustained. The identification of the present determines the nature of the philosophical task. Reciprocally, the nature of the philosophical task will have a determining effect on the construal on the present. One cannot be thought without the other.

As yet, however, the need for taking up this particular emergent connection between time, task, and writing is yet to be announced. It is not as though need is yet to be given a specific determination within philosophy. Among other possibilities, need can be taken as opening the Cartesian and the Hegelian philosophical projects. (Its presence in Heidegger and Benjamin will be just as insistent.) In both instances, need is present as what advances a necessity that orients the project and which in its projections continually comes to be addressed by them. As such, it is maintained within, while maintaining an ineliminable reciprocity. In both instances, need is a demand given by the present—the present being the construal of the contemporary at (and as) the time of writing, again needs time. As such, the response to need is itself contemporary.[1] With need, with its instantiation, its having a time at a given instant, a relation to the given is established. In other words, if need is a response to what is given—the gift of tradition creating the specificity of the moment—then the response occurs at a particular instant. While bearing a date, the instant is not the present as such. The reason for this being the case is that thinking the present will necessitate taking up the construal of the given and its (the given as construed) enjoined response. Articulated as need, the response can be formulated as a specific stand in relation to a particular repetition. Repetition here is the reiteration of the already given. Need exists in relation to the gift and yet the gift, that which is taken to have been given, is itself determined by need: again, the presence of a founding and original reciprocity. Accepting the generality of this description cannot obviate the necessity of giving it specificity and thereby opening up the multiplicity inherent in the stance. Indeed, what must be maintained is the suggestion that it is only in terms of its actual specificity—the effective interplay of dating, present, and need—that any philosophical thinking of the political will come to be acted out, because it is the differences given at the level of this interplay that mark the primordiality of conflict. (It is this possibility that will be addressed in detail in the final chapter.) Regarding their actual projects, the point of connection and divide between Benjamin and Heidegger can be located at this point. Multiplicity therefore becomes the site of conflict. Once given a precise designation, it becomes a site that resists the possibility of any automatic synthesis.

In sum, and if only to provide a name with which to work, the present as giving rise to a specific task—where that specificity is itself molded and determined by the construal of the present—will be termed, as has already been suggested, the *epochal present*. Such a present gives itself. It is given within its own self-conception. It is *not* the giving of that which is distanced because of its being either originating or primordial, and whose presence and hence its being present (were it ever to be present) would then become the epochality of its founding and maintaining origin. In working with the abeyance of such a conception of epochality, and, moreover, in allowing for the determining interplay of the epochal present and the *nunc stans* (the latter being the time of dating, the temporality of the instant), this will serve to maintain the ineliminable presence of a different politics insofar as this other possibility (a politics thought within a different philosophical frame) can be reworked as the primordial conflict over the nature of the present. Such a reworking sustains the present as that site, while at the same time providing a different instantiation of the primordial. What is proposed is a conflict that cannot be resolved by a simple deferral to the instant. The conflict staged between Benjamin and Heidegger is political for precisely this reason. The inability of the instant to resolve conflict opens up the necessity not just to rethink its presence, but to take its presence as determining and thus as real. However, the reality in question is not coextensive with the instant (which marks both the ontological as well as the temporal location proper to the time and the place of dating). As a name, the epochal present names another, yet related, reality.

The ineliminable reciprocity between action and the ontology of the present, where the former is a constitutive part of an inherent actative dimension forming an integral part of the present, is of an order such that it will sanction the possibility that this engendered construal may become the present within philosophy's history. The actative is simply the constitutive part of the present that will demand action and thus be what gives rise to a task while at the same time sanctioning its reality. As a consequence, the epochal present will always attempt to legitimatize actions done in its own name. An additional point must be made, namely that it will always be possible for the epochal present to be declared to be, in all senses, commensurate with the time marked by "calendars" and "historical occurrences." However, such a conception becomes no more than the intended, unmediated positing of objectivity, which, in the attempt to rid the present of its construction and thus of its proper reality, in the end only maintains that relation and with it the distance between the present and the instant by representing it in the guise of objectivity (reality here marking out the space of conflict). The doubling of objectivity resists exclusion. Thus, the positing of objectivity will always occupy the space of construction. Objectivity, in other words, becomes a part of an interpretative structure given by construction.

What is central within this opening, in its having opened an approach to the present as it figures in Benjamin and Heidegger, is that it entails working through the site of the task's founding formulation; in other words, the task and its interpretation demand working through the foreword.[2] Even in allowing for a certain plurality, namely an oscillation between the formal (an actual foreword) and projection (an intended project), the foreword always has an attendant risk. This risk lies in that the foreword may always be viewed as being either provisional or redundant and hence as no more than an addition that can be either subtracted or added; it could even become a gratuitous afterword. Nonetheless, it is by beginning with a foreword that Benjamin will set the scene for his writings on *Trauerspiel*, Baudelaire, Paris, and the nineteenth century. As he indicates in a letter to Scholem, which links the foreword to the *Passagen-Werk* to the much earlier foreword to *The Origin of German Tragic Drama*, writing these forewords was a necessary undertaking (*CS*: 159). Both works brought with them their own "theories of knowledge" as an integral part of their work.

In Benjamin's case what would seem to jeopardize the real or envisaged works that take place after these forewords is that the form these works will have to take is marked by the difficulty of enacting, if not the potential impossibility of realizing, then the project set out in and thus demanded by the foreword. (A similar problem is also presented in Heidegger in the case of "Time and Being.") Within Benjamin's work, the complex relationship between allegory and symbol, the use of the monad as a mode of presentation checking the power of representation, the privileging of showing and image over expression, narrative and stories have at least one straightforward consequence: the question of whether the text could ever contain, in the way envisaged, that which the foreword sets up as the project. As has already been indicated, the problem is reducible neither to style nor to genre but pertains to the construal of a task and thus of its present and then to how that task comes to be enacted.

It should not be thought that the question of presentation has to be added to the work of either Heidegger or Benjamin. Benjamin's study of the German *Trauerspiel*, for example, begins by locating the necessity for philosophy of "representation" (Darstellung). "It is characteristic of philosophical writing that it must continually confront the question of representation [*die Frage der Darstellung*]" (*OT*: 27/ *GS* 1: 207). In writing to Scholem, Benjamin expresses a doubt that can be seen as touching on precisely this point—the task's possibility, its own effective realization—in relation to what is there identified as the "Arcades" project. Of this *Passagen-Werk*, he states: "I can foresee neither whether it will find a form of representation of its own [*eine selbständige Darstellung*], nor to what extent I may succeed in such a representation" (*CS*: 159). While this letter was written in 1935, four years before the final drafting of the *Passagen-Werk*, it remains the case that the question of success, let alone the criteria for that success, remains as open after the drafting as it did before.

The foreword's own reiteration of a projected impossibility of completion—of a textual enactment in narrative—will demand a response, a response to the text, a response, perhaps, to the text's own interpretations, that has the intention of distancing both the interpretative and the hermeneutical and their subsequent replacement by experience. It is the presentation of the problematic status of interpretation and the centrality of experience that brings Heidegger and Benjamin into a specific philosophical relation. Despite the problems that will emerge in pursuing it, it is this relation—the relation given within experience—that will be of central importance.

In Benjamin's "A Berlin Chronicle," the limits of narrative and a certain construal of the politics of memory are advanced. The analogy of archaeological investigation is central to the text's effect because such investigations will demand that the politics of display—incorporating display's time—be taken up. "Fruitless searching is as much part of [excavating] as succeeding, and consequently remembrance [*die Erinnerung*] must not proceed in the manner of a narrative [*erzählend*] or still less that of a report, but must, in the strictest epic and rhapsodic manner, assay its spade in ever new places, and in the old ones delve to ever-deeper layers" (*SW* 2: 611/ *GS* 1: 486). There are two difficulties with this passage. The first is understanding the claims being made. The second is tracing their consequences. The presentation of Benjamin and the related consideration of the present—the interrelationship between politics and time as constitutive in any attempt to take up the ontology of the present—will continually have to return to these difficulties, returning, perhaps, by readdressing them.

Returning to the present means working with the recognition that the presentation of a task, and, consequently, its writing, take place in time, a time that is complex from the start. Complexity arises because this is a time, which, while it may occasion a date, at times even enjoin one, is nonetheless to be distinguished from that which is dated. Within the passage of time, the self-conception of the task to be enacted is instantiated. It is this self-conception that will be of concern here, for with it what arises is the time of the task; in other words, the conception of the present in which the task is to be enacted at the present, and with it, therefore, of the present as that which sustains and maintains the task and its self-enactment. The reciprocity here is essential. Presenting these interdependent elements in this way will allow for the possibility of thinking through the nature of the relation between the present and "now-time" (*Jetztzeit*). While cited in a number of entries, within the framework of "Konvolut N" "the present" (*die Gegenwart*) is, for the most part, a term that is still to be clarified. This lack of clarity should not obviate the necessity of recognizing the weight that it has to carry, a weight indicated in the following examples:³ "the present" (*die Gegenwart*) is included within the historical task. "The present" is that which is placed in a "critical condition" by "the materialist presentation of history" (*N* 7a, 5). Moreover it is "the present" that "polarises the event into fore and after history" (*N* 7a, 8). The question that endures concerns what it is that this "present" is taken to be. In addition, it will have to include a consideration of the link between "the present" as a temporal moment, the moment within the temporality of the instant and thus a moment that also brings its own ontological considerations with it, and that which is presented, where the latter involves a presentation of and thus also within the present: present instantiation.

The "present"—in part, Benjamin's construal of what has been designated the epochal present—and presencing are inevitably linked in his work to the presence of critique. Part of the critique of Jung that takes place in "Konvolut N" and elsewhere concerns how presencing occurs, and with its occurrence what is thought to have been carried over into the present: "translated into the language of the present" is Jung's own expression, a line quoted by Benjamin (*N* 8, 2) to establish a critical distance from Jung. For Benjamin, Jung's error lies not in the preoccupation with incursions into the present but in the way both the process and the content of presencing are thought. An intrinsic part of the critique of Jung is the effective presence of a construal of the present in which, perhaps *for* which, Jung's project is not simply vulnerable philosophically but reiterates a politics—the politics of a particular expressionism—that is once again the subject of critique. It is a stance that forms a part of Benjamin's general critique of expressionism. And yet with Jung—with a more generalized preoccupation with Jung in the *Passagen-Werk*—what is involved is more complex. A way of formulating this problem would be to suggest that Jung allows for a present in which what is received from outside of it—the outside as an archaic past, presencing in Jung's words as "an unconscious animation of the archetype" (*N* 8, 2)—becomes, despite the appearance of difference, a repetition of the Same.

In less specific terms, it will emerge that in taking up repetition, the present, and hence the differing conceptions of the epochal present, works within the complex of repetition. In other words, repetition will contain the very differences that serve to work the present as a site of conflict. With repetition, even in its complexity, experience is introduced, because experience delimits the stance in relation to repetition and this despite the stance's textual and thus written formulation. Furthermore, forming a fundamental part of what is involved in any consideration of the present is the reciprocal conception of experience that such a present demands. A way into this present will stem from the recognition that, with Benjamin and Heidegger, it is the place and thus the time of "showing." With this showing, what remains open is how the experience of showing is to be understood. What is it, therefore, to experience the shown as such?[4]

Heidegger's Present

Although they may lack any predetermined and therefore pregiven presentation, aspects of this initial taking up of Benjamin's work are, in the first place, intended to connect, reconnect, albeit on a general level, the projects of Heidegger and Benjamin. Connecting and reconnecting occur insofar as a constitutive part of each project is the relationship between showing and experience. Nonetheless, it goes without saying that the specific formulations of that relationship serve to open up an important difference between their projects, thus forcing a consideration of how that difference is itself to be thought. As difference eschews simple positing, its location is paramount. Here it turns on the present. More concretely, this particular point of departure is also intended, in the second place, to take up, again as an example, Heidegger's *Nietzsche*, in particular the final part of the section entitled "European Nihilism," a text in which "metaphysics," the history of metaphysics, bears on by bearing the present.

Before pursuing Heidegger's own formulation it should be noted that this presentation is itself intended to take up significant aspects within Benjamin's own philosophical forewords—though, more emphatically, the relationship between the forewords and that which the forewords intend to have follow them. Because it can be taken to harbor the project itself, the foreword inevitably becomes more than a given site—even a preliminary site—within a textual topology. It is the latter component, the inherent complexity of the foreword, which, as has already been indicated, must form a fundamental part of any real philosophical engagement with it. Here the work of Benjamin and Heidegger is such that one tracks and tacks on the other. Neither their opposition nor their similarity can be taken as given. Sails will always have to be trimmed. The problem will always pertain to the nature of the calculation.

Heidegger's final considerations of Nietzsche's metaphysics could be said to incorporate "today"'s location.

> "Today" [*Heute*], reckoned neither by the calendar, nor in terms of world-historical occurrences, is determined by the period in the history of metaphysics that is most our own: it is the metaphysical determination of historical mankind in the age of Nietzsche's metaphysics. (*N*: 195/ *GA* 6.2: 254)

The actual quality of this "today," its uniqueness, is clarified in the lines that follow. "Our epoch reveals a particularly casual matter-of-factness with respect to the truth of being as a whole" (*N*: 195/ *GA* 6.2: 254). And yet within the frame of the same formulation, this casual attitude is mediated by the presence of another and greater "passion." Again it attests to the age by giving it a specific particularity. "Such an indifference [*Gleichgültigkeit*] to being in the midst of the greatest passion for beings testifies to the thoroughly metaphysical character of the age" (*N*: 195/ *GA* 6.2: 254). The particular force of this description, one to which it will be necessary to return, is that for Heidegger it is a characterization that comes from being, one that is sent by it. For Heidegger, the present is, therefore, always already given by the history of being. As such, it is in part constitutive of that history. It is the precise nature of the given coupled to the mode of access to it that is presented at the end of the text.

> The age of the fulfilment of metaphysics—which we descry when we think the basic features of Nietzsche's metaphysics—prompts us to consider to what extent we find ourselves in the history of being. It also prompts us to consider–prior to finding ourselves—the extent to which we must experience [*erfahren müssen*] history as the release of being into machination, a release that being itself sends, so as to allow its truth to become essential for man out of man's belonging to it. (*N*: 196/ *GA* 6.2: 256)

For Heidegger, the quality of the present resides in what could be described as a *giveness* that is always more than the simple instantiation of the given. Again, its quality discloses itself in its forming the present, yet forming it in such a way that its "originality" can always be shown as present. The predicament of human being—a predicament that can be described as the being of human being (identified earlier by Heidegger, in *Being and Time*, for example, with the term *Dasein*)—is given by being; it is part of being's destiny, in that human being belongs to being. In Heidegger's terms, grasping that this is the case will necessitate that "experience," in which what is proper and original to human being is taken over in its propriety as establishing, though in a sense also reestablishing, the "original" belonging together of being and human being. The reluctance to separate establishing and reestablishing in any systematic way indicates the extent to which propriety is in some sense already there. The belonging together of being and human being—the latter as the being of being human—has already been worked through in *Being and Time* in terms of questioning. There, Heidegger presents Dasein as that being for which the question of being, and with it its own being, is always, that is, originally, a question. Ontology takes the place of any simple humanism.

The expressions "indifference," "casual matter-of-factness" and "passion for beings" as employed by Heidegger attest to the present epochality of being. Yet they can also be taken as descriptive of the present, the time of writing. Remembering the functional reciprocity between description and task, it becomes a description that demands a particular task. The demand is located in expressions of the form "we must experience." In marking the intended elimination of "indifference," the "must" brings the inherently actative dimension within the present to the fore. It is this dimension that gives rise to a specific task, a task formulated by the present and thus forming a fundamental part of its constitution. As such, this reciprocity takes the present beyond Heidegger's own description. Heidegger's present is no longer either the "today," or the "age," or the current epochality of being. Rather, they are all interrelated with the task they demand (to give one side of the reciprocity) and thus, for Heidegger, form the epochal present. The constitutive elements must be retained and examined within their given reciprocity.

The "passion" Heidegger identifies is for the other side of the divide within ontological difference. Consequently, while this passion may define the age, it is because of its place within that divide that, at the same time, it gives rise to a task. Present and task are interarticulated. One works within the other. What this entails is, first of all, an overcoming of the given "indifference" and stemming contemporary passion, and, second, thinking being in its differentiation from beings and thus as differentiated from them. The force of the description that presents "today" as the "release of being" allows for the recognition of the current epochality of being, that which being "today" forms and informs, while indicating that it is within the very structure of this presencing, because of what it is, that it becomes possible to consider the conditions of possibility for the thinking of being itself. (The epochal present will always have recourse to a form of the transcendental, since what such a conception of the present will give are conditions of possibility—conditions in which the present is also given.) The latter possibility arises out of "today's situation, the present, and is, moreover, predicated upon experience: more significantly, upon an experience that 'we' must have." (Again, a separate though important line of inquiry would concern the identity and thus the ontology of this "we"; not the question of who we are, but of who is the intended subject of this experience.) The difficulty that resides in experience, in what the term stakes out, pertains to how it is to be understood. This is a difficulty that arises with the acceptance, as a point of departure, that experience cannot be posited. Perhaps more significantly, however, there is the related problem of how that experience's intended effect is to be realized. What is the registration and what is it that is registered in the experience that "must" be had? The recognition of the actuality of such experience, leaving the question of its specificity to one side, is what locates the present as the present. Recognition works to intensify it. And yet the temporality of this intensity is far from straightforward. As will be indicated, it is an intensity that, for Heidegger, is released within an openness and thus within the calm of having experienced. In their link to the future, calmness and the open are given as originally determined by propriety. Present intensity for Benjamin will be significantly different.

Allowing for the present as given by the "release of being" locates the present as historical. The quality of the present—and thus of Heidegger's formulation of what has already been described as the epochal present—is determined in advance. However, what is determined must be experienced as such, as that determination. It follows that once that experience has taken place and only within the actual terms given by what it is that will have been experienced, it then becomes possible to think, for Heidegger, the condition of the present itself. More accurately perhaps, it is then possible to think at the present that which gives to it—the present—its present determination. Such a thinking is essentially futural in the precise sense that it breaks up the present by taking the present's propriety—that which is proper to the present, namely being—as its own exclusive object of thought. It will be a thinking of the present that takes place at a particular point in time, a date, which will serve to differentiate the present from itself. In the thinking of being the future is possible. Although this is to employ terms such as *present* and *future* beyond the purview of Heidegger's own specific use, it nonetheless accords with the implicit construal of the future—future possibility—that is at work, for example, in a text such as "Time and Being," a text that is of fundamental significance for any serious attempt to understand what it is that a foreword may be and thus to plot the relationship between time and task. It can be added that the project and thus the strategy of "Time and Being," along with, for example, the programmatic claim in the opening section of "On the Way to Language," in which the project is advanced as an "experience" with language and thus within the distancing of the said remaining open to the saying, work to reorient the task away from interpretation and the textual and toward experience and action. With any encounter with Heidegger's text, the precise nature of this experience endures as the dominant interpretative problem.[5] With it, the question of the hermeneutic status is reopened.

The importance of "Time and Being" lies in the fact that it is a foreword to a text that in some sense has yet to be written—there is even the real possibility that it cannot be written—and, to that extent, the possibilities that it holds open the future, while at the same time indicating the nature of the task that is given. What is meant by doubting the possibility of its being written pertains to Heidegger's understanding of the "propositional statements" (*Aussagesätze*) that characterize philosophical writing. The text reiterates the impossibility of such "statements" doing justice to the task at hand. The difficulty is stated in the text's opening and is announced again at its end. In Heidegger's terms, "statements" is one of a number of "hindrances" to the task that is given. The task is thinking being "without relation to metaphysics" (*ohne Rücksicht auf die Metaphysik*) (*TB*: 24/ *GA* 14: 29). It is the "without"—thinking "without"—that is of singular importance here.[6] Before taking it up, it is essential to examine what the distancing—establishing the limits—of philosophical writing is going to entail. These entailments work to construct an important link to Benjamin's foreword. Moreover, they seem to forge a bridge to presentational method. In both instances they will be connections that distance.

"Time and Being" was initially a lecture. Responding to it was intended to be a different exercise than the one demanded by reading. Indeed, because the practice of reading means that, within it, there is the necessity of being forced to respond to the movement of statements and propositions, it is, as a consequence, inherently problematic (again the difficulty of any immediate reconciliation of interpretation and experience). Heidegger takes up the difficulty of what he is about to present, to say, in the following way: "Let me give a little hint on how to listen. The point is not to listen to a series of propositions, but rather to follow the movement of showing [*dem Gang des Zeigens*]" (*TB*: 2/ *GA* 14: 6). This formulation of Heidegger's recalls the frequently cited though nonetheless still difficult passage from "Konvolut N," in which Benjamin describes the method of his own work. The possible paradox inevitably generated by Benjamin's juxtaposition of method and montage needs to be remarked on from the start. What is noted, therefore, is the possibility of holding method and montage together. Were they to fall apart then the way demanded by the foreword would be a way that would always prove to be impossible to follow. "Method of the project: literary montage. I need say nothing only showing [*nur zeigen*]" (*N* 1a, 81). Benjamin's showing is significantly different. What then of Heidegger's showing? What does the showing itself display? Asking what is shown is to recognize—though here this recognition is neither Benjamin's nor Heidegger's—the presence of an ineliminable doubling within showing itself. It should be remembered that the central issue here is the present, the task's time and thus the epochal present (in Heidegger's own formulation). The doubling is the complexity engendered by what the showing shows. It is thus equally, at the same time, generated by it, a reciprocity demanding another take on complexity.

Heidegger's "Age"

Heidegger's concerns at the end of "European Nihilism" can be read as yielding a construal of the present in which the present has the quality of having been given by being even though the "age" remains "indifferent" to the question of being. The nature of the present as that which is constituted by being forces through the present the task of thinking being, thus causing the present to become reconciled with itself (where this becoming brings with it a complex future). The reconciliation is premised on the forced actualization of what was described earlier as thinking "without." The task as formulated in "Time and Being" turns around the "without." Heidegger formulates it thus: "To think being without [*ohne*] beings means to think being without regard to metaphysics" (*TB*: 24/ *GA* 14: 29). The "without" can be taken, at least provisionally, as the overcoming of "indifference," the stemming of "passion," and so on. In the end it will involve a similar movement to the one occurring (perhaps envisaged) in what, in the same text, Heidegger describes as "leaving metaphysics to itself." And yet, this "metaphysics" is not just an option for thinking, a way of doing philosophy, though clearly it is that as well. Here, "metaphysics" is a description of the "age" and consequently it involves the present. It circumscribes the epochal present. "Leaving metaphysics to itself" or doing "without" it is an act in the present that opens the future, but opens it toward a possibility that is in the present even though by definition it could not occur either "in" the present or "as" it is. The future becomes the space for the realized possibility of a reconciliation between that which gives the present—the epochal present—its present determination and to which the present is "indifferent." In the end, what must occur is a reconciliation with that which is proper to human being; that is, the taking over of the question of being itself. Being reconciled with what had already been there. Nothing will have been rescued, the work of return will have been precluded, the present will have been sacrificed, given away.[7]

The intensity of the present is generated by its being the site of misidentifications (being as "idea," *energia*, "will," etc.), and the perpetual repetition of irreconcilability; a state whose existence must be experienced, acknowledged ,and then perhaps even resolutely affirmed. In taking over the present, in taking a stand within it, the present projects a future. The present will never be worked back onto itself. In "Time and Being," Heidegger is scrupulous in recognizing the possible incursion of the retroactive—what will reappear beyond his immediate concerns as the movement of *Nachträglichkeit* (iterative reworking)—and then in attempting to rid those concerns of precisely that possibility. Hence the importance of "originality," of the already there. The privileging of original propriety over the effective of iteration—iteration's work—is signaled by Heidegger in "Time and Being" that what is proper to being and time in the sense of "what determines time and being in their unique propriety [*in ihr Eigenes*]" (*TB*: 19/ *GA* 14: 24) is not what he then describes as a "relation retroactively [*nachträglich*] superimposed upon being and time" (*TB*: 19/ *GA* 14: 24).⁸

The present must—and the "must" here is the sign of the task as well as the necessity for resoluteness—abandon itself, leave itself behind, do without itself for the future. In so doing, it emerges as the future. "Time and Being" precedes that which it cannot state and, moreover, that which cannot be stated. It follows, therefore, that the text is almost, in a literal sense, a foreword indicating what is to be done while at the same time not doing it. As a text it identifies what will hinder the effectuation of the task, and in the act of identifying it indicates what might be involved in order that its restrictive and blocking powers be diminished. The present must be differentiated from itself. The problem lies with what sustains the differentiation. To be maintained, the "without" enjoins either forgetting—a forgetting of that which will have been done "without"—or sacrifice, a task involving metaphysics having been given away: from *Aufgabe* to *aufgibt*, then. Tracing the necessity of either sacrifice or forgetting enables the development of a critical stance in relation to Heidegger's construal of the epochal present. Their necessity becomes an important limit.

Sacrifice and the doing "without" are necessarily connected. They are tasks demanded by the specific construal of the epochal present. For Heidegger, they enjoin the future. It is this link to the future, a future opened up by the necessity of what is presented, that must be seen as arising out of the project engendered by the text's foreword. The projected impossibility lies in the relation to what it is that must be experienced and the impossible eventuality of its being given within the language of philosophy and thus within metaphysics. It is only with Benjamin that the linkage among experience, future, and reconciliation will be sundered. It will be broken up by the necessity of destruction and thus of the caesura. To deploy the phraseology of the final part of the "On the Concept of History," the future is forbidden precisely because it cannot be thought outside of the twofold possibility of progress and ultimate reconciliation.⁹ It is precisely this state of affairs that is captured in the presentation of "dialectical experience": "It is the unique property of dialectical experience to dissipate the appearance of things always being the same. Real political experience is absolutely free from this appearance" (*N* 9, 5).

Benjamin, Monad, Repetition

For both to maintain the difference between Heidegger and Benjamin and so as to give it philosophical force, what must be taken up is the present within Benjamin's own presentation of the term. At the same time, any such move will open up the epochal present in Benjamin's writings (in this instance "Konvolut N" of the *Passagen-Werk*, its "foreword"). Here, the presentation of the term *present* is announced as part of a particular task that is located in what amounts to a foreword. In other words, retaining the importance of the actative involves taking up the interplay of ontology and action announced within the recitation of "the present"; that is to say, positioning another epochal present itself positioned as projecting a task to be completed in writing. At a later stage in the drafting of the notes that comprise "Konvolut N"—the period 1937–1940—"the present" is drawn into the consideration of history in ways that serve to highlight "the present" as a site, while at the same time attempting to distance continuity construed as either sequence or repetition.

> For the materialist historian, every epoch with which he occupies himself is only a fore-history of the one that really concerns him. And that is precisely why the appearance of repetition [*Wiederholung*] doesn't exist for him in history, because given their index as "fore-history" those moments in the course of history that matter most to him become moments of the present according to whether this present is defined as catastrophe or as triumph. (*N* 9a, 8)

A beginning can be made with this "present." Here, something becomes a moment of the present; it becomes it because of its introduction into "the present." The question that emerges is the extent to which this introduction is constitutive of the present and is thus to be taken, in this aspect of Benjamin's work, as forming an integral part of the construction of the epochal present. Any attempt to take this question up will necessitate considering the status of "fore-history" in its differentiation from "after-history" and, therefore, in its being formulated as that which in some sense precludes repetition. It is essential that "repetition" (*Wiederholung*) be given the specificity that is demanded by the passage, rather than its being assumed to mark out repetition in general (as if there were repetition in general). It will be necessary, therefore, to return to this "repetition," a return signaling the abeyance of essential thinking.

The distinction between fore-history and after-history figures in a number of places in "Konvolut N." Almost invariably it is linked to either "the present" or the attempt to formulate historical time. For example: "It is the present [*die Gegenwart*] which polarises the event into fore- and after-history" (*N* 7a, 8). And again: "The present [*die Gegenwart*] defines where the fore-history and the after-history of the object of the past diverge in order to circumscribe its nucleus" (*N* 11, 5). At a slightly earlier stage, the "foundation of history" is linked to what is called the "afterlife" of the object of historical understanding. "Historical understanding is to be viewed primarily as an afterlife [*Nachleben*] of that which has been understood; and so what came to be recognized about works through the analysis of their afterlife, their "fame," should be considered the foundation of history itself" (*N* 2, 3). The "foundation of history" is then that which is to be located not beyond the original—as though there could ever have been an original founding moment to which a return could be made let alone a moment of original propriety—but in a present incursion. The continual repositioning, the privileging of the afterlife in the place of "life," is not intended to be taken as an anti-realist gesture that in some way denies reality by countering the material with the ideal. Rather, reality comes to be invested with a different power, one that will complicate the nature of that reality. The power is Messianic. As Benjamin states, the method proper to a "commentary on reality" (*der Kommentar zu einer Wirklichkeit*) is theology. As opposed to philology, theology concentrates on the "*nach.*" With this concentration, however, there arises the inevitable question of limits. Does a *Nachleben* always survive? Is there a limit therefore to this "*nach*" and thus to any *nach*? Can the life of the afterlife (*Nachleben*), the after-history (*Nachgeschichte*), come to an end? These are questions for Benjamin's own formulation of time. The problem to which they allude concerns the twofold possibility of fulfillment and reconciliation.

In their varying forms these questions turn around the Messianic, turning in the end towards *the* Messianic question. And yet, what is at stake here is not theology as such—understood as either the language of/for God, or God reasoning—nor the Messiah as the redeemer of a fallen humanity. Here the intersection of time and politics is thought, provisionally, within the framework of the theological in which the Messiah may be present but only as a figure; figuring, perhaps, in the same way as the "Flâneur" or "Lumpensammler." What is intended by this frame is that the Messianic is descriptive of the power that enables the "event" to have an afterlife; its capacity to live on is explicable in terms of Messianic power. That power is not theological. It is not the consequence of God's word or deed. Indeed, it can be added that a limit to Benjamin's own adventure lay in his having to have recourse to the figure of theology to explain this occurrence rather than to the ontology of the "event"—the limit that becomes, therefore, the limiting of the philosophical within his work.

A significant number of the theological motifs that Benjamin employs turn on time. In a sense this is not surprising, given the contention that theology is the site in which the thinking of time is sustained in his writings. However, the presence of such motifs brings with them a number of attendant problems, not the least of which is the nature of the relationship between motif and motive. This emerges quite clearly with the term *apocatastasis*. Despite its decontextualization—perhaps a move evoking another afterlife?—it remains the case that the word is essentially Christian. One unproblematic occurrence of it in the Christian Bible is *Acts* III:21: "until the time for restoring everything [ἄχρι χρόνων ἀποκαταστάσεως πάντων]." What is evoked is both a fall and a restoration located within totality. (Here πάντων is the Absolute, its having become actual, the giving of the totality gathered in time, given as the place of complete reconciliation.) What is designated in this instance in the Christian biblical context is the restoration of a totality that had come apart. The intended reality of absolute reconciliation is projected. (In this regard, it will be vital to try to differentiate between the Christian concept of "apocatastasis" and the Judaic or, more properly, Kabbalistic concept of "tikkun." Although the distinction may not be immediately self-evident, maintaining the difference, it could be argued, is of considerable importance. Within the Christian framework, the absolute nature of the term is essential, as indeed is the fall from completion. What is restored is that original completion and reconciliation of Man and God. What is restored is that which was originally always already there in Man though retained after the fall, in part in terms of the "image of God" and, in part, in terms of that image involving a transcendence, which denied to the material present the possibility of its own redemptive and, therefore, Messianic possibility. Partiality is excluded as is a possible infinity. In the restoration of the "all" the necessity for the continuity of any afterlife would have ended. The transformative and continually destructive power of "now-time" (*Jetztzeit*)—a destruction already indicative of a denial of any impartiality and therefore, in addition, also of a resisted universality—would have become otiose.

What then of Benjamin's use of the term? With this question the problem of the "nach" is compounded for the question of the nature—that is, the ontology—of what it is that is unending. As it does not instantiate the theological, thought as the sacred—the sacred in its disassociation from the mundane—it must follow that in the end the enforced actuality of the Messianic will simply not do. Maintaining theology as the language and reasoning concerning God, were that to be a possible option, would involve thinking its relation to politics rather than taking it as that which provided politics with its temporality. These considerations, ones that will take Benjamin's concern beyond the limits he has provided for them, come to the fore with the use of a term such as *apocatastasis*.

In "Konvolut N," the word *apocatastasis* occurs as part of what is described there as a "minor methodological recommendation," concerning the contrasting and then the recontrasting of the putative positive and negative parts of an epoch. The point of this movement was to indicate that one only has value against the backdrop of the other. Retaining the negative—the "backward" and "extinct" parts—will involve contrasting them with different "positive" elements in order that they be positioned anew. Original oppositions are thereby broken up. This breaking is at the same time the critique of historicism—be it Ranke or Hegel—and indicative of the radical nature of Benjaminian destruction. Benjamin concludes this recommendation in the following way: "And so on *ad infinitum* until all of the past has been brought into the present [*die Gegenwart*] in a historic apocatastasis" (*N* 1a,3). The value of this recommendation, which repeats the structuring force of the archaeological analogy from "A Berlin Chronicle" by bringing the past to the present as though to the surface, is that it allows for the effective distancing of oppositions such as major/minor, good/bad, and so on, when they are put forward as no more than the constitutive parts of an either/or, especially the either/or given by tradition.[10] Contrasts are to be dialectical and not straightforward oppositional juxtapositions (positing and counterpositing). These contrasts may, Benjamin suggests, be as elementary as "nuances." What these contrasts allow for, however, is a continual renewal. As he puts it, "it is from them that life always springs anew" (*das Leben immer neu*) (*N* 1a, 41). It is precisely this type of formulation that raises difficulties, because what it demands is a confrontation with the question of how the finality and totality of apocatastasis is to be squared with the continual renewal of life—the continuity of the "*nach*," the "always new" (*immer neu*)—especially because it is buttressed by the effective presence of the "*ad infinitum*." (The difficulty of answering this question in part indicates why residues of historicism are thought by some commentators to have been retained by the process marked out and thus enacted by the term *apocatastasis*.)[11]

What arises is in the first place the impossibility of "all the past" ever being brought into the "present." It is not just that the reference to infinity renders it impossible; more exactly, it is that the methodological procedure being suggested is precluded first by this type of finality and second by the "monadological structure" of the "historical object" (*des historischen Gegenstandes*) (*N* 10, 3). (It will be essential to return to the question of the monad, for with the monad the force of the disruptive nature of Benjamin's construal of time will emerge.) What is wanted by Benjamin is not a continual restoration that intends to restore the original paradisiac site or aims at completion—a completion invoked by the "all"—but a continual restoration in which each restorative moment is new, in the precise sense of a renewal of life as the afterlife. This particular theological term, therefore, while gesturing toward a state of affairs that is demanded methodologically, nonetheless belies the force of what is wanted. Benjamin uses theology to think the relationship between politics and time. As a consequence, he presents the challenge of thinking time and action beyond the conceptual purview of theology, thereby freeing theology for God.

In the passage under consideration (*N* 9a, 8), the relationship between fore-history and after-history is given in terms of the present as either catastrophe or triumph. What is located outside of their possible interconnection is "the appearance of repetition" (*den Schein der Wiederholung*). But what is repetition? It is that which is obviated in the first place by the existence of a dialectical image (the singular insistence and synonymy of Now and Then) and, in the second, by the possible continuity of the always the Same. The use of fore-history intends to rid history of repetition. Yet, even with this twofold exclusion of repetition, the question that still endures is the following: How is the after-history or afterlife to be thought? In terms of what concepts and categories is it to be thought?

The question strikes at the heart of this attempted extrusion of repetition since it would seem to be the case that the "after," the whole strategy of the present constructed by another giving, is itself unthinkable except as a form of repetition. Given this possibility, what will then have to be argued is that what is involved in the distinction is a reworked concept of repetition. What this will entail is a repetition that has been subjected to the process marked out by the distinction between fore-history and after-history. It is only the interpolation of such a construal of repetition that will allow further insight into Benjamin's response to Horkheimer's insistence of a dialectical formulation of incompleteness and completeness and why Benjamin's introduction of "a form of memoration" (*eine Form des Eingedenkens*) checks the dialectical presentation of history via the introduction of memory, but in so doing maintains the dialectical image as the ground of the historical itself.

The problem of repetition can be taken a step further by taking up the reference to Benjamin's already cited insistence on the "monadological structure" of the "historical object." Leaving to one side Benjamin's examples, as well as the question of the continuity of references to monads throughout his work, the passage in question positions the object, "the historical object," in relation to its fore-history and after-history in the following terms:

> If the historical object is blasted out of the historical process, it is because the monadological structure of the object demands it. This structure only becomes evident once the object has been blasted free. And it becomes evident precisely in the form of the historical argument which makes

up the inside (and, as it were, the bowels) of the historical object, and into which all the forces and interests of history enter on a reduced scale. The historical object, by virtue of its monadological structure, discovers within itself [*findet es in seinem Innern*] its own fore-history and after-history. (*N* 10, 3)

Present here is an ontological formulation of the "historical object." The "demand" that it makes is not a contingent possibility. On the contrary. It is a demand that stems directly from the mode of being proper to the historical object in its being a historical object. What must be questioned, therefore, is the nature of this monad. What earlier is the monad in question? It is the enormity as well as the centrality of this question that suggests an approach, which, while maintaining history and acknowledging the importance of memory, is concerned nonetheless with the nature of the "object" and thus with ontology and time.

References to the monad inevitably raise the possibility of a relation to Leibniz's own formulation of the monad in the *Monadology*.[12] What must be sought here is that which in Leibniz's own philosophical writings offers a type of illumination. (The possibility of a historical continuity, or the attempt to establish the same, even the continuity of influence, must be recognized for what it is.) As what is involved is the internality of the historical object, the obvious point of entry is Leibniz's own construal of the internality of the monad. In section 11 of the *Monadology* Leibniz argues that "the natural changes of the monads come from an internal principle, since an external cause could not influence their inner being." Slightly later, at *Monadology* 15, this "internal principle" is described as "appetition" and then further clarified as what "causes the change or passage from one perception to another." What is significant about these descriptions is that the monad's change or development comes from within the monad itself. Change—and change, if it is translated into a different idiom, is going to involve the monad's afterlife—will be an afterlife that is itself already part of its life in the strict sense that it is a possibility that is already within the monad. Furthermore, when Leibniz argues that the monad reflects the totality and thus, in some sense, contains all of its possibilities within it, it looks as if Leibniz as well as Benjamin construe monads in a similar way. However, there is a fundamental difference. In this instance it is a difference involving time; not the temporality of the monad as such, but the temporality of that in which the monad plays a constitutive part. Constitution here means that time brings ontological considerations with it.

The time in question pertains to what Leibniz identifies within his writings as "pre-established harmony." In other words, time here pertains to the time of this harmony. It will be a time that precludes a straightforward singularity. In

Monadology 59, the "universal harmony" is presented as that according to which "every substance exactly expresses all others through the relations it has with them." For Leibniz, this mutuality of infinite relations expressed in the monad opens up the need to distinguish each monad from God since, if this infinite—the infinite of both "division" and "subdivision"[13]—were clear to each monad and, in addition, the necessary presence of distance did not introduce a type of confusion, it would then follow, as Leibniz himself suggests at *Monadology* 60, that "each monad would be a deity." (This is an identity established and secured by Leibniz's own law of the identity of indiscernibles.) The relation of monads to the infinite is more complex and explicable in terms of "appetition"; in terms, that is, of the monad's internality, and thus of the ontology of the monad. The interpretative difficulty within this explication stems from having to recognize the abeyance of stasis and with it the centrality of the ontology of becoming. "In a confused way they all go after/towards (*vont à*) the infinite, the whole; but they are limited and diffcrentiated through the degrees of their distinct perceptions."[14] The movement is harmonious. Moreover, it follows from Leibniz arguing in *Monadology* 7 that, because the source of all change is internal to the monad, all changes have to be reflected in the whole, such that the totality accords with itself. Again, this is possible only for ontological reasons. In sum, it is only because the monad, as Leibniz writes in the opening line of *Principles of Nature and of Grace*, is "a being [*un être*] capable of action."[15] Action is not a contingent predicate of substance. The actative is, in part, constitutive of the monad itself. The internal and complete accord—an accord *in toto*—is "pre-established harmony." The difficulty here is God. It is, however, a very precise difficulty. If the totality is present in God then, in some sense, the infinite toward which all substance moves—a movement that, as the consequence of desire, is itself explicable in terms of the monad's inscribed desire for completion and thus, in a sense, to be God—is already present for God. In being present for God, and even if appetition provides the continuity of completion, it remains the case that for God the completing harmony is in some sense already complete. (Although there may be an ambivalence in Benjamin's work with regard to how reconciliation is to be understood, Leibnizian teleology would, nonetheless, be an untenable proposition.)

Although the ontologico-temporal considerations proper to God raise important problems for any sustained interpretation of Leibniz, it is nonetheless also directly relevant for understanding the time of "pre-established harmony." (It is the time proper to this harmony that will establish and maintain the significant divide between Benjamin and Leibniz's respective conceptions of the monad.) The harmony is continued and continuous self-completion—completion, as it were, to infinity—it is always already enacting the completing that is proper to it (thereby establishing a necessary link for Leibniz between ontology and the actative). Although this does not preclude free will, what it does render impossible is the existence of that act in which the time of completion and thus with it both the ontology and the temporality of harmony—an always already preexistent harmony—could be subverted, destroyed, let alone blasted apart. It is precisely this possibility that, Benjamin argues, can occur precisely because of the monadological structure of the "historical object."

It is possible to argue that for Leibniz, what could be described as the temporality proper to freedom—the time in which, for example, evil and good acts are committed—is historical or chronological time, while the temporality of preestablished harmony is the time of the universe held in infinite time with God and as such is not a time in which actions with determining results can occur. The reason for this impossibility is almost definitional insofar as the implicit Leibnizian conception of the universe and the temporality proper to it are such that they incorporate the totality of substance and therefore the totality of actions. With Benjamin, however, the temporal structure is importantly different. If there is any connection to preestablished harmony within a philosophy of history, then it would lie in the move that would turn the past into a given historical continuity that remains impervious to intervention or disruption. It would be as though the historical past created an accord that determined the historical task as the necessity to reproduce that founding and already existent accord, such that the reproduction itself accorded with the past. The historical object, the object of/in history, would therefore only reveal itself—reveal itself as it is, a revelation demanding the effective presence, *contra* Leibniz, of the ontology of stasis—in that founding accord.[16]

Benjamin's Repetition Again

Even though there is an important difference between them that arises here, it is at this point that the complexity of Benjamin's debt to Leibniz emerges. It is precisely the status (the ontology) of what Benjamin calls the *historical object* that, in allowing for that founding accord—the putative naturalizing of historicism—at the same time occasions the object being "blasted out" of that pregiven continuity in order then to reveal itself—and thus to reveal that which is reflected in it—in another setting. The revelation in another setting, a revelation constructed by that setting, is the explosive "now-time," the instantiation of the present by montage; by the movement of montage (a montage effect whose determinations are yet to be fixed). It will be a montage that involves temporality as well as objects and images. Consequently, it is not just that this present remains complex; there is a more insistent problem, namely whether montage could ever be provided in a sustained and intentional way such that it avoided being simply arbitrary and, as such, no more than a weak imagistic flutter. In other words, could there be a "method of montage" that worked to preclude any response other than "dialectical experience"?[17]

It is with these questions that the problem of the foreword, as the site where the task is announced such that what proceeds from it is the task's enacting, returns. Again, this is not a state of affairs simply added on to Benjamin's concerns; indeed, the framework in which a return can be made is provided by Benjamin (*N* 1, 9) by bringing "project" (*Arbeit*), "theory" and "montage" together in order to provide a formulation of the undertaking, as a foreword: "This project must raise the art of quoting without quotation marks to the very highest level. Its theory is intimately linked to that of montage."

If the approach indicated in this passage is taken up, what remains problematic is the relationship between "quotation" and the monad. A way of addressing this is provided by thinking through the difference between quotation and "quoting without quotation marks." Although allowing for its being descriptive of images and pictures, montage is, in the end, not merely descriptive of images or pictures. In moving from images and pictures while at the same time incorporating them, it will have become a description of time. In other words, independently of actual montage, Benjamin's "montage" will be a way of constituting the present (the epochal present rather than the instant, the dated present). It will awaken a possibility in which the present as temporal montage will reorient itself in relation to the given and thus to that which is given to it. It is this eventuality that can be identified as present at the beginning of "Konvolut N."

> "Comparison of others" attempts to setting off on a sea voyage in which ships are drawn off course by the magnetic North Pole. Discover that North Pole. What for others are deviations, for me are data by which to set my course. I base my reckoning on *the differentia of time [den Differentialen der Zeit]* that disturb the "main lines" of the investigation for others. (*N* 1, 2; my emphasis)

The possibility gestured at here is that the "differentia of time" could be temporal montage, the copresence of different times. (If this state of affairs can be maintained then there will be no necessary link between temporal montage and the specific art form of imagistic montage.) The link between montage and time—temporal montage—will have to be taken up at the same time as returning to the foreword and attempting to plot the effect of the presence and absence of "quotation marks."

These three elements combine in an important way. The quotation marks raise the problem of repetition. The "differentia" gesture toward a complex time at/as the present. Although the foreword instantiates the methodological and thus projective problems that are sustained by one take on "quotation marks" and "differentia," these problems are overcome by another take. With this other take, the problems will come to be distanced by the repetition of what is marked by quotation marks and differentia. As the term that is to be restricted if not dismissed as long as it remains in quotation marks, *repetition* will turn out to play a redemptive role within the project, projected and projecting beyond its given confines, though only once the quotation marks are removed. Moving from "repetition" (*N* 9a, 8) to repetition crystallizes the general problem of understanding the loss of "quotation marks." To juxtapose images, it may be that the crystal works as a *mise-en-abîme*. The radical consequence of this opening up of repetition, presented within the play of quotation marks, the continuity of their own oscillation, is that, again, though now for slightly different reasons, merely rehearsing Benjamin's own undertakings should not be assumed, in any real sense at all, to be continuing the project of the *Passagen-Werk*. Moreover, if they are repeated then their viability will not be able to be assessed in straightforwardly Benjaminian terms. Once more, it is not that Benjaminian montage amounts to the sustained juxtaposition of chronologically separate images; rather, it is that *montage* is a term that pertains to time. The importance of montage lies not in the chronologically disparate nature of the images but in the presence of the chronologically disparate being present.

The possibility of "quoting without quotation marks" is another formulation of Benjaminian destruction. A movement that as has already been noted involves blasting "the historical object . . . out of the historical process" (*N* 10, 3). Here, in opposition to either Cartesian destruction, which is the attempt to differentiate the present from itself in an absolute and all-encompassing manner, or Heideggerian sacrifice, in which the present ("metaphysics") is given away for a specific end (the thinking of being), Benjamin's "destruction" will necessitate the centrality of relation and with it of repetition. For Benjamin, destruction, it can be argued, is maintained by relation. Both the dialectical image and "now-time" are relations. And yet they are more than mere simple relations. In part, the departure from simplicity pertains to time and, in part, to repetition. It goes without saying that these two parts are related. Opting for the distinction within quotation—the absence and presence of marks as always signifying more than that which is given by the either/or of absence/presence—will capture these two interrelated parts. What has to be taken up, therefore, is quotation, to be understood as a form of repetition.

In its most general sense, to quote means to restate what has already been stated. Any citation, therefore, must also re-cite. And yet, with citation there is a convention; this is the presence of tradition. Apart from introducing the continuity of convention, the use of quotation marks works, conventionally, to mark the act of recitation and hence of what could be described as a re-situation. What the convention brings with it, in addition to itself, is a form of continuity. The quotation marks indicate that what is cited (and re-cited) is not new but is the reiteration of what has already been; an intended repetition of the Same in which the singularity of the past's content is itself maintained. (As will be indicated, it is Benjamin's description of the "historical object" having a monadological structure that will render this singularity impossible. It should be added that this is an impossibility derived from ontological considerations.) The absence and presence of quotation marks within a given narrative indicates the presence of different moments of historical time—chronological time—which are made present as continuous and thus as part of a more general continuity within narrative. Benjamin can be taken as addressing precisely this possibility—the effective presence of enforced continuity—at N 19, 1: "It could be that the continuity of tradition is only an appearance. But if this is the case, then it is precisely the persistence of this appearance of permanence that establishes continuity." The force of this description is that it gives to tradition the structure of narrative, namely a structure in which tradition is present as a continuous and therefore unfolding sequential temporality. It is in this sense that tradition incorporates progress, albeit its own progress. The intricacy of the link between tradition and progress is that their reciprocity provides further constitutive elements of Benjamin's construal of the epochal present. Here, both progress and tradition are themselves part of the necessary interarticulation of time and task.

The use of quotation marks sustains the continuity of tradition—its "permanence"—while allowing, as has been indicated, the intrusion of the discontinuous. It is, however, a discontinuity that is absorbed and, as such, becomes part of the "permanence." Another type of discontinuity—itself discontinuous with the type cited earlier—is present in "quoting without quotation marks." In this instance, the discontinuity is intended to endure. (It is thus that narrative and monadological structure are in a fundamental and effective opposition. Each will demand a different time and, with this different time, a different ontology, such that their difference is really only explicable in ontologico-temporal terms.) The absence of quotation marks signals the disruption of context. And yet, on its own the interplay of absence and disruption is far from sufficient as a description. The absence of quotation marks is not the only determination. Despite this absence, there is still a quotation and thus a form of presence. All that is missing is that which maintains the quotation as a quotation, namely the quotation marks. In this context, absence and presence are not mutually exclusive. What this means is that the contrast—the absent and present quotation marks, coupled to the continuity of quotation—is between two fundamentally different forms of repetition. What is emerging, therefore, is that, far from providing either a false path or the simply peripheral, repetition, though more significantly the an originally present divisions within repetition, can be taken as central to any understanding of Benjamin's construal of the task at the present, a construal that demands the recognition of the ineliminable presence of reciprocity. The centrality of repetition plus repetition's constitutive divisions will allow the larger problems raised by Benjamin's use of such terms as *apocatastasis* to be redressed with greater precision. The problems are inevitably linked to the unstated and therefore unacknowledged presence of repetition. What remains, however, is to set up the differing types of repetition and their enacted interrelation with time and the announced task (the site of the foreword). Enactment here is intended to mark out the ineliminable presence of the actative. Action will always be part of the present's weave.

Once thought beyond the purview of the Same, repetition opens up the possibility that what is given, repeated, is presented in such a way that its occurrence may be the result of a working through or a reworking that is itself no longer contained by the Same. What is given is given again. This re-giving is neither simple iteration nor a repetition of the Same. Work is the divide. The re-giving therefore needs to be thought as an iterative reworking. The process of reworking represents the given in such a way that other possibilities that are in some way already inscribed within and thus brought with it are, as a consequence of that work—and thus also as constitutive of the work—able to be revealed. It is this possibility that is based on the "monadological structure" of the "historical object." The affinity here is with Freud's conception of "working-through" (*Durcharbeiten*) and the way in which the temporal structure of *Nachträglichkeit* is incorporated as the temporality of "working-through." Perhaps the most important way of examining the prospects held open by iterative reworking (the other repetition) and the monad is by reintroducing the concept of the foreword and, with it, the relationship between foreword and repetition.

With Heidegger, the foreword presented that which could not be followed. This has to do with the language of metaphysics and the way in which experience in opposition, and thus in contradistinction to writing and language, functioned in his formulation and presentation of philosophical work. For Benjamin the problem of the foreword, while different, still raises problems touching on the possibility of the realization of the task demanded by it. In Benjamin's case, this will be linked to the nature of montage and with it to the possibility of methodological montage. Again, experience will play a pivotal role in any understanding of this complex set up. In both Heidegger and Benjamin, the present is to be differentiated from itself. In Heidegger's case this differentiation will be necessary since the present is taken to be metaphysics—the "age"—and therefore the task involves "leaving metaphysics to itself" and thus thinking "without" it. Here there is a differentiation that necessarily eschews relation. With Benjamin the differentiation occurs by an act of repetition, a repetition that can be thought and thus presented in a number of different ways: as "memoration," as "quotation," as "awakening," for example. In each instance there is a juxtaposition or constellation that breaks the effect of continuity.

If what has been identified as temporal montage, taken in conjunction with "quoting without quotation marks," and formulations of a similar nature are themselves all linked—a linkage that, in the end, will come undone for reasons both ontological and temporal—to the "dialectical image," then that constellation can be pursued in order that constitutive elements be taken both together and in their sundering. Of central importance here are the methodological components provided in the formulation of the image. The significance of this particular adventure is that it highlights the problem of the interplay of method and experience. "The dialectical image is a lightning flash. The Then must be held fast as it flashes its lightning image in the Now of recognisability. The rescue [*Die Rettung*] that is thus—and only thus—effected, can only take place for that which in the next moment is irretrievably lost" (*N* 9, 7). The epochal present for Benjamin comprises, therefore, the unfolding of a continuity that can be blown apart at any moment. Coupled to loss, the irretrievable loss, the flash of lightning harbors that residue of apocalyptic thinking that also inhabits the use of the term *apocatastasis*. The question is whether Benjamin is only an apocalyptic thinker. Answering the question necessitates attending to a divide in the work. To the extent that this conception of the "dialectical image" is retained, then there can be no text, no enacted writing, that follows from this "image" presented and thus serving as a foreword and thus not presented as itself. The apocalypse is not methodological. Not even the presentation of forced and enforced juxtapositions can rehearse the potential of "lightning." Irony is too strong to allow this rehearsal—the forced enforcement—to function unproblematically. On the other half of the divide, however—a divide in which the elements present in each half will always in here in the other—there is the potential inherent in the "historical object." Potential pertains to the ontology of the object. It goes without saying that the historical object and the dialectical image are not the same. The latter pertains emphatically to experience, while the first brings different ontological and temporal considerations to bear. It is the "monadological structure" that can be taken as allowing for the dialectical image and yet—this will be the point of greatest significance—it does not have to have that result. The monadological structure will allow, equally, for another repetition: repetition as iterative reworking. (Here repetition has come to be subjected to the process that it names.) This time it will be a repetition in which, to redeploy the same language, continuity has been "blasted" apart because of the presence of a quotation, which, while referring to its context and thus while bringing its context with it—a bringing to be thought as a reflection to be released—comes to be released at the present. Its release is, therefore, at the same time, an integral part of the present. This other repetition arises because of the ontology of the monad, Benjamin's monad.

Although there can be no foreword and thus no afterword to the apocalyptic, there can be nonetheless a foreword that incorporates and acts out the rescue and thus the redemption of repetition. With repetition, the present will always be characterized by the "differentia of time." It will be repetition that, while eschewing prediction, will give the present as the site that is given in being worked through. Benjamin's construal of the epochal present can, therefore, be taken as bearing on the present, bearing it. In sum, therefore, and returning to Benjamin's initial formulations, it is the "present" as that which "polarises the event into fore- and after-history" that becomes a site sanctioning its own constitution, though always as a further and furthering reconstitution, taking place and thus having a place through repetition. It is thus that the future is forbidden. This constitution, the act of constitution, not only introduces the primordiality of conflict, the flight from the homogeneous into the present, it allows at the same time the present—the present's potential—to stand apart from the homogeneous passage of time. There are two levels of destruction. Both are necessary if conflict is to be maintained and simultaneity sundered. Both enact the departure from the preestablished. It is the twofold nature of destruction that is announced in *N* 9a, 6. It is a destruction that is the province of historical materialism, the other name, for Benjamin, for the copresence of politics and time. "Historical materialism has to abandon the epic element in history. It blasts the epoch out of the reified "continuity of history." It also blasts open the homogeneity of the epoch. It saturates it with ecrasite, that is, the present [*Gegenwart*]. Even recognizing the intrinsic difficulties of its formulation the present—the epochal present—is the site of an action connected to experience.

What then of showing? Remembering, if only as a contrast, that Heidegger's showing pertained to the presence of that which had already happened; showing was linked to the already there. The refusal of the retroactive was intended to maintain that "originality." Its refusal can be understood, if only initially, as the attempt to rid the historical and experiential of that form of repetition identified by the term *Nachträglichkeit*. Having cited part of the section concerning showing (*N* 1a, 8), its complex mediation needs to be introduced. The extract is completed in the following way. "Only the trivia, the trash—which I do not want to inventory, but simply allow to come into its own the only way possible; by putting it to use." The reference to the marginal brings back not simply the allusion to archaeology and the need to investigate the castings but the whole—if the use of such a term is not here oxymoronic—of allegory (the whole being both the ontology as well as the temporality of allegory). At this stage, this is not the central point. Rather, it is the contrast between something obeying its own law "coming into its own" and being "put to work to use." The contrast here is stylistic. The opposition vanishes with the recognition that one is the other. The propriety of what is, is its being used. Showing is use. The doubling of showing, in showing, to which allusion was made above, is now affirmed. Showing cannot eliminate reworking and can never obviate the process of a retroactive and thus iterative reworking. The recognition of this ineliminable possibility will occasion another reworking of experience. The present is partial and intense because it is the site of repetition, the place continually structured by repetition as a working through, iterative reworking, and thus as the potential site of its disruptive continuity. In other words, the present maintains, by articulating, the structure of hope. This is Benjamin's potential. The "without"—the philosophy working with without—founders, yielding its place to the inevitability and ineliminability of the other repetition, as that which works the present.

Notes

The present chapter was originally published in Andrew Benjamin, *Present Hope: Philosophy, Architecture, Judaism* (London: Routledge, 1999). It is reprinted here with permission from the publisher.

1. The importance attributed here to writing is not intended to rehearse the issues involved in authorship. Nor, moreover, is it envisaged as raising generic problems: the relationship between philosophy and literature, for example. Here, writing attests to the necessarily textual nature of philosophy's presentation. Writing is, therefore, the site where the task—the philosophical task—is announced.
2. Here, "Konvolut N" of Benjamin's *Das Passagen-Werk* and Heidegger's "Time and Being" are, for reasons advanced at a later stage, attributed the status of forewords. See also Heidegger, *TB*.
3. Part of the weight is the recognition that within these passages from "Konvolut N" "the present" even, while not made specific, nonetheless marks out and therefore incorporates the site of the task's enactment. Given that the project here involves thinking through the ontology of the present, the present itself has, in virtue of that project, a double burden.
4. In the end, what experience will demand is to be rethought in terms of the problem of agency. What this involves is a rethinking that arises out of the

impossibility of singularity, even a complex singularity, of agency. Although it is a problem of considerable intricacy, it is still possible to argue in general terms that another limit within the work of Benjamin and Heidegger concerns agency. With Heidegger, it is the retention of the necessary singularity of the agent, while for Benjamin it will emerge as the inability to account in his terms for the agency of "dialectical experience."

5. Although it cannot be pursued here, it is worth noting that Heidegger's emphasis on experience is presented most systematically in the opening of "The Nature of Language."
6. I have pursued in greater detail the interpretative problems opened up by this "without" in Andrew Benjamin, *The Plural Event* (London: Routledge, 1993), 140–157.
7. Although the projects are different, the discussion of reconciliation presented here has been greatly influenced by Rebecca Comay's remarkable paper, "Redeeming Revenge: Nietzsche, Benjamin, Heidegger and the Politics of Memory," in *Nietzsche as Postmodernist*, ed. C. Koelb (Albany, NY: State University of New York Press, 1990).
8. For a more sustained treatment of *Nachträglichkeit* within psychoanalysis, see the recent collection of papers by and about Jean Laplanche, edited by J. Fletcher and M. Stanton, *Jean Laplanche: Seduction, Translation, Drives* (London: ICA, 1992).
9. The reference here is to Benjamin (*SW* 4: 397/ *GS* 2, 703). Although the passage warrants a detailed analysis, it is nonetheless essential to note the way in which the question of time—to be understood as the question of the present of historical time—is, within it, reposed away from a simple gesture toward the future:

> The soothsayers who queried time and learned what it had in store certainly did not experience it as either homogeneous or empty. Whoever keeps this in mind will perhaps get an idea of how past times were experienced in remembrance—namely, in just this way. We know that the Jews were prohibited from inquiring into the future: the Torah and the prayers instructed them in remembrance. This disenchanted the future, which holds sway over all those who turn to soothsayers for enlightenment. This does not imply, however, that for the Jews the future became homogeneous, empty time. For every second was the small gateway in time through which the Messiah might enter.

10. Tradition may seem to admit plurality, that is, it may seem that there are many traditions. And yet, any such description misses the role of power within tradition. There is a dominant tradition. Its unfolding is construed as the site of continuity, the continuity of certain power relations. Blasting it apart, therefore, is more than the simple critique of a posited singularity.
11. See in particular H. D .Kittsteiner, "Walter Benjamin's Historicism," *New German Critique* 39 (Fall 1986).
12. References to Leibniz are to P. Janet, ed., *Oeuvres Philosophiques de Leibniz*, vol. II (Paris, 1866). The English edition of *Monadology* used is that edited and translated by E. Latta as *Leibniz's Monadology* (Oxford: Oxford University Press, 1972).
13. Leibniz, *Monadology*, 65.
14. Ibid., 60.
15. Leibniz, *Oeuvres*, vol. II, 608.
16. The position under attack is brought out in Benjamin's quotation of Grillparzer:

> To contrast the theory of history with Grillparzer's comment, translated by Edmond Jaloux in "Journaux intimes" (Le Temps, 23 [Mai 1937]): "To read into the future is difficult, but to see purely into the past is even more so; I say purely which is to say without mixing that retrospective gaze with everything that has happened in the meantime." The "purity" of the gaze is not so much difficult as impossible to attain. (*N* 7, 5)

The impossibility in question is not explicable in terms of the historian's failure. In other words, the point being made does not concern the ability or inability of the historian to complete a specific task. Furthermore, various historians and philosophers will always claim to have achieved the "gaze" that Benjamin is describing here as impossible. The reason for this impossibility has, in part, to do with the ontology of the "historical object" and, in part, with the way memory works both to inform and construct the present.
17. The substantive methodological point here is that any presentation of works—even if these were accompanied by written text—which oriented itself around the juxtaposition of images, drawings and photographs, in the belief that this illuminated Benjamin's project, would have taken the references to montage far too literally. As such, it would miss what is essential to montage, namely time.

PART IV

Hölderlin

SEVEN

WHO WAS FRIEDRICH HÖLDERLIN?

Walter Benjamin, Martin Heidegger, and the Poet

Antonia Egel

For H. G. –just dwelling

When Benjamin and Heidegger write about Hölderlin, they both write about *the poet* as a concept far more than about a single, very special and individual personality, who as a human being wrote what we regard as Hölderlin's poetry. The question, "who was Friedrich Hölderlin?" appears naive in comparison. One then asks about the biography of the man who was meant to become a protestant priest but fled his school instead in order to gain the world. Out there he met the unhappy love of his life and out there, probably on his way back from the French Atlantic coast, he lost what other people called his mental health.[1] For many romantic intellectuals, to which group Heidegger belongs,[2] it was this latter biographical detail, which attracted them, and which they glorified (cf. *HP*: 59/ *GA* 4: 42).[3] Besides this, Heidegger seems to be especially interested in Hölderlin's travels, to which he often refers at the beginning of his interpretations. As a result, Heidegger mainly interprets Hölderlin's poems on movement.

Ultimately the question "Who was Friedrich Hölderlin?" asks about what Hölderlin wrote. Biographical details are of no interest, unless they assist with the interpretation of the poems. "Who was Friedrich Hölderlin?" then means to ask about the poems written by Hölderlin. Isn't that exactly what both Benjamin and Heidegger did? Yes, and both tell us a lot about Hölderlin's poetry. And both at the same time show something else. They show that the interpretation of poetry has its own preconditions, just like the production of poetry itself: historically, personally, politically. To write about two interpretations of great poetry by two great thinkers is, then, an attempt to understand what both understood; to ask whether their interpretations are convincing; to see where interpretation ends and where philosophical conceptions independently from interpretation take over; to see how these conceptions are rooted in their times and philosophies. At the end, it means to interpret two interpretations. How, if not in going back to the object that was interpreted, is it possible to clarify these interpretations? And that, in the end, means to ask which Hölderlin is to be found in Benjamin's and Heidegger's interpretations and to what extent is this Hölderlin, we—and that in this case only can be I myself—find in reading Hölderlin's poetry today with our—mine—own preconceptions. Admitting this, is not meant to be a justification of subjective reading, but to describe a hermeneutic operation.

In comparing Benjamin's essay on Hölderlin to Heidegger's thinking about Hölderlin, which he articulated in several different long lectures, one faces certain difficulties: Both deal with different poems. Both interpret Hölderlin's poetry at different points in their lives and thinking. And yet, there are similarities and comparable aspects, both in the motivation to integrate Hölderlin's poetry into their thinking and also in the way they understand it. And at the same time there are unbridgeable differences between both interpreters. So, the leading question in the following is: What is it that helps us understand Hölderlin better in comparing both Benjamin's and Heidegger's interpretations? I will compare Benjamin's essay "Two Poems by Friedrich Hölderlin: 'The Poet's Courage' and 'Timidity'" [*Zwei Gedichte von Friedrich Hölderlin. "Dichtermut"-"Blödigkeit"*] (*SW* 1: 18–36/ *GS* 2: 105–126) with one of Heidegger's lectures, namely "Homecoming/ To Kindred Ones" [*Heimkunft/ An die Verwandten*] (*HP*: 23–49/ *GA* 4: 9–31), because the motives in these interpretations exhibit the similarities and differences I noted earlier.

Benjamin

"The Poet's Courage" and "Timidity" are two poems that deal with the poet's place in the world. Walter Benjamin wrote about them at a young age—if thinkers do have an age at all—and in a special—both historically and personally—situation. What later became World War I had just broken out and caused Benjamin's pacifistic friends Fritz Heinle and Rika Seligson to commit suicide.[4] With Hölderlin in hand, Benjamin wrote a text meant to be read by few fellow Georgians (cf. *GS* 2: 921–922) and asked himself these crucial questions: Where in this hellish world is the poet's place? And, how could Heinle and Seligson could have survived a little longer?

This biographical motive for Benjamin's early essay on Hölderlin could seem illegitimate. But bringing biography into play here is on purpose, because Benjamin's reflections on Hölderlin mirror it, especially in those parts that seem to be most abstract. A shocking experience in his life made Benjamin write about two of Hölderlin's poems. Maybe, experiencing a groundless situation in his life, Benjamin felt grounded with Hölderlin; maybe he found in Hölderlin a comrade questioner; maybe he was consoled by poetry, maybe disturbed, who knows—to decide, we have to turn to the text closely.

Benjamin concludes his essay by saying that the poem "Timidity" aimed at overcoming the Greek elements of "The Poet's Courage" with an "oriental element," which consisted in the images, the ideas and the "new meaning of death" in this poem (SW 1: 35/ GS 2: 126). What, specifically is this new meaning of death?

Benjamin calls "Timidity" a "detailed, special treatment of dying [*ausführliche Sondergestaltung des Sterbens*]" (SW 1: 33/ GS 2: 122). How, then, is this special treatment of death to be thought? Creating poetry itself is understood as dying. In "The Poet's Courage" the poet's death is, says Benjamin, the poem's center, from which the world of "poetic dying [*dichterisches Sterben*]" (SW 1: 22/ GS 2: 109) emerges. Simultaneously, Benjamin emphasizes that poetry originates from life (SW 1: 19–20/ GS 2: 107). To understand the new meaning of death then means to understand how life and death are connected. This makes Benjamin think and write about the "poetized [*das Gedichtete*]" as space. He calls it a sphere or realm, which is so wide that the "living [*die Lebendigen*]," gods and—think!—even poets can dwell together (SW 1: 25–26 and 27/ GS 2: 113 and 115). The connection of life and death in the poetized makes life and death, there, in the realm of poetry, indistinguishable, even identical. This leads Benjamin to write of the living on the one hand and the poets (and not the dead) on the other.

Benjamin tries to show that "The Poet's Courage" as a poem dealing with the poet's ability to die in a stoic way is only the first step in a development that leads to "Timidity," where the poet's death is no longer performed or sung of, but is just there, as the object, which is the poetized. In "Timidity" the one realm where death, life, heaven, and earth are no longer distinguished is realized as a spiritual realm in a distinguished objective form. The poem then is the place for those left behind: the poem's spatiality provides room, in which the living can stroll around (cf. SW 1: 27/ GS 2: 115). In providing this space, it is an "almost wholly new figuration of the most concrete life [*eine fast Neugestalt des konkretesten Lebens*], the innermost essence of the poet (as his limit with respect to existence) [*(das) innerste Wesen (des) Sängers (als) Grenze gegen das Dasein*]" (SW 1: 27–28/ GS 2: 115).

If the poet's death is the center of "The Poet's Courage," in "Timidity" this center shows itself as space in which there is room:[5] "center and extension [*Mitte *und Erstreckung]*" "in one form" (*SW* 1: 28/ *GS* 2: 116). And this is not another world, even not a spiritual sphere, barely to grasp, but "the sensory order of sound [*die sinnliche Ordnung des Klanges*]" (*SW* 1: 29/ *GS* 2: 117). The poem in its materialness is "'rhymed for joy [*Sei zur Freude gereimt*]'" (*SW* 1: 29/ *GS* 2: 117).

And Friedrich Hölderlin is the one who made it? No, says Benjamin, because no "individual" causes poetry (*SW* 1: 35/ *GS* 2: 126) but the life of the poem is autonomous and anonymous in itself. And furthermore, the poem's objectivity is carried by the living [*Lebendigen*] (*SW* 1: 29/ *GS* 2: 117). In interpreting Hölderlin's poem, Benjamin contemplates this eternal piece of poetry and thus renders it to the living human beings, to those who stay on earth. At the same time he connects himself for all times with his gone friends who will live in their poetry, if that is contemplated by those who are alive. Benjamin, as the performing, mourning contemplator, shows himself between the earth and humankind. Just in that sense he presents a final quotation from Hölderlin: "'Myths, which take leave of the earth,/ . . . they return to mankind [*Die Sagen, die der Erde sich entfernen, / . . . / sie kehren zu der Menschheit sich*]'" (*SW* 1: 36/ *GS* 2: 126).

Heidegger

Just like Benjamin, it was a shocking experience—albeit of a very different kind—that made Martin Heidegger to turn to Hölderlin's poetry. In a both historically and personally extraordinary situation, Heidegger started to cling to Hölderlin's poems attempting to see a deeper sense in the deadly senseless historical events of the early 1930s—events that not only engulfed him but of which he was a part. Germans had voted for Hitler, Heidegger had been at the very core of this regime's early strategy to gain ground everywhere, for instance at universities, but gave up as a rector of Freiburg's university after a few months.[6] During his time as a rector he did execute the regime's politics (cf. *GA* 16) and he must have known at the time that he was part of a system that forced thousands of people to leave the country. Many of Heidegger's dear friends and many of his students, some of them beloved ones, flew, and he knew about it. Clinging onto Hölderlin in that situation is, I want to show, both the repellent attempt to justify the historical situation as the fateful way toward the destiny of a "people," which he wanted to root in Hölderlin as its foundation, and at the same time the attempt to overcome the loss of many close friends and to flee from politics into the realm of poetry.

Heidegger indicates this in a subtle way, when he exposes his reading of Hölderlin with significant quotations. To create poetry, he argues, with some of Hölderlin's lines is "'the most innocent of all occupations'" (*HP*: 51/ *GA* 4: 33) that handles with "'the most dangerous of goods'" (*HP*: 51/ *GA* 4: 33), namely, human language. Poetry has to create precisely the danger that it is to be overcome with poetry. Creating poetry is a "play" and a "dream" (*HP*: 53/ *GA* 4: 35) with no effect. It is, in other words, no deed in the political world. But at the same time, this innocent and harmless doing has a "realm of power [*Machtbereich*]" (*GA* 4: 34)[7]; what Heidegger aims at is to convince those who listen to him to put themselves under this "realm of power of poetry [*Machtbereich der Dichtung*]" in a decisive way (*GA* 4: 34–35). What can be the aim of such subordination? Is it politics or freedom beyond politics? Does emphasis lie on the "realm of power" or on "poetry"? To understand Heidegger's approach to Hölderlin, one has to keep open this ambivalence.

Strangely enough, Benjamin and Heidegger have different motivations to turn to Hölderlin's poems and at the same time in both cases death and devastation are central. And it is even stranger that there are striking similarities in both interpretations. Both interpreters share Norbert von Hellingrath's and Stefan George's views on Hölderlin.[8] But still there must have been a common ground, which reaches farther. And, no doubt, there are also striking differences.

Whereas Benjamin engages with two poems on the poet's *place in* the world, Heidegger deals in his many essays and lectures about Hölderlin more with the poet's *way through* the world (from an origin or a river's source to its mouth, or from the god's realm to the earth, from the mountain to the valley, from the strange to the homely, or from orient to occident). Those of Hölderlin's poems that Heidegger chose to interpret are mostly poems about time and movement, such as "Heimkunft," "Ister," "Germanien/Der Rhein," "Die Wanderung," whereas Benjamin, as shown above interprets the two chosen poems spatially.

And yet, there is also Heidegger's need for a place: "'Reluctantly/ that which dwells near its origin departs [*schwer verlässt/, was nahe dem Ursprung wohnet, den Ort*]'" (*PLT*: 76/ *GA* 5: 66)—this line is only one example of this need. In his interpretation of the poem "Die Wanderung," for instance, Heidegger emphasizes both being and staying, going away and coming back. The world is showing itself as space in that poem. And like Benjamin, Heidegger writes about the poetized as a field [*Feld*] and realm [*Bereich*] (*HP*: 53–54/ *GA* 4: 35), not to mention that the notion of dwelling is profoundly important to Heidegger's reading of Hölderlin. To ask what exactly it means to dwell poetically however leads, again, to a different notion of space and dwelling in the two thinkers. The aspects of time in Heidegger, on the one hand, and that of space in Benjamin, on the other, are to be distinguished, but at the same time there are overlapping contours of both aspects, which are to be shown in the following.

First, let us take a close look at one of Heidegger's interpretations. "Homecoming/ To Kindred Ones" is a poem about coming home—despite the fact that

Heidegger thinks it was a poem that *is* "the homecoming itself" more than being one *about* "homecoming" (*HP*: 44/ *GA* 4: 25). But exactly that distinction tells us a lot about Heidegger's reading of the poem. For Heidegger, the poem *is* coming home. Here, in reading the poem, Heidegger seems to feel at home, to dwell in letters. Has he found the poet's place that also Benjamin was looking for? How is it to be understood to dwell in letters? What Heidegger regards as coming home is an endless coming and never being there. In that sense, dwelling has always to be and never is already realized. Therefore he calls the poem a "'workshop' of what is rather unhomelike ['*Werkstatt' des Unheimischen*]" (*HP*: 32/ *GA* 4: 13) and emphasizes the poem's notion of the "'reserved [*gespart*]'" (*HP*: 43/ *GA* 4: 24): what is to reach or to happen is never already there. For Heidegger, there has to be an abyss within and toward poetry, because poetry is an origin for his thinking,[9] so the never being there is to maintain the origin longed for (see *HP*: 43–44/ *GA* 4: 25).

To read the poem in such a way allows Heidegger to emphasize the historicity of that event, which is poetry. Because something historically is to come with or for those who read or listen to Hölderlin's poetry, such poetry always has to be fluid, performing history. How does this happen? Heidegger thinks that it happened through the poetized. The poetized, one could argue, is something like a content of the poem.[10] But Heidegger shows that he gains his interpretation directly from the text's surface and not from something represented by it. The ambivalent line "and the cloud,/ Thickening joyfulness" (my translation) or "and the cloud,/ Composing poems full of joy [*und die Wolke,/ Freudiges dichtend*]" (*HP*: 25) is taken for granted only in one way (and, as I would argue, also misread, because the cloud is just taking away light from the lit valley and only in a second step maybe is to be connected with the creation of poetry).[11] Because the cloud is the subject of "dichten," Heidegger identifies the poetized with "Joyfulness [*das Freudige*]." At the same time the poetized is "tuned by joy into joy [*aus der Freude in diese gestimmt*]," and it is "what is rejoiced in [*das Erfreute*]," as well as "what rejoices [*das Sichfreuende*]" and that what "brings joy [*anderes erfreuend*]" (*HP*: 34/ *GA* 4: 15). The poetized is, in other words, autonomous. Or, almost, because it can only appear autonomous, because something else, the open, was adding itself to it.

And is Hölderlin the one who did it? No, it was the cloud. The poem, like the cloud described in the poem, Heidegger tells us, has opened itself toward the clearing above itself from where the joy, which in the end is the poetized, comes into the poem. This metaphysical (yes!) conception of the creation of poetry lies, says Heidegger, only in the poem itself; but there it lies, because the poem itself encloses the openness from where it also has its source. This is like the danger that is opened only through the poem only to be overcome by the poem. The poem, then, is a world in its own right.

In this respect Heidegger's interpretation is not that different from Benjamin's. But it is very different in its conclusion. Heidegger also calls forth mourning. The joy, which is the "poetized," he writes, is a "mourning joy [*trauernde Freude*]" (*HP*: 45/ *GA* 4: 27). This still could be interpreted as the poem that carries its own possible danger in itself. But there is a rather strange conclusion that leads Heidegger to identify the homeland's sons, the dying or almost dying soldiers, as the poet's relatives (*HP*: 48–49/ *GA* 4: 29–30). So every single dying individual who would have thought about Hölderlin before death would die like a poet—in a poem? This historical reduction is, I think, the attempt to give some consolation to people listening to Heidegger's lecture and at the same time worrying or even mourning about their sons at the front.

But at the same time, it is something different. Heidegger seemed to think about Hölderlin's poetry as an alternative to the political. He thought that Hölderlin would lead people to some sort of new and different dwelling in the world. But, where could this world be? Is the poet's place in the world—the poem—a place for all? Despite the fact that Heidegger scandalously thinks of Hölderlin's poetry as a place for Germans only, the question is: Which world could this be where people could dwell poetically, and this in a historical sense?

Heidegger starts his essay on "Homecoming" by stating that the homecoming is enclosed by a "mountain range consisting of verses [*ein Gebirge von Versen*]," which illustrate the "Alpine mountains" on one side (which is the first stanza) and the word "'not [*nicht*]'" (*HP*: 32/ *GA* 4: 13) on the other (which is the last stanza). In Heidegger's interpretation, homecoming, as this poem performs it, is a dwelling between the alpine mountains and the nothing. It is a dwelling above or even in the abyss. So the poem as a world could have been a flight from the historical world into the aesthetical. For Benjamin, the realm of poetry provides exactly this: the shelter for those who have no place in the world. Poetry, then, would be a separate world untouched by history. For Heidegger it seems to be similar to a certain degree, but in the end, Hölderlin really has to be the founder of a new historical world. How much this was accepted is shown by a reaction to one of Heidegger's Hölderlin-lectures by the painter Julius Bissier, who wrote to his friend Oskar Schlemmer about Paul Klee as the founding father of modern painting and adds: "He was a Hölderlin [*Er war ein Hölderlin*]."[12] Hölderlin here is not a *pars pro toto* for the poets but rather for those who found a really new "world." As long as the aesthetical is concerned, such foundation might be possible, but applied to politics and history and thus transferred to the concept of leadership, such thinking ended in catastrophe.

To think of poetry as of a world in its own right means to think of poetry spatially, like Benjamin did. But then, time is overruled and the space of poetry is one in space as such. To think of that space timely and so historically, like Heidegger did, is rather absurd: where and when should that special world be?

Comparison

A closer, comparative look on the autonomous realm of poetry may be helpful to clarify this. Benjamin defines "poetized" as "a limit-concept [*Grenzbegriff*]" (*SW* 1: 19/ *GS* 2: 106) toward the poem. There is a fine line drawn between the poem as an object and its inner structure, the poetized—like a stone at its edge has a line that separates it from the air, but more like the silver lining of a cloud that is just a little more water in the air than the surrounding air contains. So the poetized as a world is not very solid and at the same time very impermeable.

Benjamin writes about this world: "It is difficult to gain any kind of access to this fully unified, unique world [*Schwer ist es, einen möglichen Zugang zu dieser völlig einheitlichen und einzigen Welt zu gewinnen*]" (*SW* 1: 24/ *GS* 2: 111). And Heidegger seems to confirm this in citing from "Die Wanderung": "difficult to win, what is self-reserved [*schwer zu gewinnen, die Verschlossene*]" (*HP*: 32/ *GA* 4: 13).

Heidegger's famous conclusion of *The Origin of the Work of Art* then speaks from the other side: "'Reluctantly/ that which dwells near its origin departs [*schwer verlässt/, was nahe dem Ursprung wohnet, den Ort*]'" (*PLT*: 76/ *GA* 5: 66). Again, similarity and difference lie extremely close in both interpretations. Heidegger and Benjamin both write about a realm difficult to gain. Whereas Benjamin makes clear that this realm is an aesthetical one, Heidegger interprets the origin as "homeland [*Heimat*]" (*HP*: 32 and 48–49/ *GA* 4: 13 and 29–30) in a literal sense. Coming home is going back to the realm of childhood and finding it as closed. But exactly this closure is the condition thought paradoxically of being near the origin, which is tantamount to dwelling poetically, because the condition of the latter is precisely the not being there but only being near.

Whereas Heidegger thinks of this origin literally and even historically, Benjamin does so aesthetically. For Benjamin the poem's realm is a "hermeneutical space"[13]: "the particular and unique sphere in which the task and precondition of the poem lie will be addressed. This sphere is at once the product and the subject of this investigation. It itself can no longer be compared with the poem; it is, rather, the sole thing in this investigation that can be ascertained. This sphere, which for every poem has a special configuration, is characterized as the poetized" (*SW* 1: 18/ *GS* 2: 105).[14]

This realm is also described as "world [*Welt*]," a "domain [*Bezirk*]," and "'truth [*Wahrheit*]'" (*SW* 1: 18–19/ *GS* 2: 105). Benjamin marks the latter as weak or even wrong, because he wants to argue that the poem is not representing any truth, but rather is "the objectivity of their [the artist's] production, as the fulfillment of the artistic task in each case [*die Gegenständlichkeit ihres (der Künstler) Schaffen, als die Erfüllung der jeweiligen künstlerischen Aufgabe*]" (*SW* 1: 19/ *GS* 2: 105). The poem is likely to cause revolution in this, the objective world of the poem, which can only be described aesthetically. The poem is "a perceptual-intellectual order, the new cosmos of the poet [*die anschaulich-geistige Ordnung, der neue Kosmos des Dichters*]" (*SW* 1: 24/ *GS* 2: 111) and a "new order of poetic figures [*neue Ordnung der dichterischen Gestalten*]" (*SW* 1: 25/ *GS* 2: 113). But, unlike Heidegger, Benjamin thinks of that revolution in aesthetical terms only. What is at stake in Benjamin is not a new historical world, or a destiny of a people but a new poetical shape, a new *poetical* cosmos.[15]

Hölderlin

What about Hölderlin? Did he provide a new world, a real realm, or a guideline to "new" politics? Hölderlin speaks about politics in his poems and also about homeland and about war and peace, battles and gods and angels and nature. And in doing so, Hölderlin speaks about himself all the time. He, as a poet, had to find his place in the world—between heaven and earth, amidst people who gave advice to avoid things such as singing about beauty, amidst people that were bound to social restrictions and wanted him to be so, too. Hölderlin, like every poet, had to come to terms with "inspiration," that is, with nature, gods, angels, with beauty that made him sing, despite manmade horrors. This poetical world is a special world to live in indeed. But it is a self-referring world in its own right, which cannot be taken to do justice to any ideological understanding of history or politics.

Not much is gained in saying this; rather we have to examine how far we are able to follow Heidegger's and Benjamin's interpretations as plausible interpretations of Hölderlin's poetry and where there is a limit, especially in Heidegger, to follow.

Heidegger's essay on "Homecoming" ends with a quotation from "The Poet's Vocation" to emphasize that poets imagine contemplators, who are supposed to help us understand what the poets are doing (*HP*: 49/ *GA* 4: 31). In many passages of Heidegger's essay he does help us understand Hölderlin's poetry and, mostly indicated by a logical gap in his argument, suddenly for the reader of his interpretation there is nothing understandable at all. In Heidegger's argument the strange conclusion is that Hölderlin helps people at war dying. And at the same time he cites the pacifistic lines of "The Poet's Vocation": the poet who dares to be what he or she is, needs neither weapons nor cunning, but is what he or she is (*HP*: 47/ *GA* 4: 28). This attitude is called "simplicity [*Einfalt*]" in "The Poet's Vocation," which is in some respects similar to the word *timidity*, the title of one of the poems Benjamin wrote about. Hölderlin writes about the poet in that sense as about someone—whom others could call naive—who is not able to take his or her place in the world like everyone else, but who is unarmed and bold and therefore in conversation with (even lacking) gods.

This radicalness—Hölderlin describes himself sometimes as part of nature, indistinguishable from a tree or a flower—must have been something Heidegger also wanted to show, when he took up exactly this poem at the end of his essay. What would that have meant, if the conclusion of the essay, which is irritating massive, were not there?

If so, the essay would end with a description of the poet as someone "alone before god," unarmed and still without fear, waiting for the help of the gods who are not there. That could be understood as a flight from the surrounding political world, a stoic retreat. I would understand also the last line of "Homecoming" in the same sense. Here the poetical "I" separates itself from "the others." The poet bears sorrows that only he or she has to bear, which is how to sing about what she or he experiences, sorrows that are relevant to poets only. And even if one interprets the sentence in its second sense, which would be to understand it in such a way that the poet has to bear only sorrows that deal with the question of how to sing adequately, and not such sorrows as how to get food, clothing and so on, sorrows that everyone else has to deal with, even then, Hölderlin would have shown a deep gap between the poet and his poem and the rest of the world.

Exactly this, for Heidegger, is the starting point to assert, without further explanation, that the others have to listen to Hölderlin. Because there is no bridge between the others and the poet, there is something to listen to. It may be plausible for a philosopher who reads poetry in order to stand on solid ground—for a philosopher who is, as a philosopher, a reader in an emphatic sense—to step back from "the world" and to think about it slowly and "thoughtfully [*bedachtsam*]" (*HP*: 48/ *GA* 4: 29). But the same is by no means plausible as a collective, historical founding for one specific people and even less in order to justify the dead soldiers as sacrifice to that absurd history (*HP*: 48–49/ *GA* 4: 29–30).

Benjamin also writes about a distance, but this distance is not an unbridgeable gap. He emphasizes the distance between life as the ground of poetry and poetry but at the same time he conceives the poetized as a "transition [*Übergang*]" (*SW* 1: 19/ *GS* 2: 107) between both. For Benjamin, the poetized in that sense connects the poet and the others, which are called the "related [*verwandt*]" in "Timidity" and "The Poet's Courage." Whereas "Homecoming" indeed shows the difference between the poet and the others, "The Poet's Courage" and "Timidity" emphasize the relatedness of the poet and the living. Whereas Heidegger tries to make the relatives of the poet those who die in the name of a certain politics, Benjamin emphasizes the connection between the poets and the living.

Hölderlin himself did both: he wrote about the connection and the separation with the others and, in the case of "Homecoming," which starts with a whole stanza of oxymora, both is meant in one poem. He must have known about coming home with a whole gamut of experiences he could not tell to anyone, so he chose to tell them to everyone. And there he is, in his poems only, as "duration [*Dauer*]" (*SW* 1: 31/ *GS* 2: 119), or as Benjamin puts it, as a "moment of inner temporal plasticity [*Moment innerer Plastik in der Zeit*]" (*SW* 1: 31/ *GS* 2: 120). As one of those who dared "To give oneself form—that is the definition of 'hubris' [*Sich selbst Gestalt geben, das heißt 'hybris'*]" (*SW* 1: 32/ *GS* 2: 121). And, thank god, some do so.

Notes

I am grateful to Andrew Benjamin and Dimitris Vardoulakis for their meticulous and helpful revision of the text.

1. Cf. Thomas Knubben, *Hölderlin. Eine Winterreise* (Tübingen: Klöpfer und Meyer, 2011), 9–17.
2. See Hannah Arendt, *What Is Existential Philosophy?*, in *Essays in Understanding*, ed. Jerome Kohn (New York: Harcourt, 1996), 163–187, p. 187.
3. Heidegger does refer to Hölderlin's illness, but differently than others (see Shane Weller, "Literature and the Politics of Madness: On the Twentieth Century Reception of Friedrich Hölderlin in France and Germany," in *Comparative Critical Studies* 5, 2–3 (2008), 193–206, p. 195: "Heidegger's commentaries on Hölderlin are notable not least for their dismissal of the question of madness and its possible relation to the work"). Heidegger addresses "the night of madness [*die Nacht des Wahnsinns*]" as "protection [*Schutz*]" or shelter (*HP*: 59/ *GA* 4: 42). In such expressions, Heidegger's attempt to flee from politics in turning to Hölderlin is evident. But this is only one side of Heidegger's Hölderlin.
4. Cf. *GS* 2: 921 and Willem van Reijen, *Der Schwarzwald und Paris: Heidegger und Benjamin* (Munich: Fink, 1998), 155.
5. The distinction between "space," "space as such," and "room" derives from an ongoing conversation that I have with Günter Figal about his work in progress on space.
6. Cf. "Chronology of Heidegger's Life," in Günter Figal, ed., *The Heidegger*

Reader, trans. Jerome Veith (Bloomington, IN: Indiana University Press, 2009), 334–340.
7. Keith Hoeller translates "Machtbereich" as "sphere of influence" (*HP*: 52). That neglects the political implication of the German "Macht" (power).
8. See the most illuminating dissertation: Sara Jean Ogger, *Secret Hölderlin: The Twentieth-Century Myth of the Poet as Authored by the George Circle, Walter Benjamin, and Martin Heidegger*. Department of Germanic Languages and Literatures at Princeton University. (Ann Arbor: UMI Dissertation Services, 2000).
9. Cf. Antonia Egel, "Das 'eigene Mäh' der Kunst. Zu den literarischen Quellen," in David Espinet and Tobias Keiling, eds., *Heideggers* Ursprung des Kunstwerks: *Ein kooperativer Kommentar* (Frankfurt: Vittorio Klostermann, 2011), 186–199, esp. 194.
10. So does Nikola Mirkovic, "Heidegger und Hölderlin: Eine Spurensuche," in Espinet and Keiling, eds., *Heideggers* Ursprung des Kunstwerks, 174–185, esp. 176.
11. Hoeller's translation of "dichten" as "composing poems" is already a Heideggerian interpretation of Hölderlin's poem; The German "dichten" is, especially in respect to the mentioned image of a cloud, also possibly translated as something like bringing density to the sky (cf. "verdichten," especially used in meteorological contexts), maybe to be translated as "to thicken" or even "to tighten."
12. Julius Bissier to Oskar Schlemmer, 13. 07. 1940, in Julius Bissier and Oskar Schlemmer, *Briefwechsel*, ed. Matthias Bärmann (St. Gallen: Erker, 1988), 49.
13. Cf. Günter Figal, *Objectivity: The Hermeneutical and Philosophy*, trans. Theodore D. George (Albany, NY: State University of New York Press, 2010), 121–153, esp. 138–139.
14. Cf. Günter Figal, *Erscheinungsdinge: Ästhetik als Phänomenologie* (Tübingen: Mohr Siebeck, 2010), 155–156.
15. Cf. Donatella Di Cesare, "Memory, Language, Feast. Benjamin's Revolutionary Judaism," *Naharaim* 6.2 (2012), 208–246, esp. 209.

EIGHT

SOBRIETY, INTOXICATION, HYPERBOLOGY

Benjamin and Heidegger Reading Hölderlin

Joanna Hodge

"Hölderlin's translations in particular are subject to the enormous danger inherent in all translations: the gates of a language thus expanded and modified may slam shut and enclose the translator in silence. Hölderlin's translations from Sophocles were his last work; in them meaning plunges from abyss to abyss until it threatens to become lost in the bottomless depths of language" (Benjamin, SW 1: 262).

This minatory citation concerning the dangers of translation is drawn from Walter Benjamin's essay "The Task of the Translator," written in 1921, in which Benjamin introduces his discussion of translatability. This notion of a modal potentiation, as distinctive of Benjamin's writings and inquiries, is the focus for the study by Samuel Weber, *Benjamin's -abilities* (2008), which, in its title, neatly marks up the displacement in Benjamin's inquiries of the Kantian faculties, sense, understanding, reason, judgment, by a proliferation of capacities, and potentialities, in process of formation, rather than given in a set of fixed relations one to another. Instantiation of these capacities are conditional on certain states of affairs and developments in the world, but require for their actualization the development of a distinctive mode and practice of thinking, and writing, that of Walter Benjamin, which itself must always be a process of transmission, and not a completed fact. Weber identifies a pull between Benjamin's preoccupation with tracing out a movement of language as signification, on the one hand, and, on the other, the patient attention to text as repository of an anterior meaning, to be retrieved and redistributed in translation. Weber marks up the manner in which "each self-contained unit of meaning is always exceeded by the way it is meant," going on to cite a passage immediately preceding the passage cited above from "The Task of the Translator."[1] Weber marks up how in the early essay on Hölderlin, "Two poems by Friedrich Hölderlin" (1914–1915), to which this essay will return, Benjamin introduces Kant's notion of determinability (*Bestimmbarkeit*), which then forms a model for marking up these other potentialities. Weber analyzes a contrast between a precarious "now" of knowability (*Erkennbarkeit*) as giving way in Benjamin's inquiries to a meditative, temporally protracted process of readability (p. 19). This contrast between an instant of recognition, or knowability, and a drawn-out and potentially incompletable meditation on meaning is one that draws attention to differential modalities of time and differential modalities of meaning.

These differential modalities of time and of meaning are in dispute between Benjamin and Heidegger who, in their contrasting readings of Hölderlin, develop contrasting accounts of the need to rethink modality, as a rethinking of time and of meaning. In this chapter, a contrast is developed between the sobriety of Hölderlin's writing, as underlined by Benjamin, and the intoxication of a return to the Greeks, attended to by Heidegger, for whom Hölderlin is closer to the Nietzsche of *The Birth of Tragedy*, than to the Nietzsche of incipient collapse marked up in *Ecce Homo*. For Heidegger, the richness and strangeness of the Hölderlinian register is all gain; for Benjamin, there lies the danger of being once again enclosed in an infantile incapacity to communicate, an inability to impose oneself on the linguistic registers of the day and aspire to independent self-expression. By contrast to these two, and drawing on Beatrice Hanssen's readings of Benjamin, this chapter identifies in Lacoue-Labarthe's insistence on a Hölderlinian hyperbology, an intensification of movement, transforming meaning by reiterating a moment of invention and innovation. Here there arrives in the analysis of time, meaning, and modality the childhood discovery of linguistic potency, and there also arrives the accompanying recurring anxiety both that this lucidity will once again recede, and that it be closed down by extraneous forces put in question by such discovery. The euphoria of attaining a capacity to speak, and of asserting a certain autonomy, is haunted by the fear of its loss, by sequestration, or by its erosion in the passage of time.

The discussion in this chapter is framed by the contrast between a movement, out of infancy and infantilism, into the condition called by Kant that of maturity, *Mundigkeit*, acquiring a capacity for self-assertion in a set of recognized linguistic, legal, and civic capacities, and a movement of mourning and melancholy, in which the first intimation of independence is continually eroded and subverted.[2] A moment of redemptive illumination is to be contrasted to its loss, exposed as it is to a movement of dissolution, offering the alternates of a return to daily life or a collapse into unreason. Thereby, a clarification of a series of distinct registers and conceptions of language, and of reading and writing, may be brought into view. The moment of redemptive illumination is that of messianic time, released from any actual returning of messiah. The former movement, that of mourning and melancholy, is the focus for attention, and the mode of composition for many of Benjamin's studies, which meditate on fragments of meaning and expression retrieved from the past, seeking to bring them to a completion and fulfilment, in some register other than their own. For this task, Benjamin takes up, adapts, and transposes some of the insights he gleans from his own analyses of the concept of criticism, in the early study: *The Concept of Criticism in Early Romanticism* (*SW* 1: 116–200). The latter movement, a return to an ordinary dailyness, is the goal of the therapist's interventions, and of the processes of self-analysis to which Freud subjects himself, as reported on in *The Interpretation of Dreams* (1900). These movements, those of euphoria, of melancholy, and of a working through, advance toward, and retreat from a moment of stasis, in which conflict and process turn into an overload of meaning and into an immobilization of thought.

Such movements and interventions may be thought to constitute, indeed to generate, the dynamics of the writing careers of the three thinkers here in question: Hölderlin, Benjamin, Heidegger, while denying them any such return to normalcy. For each thinker, theoretical and linguistic innovation, while temporarily stemming a rising tide of isolation, and loss of meaning, creates a further barrier to such reentry into the dailyness of those around them. Hölderlin's career is broken in half by the collapse that leaves him in the care of the carpenter, the wonderfully named Ernst Zimmer, until his death in 1843. Benjamin's career is split between his life, ending in suicide at Port Bou in September 1940, and an afterlife, with the marked contrasts of the rejected, and the celebrated theorist, in the care variously of Theodor Adorno and Hannah Arendt.[3] Heidegger's trajectory splits him into the twin figures of philosophical giant, and political reprobate, like Dionysus, infinitely dissected.[4] Despite the political suspicion under which Heidegger's activities must fall, there is all the same a power of disruptive energy in his reading, which is to be attended to in what follows. He has a capacity to release an intoxicating energy from the texts he reads at the same time as he succumbs to the putting to work of truth, on behalf of a renewal of fascism.

Heidegger's repudiation of the work of his mentor, Edmund Husserl; and his enthusiasm for the inner truth and greatness of the National Socialist movement, reiterated in 1953, indicate, on both sides of the nervous collapse he allegedly suffers in 1946, a curious indifference to the values and standards of conduct more common to his epoch.[5] All three, Hölderlin, Benjamin, and Heidegger, sacrifice ease of assimilation and acceptance by their contemporaries, in the pursuit of their programs of study and trajectories of inquiry, as writers and thinkers. They are also distinctive in not easily finding a place in any collectively describable research program. Hölderlin fits easily neither into the program of Romanticism, nor into that of German Idealism, nor into those, more broadly understood, of Schiller and Goethe, in their contributions to the development of a distinctively German culture. Benjamin's difficulties with Horkheimer and Adorno, Arendt and Scholem are legend; and the customary trope is that of splitting his work up into the opposed modes of revolutionary activism, with Brecht, and a mystic redemptiveness, with Gershom Scholem. "Heidegger" is the name for an utterly distinctive reception of both Husserlian phenomenology, and of Nietzsche's inquiries, insisting that the latter are through and through philosophical and metaphysical, while transforming phenomenology into a meditation on meaning, thus defying the more customary distinctions between philosophy and psychology, literature and writing. It is as though he seeks to change places with Nietzsche, to confine Nietzsche to the lecture theater and, himself, to become the free spirit Nietzsche's writings anticipate. Heidegger's Hölderlin, like his Nietzsche, is an unprecedented figure who, while given the task of retrieving the Greek inception of philosophy into a properly German word, nevertheless traces out the signs of hope and reinvention, as much as nostalgia and melancholy.

Benjamin's early essay on Hölderlin, from 1914 to 1915, "Two Poems by Friedrich Hölderlin: *Dichtermut* and *Blödigkeit*" (*SW* 1: 18–37) will form one focus for discussion, and Heidegger's commemorative essay *Andenken*, from 1943, another.[6] For Benjamin, these two poems offer versions of a single *Gedichtete*, Hölderlin's term for that which is to be expressed, or exposed within the constraints of the expressive powers of a given natural language. The reflections on Hölderlin then inflect Benjamin's "The Task of the Translator" (1921), the introduction to his translations from Baudelaire, and arrive in midst of the treatment of Goethe's *Elective Affinities*, from 1919 to 1921. For Heidegger, too, the notion of the *Gedichtete* is compelling, but within a broader context of discussion, where the fate of art itself and the fate of the human are in question. The flight of the gods, treated by Benjamin as allegory, for Heidegger has an urgency that leads him to invoke the need and necessity for the return of a godhead, in his posthumously printed interview, "Only a God can save us now."[7] He theorizes a decline of onto-theology as the potential for a return of a binding religiosity. The task for this chapter is to consider these differing accounts and moods, a contrast that is already prefigured by the juxtaposition, in the collection *Walter Benjamin and Romanticism* (2002) of versions of essays on Benjamin by Beatrice Hanssen, first published in 1989, and of Philippe Lacoue-Labarthe, on Benjamin and Heidegger, first published 1993, under the title "Poetic Courage."[8] Hanssen's essay marks up Benjamin's attention to a sober connectedness, and to the sacral sobriety, invoked by Hölderlin; whereas Lacoue-Labarthe attends more to the implications of a fissioning of Hölderlin's undertakings in Heidegger's distinctly erratic readings. For Heidegger, too, the notion of *Nüchternheit*, sobriety, or indeed neediness, arrives emphatically for attention, in conclusion to his essay "*Wie wenn am Feiertage*" (As on the Day of Celebration), from 1941.[9] The task is to permit the deeply contrastive notions of language, and of translation, to come into view, and to mark up the return in Heidegger's readings of a dangerous but irrepressible intoxication, which disrupts any attempt to soothe the turbulence of Hölderlin's vision.

Heidegger lectures three times on Hölderlin's hymns, and in the last series, on *Der Ister*, from summer 1942,[10] he cites the first strophe of *Dichterberuf*, here given in Michael Hamburger's translation:

The banks of the Ganges heard the triumph of the God of Joy when, all conquering, from Indus young Bacchus came, rousing the peoples from sleep with holy wine.[11]

The sobriety of the matriarch, Juno, marked up by Hanssen, is to be contrasted to the youth and joy of Bacchus. This sets up a contrast between Benjamin's emphasis on sobriety, and Heidegger's recklessness when, in 1933 to 1934, and in 1941 to 1942, in his forties and fifties, he is willing to entertain dark forces that cannot be contained within the ordered domesticated domains demarcated by separations between hope and fear, poetry and philosophy, religion and politics. For it is politics, in the grand style of Nietzsche's imagining, which is here at stake: not just the politics of a current configuration, in which agents deliberately maneuver within a well-formed field. In the grand style of politics, there is a current conjuncture and, within that, a series of relays of unnoticed unmarked forces, out of which unprecedented eruptions may arrive, derailing the ordered expectations of those engaging in politics in the minor mode. Gaining access to these concealed forces is an undertaking in common between Hölderlin, Benjamin and Heidegger. A return to the past in the mode of legend relays these vanished powers into the future, in a way that keeps them in circulation; a return to the past in the mode of myth seeks to contain and control what can be passed forward, thus controlling the image, but not the forces that arrive out of the future. This is the status of Hitler's imagining of a Thousand Year Reich, and the attempt thus to control the uncontrollable contributes to its defeat. These processes of retrieval and reinvention tap into the otherwise unnoticed processes of transmission of forces at work, which more usually escape individual and indeed collective human attention.

Sobriety and Intoxication

It is worth underlining that these three, Hölderlin, Benjamin, Heidegger, while sharing a common language, German, write and think in markedly distinct registers. For Benjamin, as is well known, his early reflections on tragedy, and on the work of translation lead to an invocation of a pure word, as such, which, as indicated in the title to his 1916 essay, "On language as such and the language of human beings," is to be contrasted to the words of human languages. This thought of a pure word of language is in part derived by him from a response to reading Hölderlin, marked up in the early essay from 1914 to 1915, "Two poems of Friedrich Hölderlin," (*SW* 1: 18–37). In this essay, he explores the thematics of sobriety, indeed of a sacred sobriety, which arrive in Hölderlin's curiously prescient poem *Hälfte des Lebens* (The mid-point of life) from 1803:

> With yellow pears and full of wild roses the land hangs down into the lake, you lovely swans and drunk with kisses, you dip your heads into the holy and sober water [*Ins heilignüchterne Wasser*]. (242)

This again is Michael Hamburger's translation, from 1961, revised 1986, and it is important to point out both that the specific reference is added by the translators of Benjamin's text into English, and that there are other references to this holy sobriety in Hölderlin's writings. For Benjamin, the pure word is invoked sometimes through a work of citation, and sometimes through that of translation. The citation from "The task of the translator" at the beginning of this chapter indicates that translation taken to the limit opens up a dangerous realm, in which there is no longer a circulation of shared meanings, held in place in the collective practices of functioning communities. This is Nietzsche's hyperborean realm, survival in which presupposes strong nerves, good fortune, and a character inclined to solitude.

In his essay "The Role of Language in *Trauerspiel* and Tragedy," also early, from 1915 to 1916, and also unpublished in Benjamin's lifetime, Benjamin describes the language of tragedy thus: "Every speech in the tragedy is tragically decisive. It is the pure word itself that has an immediate tragic force" (*SW* 1: 59). The context provided by the immediately preceding reading of Hölderlin suggests the strong contrast between the Greek tragedies of Sophocles, as translated by Hölderlin, and the baroque mourning plays discussed by Benjamin at greater length in the later

Origin of German Tragic Drama (1928). The line preceding the citation provides a clue to the dynamics of this claim. Given in full, the citation reads:

> In tragedy, speech and the tragic arise together, simultaneously, on the same spot. Every speech in the tragedy is tragically decisive. It is the pure word itself that has an immediate tragic force. (*SW* 1: 59)

The difference between speech in tragedy, and language in the mourning play is underlined by contrasting the mixing of feelings (*Gefühlen*) to be found in the mourning play, to the unity of style, which "in the sense of a unity beyond feelings, is reserved for tragedy" (*SW* 1: 61). A unity beyond feelings strays close to the model of the unobtainable ego ideal, in psychoanalytical theory. Less obvious is the link back, via the invocation of the pure word, to the essay on the art of Hölderlin, its tragic force resulting from a unique binding together of mythic connectedness, meaning and life. The brief commentary concludes, drawing out the contrast between worlds:

> The world of the mourning play is a special world that can assert its greatness and equality even in the face of tragedy. It is the site of the actual reception [*Empfängnis*] of the word and of speech in art; the faculties of speech and hearing stand equal in the scales and ultimately everything depends on the ear for lament, for only the most profoundly heard lament can become music. Whereas in tragedy the eternal inflexibility of the spoken word is exalted, the mourning play concentrates in itself the non-finite [*endlose*] resonance of its sound. (*SW* 1: 61, trans. mod.)

The eternal inflexibility of the spoken word is juxtaposed to the modulations of a resonance between ear and hearing, receptivity and understanding.

The world of tragedy is that of a unified moment in time, interrupting human ordering, in which finitude is transposed into a fulfilled time of immortality. This figure turns out to be of the greatest importance to Arendt, who, in *The Human Condition* (1958) conceives the point of politics as the quest for such immortality.[12] This then is her version of the greater politics, which Nietzsche seeks to install, whereby not just the immediate aims and concerns of given human beings are in question, but the very destiny of humanity. The resistance displayed by Hölderlin, Benjamin, and Heidegger to inclusion in some collectively describable research project then is the consequence of their preoccupation with this larger question: What shall become of the human? The world of mourning by contrast is that of a play of feelings, which, because conflicted, cannot be simultaneously experienced, nor yet expressed, but which requires a lapse of time, and lack of synchrony, through which an incompleteness of meaning can be worked through. The notions of echo and reverberation play a role here in marking up changeability and alterability dependent on modes and contexts of reception.

In the finite contexts, of actual lives, sound resonates by encountering the acoustic limits of its domain, and this provides a model for thinking the time lags and reverberations through which meaning arrives. The feelings of hope and despair, joy and sorrow, fullness and emptiness alternate: this is a domain of change and alteration, in which the consequences of an intertwining of fate and destiny are as yet obscure. By contrast, in the eternal inflexibility of tragic spoken word, all has already been decided: this would be the moment of the Lacanian real, from which there is no return, but which, when staged in the rite of tragedy, becomes negotiable and appropriable. The difference between tragic speech, designed for public performance, with a precisely delimited audience, its responses providing a context for a collective reception, and tragic speech, ordered into a process of translation, is decisive. For when Sophocles' plays are performed, their function within a community is thus guaranteed by the institution of their presentation. By contrast when Hölderlin seeks to transpose this experience of speech, preserved in the textual remains of that institution, into an experience of a contemporary German language use, marked by Luther, and by the Athenaeum, and about to be embroiled in a war of liberation from French invasion, this is a quite other mode of engagement. Hölderlin contrasts the moment of the fire from heaven, in which fate is decided, to the time of the task of presentation, and its mode of clarification (*Klarheit der Darstellung*).

Hölderlin's writings, and struggles to translate Sophocles, convert the exaltation of the moment in a spoken word into a relay of echoes between poems, and translations, drafts and texts, with a series of resonances between their distinctive moods and moves. The title of his collection *Nachtgesänge* (1805) is thus prophetic: there is no shared daylight in which these meanings may circulate. The processes of testing out meaning and its communicability are fraught with difficulty, and haunted by specters of both an irretrievable past and an unattainable, unimaginable future of reinvented community, breaking with a history of loss. There are then three, not two, registers here: that of tragic speech, that of the mourning play, and that of the work of translation, which, as intimated, has some strange connection to the as yet to be invented techniques of transference (*Übertragung*), and of working through (*Durcharbeiten*), which are imagined by Freud, and decisively transposed by Jacques Lacan. Hölderlin himself, as the sounding board on which this relay of resonances takes place, becomes immobilized, and pays the price of a radical isolation, of his own making, locked into an endless night of a captivity.

He moves beyond the reach of the talking cure; but perhaps not beyond the reach of a Lacanian analysis.[13]

As Benjamin develops his thinking, he gets caught up in the gesture of both mourning, and replicating Hölderlin's move into increasing isolation. His seven-year peregrination after his departure from Hitler's Germany in February 1933, and his demise in 1940, attempting to escape the long arm of the Nuremburg Laws, provides a stark contrast to the outward stability of Heidegger's position from 1928 onward as Husserl's successor in Freiburg im Breisgau. Heidegger's one excursion into foreign lands, in 1936, provides him with the occasion to pronounce his most emphatic declaration that Hölderlin is the most poetic of poets, and the most German of Germans, in the paper "Hölderlin and the Essence of Composing" Rome, April 2, 1936.[14] This analysis, had he known of it, could only confirm Benjamin's view that no piece of the cultural heritage could be deemed safe in Heidegger's hands. Benjamin is stinging on the topic of Heidegger's treatment, in the 1916 Habilitation Thesis, *The doctrine of categories and meaning in Duns Scotus* (1916), actually on Thomas of Erfurt and the theorisation of a *modus significandi*, Art des Meinens, or mode of indicating (see *GA* 1). He is savage about Heidegger's, to Benjamin, pitiful attempt to think the specificity of history.[15] Benjamin writes in a letter to Scholem, January 1920:

> It is unbelievable that someone can be habilitated with such a work. For its completion all that is needed is great assiduousness, and a mastery of scholastic Latin; despite a lot of philosophical grandiloquence, it is only a bit of good translation work. The undignified crawling of the author to Rickert and Husserl does not make it any pleasanter to read. (*GB* 1: 246)

Heidegger at this point is clearly better equipped than Benjamin to succeed in the minor politics of pleasing his examiners. On the dispute concerning history, there is a remark in a letter, in French, to Scholem, almost exactly ten years later, January 1930, when, writing of the proposed *Work on the Paris Passages* (*Passagenarbeit*), Benjamin remarks that:

> [F]or this book as much as for the *Trauerspiel* book, I cannot dispense with an introduction which will treat of a theory of knowledge (*connaissance/Erkennen*) and this time above all a theory of knowledge of history. It is there that I will find Heidegger on my path and I anticipate certain sparks to fly from the clash between our two modes, so very different, of considering history. (*GB* 2: 506)

This gains further definition, if it is still needed, in the following remark in a letter from April 1930, again to Scholem. Benjamin announces, once more in German, the plan for a reading group: "There is a plan here for this summer in a small critical reading group, led by Brecht and me to reduce Heidegger to rubble" (*GB* 2: 513). The *Work on the Paris Passages* addresses itself to the epistemological problems thrown up by the gap between language as such and the language of human beings. The local, restricted scope of meaning in all so-called natural languages is to be overcome by the work of citation, which converts that meaning into the pure word, naming the intimated thought, flaring up brightly, if ephemerally, in the domains of human beings, in a shock of recognizability. The work is strictly one of mourning, for the event is determinately past, fragile and subject to both forgetting and decay. Here knowing (*Erkennbarkeit*) requires the supplementation of retrieval and transposition, from pure word to linguistic expression.

By contrast to Benjamin's meditations on mourning and tragedy, Heidegger's analyses of the work of translation, and, in particular, his responses to Hölderlin's work, transposing Pindaric elegy and ode, and Sophoclean tragedy into a modern idiom, take the form of a celebration of a future potentiality. For Heidegger an understanding and adequate response to Hölderlin's challenge is yet to come, and he and Benjamin at least agreed that the biographical style of matching events in Hölderlin's life to poetic innovation is a grossly inadequate method of analysis. Heidegger emphasizes the role in Hölderlin's writings of drink and friendship, joy and affirmation, bound together in the figure of Bacchus. The forces of forgetting and of decay are to be turned around. They are not just processes to which all human endeavor is subject: they are ontological conditions of possibility, and the mode of temporalization itself. They are thus to be made over into the characteristics distinctive of a whole trajectory of thinking, beginning with the philosophical wonder, and the intensification of meaning into thinking, which for Heidegger first dawns among the Greeks. This is a singular dawning, as he is utterly closed to the thought that other such dawns may have come and gone, escaping the attention of the clever spirits of Northern Europe. The Germans, for Heidegger, are those at the dwindling of the light who still have an attunement to this initiatory word. The dynamic of the dawning of history, in the Orient, and its waning, at twilight, in an occidental land of the evening darkening (des *Abendlandes*) is a strong and continuing motif for both Heidegger and Nietzsche, and indeed Hölderlin.

There is then a presumption that those who survive, by virtue of commemoration, are vindicated by that redeeming destiny, a thought utterly foreign to both Hölderlin and Benjamin, who struggle to maintain a connection to the stuttering light of their precursors. There is here, too, a difference of vector with respect to an affirmation of a spirit of Germanness: Hölderlin's wars are those of Napoleon, and the *Freiheitskriege*, the war of emancipation, is a freeing from French and indeed from absolutist dominion, at a time when there is no German nation; Benjamin's war is World War I, the clash of empires, and the destruction of a generation of young men, again without the quite specific spin, which Hitler's plan for a Thousand Year Reich gives to any notion of a German-speaking hegemony. The context of Heidegger's reading of Hölderlin is then unbelievably that of Heidegger's endorsement of Hitler and Hitler's regime in 1933, and of Heidegger's attempt to retreat from Syracuse in 1934; of the German invasion of Poland and Russia, and the defeat and failure to retreat from Stalingrad in winter 1943. As noted the lecture, "Hölderlin and the Essence of Composing" dates from 1936; and as also noted Heidegger lectures three times on Hölderlin, on the hymns *Germanien* and *Der Rhein*, from 1801, in the 1933 to 1934 lectures; on *Andenken*, from 1803, in the 1941 to 1942 lectures, and on *Der Ister* and on *Dichterberuf*, also probably from 1801, in the summer of 1942, publishing a long essay on *Andenken* in 1943, the centenary of Hölderlin's death. In addition the lectures *Introduction to Metaphysics* (1935) have a long section responding to Hölderlin's translation of Sophocles' *Antigone*. Heidegger's attempt to reinvent the language of meditation owes as much to his readings of Hölderlin as to his readings of Nietzsche, Schelling, and Kant.

Andenken may be variously translated as "remembrance," "commemoration" or, indeed, with the name "*Mnemosyne*," Memory, the mother of the muses, to whom Hölderlin also dedicated a hymn, in at least three versions. The commemoration that Heidegger dedicates to Hölderlin does not take up the vexed issue of the female embodiment of the daughters of Memory and Zeus, although he does contrast the "brown women" of the foreign location of Hölderlin's exile to the receptivity of German women, to whom Hölderlin may return. A further intent of this essay is to consider a retranscription of the various arts, history, astronomy, tragedy, comedy, dance, epic poetry, erotic poetry, sacred and lyric song, the nine daughters of Memory. The arts may be refigured along with memory as technically modified forms of human embodiment, enhanced by prostheses of all kinds, but all still as modes of being human, rather than as objectified genres of reified results of activity: books, symphonies, statues, pictures. This transformative thinking of art as a physical emanation of determinately embodied human beings poses a challenge to classical notions of language, as principally a means of fixing and communicating thought, and supports a notion of language as more a medium for self-discovery, in a strong sense of self-forming. This would connect back to the modal potentiation marked up for attention by Sam Weber in his reading of Benjamin. In language, as a medium for self-discovery, what is important are the transitional modes of articulating meaning, for which the moment of innovation not the repetition of the already codified is the focus for attention. For Heidegger, too, the arts of language use are to be responded to: they are activities, rather than presenting a series of completed dead inscriptions to be deciphered. For Benjamin, the challenge is to detect a dynamic, a life force at work in language in which a living memory of past epochs is preserved and transmitted as contraband, defying the barbarisms of his day.

Monstrous Couplings

For Sophocles, what is monstrous is the coupling of the son with the mother, generating the drama of Oedipus, for Aeschylus, the monstrous is the murder by the father, Agamemnon, of the daughter, Iphigenia, revealing that the Atreids are doomed, and have been ever since the founder of the line; Tantalus, son of Zeus and the nymph Plouto, tricked Demeter, goddess of fertility, into eating human flesh. This lineage is thus fated to achieve greatness only through sacrilege, and at the cost of self-destruction. Clytemnestra, Iphigenia's mother, abandons Agamemnon for his cousin, and foster brother, Aegisthus, who is both son and grandson of the incestuous Thyestes. Here, there is a multiplication of incests, and, by contrast to Oedipus and Jocasta, son and mother, the incest is between father and daughter, Thyestes and Pelopia, who is both mother and sister to Aegisthus. For Hölderlin, what is monstrous is the coupling of the human and the divine, usually but not always the female human and the male divine, from which follows the procreation of demi-gods and of the mixed generations of the distinctly complicated Olympian genealogy. The task of the poet is to depict this encounter between mortality and divinity, and to anticipate its reinvention. In the twenty-first century, in vitro fertilization and biogenetics play the same role today of revealing an artifice in the delimitation of what counts as a natural procreativity, shocking their opponents into testifying to what seems to them to be fixed natural law.

These monstrous couplings, son with mother, mortal with divinity, test tube and womb challenge the divisions of nature and notions of natural orderliness. At some stage an attempt must be made to anticipate a reinvention of a parthenogenesis, a giving birth, unmediated by sexual difference, or at least unmediated by any naturalized, mythological, and, in Benjamin's terms, fascist notion of sexual difference: the one that preserves an old outmoded order. Benjamin and Heidegger reading Hölderlin, then, is another monstrous coupling, where opposed forces are brought together to reveal a common reluctance to address a fear of infantilization. Procreation here has various modularities, men without women, women without men, insiders without outsiders, outsiders without insiders, the indigenous without the foreign, the foreign without the indigenous. Implied, too, are a concern with all the different modes of suicide and self-disfigurement, collapse, and survival as immortalized in tragic reiteration. It is important to trace the violent rage with which such refiguring is sometimes greeted. An exploration of the figures that arrive in such a retreating of sexual difference is then part of a larger program, designed to trace a process of reinventing sexual difference, no longer thought of as an ontological difference mirroring an ontical, given biological fact, but as differentiating processes of regeneration, in all these modularities. The tragic tradition barely contains the forces of self-transformation and reinscription of humanity now available for human beings. The gap between a naturally given human species and a self-transforming humanity has never been narrower.

For Heidegger, there is a potentiality for a return to a pagan affirmation of *phusis*, as all that surges and grows, decays and regenerates, which he traces out in Hölderlin's invocation of it, as older than time, and preceding any distinction before east and west. For Benjamin there is no need for such a route back into an archaic past, for the history and hereditary cruelty of these chthonic gods is, to paraphrase William Faulkner, not only not over, it is not even past. Their thinking of the self-forming of humanity is prompted and accelerated by their responses to Hölderlin responding to the Greek inception. The last line of Hölderlin's hymn *Andenken* runs: "*was bleibt aber stiften die Dichter*" (what remains is poetic ordaining). Here then is the clue to the thematic pivot for this essay: for all three, Hölderlin, Benjamin, and Heidegger, there is a question of how meaning may be secured, with the implied corollary of an anxiety that meaning is utterly fragile and ephemeral, dependent on an attunement to its reverberation. The link between securing meaning, generating innovative language use, and refiguring a monstrous procreativity remains to be made out. The one who secures meaning, both inventing and retrieving meaning, is to be accorded the status of poet, but with a vastly expanded notion of the task and scope of poetic activity: no longer a task, *Aufgabe*, but a *Spielraum*, a field of activity. This activity of securing, inventing, and retrieving meaning presupposes a transformative capacity for reading, responding to, and translating the writings of others, with a sensitivity to what cannot yet come to expression in that writing, and for an as yet unreleased potentiality, thus invoking meanings that have not as yet arrived. These transformative practices presuppose the skills of the poet, the philosopher, and critic, which Hölderlin, Benjamin, and Heidegger combine in their different inflections and variations. What is not constant is the relation between human and human, between humanity and divinity, and the place of a thinking of divinity in relation to conceptions of time and history. For Hölderlin invokes a notion of nature, to which the poet must respond, as above time and history and above the division between mortals and gods.

The human, as the strangest of beings, is analyzed by Heidegger, in his lectures, *Introduction to Metaphysics* given in summer 1935, through a reading of Sophocles *Antigone*, as translated by Hölderlin (see *IM/ GA* 53). Here Heidegger depicts human beings, men and women, Oedipus and Antigone, as destined to suffering, and to a transformatory self-overcoming.[16] Unlike Hegel's Antigone, this is no empty vessel, designed to catch the reject and mirror image of a concept of masculine personality, into which the positive of the feminine has been reappropriated and absorbed, *aufgehoben*. Antigone, as daughter and sister of Oedipus, suffers her own distinctive fate, and is not bound, as Hegel would have it, solely to the fates of her half-sibling, Oedipus, and her full siblings, Eteocles and Polynices, the one murdering the other while Antigone escorts the now blind Oedipus to transfiguration at Colonnus. Having effected the transfiguration of Oedipus, she then returns to engage in the politics of state and family, insisting on burying the secessionist brother. Heidegger also writes on Hölderlin's incomplete hymn, "*Wie wenn am Feiertage*" (As on the Day of Celebration), dated 1799, which he reports was frequently delivered as a lecture between 1939 and 1940, first publishing it in 1941. This reading insists on the poet's capacity to learn not just from human teachers, but from an all-encircling mighty, divinely shining nature, which for Hölderlin is the chthonic force of *phusis*, not the series of relations studied in laboratories by many in his generation. In this Hölderlin, like Heidegger, adopts an archaising distance from the scientific innovations of his age.

There is a claim on the poet that transcends immediate historical and political context. The second strophe, in Hamburger's translation, begins:

> They stand under a favourable climate, the ones taught not simply by a master, but in a gentle embrace by the wondrous all-encircling mighty, divinely shining nature. (77, trans. mod.)

The poet is thus marked as open to nature in a distinctive way, and especially so on days of celebration, when the daily cycle of work is suspended. When mourning comes, as it does in this second strophe of "*Wie wenn am Feiertage*," it is twinned by an intimation that renders the poet solitary, but able to anticipate a future, and therefore still capable of joy. The strophe continues:

> So when (nature) seems to sleep at certain times of year, in the sky, or among plants or the peoples, the poets' faces also will mourn; they seem to be alone, yet always they are foreknowing. For she herself foreknows as she rests. (77–78, trans. mod.)

Thus the poet is supposed to share a kind of intimation of cyclical renewal, through which the poet's powers like those of growth and decay are renewed, discharged, and allowed to lie fallow, to be summoned into action again by the changing of seasons and the arrival of clement weather. The modern day cycles of full- and underemployment have taken the place of any natural cycle of work and the curse of unemployment then would feature as a modality of the actual and ontological homelessness, loss of orientation. This homelessness and the status of the work Heidegger begins to thematize at this time, without remarking the hideous contribution of his chosen party, in its invention of an ultimate exile.

It is in the third strophe that Hölderlin locates nature as older than the ages, and above the gods of both occident and orient, nightfall and dawn, west and east (*Abends und Orients*):

> For she herself who is older than the ages and above the gods of Occident and Orient, Nature now has awoken with clamour of arms and from the heights of aether, down to the lowest abyss, according to the rigid law, engendered out of holy chaos as once she was, the all-creative, feels her own fullness of spirit anew. (78, trans. mod.)

The temptation in the current context to translate this as "USA and China" is strong, for this would underline the futility of Heidegger's obsessive denunciation of "Americanism," which stretches from the 1935 to 1936 lectures, into this essay from 1941, and the lectures on *Der Ister* and beyond. From the current stance where U.S. hegemony is over, a new play of forces constitutes the domain of greater politics. The draft of this poem breaks off, with the words: *Doch weh mir* . . . , marking the sorrow of one to whom a modest contentment is denied. The change of tone is stark, the work incomplete, but this is not Heidegger's focus of concern. For in the concluding passages of his essay on "*Wie wenn am Feiertage*," Heidegger invokes the self-same *Nüchternheit*, which is important for Benjamin's reading of Hölderlin. He cites a passage from Hölderlin, a fragment entitled "*Deutscher Gesang*" (German song):

> for he sits in deep shadows
> when above his head the elm tree rustles
> by the coolly breathing stream, the German poet;
> and he sings, when he has drunk deeply enough
> from the holy sobering [*des heiligen nüchternen Wassers*] water
> resonating deeply into the tranquil silence
> a song of the soul. (74)

The *Seelengesang*, the song of the soul, gets a whole new inflection when sung in canon with BB King at the White House, by the first black president of the United States. It is worth following Heidegger's comment on this in some detail:

> The "deep shadows" rescue the poetic word from the excessive brightness of a "heavenly fire." The "coolly breathing stream" protects the poetic word from the overwhelming heat of the "heavenly fire." The coolness and shadiness of this sobriety corresponds to the holy. This sobriety does not deny itself a certain fullness of spirit. This sobriety is the basic mood [*Grundstimmung*] of readiness, which is at all times ready, for that holiness. (74)

Heidegger proposes that Hölderlin's distinctive register of the hymn is not addressed to a deity but is itself an expression of the holy, of that which heals both body and spirit; he concludes:

> Hölderlin's distinctive word speaks holy healing, and thus names the singular time-space of an initiatory decision in favour of the essential articulation of the coming history of gods and human kinds [*Götter* und *Menschentümer*, both plural]. This word is, still unheard, preserved in the twilight language of the Germans. (74)

This double movement of preservation and preparation is the preserve of the poetic word. Where Benjamin reads this holy sobriety as the hidden imperative of the meaning of the two poems, finding in it a localized *a priori*, determining order and meaning, Heidegger finds in it a new register for the *Grundstimmung*, out of which he supposes there arrives an innovatory human attentiveness to the danger and future of humanity.

From Courage to Diffidence

In her decisive discussion of Benjamin's 1914–1915 essay, "Two Poems by Friedrich Hölderlin: *Dichtermut* and *Blödigkeit*" (*SW* 1: 18–37), Beatrice Hanssen marks up its place in Adorno's response to Benjamin's writings, and in Adorno's development of various of Benjamin's motifs. This careful reading traces out the work of this *a priori* of meaning, the *Gedichtete*, or *dictamen*, to which these two poems respond. The reading attends to the movement of sobriety (*Nüchternheit*) in both Hölderlin's and Benjamin's attitudes to what they read, a sobriety oddly attributed by Hölderlin in a letter to Bohlendorff, to Juno, mother of the legitimate gods. Benjamin cites the passage at length in the later essay on Goethe's *Elective Affinities*, in which he is seeking to delimit a notion of expressionlessness: that which has exhausted all connotative meaning in a fullness of articulation.

> Only the expressionless completes the work, by shattering it into a thing of shards, into a fragment of the true world, into the torso of a symbol. As a category of language and art, and not of the work or of the genres, the expressionless can be no more rigorously defined than through a passage in Hölderlin's *Annotations to Oedipus*, whose fundamental significance for the theory of art in general, beyond serving as the basis for a theory of tragedy seems not yet to have been recognised. (*SW* 1: 340)

He then cites from Hölderlin's *Annotations to Oedipus*:

> The passage reads: "For the tragic transport is actually empty, and the least restrained. Thereby in the rhythmic sequence of the representations wherein the transport presents itself, there becomes necessary what in poetic meter is called caesura, the pure word, the counter-rhythmic rupture—namely in order to meet the onrushing change of representations at its highest point in such a manner that not the change of representations, but representation itself (trans. mod.) very soon appears." The "occidental Junoian sobriety"—which Hölderlin, several years before he wrote this, conceived as the almost unattainable goal of all German artistic practice—is only another name for that caesura, in which, along with harmony, every expression simultaneously comes to a standstill, in order to give free reign to an expressionless power inside all artistic media. (*SW* 1: 340–341)

Benjamin goes on to contrast a capacity in lyric and hymn to reach for this expressionless standstill, to a movement of beauty, as captured by Goethe. He then remarks the danger of a descent into madness at one extreme of this juxtaposition and into fakery at the other: "What sits beyond this limit is, in one direction, the offspring of madness, and, in the other, the conjury of semblance" (*SW* 1: 341). For Benjamin, it is clear, Hölderlin enacts the one and Goethe inclines to the other.

This emphasis on sobriety should not be taken to imply a lack of innovating self-confidence in each, Hölderlin and Benjamin, for they both dare to take language, as they find it, and transform it into something other than it was. Indeed, Hölderlin contrasts the sobriety of Juno to the disruptiveness of a less ordered source of inspiration, coming from further east: the twice-born double figure of Dionysus/Christ. Hölderlin's and Heidegger's willingness to put the Christian figures of the divine on a par with those of the Olympian and pre-Olympian chthonic deities should also be remarked. There is a close connection to be traced out here between the task of translation, an acceptance of the departure of the Greek gods, as a prelude to the arrival of other modes of figuring divinity, and that of an affirming, transformatory potency in the invention of meaning, in which current meaning is pushed up to, and beyond some kind of limit, currently sustaining its given state of well-formedness. For Hölderlin and Benjamin become the writers they are in part by translating Pindar and Sophocles; Baudelaire and Proust, opening German up respectively to Greek and to French. Heidegger, in his meditations on Hölderlin's efforts to transpose Greek linguistic forms and genres of poetry into German, demonstrates his commitment to transforming language and currently available registers of philosophical enquiry, to make ready a response to radically altering circumstance, and unprecedented exigency.

A first move to make with respect to the reading of Benjamin on Hölderlin is to question the adequacy of the translation of *Blödigkeit* as timidity, the choice made by the editors of the English translation in the *Selected Works*, following, as Hanssen indicates, the French translation of it as "*timidite*." For these may be false friends. Michael Hamburger, in his translation of this late ode, offers "Diffidence," which better captures the mode in which the poet addresses himself to himself and to his art.[17] The final stanza of this ode, with apologies and modifications to Hamburger's version, runs:

> We too are good and sent/fated, as someone destined for something, when we come, with this skill, bringing that someone with us from the eternal realm. For we bring our own destinal capacity. (239)

These violent alterations to Hamburger's version are designed to underline his observations concerning the work of the terms *geschickt*, *Geschick*, and *schicklich*, with their connotations of a divine gift, a fate and a singular capacity, and the inspiration deriving from the arrival of a god. This is not the voice of someone timid; but diffidence with respect to the gift of a divine insight would assuredly be in order. There can be no doubt but that Hölderlin and Benjamin paid a high price for their resolute commitment to their respective undertakings.

There is here a resonance rather to the ingenuousness of a holy fool, daring what most would hesitate to undertake. It is worth noting that one of Benjamin's early publications, in 1921, is a short piece on Dostoevsky's *Idiot*, which concludes:

The entire momentum of the book resembles the implosion of a giant crater. Because nature and childhood are absent, humanity can be arrived at only via a catastrophic process of self-destruction. The relationship of human life to the living, right down to their total destruction the immeasurable abyss of the crater from which mighty energies may one day be released on a grand human scale—this is the hope of the Russian nation. (*SW* 1: 81)

These returns to nature and to childhood will require a reassessment of Benjamin's iteration of thousands of years of casual exclusion of women from the working through of mourning, and meditation on tragedy, and of a casual assumption that only the childhoods of men are worthy of attentive interpretation. For it cannot simply be assumed that only men can emerge renewed from the challenge of an encounter with death and despair. The roles of women and men in tragedy are distinct, and the childhoods of men and of women may turn out to have quite distinct dynamics, relating to contrasting, non-naturalizable notions of nature, that is of *phusis*, of all which grows and decays, and gives rise to these emergent potentialities marked up in Benjamin's and Weber's attention to modal potentiation. These childhoods and their denaturalization will respond to distinct modes of revivification. At some point it will be necessary to challenge the Benjaminian image of childhood, which, apparently sexless, is all the same resolutely masculine.

From Theology to Theiology

Hamburger dates *Blödigkeit* from 1803, Hanssen dates *Dichtermut*, poetic courage, from around 1800, and *Blödigkeit* from 1802, presumably after Hölderlin's return in July 1802 from his stint as private tutor in Bordeaux. There is general agreement that *Dichtermut* precedes *Blödigkeit*, and thereby that courage is superseded by diffidence. It is the latter, *Blödigkeit*, which is printed in the 1805 collection authorized by Hölderlin, *Nachtgesänge*, *Night lyrics*. Benjamin and commentaries on Benjamin trace a shift of tone from the earlier to the later version, from a celebration of a poet's death to a celebration of the poet's undertaking. Lacoue-Labarthe in his essay "Poetic Courage" (68), surmises there is an intervening version of the poem, without indicating which. It is tempting to suppose he might be thinking of the lyric "*Dichterberuf*" ("The Poet's Vocation," 1801), also translated by Hamburger, which plays an important role in Heidegger's reading of *Der Ister*, in the summer 1942 lectures reading Hölderlin, and in the commemorative essay, entitled *Andenken*, from 1943. It is worth noting that by summer 1943, Benjamin is already dead, and the German armies are on their way to disaster, and defeat at Stalingrad. Reading Heidegger's essay after the defeat of Nazism, it is scarcely possible not to think of the sacrifice of Benjamin on the border between France and Spain, and the disorderly disruption of Hitler's plans by these forces coming from the East. The work of Nazi myth is disrupted by the return from the East of this oriental principle of disruption, and of a legendary power, left unread by Hitler and his advisers.

What both of these commentaries fail to note is that Benjamin concludes his essay by citing one of the poems from the time of Hölderlin's derangement, when he was inclined to give impossible dates for his work and, like Nietzsche, to sign himself in all the names of history. The lines in question, citing Hamburger, are:

> The legends, which depart from the earth, of the spirit which has been and returns again, these turn to human kind, and we learn much from time, which busily consumes itself. (258)

These lines Benjamin cites in ellipsis, leaving only: "Legends, which depart from this earth, . . . turn themselves back to human kind." Benjamin writes of these lines, "But if there were words with which to grasp the relation between myth and the inner life, out of which the later poem sprang, it would be those of Hölderlin, from a period still later than that of this poem," then citing these lines (*SW* 1: 35–36). The citation is taken from the opening strophe of a lyric, entitled "Autumn," which stands between one entitled "Summer," dated March 9, 1940; and one entitled "Winter," dated April 24, 1849, both dates postdating Hölderlin's demise, and both signed off, *Mit Untertänigkeit Scardanelli* (Your Humble and Obedient Servant, Scardanelli). These dates and signatures Benjamin passes over in silence, a silence then extended in commentary to the whole perplexing move. This then is another candidate for the poem to which Lacoue-Labarthe gestures in his remarks that there is a third poem in the frame in Benjamin's discussion: a poem from the time of Hölderlin's derangement, placed by Hölderlin himself somewhere between 1940 and 1849. This disruption of an ordered time, and a severing of historical incident from the order of chronology are worthy of attention. The appearing of the deity in a poetic theology disrupts the ordering of what there is in any political theology, and it is this tension to which the juxtaposition of Benjamin's and Heidegger's responses to Hölderlin points.

As Hanssen indicates, what is key to Benjamin's reading here is a connection between writing, life and a mythic meaning, given in the transmission of legend, *Sagen*, that which is handed down in oral form, which ought to be, but is not yet given determinate written fixity. Legend thus provides a fourth register, alongside tragic speech, the mourning play, and the work of translation, which oddly will provide Benjamin subsequently with the means to consider the logic of film, that latter day offspring of the mother of the muses, memory, or commemoration, *Mnemosyne*, and the father of Olympian theocracy, Zeus. Mythic connection and the word of legend would defy the customary ordering of dates, disrupt the presumption that death ends effectivity, and put in question the thought that time and history form a single unified structure. Hanssen draws attention to Benjamin's analysis of the tension, outweighing balance, between Hölderlin's invocation of a Greek plasticity, or forming power, and an oriental mystical principle, which binds together the forces of destiny. The contrast runs:

> And in this world every function of life is destiny, whereas in the first version, in the traditional way, destiny determined life. That is the Oriental mystical principle overcoming limits which in the poem again and again so manifestly sublates the Greek shaping principle that creates an intellectual cosmos from pure relations of intuition, sensuous existence, and in which the intellectual is only the expression of the function that strives towards identity. The transformation of the duality of death and poet into the unity of a dead poetic world "saturated with danger" is the relation in with the poetized of both poems stand. (*SW* 1: 34)

Here Benjamin contrasts a plastic notion of destiny, working itself out in a transmission across generations, and an overflowing Oriental energetic, which invites consideration of forces other than those of intuition, sensuous existence, and a limited intellectuality. The forces will be libidinal energy, reptilian memory, and invention of new modes of existing, new embodiments for newly figured muses, to be reborn in a new conjuncture of memory, Mnemosyne, and the sky god, in these unprecedented times.

For Hölderlin the contrast is between the plurality of the Olympian gods, chthonic deities, and titans versus the Oriental figure of the god who takes rebirth, Dionysus/Christ, who departs and returns. In Freudian terms this Oriental principle marks the arrival of the death drive, and its dispersion throughout a population, no longer reserved to sacred figures of the scapegoat, the doomed poet and the divine monarch. This disseminated repetition permits a radical refiguring of the identity, or identities of the one under process of self-discovery. This need not necessarily terminate in death, but may rather be thought as the moment of taking a rebirth, as a conversion experience, or as a transfiguration, an entry, like Oedipus at Colonnus, into the domain of the gods, or, like Aphrodite emerging from the waves. A modern equivalent would be the increasingly common place emergence from gender reassignment surgery. When life overflows the limits set out for it by destiny, or by everyday proscription, then meaning and history arrive intertwined. Benjamin subsequently marks up a hesitation with respect to the use of the distinction between Hellenism and an Oriental mysticism, with its echoes of Nietzsche's mobilization of the principles of Apollo and Dionysus, but it is worth preserving a contrast between a Greek shaping principle, or plasticity, which goes to work on existing materials; and another principle, this so-called Orientalism, figured as overcoming limits.

For Benjamin, as Hanssen demonstrates, what is important is to effect a transition from meaning dominated by myth, to a myth like connectedness. For both Benjamin and Hölderlin, there is a transition from a domain of inquiry in which myth and history are opposed to one another, to one in which the energetics of myth are transposed into the delineation of historical order, such that history itself might rotate on a pivot, and permit the inauguration of a new emancipatory historical formation. This caesura of the pure word, in a return of what is preserved in legend, might permit the arrival of a new configuration of divinity, in which the installation of patriarchal myth as religious truth is no longer determining. This is the work of theiology, a new appearing of divinity, as opposed to theology, an appropriation of a given divinity. For Hölderlin the contrast is one between the Olympian gods and the titans, as co-terminous with the natural forces of wind and sun, river and ocean, underworld and sky; and the gods of the mysteries, who transgress this natural limit. The Olympian order permits an elaboration of the hidden sides of these chthonic powers, the darkness of Hades, the disaggregating forces of Dionysus as twice born, figuring forms in the shadows, which follow the trajectory of the sun god, Apollo, across the sky.

There is then a transition from the localized gods of Greek city states, to those that can accompany human beings on their wanderings, beyond the claustrophobic relations imposed by those empowered within those city walls: Hölderlin's Bacchus and Benjamin's melancholy angel for example. The sobriety of Juno is of one who does not thus wander into heterogenesis and hybridism, does not permit or invite dissolution, nor yet urge a self-overcoming of a female principle. Juno is not party to the Olympian procreative surge, generating the demi-gods of Hölderlin's streams and rivers, woodlands and mountains, and mixing with the titans, who dare to defy the gods, Atlas, who holds up the world, Prometheus who steals fire, Epimetheus, who seeks to rescue his brother. When Zeus gives birth to himself as Athena, splitting open his own head with an axe, it is tempting to see a reversal of a previous process whereby Rhea gave birth to herself as a sky god, called Zeus, by cutting open time, Chronos. To open Junoian sobriety up to these forces, to permit her to take rebirth, would require Benjamin to reopen the reevaluation of death, to which he pays such close attention in this reading of the two poems, to a reevaluation of birth, and rebirth, and of whom may take rebirth.

In his essay "The Poet's Courage," Lacoue-Labarthe is keen to mark up the differences between Benjamin's and Heidegger's responses to Hölderlin, which he articulates through differences concerning the role and status of political theology, and differences between myth making, and fixed mythology. These differences provide him with a way to begin unpicking the invisible work of naturalization of political historical process. There is a link, too, to the program announced by Lacoue-Labarthe and Jean-Luc Nancy in 1982, under the title "retreating the political," designed, with full awareness of the comedy of its own attempt, to suspend engagement in the domain of minor politics, of deliberate engagement in an established field, in order to consider and reveal the constitution of the field itself: the move, in short from minor to greater politics. This move replicates the one, marked up by Benjamin, in his analysis of *Elective Affinities*, from following the play of representations, to identifying the function of representation itself. Lacoue-Labarthe shows both Benjamin and Heidegger attending to Hölderlin's focus on a turning of time (*die Wende der Zeit*), arriving in the break (caesura) in the line of meaning. Citing again from *Blödigkeit*, Hölderlin invokes the Sky God:

> Who grants the thinking day to poor and rich alike, who, at the turning point of time, keeps us, the sleepy, upright as one keeps children, with golden leading strings. (239)

Attunement to this breach of time is in principle open to both poor and rich, but it is perhaps as children that we are most receptive to the dynamics of such a complete standstill and reversal of time.

This then provides a clue to the third component of a response to Hölderlin, Benjamin and Heidegger, alongside analyses of their sobriety and intoxication: there must also be in play here a response to Lacoue-Labarthe's reworking of the pure word and countermovement, in his identification of what he calls a hyperbology in Hölderlin's writing: an intensification of movement in meaning.[18] The proposal here is to locate access to the full impact of such hyperbology in a reopening of the moment of an insertion, in childhood, into language and, more broadly, into a symbolic order. For children, acceptance of a given order of meaning is still a relatively recent accomplishment, one that still bears the markers of the movements by which it has been acquired. Meaning has not yet become a standing reserve, without movement, immobilizing thought in restrictive and restricted conventions. The immobilization of meaning thematized and enacted by Hölderlin,

Benjamin and Heidegger may thus be converted into movement, as a struggle over how to reconceive politics, by revisiting the processes of emergence, from nature, and night, sleep, and childhood. In that movement, as intensification and struggle, the order in any logical ordering securing meaning turns, opens up, and provides the pure word, the counterrhythmic intrusion, the gap through which, on Lacoue-Labarthe's reconstruction, these processes of emergence, of invention and indeed futurity itself may arrive into view. This is the moment of monstrous disruption, in which what is shown, because it cannot be captured in existing terms and categories, opens meaning up to its own generative transformation. It is the world in which a child acquires a language, or languages, in which partially to articulate what arrives. Sometimes what arrives will be experienced as genuinely monstrous, obscene, unthinkable, disgusting, to be marked up as more properly lying off stage: in short, as the disturbing figures of Benjamin, as childlike scapegoat, over whose custody the various parents battle, and of Heidegger, as prophet and betrayer of a renewal of political life.

Benjamin's warning about the silence at the heart of the task of translation, which threatens to enclose the translator in an irreducible solitude is well-enough known. The contrast to Heidegger's drive to transpose the origins of Greek thinking into a contemporary German idiom is not so often remarked. Examining that contrast through the focus of their respective responses to Hölderlin's innovations brings out a further contrast between the workings of legend, that which might be but has not yet been put into writing, of an oral transmission, in which unacknowledged strands of an inheritance may be preserved, and Heidegger's emphasis on the power of the word, or apothegm, Nietzsche's word, God is dead; or the remark, where the danger grows, there, too, is rescue and redemption, from the opening of Hölderlin's great elegy, "Patmos." These titans of the spirit are indigenous to the flow and growth of language itself, and, pivotal in their responses to Hölderlinian sobriety, are the utterly distinct registers of language to which they attend. The one is at work in the laboratory of citation, responding to and expanding on the allegories of industrialization and commerce; the other intent on espying a new dawn at the darkest hour, in a reworking of Hölderlins titans as distinctively German sources of regeneration.

Attention to Benjamin's and Heidegger's respective responses to Hölderlin opens out these distinctions between legend and myth, allegory and fable, and their potentiality for a challenge to a narrowing of the scope and understanding of the domain of politics, to that of explicit transactions, communication, information, formulation. The irrational and nonrational processes, beyond communicativity and information, glitter on the surface of daily life, in investments of energy in pageantry and militarization, sporting events, and the manipulation of populations. The monstrous forces generating an unpredictable future lie here in waiting to be excavated. This focus on differences between Benjamin and Heidegger, specifically in response to Hölderlin's innovations might provide access to these forces, and permit a more detailed specification of the differences between a greater politics, derived from returns to and reinventions of traditional patterns of political theology, and a more genuinely innovatory greater politics through which to give expression to the unprecedented challenges of the day, posed by economic idolatries of various kinds, and mass movements of populations, by the privatization of the wealth of nations, and the immiseration of public life. The reinvention of humanity by interfering in the biogenetics of the human species provides an entirely twenty-first-century version of the miscegenation of divinities with mortals, rivers with sky gods, of Hölderlin's imaginings, and of sons with mothers, and fathers with daughters, of Greek myth. The sacral status of incest for Greek tragedy and the hereditary doom of its offspring are to be contrasted to the political economy of population management and the need to reinvent childhood as the powerhouse or destruction of self-generating innovation. Furthermore, the arrival of the thematics of sexual difference poses a question to the contrasting fates of the sons and the daughters of Oedipus' incest. The contrasting fates of his sons, Eteocles and Polynices, are charted in Sophocles' plays; the contrast between the fates of Iphigenia and Antigone, by contrast to those of Ismene and Electra, the daughters sacrificed, and the daughters who live on, remains to be retrieved. This would presuppose a differentiation of the figure of childhood, and of the threat of infantilization, to fill out the partial gesture made in psychoanalysis, of seeking to install an Electra complex alongside that of Oedipus. Attention to a proliferation of daughters' destinies would pose the need to rewrite Sophocles even more emphatically than the rewriting effected by Hölderlin.

Notes

1. Samuel Weber, *Benjamin's -abilities* (Cambridge, MA: Harvard University Press, 2008), 91.
2. Kant discusses the aspiration to maturity of a people, and of the individuals constituting that people, in the short essay "An Answer to the Question: What is Enlightenment?" (1784), which begins with the claim "Enlightenment is the emergence of human beings from self-incurred immaturity [*Umundigkeit*]," literally lack of voice. See Immanuel Kant, *Political Writings*, ed. H. B. Nisbet (Cambridge: Cambridge University Press, 1998).
3. Theodor W. Adorno, while dashing Benjamin's hopes during his lifetime for a

positive reception of his study of the Paris of Baudelaire, published with Gershom Scholem the posthumous two-volume edition of Benjamin's *Schriften* (Frankfurt am Main: Suhrkamp, 1955), and a two-volume edition of letters again with Scholem also with Suhrkamp, in 1966. Hannah Arendt edited and wrote the introduction to the 1968 English translation of a selection of Walter Benjamin's writings, under the title *Illuminations*, trans. Harry Zohn (New York: Harcourt and Brace, 1968). In it there appeared a translation of Benjamin's "Historico-Philosophical Theses," of which he had entrusted a copy to Hannah Arendt when they met in Marseilles in early autumn of 1940, Arendt to board ship for Lisbon, Benjamin to walk over the border into Spain.

4. For a recent revival of this process, see Emmanuel Faye still at work in his recent piece, "Being, History, Technology, Extermination in the work of Heidegger," *Journal of the History of Philosophy*, 50.1, (2012, 111–130). The combination of careful scholarship and extravagantly distorting reading shows that the process of fissioning is transitive, from subject to commentator.

5. For the infamous phrase printed in the published version of lectures from 1935, see Martin Heidegger: *Introduction to Metaphysics* (1953), new translation by Gregory Fried and Richard Polt (New Haven, CT: Yale University Press, 2000), 213; for the nervous collapse, see Hugo Ott, *Martin Heidegger: A Political Life*, trans. Allen Blunden (New York: Basic Books, 1993).

6. Martin Heidegger, "*Andenken*" (1943) in *GA* 4. Published as the fourth essay in the 1951, and subsequent editions of *Elucidations of Hölderlin's Poetry*, ed. and trans. Keith Hoeller (Amherst, NY: Prometheus Books, 2000).

7. See Martin Heidegger, "Only a God Can Save Us Now," in eds. Gunther Neske and Emil Kettering, *Martin Heidegger and National Socialism: Questions and Answers*, trans. Karsten and Lisa Harries (New York: Paragon House, 1990), 41–65.

8. See Beatrice Hanssen, "*Dichtermut* and *Blödigkeit*—Two poems by Friedrich Hölderlin, Interpreted by Walter Benjamin," in Beatrice Hanssen and Andrew Benjamin, eds., *Walter Benjamin and Romanticism* (London: Continuum, 2002), 139–162; and, Philippe Lacoue-Labarthe, "Poetry's Courage," in Hanssen and Benjamin, *Benjamin and Romanticism*, 163–179; and also in Lacoue-Labarthe, *Heidegger and the Politics of Poetry*, trans. and ed. Jeff Fort (Urbana: University of Illinois Press, 2007).

9. "*Wie wenn am Feiertage*," Heidegger's lecture on Hölderlin from 1941, is printed as the third essay in *Elucidations of Hölderlin's Poetry*.

10. Martin Heidegger, *Hölderlin's Hymn Der Ister*, trans. and ed. William McNeill and Julia Davis (Indianapolis: Indiana University Press, 1996). This lecture from the summer of 1942 can be found in *GA* 53.

11. Friedrich Hölderlin, *Selected Verse*, with an Introduction and prose translations by Michael Hamburger (London: Anvil Press Poetry, 1986), 135. Hereafter, all references to this edition will be made parenthetically within the text, without further clarification.
12. See Hannah Arendt: *The Human Condition* (Chicago: Chicago University Press, 1958).
13. For such discussion see Foucault's review of Jean Laplanche in Michel Foucault, *Language Counter Memory Practice: Selected Essays and Interviews*, ed. David Bouchard (Oxford: Blackwell, 1978). Foucault writes of Hölderlin:

 > [H]e created and manifested the link between a work and the absence of a work, between the flight of the gods and the loss of language. He stripped the artist of his magnificent powers—his timelessness, his capacity to guarantee the truth and to raise every event to the heights of language. Hölderlin's language replaced the epic unity commemorated by Vasari with a division that is responsible for every work in our culture, a division which links it to its own absence and to its dissolution in the madness that had accompanied it from the beginning. (ibid., 58)

14. This is the second of the essays to be found in Heidegger's *Elucidations*, already in the first edition, 1944, where it follows Heidegger's essay on "*Heimkunft- an die Verwandten.*"
15. For a discussion of this see the first chapter on translatability, in Weber's *Benjamin's -abilities*, where he rehearses Benjamin's reflections on Heidegger's treatments of these topics.
16. For just two of the many studies of Antigone, and all she has been taken to represent, see George Steiner, *Antigones: The Antigone Myth in Western Literature, Art and Thought* (Oxford: Oxford University Press, 1986); and, Judith Butler, *Antigone's Claim: Kinship Between Life and Death* (New York: Columbia University Press, 2000).
17. "We too are good and sent to someone for something when we come with art, and bring one of the Heavenly with us. Yet we ourselves bring competent hands" (239).
18. For Lacoue-Labarthe on this hyperbology, see the essay "The Caesura of the Speculative" in Philippe Lacoue-Labarthe, *Typography: Mimesis, Philosophy, Politics*, ed. and trans. Christopher Fynsk (Cambridge, MA: Harvard University Press, 1989), 231. For an extended treatment of hyperbology, see John Martis: *Philippe Lacoue-Labarthe: Representation and the Loss of the Subject* (New York: Fordham University Press, 2005).

PART V

Politics

NINE

BEYOND REVOLUTION

Benjamin and Heidegger on Violence and Power

Krzysztof Ziarek

An Alternative Critique of Violence

Let me begin with two quotations: "Die göttliche Gewalt, welche Insignium und Siegel, niemals Mittel heiligen Vollstreckung ist, mag die waltende heissen." / "The divine violence, which is the sign and seal but never the means of sacred execution, may be called 'reigning' violence"; and "Das Gewalt-lose Walten." / "The violence-free reign." The first famous quotation closes Benjamin's *Zur Kritik der Gewalt*. The second, still largely unnoticed in critical debates, comes from the initial sections of Heidegger's *Die Geschichte des Seyns* (GA 69), published only in 1998 but dating from 1938 to 1940, the years marking the outbreak of the violence of World War II. I am allowing language to bring together here Benjamin and Heidegger—more frequently opposed to each other than discussed jointly—precisely with respect to the problematic of violence, *Gewalt*, and its relation to its root verb *walten*. Juxtaposed this way, the two quotations let us reflect on the fact that Benjamin's text gives priority to divine *Gewalt* (violence, rule, governance) understood specifically in terms of *walten*: of holding sway, ruling, governing. Modifying it with the adjective *waltende*, and thus naming it doubly by its own name, as it were, Benjamin draws attention to the fact that *Gewalt* signifies the gathering, indicated by the prefix *ge-*, of the operations of *walten*. It is perhaps in this sense that one can understand Benjamin's remarks about divine violence as "pure": speaking of the educative *Gewalt*, Benjamin describes it as "an extension of pure or divine power"

(*SW* 1: 250), "Eine solche Ausdehnung reiner oder göttlicher Gewalt" (*GS* 2.1: 200). Having set up an equivalence between pure and "divine" violence/power—both senses of *Gewalt*, with another possible translation as coercive force—Benjamin suggests that pure violence is nothing but the forcing and prevailing that comes to make violence what it is: it is the very movement of violence, that is, its *walten* gathered into *Gewalt*. It seems that Benjamin points out the uniqueness of divine violence as that which, free from means and ends, happens as its own sway. The divine violence is what it is by virtue of its merely holding sway and prevailing. It does not have a "what," a content, or an essence: it is its own reign and nothing else. It is this "pure sway," which radically distinguishes divine violence from other forms of violence: mythical, law-making, law-preserving, and so on. Pure violence is "median" violence, or violence as its own medium, the medium in which other forms of violence can exist to begin with.

While the end of Benjamin's texts invites us to think *Gewalt* by way of *walten*, Heidegger's remark, by contrast, telescopes attention on *walten* itself, using it as a verbal substantive and modifying it by a noun turned adjectival: *das Gewalt-lose*. In this turn of phrase, Heidegger strips *Gewalt* of its primary role, that is, as the gathering of the forms of *walten*, and turns it, in its "negative" form, into a modifier of *walten*. *Walten* becomes the principal part of the phrase, grammatically and philosophically, shifting attention from violence/power to the prevailing and working indicated by the verb *walten*. Heidegger moves to rethink this prevailing—what emerges as the "nonviolent" force of *walten*—away from violence and coercive force, and, as we see shortly, also from power (*Macht*) and eventually also from mastery/lordship (*Herrschaft*). Resetting the primary register of *walten* in relation to *Gewalt*, Heidegger proposes to think *walten* as released or freed from violence: as *das Gewalt-lose*.

Since Derrida's "The Force of Law" and especially Agamben's *Homo Sacer*, Benjamin's "Critique of Violence" has been widely debated, critiqued, and variously interpreted. It has certainly inspired a great deal of debate about violence, justice, law, and sovereignty. By contrast, Heidegger's critical engagement with power (*Macht*), violence (*Gewalt*), and mastery (*Herrschaft*), contained in a series of books written from 1936 through 1940s and only recently published in German, has received scant attention in these debates. Furthermore, the stigma of the 1933 Rectorate and support for National Socialism expressed in Heidegger's texts between 1933 and 1935, combined with the general lack of familiarity with the subsequently written but recently published and still mostly not translated works, seems to disqualify, at least in some circles, Heidegger's work, rendering it unworthy of critical engagement, and often judged a priori to be unable to offer any crucial insight into such matters as power, law, or justice. Yet my contention here is that it is precisely in Heidegger's thought—a thought that begins to respond to the planetary confrontation of powers and total war enveloping the world in late 1930s—that we find the most radically transformative challenge to the dominion of power, violence, rule, and sovereignty. A much longer critical study, taking a look at the already mentioned series of books, would be needed to clarify the importance of these works not only for understanding Heidegger but, more important, for the critique of modernity and of its idioms of power, production, knowledge, life, and so on. I can only sketch out some of these implications here and introduce them by reading Benjamin on violence in relation to Heidegger's remarks on power, violence, and mastery.

Divine Violence

Benjamin's text on violence has generated different, even contesting, interpretations. This is not surprising given the sometimes aphoristic and even cryptic way Benjamin writes, which often leaves the reader with terms qualified by various adjectives, whose resonance needs to be interpreted, if not developed. I am not interested here in a reading of the essay on violence as a whole, or in illuminating the various distinctions Benjamin introduces within the concept of violence (*Gewalt*): between mythic and divine violence, law-making and law-preserving, transformative and annihilating, bloody and bloodless (expiatory), pure and impure, and so on. Rather, I focus on the violence named in the remark closing Benjamin's text, namely divine violence, which is pure (*reine*) and "principal" or "reigning" (*waltende*). Obviously the other forms of violence enter into this consideration to the extent to which the elaboration of divine violence hinges, and at times quite precariously it seems, on the ability to distinguish it from these other nondivine, that is, human and natural, forms. This is the case because the impetus of Benjamin's text is to demarcate, by way of a very brief "history as critique" of violence, a violence that would be capable of suspending, even annihilating, and thus ending all other forms of violence. A key aspect of this setting apart of divine violence is that: "Justice [*Gerechtigkeit*] is the principle of all divine end making, power [*Macht*] the principle of all mythical lawmaking" (*SW* 1: 248/ *GS* 2.1: 198). Although mythical violence makes laws, divine violence is law-annihilating (*rechtsvernichtend*) (*SW* 1: 250/ *GS* 2.1: 199).

Crucially, this form of pure violence is not just unavailable to human beings, but it cannot even be recognized by them. "Less possible and also less urgent for humankind, however, is to decide when pure violence has been realized in particular cases. For only mythical violence, not divine, will be recognizable as such with certainty, unless it be in incomparable effects, because the expiatory force [*Kraft*] of violence is invisible [*zutage*] for men" (*SW* 1: 252/ *GS* 2.1: 203). The violence Benjamin aims at here is so radically different that it may not even be recognized in its effects; it may pass unnoticed, and not register at all as violence or power. It is apparently for those reasons that Benjamin calls it pure and divine. One way to pursue this avenue of thinking is to move the concept of *Gewalt* toward a progressive evacuation of violence and power. The other is to remark precisely, as Rodolphe Gasché does, on the ambiguity of the manifestations of this violence: "If, in the end, divine violence appears to be undecidable, it is because its own concept of pure distinction requires that it must be different from its own manifestations. Whatever Benjaminian gestures could be shown to undermine the thought of such a pure violence, they are not deliberate; they certainly are not thematized." Yet as Gasché argues in distinguishing between critique and deconstruction, this critical gesture par excellence on Benjamin's part, the gesture trying to secure pure nonmediate violence and guard it against all contamination, is bound to ruin itself: "the very 'thing' itself of a pure nonmediate violence cannot *not* yield to what it so violently excludes—the mediate, the law, the mere life."[1]

What comes to the fore here is the principal difficulty of Benjamin's text, namely the question of whether what he calls *divine violence* as "pure violence" is violence to begin with, whether it is violent at all. And if it is not, as some approaches suggest,[2] then why call it violence.[3] In his recent paper, "Life Beyond Violence," Andrew Benjamin argues that the distinction between divine violence and "mythic violence" has "a force that positions the term 'Gewalt' in its slow withdrawal from a complete identification with 'violence' and allows it to be connected increasingly to the presence of an operative sense of power."[4] "As a result Gewalt will be able to be held apart from any direct, let alone inevitable relation to terror."[5] In Andrew Benjamin's view, pure violence comes to resemble a power of interruption, an opening, and also an allowing, and thus potential for transformation. "'Pure violence' is an interruption and an allowing."[6]

This move within *Gewalt* from violence to potentiality and even allowing is indeed intimated in the term itself, which historically came to translate *potestas* (power/potentiality) and later also *violentia*.[7] The German predecessor of the word, before it acquired legal and state power connotations, was likely linked to the Indo-European root *val-* and thus can be thought as indicating being in force, capable, obtaining. The modern use of the word appears to superimpose *potestas* and *violentia*, while giving the upper hand to the latter and emphasizing the sense of *Gewalt* as: power, authority, sway, dominion, control, force, coercion, violence, restraint, strength, might. The ambiguity and possible transformation or turn within the term *Gewalt* is further highlighted by the verb form *walten*: to govern, rule, but also exercise, or be at work. The Grimm dictionary gives two explanations for the root *walten*, which allows it to be read as both "die kraft für etwas, gewalt über etwas haben": "to have the force/ capacity for something, to have power over something."[8] The complicated and complex use of *walten* and its derivatives in German is inevitably replicated to some extent by Benjamin's texts, suggesting the possibility of thinking *Gewalt* more in terms of what is at work and remains in force, rather than simply violence or coercive force. Yet, as David Krell puts it, it remains a question "whether *Gewalt* is 'violence' *plus* governance, ruling sway, sovereignty; or whether it is more likely that 'violence' lies concealed in the governance of the messianic, theocratic, critical-aesthetic, and moral word."[9] In other words, whether the sense of prevailing and working offsets the primary sense of violence and coercion, or, rather, conversely, any sense of "being in force" is inevitably "powered" by violence and coercion.

For all the ambiguity and semantic sliding inscribed in the notion of pure violence and the undecidability of its manifestations, its "location" seems to be unambiguous in the text: Benjamin repeatedly refers to it as being outside (*ausserhalb*) or beyond (*jenseits*) the law. Whether it is divine violence capable of bringing a halt to mythic violence or educative violence, law-destroying violence and even revolutionary violence, each of these manifestations—whether pure or impure is less relevant here—confirms the momentum of Benjamin's essay toward securing "pure nonmediate violence" beyond the law: "der Gewalt auch jenseits des Rechtes ihr Bestand als reine unmittelbare gesichert" (*GS* 2.1: 202). The securing of pure violence beyond the law demonstrates that and how revolutionary violence is possible and designates it "as the highest manifestation of pure violence through man": "die höchste Manifestation reiner Gewalt durch den Menschen zu belegen ist" (*GS* 2.1: 202). Revolutionary violence is not pure violence; rather, pure violence manifests itself through human beings in their revolutionary violence, though it cannot be identified with revolutionary violence. Here Benjamin puts into question the notion of sovereignty, indicating that pure violence manifests through the human exercise of power and cannot be as such a matter of mastery or sovereignty. Pure violence is not sovereign but *waltende*: signing itself with its own name, at work just by being itself, that is, simply by being.

The ending of Benjamin's *Zur Kritik der Gewalt* opens, therefore, the question of what it is exactly that manifests itself either in revolutionary violence or as law-annihilating violence in relation to law-making and law-preserving forms of violence. This *waltende Gewalt* neither preserves the law nor makes new laws, as revolutions are bound to, and thus it finds itself in a way beyond conservatism and revolution, beyond the human reach, though implicated and moving through the human domain, never reducible to human agency and yet on occasion manifesting through it, pushing it toward (revolutionary) transformation.

If we place the emphasis, like Andrew Benjamin does, on the interruptive and allowing force of pure violence, progressively taken away from the connotations of violence and coercion, does not what Walter Benjamin tries to open the door to in *Zur Kritik der* Gewalt come to resemble Heidegger's "das Gewalt-lose Walten"? It does, on the condition that pure violence begins to be taken away from some of its qualifiers in the text: divine, expiatory, annihilating. These adjectives keep binding Benjamin's pure violence to monotheistic and onto-theo-logical positions in ways that cannot be addressed here. That said, and hopefully without doing too much violence to Benjamin's text, if one follows this line of interrogation and takes the onto-theo-logical references as part of the history of various forms of violence, which Benjamin sketches by mentioning instances of mythic and divine violence, then these references appear precisely as markers of the outside and the beyond, securing the possibility of (pure) *Gewalt* outside the law. And it is specifically this securing that constitutes the very momentum of Benjamin's critique.

The key adjective "divine" (*göttlich*), framing Benjamin's discussion and excepting pure violence from other forms, remains the most difficult here. Is it a marker of "pure" outside, or of a transcendent vector of power? Does it not inevitably inscribe Benjamin's critique of violence into the metaphysical precepts of a power beyond all powers, a transcendent guarantee, whose end is justice rather than power itself? "Once again all eternal forms are open to pure divine violence, which myth bastardized with law" (*SW* 1: 300, 252). Another adjective, "expiatory," also attached by Benjamin to divine violence (*SW* 1: 252), indeed suggests a "redemptive" scenario, though typically for Benjamin, one that would end history rather than redeem or justify its "history of violence." This impression is reinforced repeatedly by Benjamin's calling divine violence "annihilating" (*vernichtend*), suggesting an all embracing power of total destruction: "pure divine violence over all life for the sake of the living"(*SW* 1: 250; trans. modified). It is the kind of violence that "does not stop short of annihilation" (*SW* 1: 250)/ "macht nicht Halt vor der Vernichtung" (*GS* 2.1: 199).[10] Because of this insistence on the possibility of annihilation, does the resonance of "divine" continue to be (onto)theological in the text to its very end, or can it still be taken as part of or a manifestation within the history of violence, which is also its critique? That is, are the terms *divine* and *pure* Benjamin's shorthand, borrowed from the "history of violence," in order to attempt a dislodging and questioning of *all* forms of violence, as some interpretations suggest? Taking Benjamin's text in this way, what we inherit is the possibility, and necessity, of thinking violence (which is not violence) as an "outside" inside history. Or "life beyond violence," as Andrew Benjamin calls it.

Beyond Violence?

Such possibility of "beyond violence" unfolds, I argue, even more manifestly from Heidegger's work from mid-1930s onward, in particular from his critique of power (*Macht*), violence or coercive force (*Gewalt*), and mastery/lordship (*Herrschaft*). Heidegger's comment on violence-free sway or force is much more explicit in seeking to release *walten* (most often deployed by him in the sense of prevailing) from the purchase of violence. In fact, Heidegger's complex deployment of *walten* throughout his work could be read as a continuing interrogation of violence, which is definitely the case after the turn of the mid-1930s. For the kind of reign or sway (*walten*) Heidegger is attributing to being (in the sense of *Seyn* played against the standard modern spelling *Sein*) is one that is violence-, rule-, and governance-free. This sense of "sway" is connected by Heidegger to the notion of event: "Ereignis und die Milde der höchsten Herrschaft, die nicht der Macht und nicht des 'Kampfes' bedarf, sonder ursprüngliche Auseinander-setzung. Das Gewalt-lose Walten" (*GA* 69: 8). "Event and the gentleness of the highest majesty, which does not need power and 'struggle,' but originary con-frontation. The violence-free reign." At this point in *Die Geschichte des Seyns*, Heidegger still holds on to the term *Herrschaft*, which he tries to think, as *Besinnung* indicates, as majesty (*maiestas*) and deploy critically against the notion of mastery or lordship.

While Benjamin attempts to unearth and take *Gewalt* toward a sense of nonviolence, Heidegger performs a similar operation on *Herrschaft*, playing *Herrschaft* as majesty and dignity against *Herrschaft* as power, rule, dominion, or sovereignty. In fact, this sense of majesty (of being) is directed specifically against the possibility of mastering. Several pages later, in chapter 57, entitled "Das Wesen der Macht" (*GA* 69: 62–74) or "The Essence of Power," after another rescue attempt, Heidegger decides to abandon the term *Herrschaft* as completely inapt and unsuitable for how he proposes to think *Seyn* (being). He starts by saying that every power is false majesty/rule or a semblance of it: "All Macht ist Scheinherrschaft." He continues by inserting a parenthetical remark about the sense of *Herrschaft* as *charis*: "(*Herrschaft* ist die χάρις des Seyns als des Seyns, stille Würde der milden Bindung, die sich nie in das Bedürfen der Macht zu versteifen braucht)" (*GA* 69: 69). "*Majesty* is the *charis* of being as of being, the silent dignity of the gentle binding, which does not need to harden into the use of power." The parenthetical remark italicizes *Herrschaft* to set it apart as majesty from sovereignty and rule. Yet immediately after the close of the parenthesis, Heidegger declares that, despite the possibility of the internal slide between majesty and mastery, *Herrschaft* as a term of thinking needs to be called into question and assigned to the domain of power, because it is totally inadequate for the idiom of the power- and violence-free relation he is trying to evolve: "'Herrschaft' wird so zum völlig ungemässen Wort und deshalb dem Wesenbereich der Macht überwiesen" (*GA* 69: 69). The inscription of *Herrschaft* into the domain of *Macht* indexes the fact that, though trying to except itself from the law, sovereignty remains inescapably part of power, power that brooks no exception to its sway, to its violence-driven *walten*.

This vacillation within *Herrschaft* shows the extent to which Heidegger thinks by submitting his own thought to a continuous questioning. Another indicator of this Heideggerian movement of thought is the shift in the term central to my discussion here, namely *Gewalt*. In the well-known reading of the Antigone chorus in Introduction to Metaphysics (1935), Heidegger speaks about the human being as violence-doing (*gewalttätig*), yet only four years later in *Die Geschichte des Seyns*, violence-doing (*Gewalttätigkeit*) becomes synonymous with brutality (*Brutalität*) and explained as part and parcel of the operations of power (that is, of metaphysics), which are to be deconstructed and transformed (*GA* 69: 76). In a couple of sections following the discussion of "the essence of power" in the twenty-six numbered sections, Heidegger links *Gewalt* to the central concept against which his thinking turns, namely power (*Macht*). "Wenn die Macht sich selbst in den Gebrauch nimmt und sich verbrauchen muss, dann wird die Macht zur Gewalt" (*GA* 69: 75). "When power puts itself to use and must expend itself, then it turns into violence." *Gewalt* as violence or coercive force is a manifestation of power, which does not have to be explicit violence in order to compel and steer. However, in either case it renders unfree, even when power, as is its tendency, dissimulates its essence, hiding its essentially violent workings: "das wesenhafte Gewaltwesen der Macht" (*GA* 69: 74). For Heidegger, *Gewalt*, most often seen as one of the modes of the deployment of power, is, like *Herrschaft*, captured within and assigned to the domain of *Macht*. Its assignment to power is "essential": it is the *Gewaltwesen* of power. The triad of *Macht*, *Gewalt*, and *Herrschaft*, which Heidegger's texts from mid-1930s interrogate, revolves around a complex sense of power (*Macht*), which works through metaphysics and its onto-theo-logical positions. This is why for Heidegger, God or monotheistic divinity, remains inscribed in the very metaphysics of power, and whether operating as *Gewalt* or *Herrschaft*, remains essentially pervaded by the operations of power, whether creative or destructive. It does not stand outside or beyond power, but, even in creating the semblance of the beyond, as *ens supremum* or *actus purus*, becomes its part and parcel, its grounding force.

In this context, all forms of violence become manifestations of power. *Gewalt* is the way power shows itself as power.

If we could think about the violence discussed in *Introduction to Metaphysics* as "mythic," then what Heidegger juxtaposes to it is not divine violence, in fact, not violence at all, but a transformation in power and violence, which he describes through the term *Milde*: gentleness. The remarkable twenty-six points about power from the chapter "The Essence of Power" (*GA* 69: 62–71) sketch out the operations of power that we have come to know from Foucault (to an extent elaborated via Heidegger's readings of Nietzsche), and which now we have an occasion to read in Heidegger's own, much earlier formulation. Some of the key points Heidegger underscores have to do with the continuing transpowering (*Übermächtigung*) of power, the fact that power operates intrinsically without aims or goals; power needs no carriers or possessors as it carries those who appear to possess it; power elevates/sublates (*aufheben*) the possibility of law, insofar as power changes the essence of law to a dissemination or distribution of power (*Machtverteilung*) (*GA* 69: 64); power is constructive and productive; it exercises itself by compelling, though not necessarily in violent or coercive manner—it often compels through production, empowering, creation, and so on; power locks the dynamics of history into the binary of power and its absence (*Ohnmacht*) (*GA* 69: 66), disallowing any possibility of something that would not explain itself as power and thus amount to either power's presence or its absence.

It is in the course of elaborating these points on power that Heidegger decides to assign *Herrschaft* to the domain of power (under point twenty-three) and do so quite explicitly in the context of his critical remarks about race and racial superiority (*Rassevorrang*). Point twenty-five of "The Essence of Power" is entitled "Power and Race" and shows the critical link between the metaphysical notion of the subject as the ground of race thinking: the subject as supposedly constituted/produced as self-identical. The production of subjectivity underlies the doctrine of race, racial differences, as well as the notion of the production of race. The understanding of subjectivity in its relation to power renders race available to calculation (*Rechnen*) and manipulation. In fact, as Heidegger remarks: "Rasse-züchtung ist ein Weg der Selbstbehauptung für die Herrschaft" (*GA* 69: 70) / "Race-breeding is a way of self-assertion for mastery/ lordship." Here clearly the term *Herrschaft* becomes associated with the "master race," and points to the implication of race thinking in the drive toward power and control. This remark indicates that a factor in Heidegger's decision to abandon the term *Herrschaft* is its association with race-breeding and mastery, or, in short, with the master race. In an appendix to "Koinon," the second text in *Die Geschichte des Seyns*, Heidegger states: "'Rasse' ist ein Machtbegriff—setz *Subjektivität* voraus" / "Race is a concept of power—presupposes *subjectivity*"(*GA* 69: 222). For those willing to read, these remarks should also point out clearly where Heidegger's thought places itself in 1939–1940 in relation to the racial doctrines of National Socialism. It is equally important in this context to expose the suppositions of Emmanuel Faye, who tries to present the very same quotes from Heidegger—and several more in the same vein—as purportedly endorsing the Nazi racial doctrine. The context of Heidegger's critique of subjectivity, as well as of nation, people, and race as extensions of the will to power from which Heidegger distances his thought, leaves no doubt as to the critical nature of these remarks, and leads one to the conclusion that Faye is either unable to understand what he reads in Heidegger or intentionally misreads him.[11]

To reinforce this point, let me mention here that a few pages after the lines cited earlier Heidegger remarks on how power drives toward the extreme either-or, its essence demanding a "life and death" struggle (*Kampf*), in which one must annihilate the other. Not threaten with annihilation as in Hegel's master/slave dialectic, but actually annihilate the other, so that, as Heidegger adds, no recognition of the other can take place (*GA* 69: 71). Given the context of Heidegger's discussion on race thought and race-breeding, there seems hardly any doubt as to the aim of these remarks, namely, the doctrine of racial superiority. In fact, the critique of the interweaving of *Macht*, *Gewalt*, and *Herrschaft* I have been outlining here makes sense precisely as part of Heidegger's critical injunction against nationalisms and socialisms, operating, in his view, as part and parcel of the metaphysics of power[12] and its *Machenschaft*. It is precisely in the context of these texts and their crucial insights and transformations, still too often ignored by those writing on this topic, that the relation of Heidegger's thought to National Socialism needs to be reexamined.[13]

It is crucial to note that there is a marked difference in Heidegger between the operations of *Macht* and *Gewalt* as *Vernichtung*, annihilation, and the *macht-los* event of being as *nichtend*: nihilating. Nihilation in Heidegger marks the originative play of time-space, each time one time and singularly given, that is, always already nihilated, opened in a futural projecting-open. In short, nihilation marks the silent force of the possible. There is a way of thinking nihilation precisely as that which singularizes, which allows what is, to be always and only onetime, *einmalig* as Heidegger puts it. This singularization of each time is the very movement of experience, it is *das Nichtige* taken away from the sense of nothingness or nothing (as absence of being) (*CP*: 173/ *GA* 65: 245) and also from *das Vernichtende* as an extreme manifestation of violence. "'Nothingness' is neither the negation of beings nor the negation of beingness, nor is it the 'privation' of being; it is not the deprivation [*Beraubung*] that simultaneously would be an annihilation [*Vernichtung*].

Rather, *'nothingness' is the foremost and highest gift of be-ing* [*Seyn*], which along with itself and as itself gifts be-ing as event unto the clearing of the origin [*Ursprung*] *as abyss* [*Ab-grund*]" (*M*: 263, modified/ *GA* 66: 294–295). This is why for Heidegger being never annihilates, only power and violence can. Being's nihilation marks the span of finitude and Dasein's own most nonrelational possibility: death. Rethought this way, nihilation is the highest gift in the sense that it allows the play of time-space to be instantiated each time as singular, as one time, and allows thinking to experience it in this way. This experience of nihilation gives/allows to be, and is sharply distinguished from annihilation as the depriving of being. What can be annihilated is precisely finitude as the experience of nihilation characteristic of Dasein. Furthermore, it is precisely the *Nichten*, the nihilating *intrinsic* to being that, for Heidegger, releases from power and violence, and not manifests it. In other words, nihilation is the vector indicated by the suffix *–los* in the phrases like *macht-los* and *gewalt-los*. As taken away from the nothing and annihilation, nihilation "works" as the possibility of the power-free.

In his thought of the event as the gentle or mild binding, Heidegger explicitly seeks a way of relating and a force that would be free of violence, governance, and domain—*gewalt-los*. This remark echoes the insistence in the earlier book, *Besinnung*, on the need to think being (*Seyn*) as beyond power and powerlessness, as power-free (*macht-los*). "The power-less is not the same as what is without-power while it is deprived of power and lacks power nevertheless and simply remains related to power" (*M*: 166). The absence of power, that which is powerless in the sense of being without power, is part and parcel of power and essentially related to it: it is the shadow of power, its verso, and its companion. The *power-less* in the sense of the *power-free* is unrelated to power as Heidegger puts it. "And being is thus beyond both power and powerlessness. And yet being is not *something that belongs to the 'beyond'* [*Jenseitiges*] since being does not need first to posit for its truth the secular [*Dieseitige*] powerful (actual) beings in order that being or the be-ing-historical projecting-opening of its clearing can have a leap-off" (*M*: 170).

To think being as *Gewalt-los*, *Macht-los*, and *Herr-los* is precisely to think that which remains released from power and violence, as well as their absence, and which at the same time does not belong to a beyond. Being has no need of a beyond, and thus also not of "this side" (*Dieseitige*), no need of the "divine" and of the "secular," which means that its event remains in some dimension untouched by power and violence—whether mythic/secular or divine violence is no longer relevant here. For Heidegger, the operations of power (*Macht*) pervade all the oppositions between "here" and "beyond," thus effectively canceling the opposition and making it a constitutive moment in the deployment of power. Even though being does not explain itself in terms of power and its absence, it is not beyond them.

Rather, it grants and gives them, in the way in which all that exists *is*, in this specific sense, *given to be*. And it is this granting and giving that remains beyond power and powerlessness without being a beyond or an outside to power.

The Gentle Bind of the Event

One of the striking gestures of Heidegger's texts from *Contributions to Philosophy* to the just published *Das Ereignis* is the idiom of the gentle bind (*milde Bindung*). *Die Geschichte des Seyns* returns several times to this idiom of gentleness, the idiom that is beginning to take shape at that time in Heidegger's texts and becomes known from his later writings as *Gelassenheit*. The juxtaposition Heidegger makes there is between power, violence, and rule-oriented relations, the complex and global scope of *Machenschaft*, on the one hand, and gentle binds, event-like relations, which bind beings in the modality of *Gelassenheit*, on the other. This modality of gentleness and mildness (*Milde*) is not to be confused, however, with powerlessness signifying the absence of power. As Heidegger puts it, this "gentleness" is *machtunbedürftig*: it has no need of power. This modality of *Milde* as having no need of power is thus located "beyond" the scope of power and without-power. It is beyond them in the sense of being unrelated to them, of another order of relating, as it were. Yet this gentle binding does not constitute a beyond but remains within power and powerlessness as the power-free. As Heidegger puts it, the power-free can never be disempowered (*M*: 168), and it is never a deficiency of power. Rather, power and its absence are not fitting or appropriate to the power-free. "[T]he name power-less [that is, power-free] should indicate that in accordance with its essence [Wesen], be-ing [*Seyn*] continues to be detached [*losgelöst*] from power. However, *this* power-less *is* mastery [*Herrschaft*]" (*M*: 170, modified). As is evident, Heidegger's texts are not free from their own ambiguities, as the above quotation from *Besinnung* predates the abandonment of *Herrschaft* in *Die Geschichte des Seyns* and signals that at this point Heidegger still tried to reserve the resonance of *maiestas* in *Herrschaft*: "On occasions we use the word 'power' in the transfigurative sense of *maiestas*, which means the same as 'mastery,' [*Herrschaft*] although even this word frequently gets lost in vagueness and approximates what is in the nature of power in the sense of coercive force [*Gewalt*]" (*M*: 170). As this remark makes clear, Heidegger's idiom, not unlike Benjamin's, vacillates between the various connotations of *Macht*, *Gewalt*, and *Herrschaft*, trying to maintain their power- and violence-free resonances, and not to lose the sense that something "transpires" or transforms in their enactment. Nonetheless, we can see clearly that what is at issue is a critique of power and violence and the possibility of "force" and "relation" that would be transformative without being *power-ful* or violent: a *Gewalt-lose Walten* and a *Macht-lose Machen*.

The difficulty of negotiating the idiom of thinking that would befit *das Gewalt-lose Walten* and *das Machtlose* has to do precisely with the way in which power pervades all relations and establishes an exclusive, that is, without exception, purchase on thought, language, and action. Power rules and governs, in the sense of *Herrschaft*, thought and language in ways that disallow anything that is not thinkable in terms of power, with a sign of either a plus or a minus with regard to power, thus inscribing it within the purview of power and its absence: "power and super-power must always necessarily and *from the ground up* mis-cognize the essence of that which is power-free . . ." (*M*: 168; modified). Explaining this in more detail, Heidegger adds: "However, since long ago man, and modern man in particular, calculates everything (and even being) according to power and powerlessness, usefulness and disadvantage, success and uselessness, he is not capable of hearing any word of be-ing [*Seyn*] and of thinking its truth without initiating his *calculation*" (*M*: 170). All thought and action calculate what they do in terms of power and powerlessness, and continue to be unable to hear anything in another tonality, namely one that is power-free. This is why Heidegger insists on the need to allow into thinking and acting ways that would not be calculable in terms of power or its impasses but would release from power and violence.

To the extent that it is neither without power nor powerful, this letting go and release from power introduces a fold, perhaps even an interruption into the workings of power. However, we must be careful with how we think this "interruptive" allowing, perhaps better seen as originative in the sense of Heidegger's term *ursprünglich*. For this originative letting is not a counter to power and also not an absence of power, but a release, a clearing in power, which does not submit to power and cannot be explained as absence of power, or as a hole in its all-embracing weave. This letting (*lassen*) is not "of" power, as it does not perform a "power-ful" or forceful interruption. It is its very "nature" of letting that can become easily miscognized in terms of power as an interruption, that is, woven back into the terms of power as its absence.

Yet the originative momentum of letting is more "radical" than any counterpower can be, precisely by virtue—Heidegger would likely say by the dignity (*Würde*)—of its refusal and letting go of the play of power. This is what, in *Besinnung*, Heidegger calls the radicalism beyond a yes and a no. Letting is neither a yes nor a no to power; neither a power-ful countering to power nor an indifferent abandon to powerlessness or absenting from power. Rather, it transforms power itself beyond power and without-power by allowing for the power-free. From the perspective of power, the power-free will be inevitably miscognized as without-power, unless and until an allowance for the power-free "events." It is precisely for such radicalism beyond a yes and a no that Heidegger calls; that is, he calls for a radicalism of letting (*lassen*), which opens the domain of power without the need for a beyond. This radicalism opens power to a frequency or better a tonality (*Stimmung*) unheard by power and unheard-of within power, the tonality that speaks neither in the loud nor the subtle voices of power, nor remains mute and thus without power. It is the tonality of what Heidegger calls the silent force of the possible, the tonality in which *es gibt*, in which there is being and beings in the play of time-space.

This is the tonality of the gentle binding, of *Gelassenheit* or letting-be, a relating no longer according to power or its absence. That at stake in this shift from violence and power to the gentle bind (*milde Bindung*) is indeed a transformation within power, can be gleaned from the fact that German allows the verbs *walten* and *lassen* to conjoin into *walten lassen*, suggesting that the primary determination of *walten* comes at this point from *lassen*, that is, from letting and allowing, and not from power or violence. In fact, one of the phrases formed with *walten lassen* is "*Milde walten lassen*," which can be rendered literally as "to let gentleness prevail" or "allow gentleness to work." Nearly a synonymous phrase is "*Gnade walten lassen*": to spare or to show leniency.[14] It is critical to note here that the verb *lassen* does not indicate, certainly not in the way in which Heidegger employs it, passivity, a disengaged allowing for something that is already there to remain as it is. Rather, *lassen* indicates a way of getting something to work without forcing or compelling it, as in "to allow gentleness to work." The difference here would be between "allowing to work" (*walten lassen*) and "making work" (where *walten* remains linked to *Gewalt* and *machen*). The more important point here is that, relying on the resources of German, it can be shown how the transformation in *walten* initiated by Heidegger takes it away from *Gewalt* (power, violence, governance), and, changing its tonality through *lassen*, allows for a different modality of relating: the gentle binding free from power. We have here a significant, even radical shift from *Gewalt/Walten* to *Lassen/Walten*, the shift that pinpoints the importance of the transformation (*Wandlung*) (GA 69: 21), which Heidegger sets out to initiate in power (*Macht*) and in its deployments through *Gewalt* and *Herrschaft*. This transformation in *walten*, which motivates the rethinking of *Macht*, *Gewalt*, and *Herrschaft*, also twists the logic of purity and contamination. *Das Macht-lose* or *das Gewalt-lose* does not indicate either purity from or contamination by power and violence, as they no longer conform to this logic, which is enforced by power. The release that allows or lets, all signified through the verb *lassen*, hinges on the valence of the suffix *–los*, indicating a move away, a letting go, and also a lessness. The difficulty for us is that this "-lessness" (*-losigkeit*) signifies precisely a release from the binary of power and powerlessness, contamination and purity: not a mixture of the two, the trace of their having always already been entwined, but "the gentle bind" of *walten lassen* that could transform the very landscape of relation.

This shift from violence/rule to letting/being at work, is what Heidegger means by the radicality of the other beginning (*der andere Anfang*), a beginning again of being/thinking/acting no longer only in terms of *Macht, Gewalt*, or *Herrschaft*, but also of the power-free. Heidegger introduces the term *Anfang* (most often translated as "beginning") first to differentiate it from *Beginn*: start or mere beginning and, second, to point out the sense of the simultaneous projective opening and sketched out capture implied by the German term. *An-fang*, often hyphenated by Heidegger, does not indicate a temporal moment in which something starts or commences, but instead an opening into an inceptual, originative projecting open and being captured (from the verb *fangen*: to capture, catch, seize) within the historical outline of this projection: a proleptic extension, which gives the momentum to what is coming and thus continues to captivate and maintain it within the tonality set at and by the beginning (*An-fang*). The first beginning in ancient Greece has influenced and shaped Western thought in its peculiar tonality of presence, idea, substance, and so on, which still resonate today through the key structuring terms of Western thought: representation, subject/object, essence, substance, presence/absence, and so on. In this sense, Greece, though inescapably Latinized, keeps "beginning" over and over again; or, to put it differently, our thinking, no matter how changed, developed, or evolved from the first beginning, finds itself repeatedly determined, as though preset, by its initial tonality. This first beginning has toned—in the sense of *Stimmung*—all of our beginnings and origins, Heidegger claims, into the terms of power and its shadow, powerlessness, forcing all relations to assume a form of power. Heidegger's remarks on the possibility of the other beginning attempt to help reset thought to a different, power-free tonality, which would breach the inceptual enclosure of the Greek beginning and possibly allow being (*Seyn*) as an otherwise to power, as projecting open and letting being be "captured" anew within its throw.

The other beginning thus originates in a different tonality: no longer the dialectic of the presence and absence of power but an essential "letting" of the power-free. This originative allowing is irreducible in its transformative momentum to a revolution, for, as Heidegger puts it "No 'revolution' is 'revolutionary' enough. . . . Everything 'revolutionary' is a dependent counter-play of the 'conservative'" (*GA* 69: 23). Both conservatism and revolution, as a response to conserving power and violence, are already captured within the first beginning, stylized in terms of power, counterpower, and powerlessness, and neither admits of a power-free doing that lets be. Perhaps if we were to continue with this tone of thinking, we could say that the power-free letting (*Gelassenheit*) indexes revolution the way, in which for Benjamin "pure violence" manifests through revolutionary violence. It transforms more radically, more inceptually, than revolution can.

Notes

Part of the material used in the third and fourth sections of this chapter appeared in my book, *Language After Heidegger*, Indiana University Press, 2013.

1. Rodolphe Gasché, *The Honor of Thinking: Critique, Theory, Philosophy* (Stanford, CA: Stanford University Press, 2007), 35.
2. Haverkamp calls the ideal of pure violence "nonviolent," while Hamacher speaks of "pure, and thus nonviolent, violence." Both Haverkamp and Hamacher read the adjective pure as indicating a nonviolent momentum, as in fact purifying violence of violence. See Anselm Haverkamp, "How to Take It (and do the Right Thing): Violence and the Mournful Mind in Benjamin's *Critique of Violence*," in *Cardozo Law Review*, 13 (1991–1992): 1159–1171; Werner Hamacher, "Afformative Strike," trans. Dana Hollander, *Cardozo Law Review*, 13 (1991–1992): 1132–1157.
3. In his response to Haverkamp and Hamacher among others, Jonathan Boyarin suggests that Benjamin keeps the term violence in order to indicate that "*the only genuinely revolutionary violence would seem to us like non-violence; he cannot call it non-violence because a positive preaching of non-violence is also an acquiescence to the rule of law.*" Boyarin, "Walter Benjamin: Justice Right, and *The Critique of Violence*," *Cardozo Law Review*, 13 (1991–1992): 1192.
4. Andrew Benjamin, "Life Beyond Violence: Notes on Walter Benjamin's 'Zur Kritik der Gewalt'" (www.cecl.com.pt/workingpapers/files/ed15_life_beyond_violence.pdf), 2.
5. Benjamin, "Life Beyond Violence," 11.
6. Ibid., 15.
7. Haverkamp, "How to Take It (and do the Right Thing)," 1159.
8. *Das Deutsche Wörterbuch von Jacob und Wilhelm Grimm*, http:// germazope.uni-trier.de/ Projects/ DWB.
9. David Farrell Krell, "Everything Great that Stands in the Storm that Blows from Paradise," *Cardozo Law Review, 13* (1991–1992): 1250.
10. It would be important to consider in this juxtaposition between the critique of *Gewalt* in Benjamin and in Heidegger the difference, striking at times, between *Vernichtung* (annihilation) and *Nichtung*. It is precisely *Nichten* or nihilating

in being, which releases from power and violence. By contrast, annihilation appears to be an extreme manifestation of pure violence.

11. This is not to say that Heidegger's texts, especially from 1933 to 1934, should not be carefully scrutinized for their proximity to several key issues and concepts employed by National Socialism: from *Stamm* and *Volk*, to *Führung* and *Kampf*, to see precisely whether Heidegger is simply taking over the terms and endorsing them or submitting them to examination and critique. It is interesting to note here that the word *Rasse* (race) appears much more frequently in Heidegger's work after *Contributions to Philosophy*, when it is unmistakably submitted to a persistent, and consistent critique, as part and parcel of the metaphysics of power. The extent of Faye's deliberate "misreading" becomes obvious if one reads the quotations he excerpts back in their context, which shows them, without a shadow of a doubt, to be critical of the very approach that Faye attempts to forcibly ascribe to Heidegger (see, for instance, p. 649), where Faye, discussing Heidegger's remarks on race thinking, immediately qualifies them by adding "racial selection" and claiming that Heidegger does so in order to legitimate both ("pour les légitimer"). That Faye's misreading is simply untenable can be seen easily in the fact that he keeps claiming that Heidegger endorses and propagates the thought of power and machination (*Machenschaft*), while in fact from the time of *Contributions to Philosophy* Heidegger is remarkably consistent in thoroughly and repeatedly critiquing *Macht, Machenschaft, Herrschaft*, or even "total mobilization"—critique that it is impossible to miss and that I have elaborated in more detail in other essays. For Faye's remarks about race in Heidegger mentioned above, see Emmanuel Faye, *Heidegger, l'introduction du nazisme dans la philosophie* (Paris: Fayard, 2005), 641–650. And for excellent critical exposition of the way in which Faye fabricates a "fiction" or even a "phantasm" of Heidegger, in the words of François Fédier, see *Heidegger à plus forte raison*, ed. Fedier (Paris: Fayard, 2007). Fédier's "Faux procès" (pp. 21–65) outlines the main procedures of misquotation, decontextualization, and insinuation, which Faye employs throughout the book. Particularly instructive is Philippe Arjakovsky's "Àpropos d'Ernst Jünger" (pp. 111–159), which demonstrates how Faye, through a series of decontextualized and intentionally misread excerpts from Heidegger's critique of Jünger and of the notion of race in volume 90 of the *Gesamtausgabe*, puts forward a distortive claim about Heidegger's supposed embrace of Jünger and of racist ideology. My essay was completed in 2011 and the recent publication (February and March 2014) of the first series of the so-called "Black Notebooks" (*GA* 94, 95, 96), which make available Heidegger's notes from 1931 to 1941, with numerous remarks on the Rektorat period, National Socialism,

and race, as well as several comments containing anti-Semitic stereotypes, will provide the context for and necessitate a careful reappraisal of the question of race in the manuscripts from 1936 to 1942 discussed here. Given the timing of the publication of these new volumes and the fact that my chapter is already in production, such an engagement is unfortunately impossible here.

12. "Die Wesensfolge der *Subjektivität* ist der Nazionalismus der Völker und der Sozialismus des Volkes" (*GA* 69: 44).

13. Some of my own texts as well as those by Fred Dallmayr have begun to examine a few years ago the complexity of Heidegger's critique of power and violence. See my *The Force of Art* (Stanford, CA: Stanford University Press, 2004); "Art, Power, and Politics: Heidegger on *Machenschaft* and *Poiesis*"; *Contretemps* 3, July 2002 (www.usyd.edu.au/ contretemps/ dir/ contents.html); "The Other Politics: Anthropocentrism, Power, Nihilation"; in *Letting Be: Fred Dallmayr's Cosmopolitical Vision*, ed. Steven F. Schneck (University of Notre Dame Press, 2006); Fred Dallmayr, "Heidegger on *Macht* and *Machenschaft*" *Continental Philosophy Review* 34 (2010), 247–267. A recent essay by Richard Polt, "Jenseits von Kampf und Macht. Heideggers heimlicher Widerstand" (in *Heidegger und der National-Sozialismus, Heidegger-Jahrbuch*, vol. 5 [Munich: Karl Alber, 2001], 155–186) provides a more developed account of the problematic of power, violence, and struggle against the backdrop of Heidegger's political engagement and can serve as a foil to Faye's statements.

14. Two phrases listed by an online dictionary: mit jdm. Nachsicht haben; gegenüber jdm. Milde walten lassen / to be lenient towards sb.; to be forebearing with sb. (German English dictionary: [http://dict.tu-chemnitz.de/]).

TEN

A MATTER OF IMMEDIACY

The Political Ontology of the Artwork in Benjamin and Heidegger

Dimitris Vardoulakis

Martin Heidegger's and Walter Benjamin's essays on art—"The Origin of the Work of Art" and "The Work of Art in the Age of Technological Reproducibility"—are not only, or even primarily, about art. Heidegger and Benjamin use the work of art to articulate an argument against immediacy. Immediacy is seen as a remnant of the onto-theological tradition that is to be destructed, according to Heidegger. The insistence on mediacy is a marker of modernity, according to Benjamin. Even though Hegel is in the background—for instance, Heidegger borrows from his lectures on Hegel, as we see later—nevertheless immediacy is not understood simply in Hegelian terms as a description of a form of subjective experience. Rather, immediacy for both Heidegger and Benjamin is presented within a political register.[1] Ultimately, for both thinkers, the argument against immediacy is a way of articulating a political ontology of the artwork.[2] And yet, divergences in the way that immediacy is construed lead the two thinkers to espouse radically different political projects.

The Autonomy of Art

The most discernible difference of their respective approaches to immediacy is that for Heidegger immediacy is discussed in terms of a forgetting of being since the translation of Greek thought into Latin, whereas in Benjamin it is articulated as an engagement with Romanticism and its aftermath.[3] These two trajectories are overlayed. Heidegger was conversant with the German Romantic tradition, as is indicated by a series of lecture courses such as those on Schelling, not to mention his work on Hölderlin from 1934 to 1935 that prefigured notions such as the "destiny of the people" found in the "Origin" essay. Benjamin, also, was conversant with the Greek tradition, for instance when he determined the allegorical impulse in modern art with reflections on ancient Greek tragedy in his book on the Trauerspiel, and in the "Reproducibility" essay itself parallels are drawn between the epic and film.[4] Yet, it is clear from the "Origin" and the "Reproducibility" essays that Heidegger focuses on the forgetting of the Greeks, while Benjamin uses Romanticism as the foil of his argument. The different referents determine the development of their argument. Heidegger in the "Origin" essay relies heavily on Greek terms such as *aletheia, techne,* and *poiesis*. Benjamin concentrates on the aftermath of Romanticism, especially from the mid-nineteenth century onward, as is also evidenced by his choosing photography and especially film as the prime examples of reproducibility. These different referents can be read as symptomatic of the different ways that they dismantle immediacy and conceive of history and politics. Hence, the entry to the inquiry into the function of immediacy in the two essays on the work of art is how they define immediacy with recourse to the Greeks and to Romanticism. In both thinkers, this is articulated as a discourse on the nature of the artwork as a thing or object that is construed in terms of denying the autonomy of art.

The question that organizes "Thing and Work," the first section of the "Origin" essay, is "What in truth is the thing, so far as it is a thing?" (*BW* 146/ *GA* 5: 5). Heidegger describes three answers given to this question. Either the thing is the connection between "substance and its accidents"; or, the thing is understood as "the unity of a manifold of what is given in the senses"; or, finally, the "thing is formed matter" (*BW* 149/ 7–8; *BW* 151/ *GA* 5: 10; *BW* 152/ *GA* 5: 11).[5] Heidegger summarizes the problem with all these conceptions of the thing thus: "These three modes of defining thingness . . . give rise to a mode of thought . . . [that] preconceives all immediate experience of being [*greift allem unmittelbaren Erfahren des Seienden vor*]. The preconception shackles [*unterbindet*] reflection on the Being of any given being" (*BW* 156/ *GA* 5: 16). Onto-theology is described as a preconception. The object, preconceived as merely a thing at hand, imprisons the thing in "immediate experience." Evading immediacy, then, is the starting point of Heidegger's reflection on the work of art.

Methodologically, this necessitates a thought that would "unshackle" the thing. As Heidegger puts it, "To this end, however, only one element is needful

... to leave the thing rest in its own self [*das Ding . . . in seinem Dingsein auf sich beruhen lassen*]" (*BW* 157/ *GA* 5: 16). Such a thought needs to go to the source of the thinking of existence in ancient Greek philosophy, prior to the translation of the Greek terms into Latin and their appropriation by the onto-theological tradition. "The rootlessness of Western thought begins with this translation" (*BW* 149/ *GA* 5: 8). This methodological insight, however, does not stand on its own. What is required in addition is a conception of the historical context in order to liberate thought from the preconceptions generated by the Latin translation. "That the thingness of the thing is particularly difficult to express and only seldom expressible is infallibly documented by the history [*Geschichte*] of its interpretation indicated above." Despite the difficulty, such a liberating history is crucial because it determines the Occident. Heidegger continues: "This history coincides with the destiny [*deckt sich mit den Schicksal*] in accordance with which Western thought has hitherto thought the Being of beings" (*BW* 157/ *GA* 5: 17). Heidegger identifies a destiny that covers over the metaphysical tradition. The origin of the work of art can only be recovered by aligning it with the historical thought that perceives such a destiny. In other words, the origin will turn out to be not in the past but in the future defined as the liberating destiny of the people. Consequently, it will be the allowing of such a destiny to unfold that will determine the political task at the end of the "Origin" essay. At the moment, all that can be inferred is that the historical understanding counteracts immediacy in order to deny the autonomy of art. Art does not exist merely in art objects, but rather pertains to the destiny of the people and hence it is political.

The denial of the autonomy of art in Benjamin's "Reproducibility" essay is also crucial for his argument against immediacy.[6] This immediacy is designated as "the here and now of the work of art—its unique existence in the place that it finds itself" (*SW* 3: 103/ *GS* 7.1: 352; trans. modified). Benjamin underlines the way that the "here and now" understood as the authenticity of the work of art gives rise to a certain conception of the historical: "The authenticity of a thing is the embodiment of all that is transmissible in it from its origin, ranging from its physical duration to the historical testimony relating to it" (*SW* 3: 103/ *GS* 7.1: 353; trans. modified). One aspect of the term "reproducibility"—one element that is *enabled* through reproduction—is the overcoming of a notion of history that sees the work of art as a discreet object inserted within a historical continuum. Benjamin refers to this as the devaluation of aura: "what withers in the age of technological reproducibility of the work of art is the latter's aura" (*SW* 3: 103/ *GS* 7.1: 352). Aura designates the conception of the work of art that relies on a notion of authenticity and leads to a certain historical conception. Reproducibility stunts the effects of authenticity and hence leads to the aura's withering. And, further, this also means for Benjamin that "all semblance of art's autonomy disappeared for ever" (*SW* 3: 109/ *GS* 7.1: 362).[7] So long as the work of art cannot be conceived as a discreet, authentic, auratic object, it is no longer possible to understand art as autonomous.[8]

The conjunction of the work of art and history "in the age of reproducibility" is related to what Benjamin promises to deliver in the first section of the essay, namely, "the formulation of revolutionary demands in the politics of art" (*SW* 3: 102/ *GS* 7.1: 350). Again, the target can be initially determined as the correlation between immediacy and politics, or what Benjamin calls in the final section of the essay "the aestheticization of the political." It is here that the engagement with the Romantic tradition can be discerned. Romanticism turns its sight to immediate experience and its contingency in order to derive the self-reflexivity of the subject. For instance, Novalis puts it as follows in his notes on Fichte: "Reflection finds the need of philosophy . . . because the need is in feeling. . . . Because otherwise it would not be the pure form of *reflection*, which necessarily presupposes a material, because [reflection] is the product of the limited thing, of consciousness in this sense—in short, of the subjectivity of the subject, the accidental character of the accident."[9] It is only through "feeling," "the material," or "the accidental" that the Romantic infinite reflection of subjectivity is attainable. One possibility of self-reflection is to designate the work of art as its privileged site. Benjamin argued against this possibility in the addendum of his dissertation on Romanticism, by saying, for instance, that "the connection of this ideal with art is not given in a medium but is designated by a refraction" (*SW* 1: 179/ *GS* 1.1: 111). In other words, the self-reflection of the subject through the work of art remains unmediated; it can lead to what Hegel would term a "bad infinity."[10] It was precisely in an attempt to quench the Romantic reliance on contingency and to avoid bad infinity that led Hegel to confine the aesthetic to the first stage of the dialectic—the stage that is characterized by the immediacy of perception.[11] The Hegelian drive against immediacy, however, does not repudiate the autonomy of art. On the contrary, it is this autonomy, designated as immediacy, that allows for its sublation in the ethico-political stage of the dialectic. In other words, the autonomy of the aesthetic is subsumed in the autonomy of the political. Adorno and Horkheimer analyzed this move under the rubric of the "dialectic of Enlightenment," whereas Benjamin identifies it in the "Reproducibility" essay as the "aestheticization of the political."

The Autonomy of the Political

The rejection of an ontology that relies on the immediacy of subjective experience explains Heidegger and Benjamin's reluctance to define the work as an object with distinct, aesthetic properties bestowed by a subject, the artist. Art is not autonomous. It also explains the parallels in the way that they reposition art, specifically in insisting that the work of art is not merely an object, but rather it is characterized by an energetic, productive element—what can be called the *work* of the work of art. In both the "Origin" and the "Reproducibility" essays this work expressly determines the confluences between art and history. Such confluences show that the rejection of the autonomy of the artwork is accompanied by a parallel rejection of the autonomy of the political.

Heidegger shows this confluence by indicating two types of relation—what he calls *world* and *earth*—that are constitutive of his notion of "destiny." In the second section of the "Origin" essay, Heidegger abandons the attempt to define the work of art through an inquiry into its status as a thing, and pursues instead an inquiry into its work-character.[12] This character is understood as a form of relationality. The organizing question is, "in what relation it [i.e., the work of the work of art] stands?" (*BW* 167/ *GA* 5: 27). The example that Heidegger chooses to illustrate his argument is the ancient Greek temple of Hera at Paestum.[13] The temple produces two kinds of relations. The first one is referred to as world and it is characterized as a "setting up [*Aufstellen*]" (*BW* 169/ *GA* 5: 29). The world is described as a matrix of relations that reveal being. The starkest expression of such a revealing is that the determination of the people is given through the relations that belong to the world of the temple: "The all-governing [*waltende*] expanse of this open relational context is the world of this historical people [*die Welt dieses geschichtlichen Volkes*]. Only from and in this world do the people first return to the fulfilment of their determination" (*BW* 167/ *GA* 5: 28; trans. modified). In other words, as Heidegger would express it more directly later, this is "the act that founds a political state" (*BW* 186/ *GA* 5: 49). Heidegger asserts that the work of art has the capacity to produce a network of relations that disclose to individuals that which determines them as a people. Only through such a determination can they constitute a people. The relations of disclosure that are organized under the term *world* also require a different, opposing set of relations that are referred to under the term *earth* and whose main characteristic is concealment. Concealment returns from the expansive work of the world back to the materiality of the work of art. With earth's relations of concealment, which Heidegger calls a "setting forth [*Herstellen*]," "the work sets itself back into the massiveness and heaviness of stone" (*BW* 171/ *GA* 5: 32). This reversion to materiality guarantees that the work of the work of art is not reducible to an object in its immediacy, but rather "unfolds itself in an inexhaustible variety of simple modes and shapes" (*BW* 173/ 34). Crucially, world and earth cannot subsist each on their own; instead, their respective relations of unconcealment and concealment exist as a productive "counterplay [*Widerspiel*]" (*BW*

181/ *GA* 5: 43). Even though they can be distinguished, still they are inextricable. Further, it is this inextricable relation between the relations of world and earth—this *relation of relations*—that provides Heidegger's definition of truth as *aletheia*. And, importantly for the argument pursued here, this relation of relations shows, according to Heidegger, how the dismantling of the immediacy of the art object through the work annuls the autonomy of both the aesthetic and the political.

How precisely does Heidegger's conception of the political overcome immediacy? The difficulty in answering this question by relying solely on the "Origin" essay consists in that Heidegger himself does not explicitly pose the problem this way. To see how immediacy can be inscribed in his notion of the political, the lecture course "Hegel, über den Staat" is indispensable. This course was delivered in the winter semester of 1934–1935, and the "Origin" essay was first delivered as a lecture in November 1935.[14] In "Hegel, über den Staat," Heidegger considers Carl Schmitt in order to determine the positioning of the political. Schmitt seeks to sustain the autonomy of the political.[15] He does so by reducing the essence of the political to the sovereign's determination of the enemy. According to the famous opening sentence of *Political Theology*, "Sovereign is he who decides on the exception."[16] The exception is the set of circumstances that reveal a threat to the state from an enemy. The role of the sovereign is to identify the enemy and to suspend the law to protect the state. This mutual act of identification and suspension is the Schmittian decision. Heidegger's response to Schmitt in the lecture on January 13, 1935, is that the distinction between friend and enemy, that is, the possibility of the decision, cannot form the ground of the political—which is tantamount to arguing against Schmitt's conception of the autonomy of the political. Heidegger begins the argument by defining the political with recourse to the ancient Greek polis:

> For the determination of the essence of the political it is paramount to return to the essence of the *state*. What's the polis? . . . We learn what the polis is already in Homer, *Odyssey*, Rhapsody 6, line 9 ff. "He erected (drew) a wall around the polis, and built houses and temples, and divided the land." Thus, the polis is the authentic middle of the span of existence. . . . The polis is the authentic, determined middle of the historical existence of a people. . . . The most essential is self-assertion. Wall, house, land, gods. It is from here that the essence of the political must be understood.

Polis is the site where all the different relations that found the state—"wall, house, land, gods"—assert themselves, giving a people its historical existence. Polis, then, designates here the opening matrix of relations that in the "Origin" essay are referred to as *world*. At precisely this point, Heidegger turns to Carl Schmitt:

> Lately, the relation between friend and enemy has emerged as the essence of the political.[17] Such a relation presupposes the *self-assertion*, and therefore it is merely an effect of the political essence. Friend and enemy exist only where there is self-assertion. Thus understood, self-assertion longs for a determinate grasping of the historical being of the people as well as of the state. It is only because there is a state for this self-assertion of the historical being of a people *and* because the state can designate the polis, that the relation between friend and enemy shows itself as a consequence. The political, however, is not that relation.[18]

Schmitt's decisionism misses, according to Heidegger, the essential relation of the polis or the world. Deciding upon the enemy is merely a consequence—that is, an empirical manifestation, an *immediate* representation—of the state. In other words, Heidegger argues that Schmitt completely misses the *relation* of relations. In that sense, he reverts back to a notion of immediacy.[19] As an onto-theological relation, decisionsim preconceives all immediate experience. The enemy is in politics what the thing at hand is in epistemology.

Heidegger rearticulates this argument in the "Origin" essay by employing the notion of strife.[20] Strife designates the antagonism between world and earth:

> The work is the self-opening openness of the broad paths of the simple and essential decisions in the destiny of a historical people. The earth is the spontaneous forthcoming of that which is continuously self-secluding. . . . The opposition of world and earth is strife. But we would surely all too easily falsify its essence if we were to confound strife with discord and dispute, and thus see it only as disorder and destruction. In essential strife, rather, the opponents raise each other into the self-assertion of their essential natures. Self-assertion of essence, however, is never a rigid insistence upon some contingent state, but surrender to the concealed originality of the provenance of one's own Being. (*BW* 174/ *GA* 5: 35)

Note that Heidegger is explicit that the "essential decision" is a modality of the world-relations that found a state understood as polis. Whereas a decision is, according to Schmitt, the act that instigates enmity or the war between sovereigns, Heidegger views this idea of enmity as the falsification of the essence of strife.[21] Strife is not simply the immediate manifestation of war, "disorder and destruction." Rather, strife constitutes a self-assertion that is irreducible to contingency. Thus, Heidegger determines the notion of immediacy in the political through a critique of Schmitt's decisionism. The distinction between friend and enemy is a decision immanent within the authority of the sovereign of an established state. Heidegger objects that a state is never simply given, nor is it concentrated within the sovereign authority. Rather, the strife between world and earth—Heidegger's polis—opens up the historical essence of a people. "The world is the clearing of the paths of the essential guiding directions with which all decision complies. Every decision, however, bases itself on something not mastered, something concealed, confusing; else it would never be a decision" (*BW* 180/ *GA* 5: 42). The relations that pertain to materiality prevent the decision. They belong, instead, to the concealment of the earth. By forgetting the earth, Heidegger suggests, Schmitt turns strife into the immediate relation between friend and enemy, and thereby guarantees the autonomy of the political as the realm of the sovereign's decision. On the contrary, by insisting on the undecidability of the earth, Heidegger exposes decisionism's adherence to immediacy and simultaneously also destructs the autonomy of the political.

The similarity and yet profound difference between Heidegger and Benjamin's political ontologies can be succinctly expressed with reference to Schmitt's grounding the autonomy of the political in the sovereign "who decides upon the exception." Both Heidegger and Benjamin are opposed to this autonomy. However, Heidegger concentrates on critiquing the decision because it reverts to immediacy, whereas Benjamin's discourse can be read as a critique of the exception. Similarly to Heidegger, Benjamin describes the work of art as establishing a network of relations, or in Benjamin's terminology, the work is a medium. This, again, leads to a reconsideration of the historical: "Just as the entire mode of existence of human collectives changes over long historical periods, so too does their mode of perception. The way in which human perception is organized—the medium in which it occurs—is conditioned not only by nature but by history" (*SW* 3: 104/ *GS* 7.1: 354, emphasis deleted).[22] Since the work of art is not conditioned only by nature, the perception of the art object is inadequate for the determination of the work's functionality. Immediacy is inadequate because perception is not *sui generis* but is rather inextricable from history. Or, more emphatically, existence and history are codetermined through common media—and the work of art is such a medium. For instance, the transition from the aura to reproducibility is effected through new media of production. In the nineteenth century, "photography freed the hand from the most important artistic tasks in the process of pictorial reproduction . . . [which] was enormously accelerated" (*SW* 3: 102/ *GS* 7.1: 351). Thus it is the medium—the work understood as an energetic field—that determines artistic processes because it forges a conjunction between modes of perception and history.

Benjamin insists, further, that the medium has always had that function. "In principle, the work of art has always been reproducible" (*SW* 3: 102/ *GS* 7.1:

351). The principle that distinguishes historical periods is not whether or not they contain a historico-political conception of the medium or the work character of the work of art. Such a conception, Benjamin suggests, has always been present in one way or another, because reproducibility points to an inherent potentiality within the work: "It has always been one of the primary tasks of art to create a demand [*eine Nachfrage zu erzeugen*] whose hour of full satisfaction has yet to come. The history of every art form has critical periods in which the particular form strains after effects which can be easily achieved only with a changed technical standard—that is to say, in a new art form" (*SW* 3: 118/ *GS* 7.1: 378). The historical is understood here neither as a retrieval of an authentic origin, nor as a development towards the future, nor—most importantly—as a combination of the originary and the futural, that is, the combination that Heidegger calls "destiny." For Benjamin, there is no opposition between an authenticity and an inauthenticity to produce historical and artistic modalities. Instead, the medium always poses an irresolvable problem—it "asks a question after its presentation" (*Nachfrage*). It is this irresolvability that produces a sense of the future as that which has "yet to come." Or, to put this another way, the future is the open question that the medium contains within itself. And that's why the medium is always mediated, it can never be reduced to immediacy. Heidegger translates this argument against immediacy to a political argument against Schmitt's decisionism. Benjamin's focus on the exception instead of the decision is due to his conception of temporality. This can be expressed in the question, what is the political import of the "yet to come"?

The question of temporality in Benjamin is linked to a consideration of exclusion. It was argued a moment ago that the opposition between the authentic and the inauthentic is inoperative in Benjamin. The objection can be raised that it is precisely the auratic that is understood as authentic in the "Reproducibility" essay. On closer inspection, however, it emerges that the objection in fact supports the argument. The reason is that only the aura conceives of its temporal dimension in terms of a relation between the authentic and its opposite, whereas reproducibility repudiates that opposition. Further, and most crucially, aura and reproducibility themselves do *not* form a relation that reiterates, rehearses, or re-creates the opposition between an "inauthentic authenticity" of the aura and an "authentic authenticity" of reproducibility. Aura and reproducibility are *not* related in terms of authenticity. Rather, they are related through the temporality of the "yet to come," the inherent potential whose unpredictable unfolding entails an undecidable future. In section VI of the essay, Benjamin points to a "qualitative transformation" of the work of art that he expresses in terms of a first and a second technology—Foucault later called them technologies of *power*. The first technology corresponds to auratic art, and the second to the reproducibility of the artwork:

> What matters is the way the orientation and aims of [the first] technology differ from those of ours. Whereas the former made the maximum possible use of human beings, the latter reduces their use to the minimum. The achievements of the first technology might be said to culminate in human sacrifice; those of the second, in the remote-controlled aircraft which needs no human crew. The results of the first technology are valid once and for all. . . . The results of the second are wholly provisional. (*SW* 3: 107/ *GS* 7.1: 359)

There are two opposing features that distinguish the two technologies. Whereas the first one appears through its effects on the human, culminating in demanding its death in sacrifice, the second decreases the effect on the human and recognizes the "play," as Benjamin calls it, within the objects themselves. Further, the effects of the first technology acquire a finality—the death that it demands is, after all, an ultimate limit. The effects of the second technology are, conversely, an open question, they live on, they have "yet to come." Benjamin extrapolates the distinction by clarifying that he is not suggesting an exclusory opposition between the two technologies: "Seriousness and play, rigor and license, are mingled *in every work of art*, though in very different proportions. This implies that *art is linked to both the second and the first technologies*" (*SW* 3: 107/ *GS* 7.1: 359; emphasis added). If there is something like a "relation of relations" in Benjamin, this has to do with the way that aura and reproducibility, the first and second technologies, are always mingled or linked. There is no outside that relation.[23]

Conversely, it will be recalled that Heidegger designates the inauthentic space opened up by the Latin mistranslation of the Greek concepts as that exteriority wherein immediacy persists, and at the same time reserves the "relation of relations" as the exclusive characteristic of strife and the polis. According to Benjamin, if the auratic was concerned with the mastering of nature, reproducibility introduced an additional element: "The first technology really sought to master nature, whereas the second aims rather at an interplay [*Zusammenspiel*] between nature and humanity. The primary social function of art today is to rehearse that interplay" (*SW* 3: 107/ *GS* 7.1: 359). There are not two types of relation—one authentic and the other inauthentic. Rather, there is in actuality only one relation, that of the second technology. In other words, the aura is, in actuality, a curtailed reproducibility—a moment that stops short of recognizing that it has "yet to come" and thereby sacrifices itself. Thus, the second technology excludes nothing, but rather proliferates the relations of nature by bringing them into interplay with humanity.

Schmitt's definition of the sovereign as "he who decides on the exception" requires the exception to be understood in terms of radical novelty as that which is new and hence uncodifiable. The critique of the decision that Heidegger pursues in "Hegel, über den Staat" and in the "Origin" essay also relies on a radical novelty—which explains why Heidegger does not criticize the exception. Heidegger's "counterplay [*Widerspiel*]" is an opposition, a strife, or, as he also says, the site where "the battle of the new gods against the old is being fought" (*BW* 181/ *GA* 5: 43 and *BW* 168–9/ *GA* 5: 29). This battle is undecidable because it points to the *relation* of relations, which can never be particularized. Nevertheless, the battle relies on the existence of *new* gods, whose emergence radically alters the relations designated as world and earth. As Heidegger put in his *Spiegel* interview, "Only yet another, a new god [*nur noch ein Gott*] can save us."[24] Heidegger's notion of the undecidability of strife, and hence his delineation of the destiny of a historical people, requires this radical, divine novelty.[25] This retains the notion of the exception, which is radically new and hence uncodifiable.[26] Conversely, Benjamin's future is not a destiny that requires a radical exclusion so that its originary dimension can be reached. Rather, Benjamin's future is produced through a realizing of the potential contained within the medium itself. The future has "yet to come" because it can never come—the potential can never be fulfilled (this would entail its being sacrificed), it is, rather, only ever provisional. The reason is that its actuality is nascent within the medium. It consists in the unmasterability that is indicated by the interplay (*Zusammenspiel*) between nature and history. From Benjamin's perspective, the problem with Schmitt's definition is not so much the notion of the decision, but rather that of the exception. The exception is the unique situation in which the law is inadequate. It is the moment something radically new and unpredictable happens—or, as it can be expressed with reference to Heidegger's terminology, the moment of the arrival of the new god. Whereas for Heidegger that new coming constitutes strife and it is the act that founds a new state, for Benjamin the god never comes. Every second is "the small gate in time through which the Messiah could enter"—but the Messiah is neither a new god, nor does he ever come (*SW* 4: 397/ *GS* 1.2: 704; trans. modified). Rather, it is the Messiah's "not coming" that accompanies the play of reproducibility, and hence the *zusammen* of its play. This possibility—the fact that he *could* come—is the condition of a temporality that is radically unexceptional. Or, to put it in the language of Thesis VIII from "On the Concept of History," the exception has become the norm.[27]

Novelty or Reproducibility

Radical novelty is inexorably linked to immediacy. The coming of the new gods reinscribes immediacy in Heidegger's ontology of the political. This new coming is signaled in the "Origin" essay as the function of the work's preservers. In the third section of his essay, Heidegger indicates a transition from possibility to an ethico-political imperative. The organizing question is: "What is truth, that it *can* happen as, or even *must* happen as, art?" (*BW* 182/ *GA* 5: 44; emphasis added). There is a move from the "can" to the "must." This transition necessitates radical novelty: "The establishing of truth in the work is the bringing forth of a being [*Seiende*] such as never was seen before and will never come to be again" (*BW* 187/ *GA* 5: 50). This bringing forth of something new is what Heidegger calls *creation* (*das Schaffen*). Creation, significantly, "*must* contain within itself the essential traits of strife," says Heidegger. This "must" of creation leads to the ethico-political imperative of the work of art. Heidegger continues: "As a world opens itself, it submits to the decision of a historical humanity the question of victory and defeat, blessing and curse, mastery and slavery. The dawning world brings out what is yet undecided and measureless, and thus discloses the hidden necessity of measure and decisiveness" (*BW* 187–8/ *GA* 5: 50). The "hidden necessity of measure" is the necessity to establish a state, for instance, to recall the Homeric definition, by erecting a wall, by building houses and by dividing the land. This founding act of a state is still not enough: "But the work's actuality does not exhaust itself in the createdness. On the contrary, this view of the essence of the work's createdness now enables us to take the step toward which everything thus far said tends" (*BW* 191/ *GA* 5: 53–54). Everything that he has thus far argued, Heidegger says, is leading toward a notion he is about to announce. That notion is the preservers as that which forges the link between the work of art and its historical and political significance, or its ethico-political imperative. "What is created cannot come into being without those who preserve it [*sowenig kann das Geschaffene selbst ohne die Bewahrenden seiend werden*]" (*BW* 191/ *GA* 5: 54). The participle turned into a substantive that is used for the preserves—*Bewahrenden* instead of *Bewahrer*—indicates the active role that the preservers assume. This activity is indicated through the etymological link between preserving (*bewahren*), truth (*Wahrheit*) and perception (*Wahrnehmung*). Immediacy was defined as that which was presupposed in perception according to the onto-theological tradition. It then emerged that what was presupposed was truth, the originary operation of strife. This operation is now shown to be carried out by the preservers. And this is what enacts a return to the perceptible (*seiend werden*)—a transition from the mere ontic to facticity. This way, Heidegger shows how his opposition to the autonomy of art and the autonomy of the political are inseparable. The two form a relation of mutual bestowing of identity. Art determines the political and vice versa.[28] And it is the preserves that set in motion this aestetico-political hermeneutic circle.

This circle requires a plurality of preserves. Or, more emphatically, preserving is political. A work does not necessarily need to have a preserver, says Heidegger, so long as "it is waiting" for its preservers (*BW* 192/ *GA* 5: 54). More emphatically: "Preserving the work does not reduce people to their private experiences, but brings them into affiliation with the truth happening in the work. Thus it grounds being for and with one another as the historical standing-out of human existence in relation to unconcealment" (*BW* 193/ *GA* 5: 55). For this *ex-stasis* or standing out, for this destiny, a plurality of preserves is necessary. This destiny *presupposes* the dialectic between the individual and the people in order for the immediacy of perception to be overcome.[29] The mutual determination through the hermeneutic circle of art and the historico-political is impossible without that presupposition: "Whenever art happens—that is, whenever there is a beginning—a thrust enters history; history either begins or starts over again. History here means not a sequence in time of events. . . . History is the transporting of a people into its appointed task as entry into that people's endowment. . . . Art is history in the sense that it grounds history" (*BW* 201/ *GA* 5: 65). Art is political because art is the essence of history. Art creates a new beginning, or makes beginning *as such* possible. Art as history means that *art is the undecidable exception*. The creation of a people or a state is interchangeable with the creation of the work of art. This is, according to Guy Debord, the structure of the spectacle, in that it "seeks to appear *at once* as society itself."[30] The connection between history and art proposed by Heidegger in the "Origin" essay provides no other criterion for recognizing art than its creating the political in the form of the destiny for a people. There is no art without a "we" and no "we" without art. This entails that a people originates through its *immediate* connection to art.[31] Even though Heidegger sought to establish the work of the artwork outside immediacy, still immediacy is reinscribed as the "at once" in the relation between a people and the work. This immediacy is not inscribed in the relations of world or earth, but rather in the relation of their relations—in strife, in the polis, in preserving.

Having developed a notion of the historical that does not rely on the exception, Benjamin can criticize the presupposition of Heidegger's discourse—namely, the dialectic between private and public that gives rise to the preserves as the representatives of the destiny of a people. Benjamin's critique also leads to a very different notion of the political that does not revert to immediacy. According to Heidegger, it is the formation of a people that overcomes the autonomy of the political because it does not conform to the immediacy of decisionism, thereby creating an authentic politics of preserving, *ex-stasis* and so on. Conversely, according to Benjamin, the auratic in its various modalities of immediacy is neither political nor historical. "Instead of being founded on ritual, it [exhibition as a function of reproducibility] is based on a different practice: politics" (*SW* 3: 106/ *GS* 7.1: 357). Again, this does not mean that the auratic is simply outside politics. Rather the auratic has not realized its potential, for instance, its historical potential: "Neither the concept of semblance nor that of play is foreign to traditional aesthetics; and to the extent that the two concepts of cult value and exhibition value are latent in the other pair of concepts at issue here, they say nothing new. But this abruptly changes as soon as these latter concepts lose their indifference to history" (*SW* 3: 127/ *GS* 7.1: 368–369). The recognition of potentiality is equated with a recognition of—an awakening to—the importance of the historical and the political. This potential, as something inscribed in auratic modes, does not signify radical novelty. It rather signifies an only ever curtailed project—and it is curtailed because it regards itself as completed, because it does not recognize the "yet to come." In addition, the insistence on novelty contained in the auratic implies a certain kind of politics: fascism. Aura and fascism are connected in that they rely on immediacy, which in turn is produced by the dialectic of private and public.

Benjamin takes up the issue of the link between immediacy, the private and the public, and fascism in an important footnote, which in turns relies on a certain reading of Marx. According to Benjamin,

> The class-conscious proletariat forms a compact mass only from the outside, in the minds of its oppressors.... In the solidarity of the proletarian class struggle, the dead, undialectical opposition between individual and mass is abolished.... The mass as an impenetrable, compact entity... is that of the petty bourgeoisie. The petty bourgeoisie is not a class; it is in fact only a mass.... [T]his compact mass with its unmediated reactions forms the antithesis of the proletarian cadre, whose actions are mediated by a task, however momentary.... Fascism... realizes that the more compact the masses it mobilizes, the better the chance that the counterrevolutionary instincts of the petty bourgeoisie will determine their reactions. The proletariat, on the other hand, is preparing for a society in which neither the objective nor the subjective conditions for the formation of the masses will exist any longer. (*SW* 3: 129–130/ *GS* 7.1: 370–371)

Benjamin suggests that the creation of a mass—the creation of "a people"—is premised on the opposition between "individual and mass." Further, the reactions of such a mass are always unmediated—they are immediate. Later in the "Reproducibility" essay, Benjamin will elaborate on this point with an unmistakable allusion to Nazi aesthetics, as they were expressed, for instance, at the Nürnberg rallies: "In great ceremonial processions, giant rallies and mass sporting events, and in war, all of which are fed into the camera, the masses come face to face with themselves" (*SW* 3: 132/ *GS* 7.1: 382). This coming "face-to-face" with oneself as a mass is what Debord referred to as the "at once" in the relation between art and society, and what for Heidegger constitutes the interchangeability between a people and the work of art. This face-to-face is the *immediate* bestowal of identity, it is the formation of a mass that lacks mediation. Such a mass is created through the bourgeois, undialectical opposition between the private and the public. And it is precisely this same process of immediacy that fascism utilizes in order to oppress. Finally, it is this immediate identification that is accomplished through the collapse of any difference between—the mutual definition of—the historico-political and art that is characterized as the "aestheticization of the political" at the end of the "Reproducibility" essay. How does the "proletariat," however, manage to avoid forming itself into a mass? How does "class consciousness" evade the opposition between the individual and the mass?

The questions can be understood to form one of the major themes of the project on the Second French Empire that Benjamin was working on, which remained unfinished and which we know as "The Arcades Project." Benjamin was interested to explore the way that city planning in Paris after 1852 relied on forms of thinking that presupposed oppositions such as that between the private and the public. Marx's *18th Brumaire*, which describes the rise to power of Louis Bonaparte in 1851, provides the background to these ideas. Indeed, Marx in the *18th Brumaire*, just like Benjamin in the "Reproducibility" essay, is fiercely critical of the exception, developing at the same time a conception of community or class beyond the opposition between private and public. Even though traditional political theory understands the exception as a response to a threat to the state, Marx shows how Bonaparte *used* the exception to propagate his power. If the use of the exception to protect the state is a tragedy because of its toll on human life, then the use of the exception to grab power is merely a farce. Marx expresses this reversal in the function of the exception with belligerent irony: "Society is saved just as often as the circle of its rulers contracts, as a more exclusive interest is maintained against a wider one."[32] Now, this critique of the politics of the exception leads to a conception of class-consciousness as nonrepresentable, or in Benjamin's terminology as class-consciousness' incompatibility with the unmediated mass:

> Bonaparte represents a class, and the most numerous class of French society at that, the *small-holding peasantry*.... Insofar as millions of families live under economic conditions of existence that separate their mode of life, their interests and their culture from those of the other classes,

and them in hostile opposition to the latter, they form a class. Insofar as there is merely a local interconnection among those small-holding peasants, and the identity of their interests begets no community, no national bond and no political organization among them, they do not form a class. . . . They cannot represent themselves, they must be represented. Their representative must at the same time appear as their master, as an authority over them, as an unlimited governmental power that protects them against the other classes and sends them rain and sunshine from above.[33]

The utilization of the exception creates a politics of representation, a politics that relies on the opposition between private and public in order to create a compact mass. It is the same process that Heidegger had characterized as the opening of a world that allows for "the decision of a historical humanity" about the "victory and defeat, blessing and curse, mastery and slavery" of a people. According to Marx, the endpoint of the exception is the representation of the masses by someone else—a dictator like Bonaparte.[34] This representation—or, more precisely, the *immediate* inscription of aesthetic values of representation in the political sphere—is like a comedy. Conversely, a class is nonrepresentable.[35] It presents itself "in hostile opposition" to those who seek to oppress it, and it forms a community in the sense that its "actions are mediated by a task," as Benjamin put it. Or, to use a figure that is prevalent in the *Arcades Project*, the political task is an *awakening*— an awakening to the immediacy with which a politics of representation creates "a people" in order to immediately bestow identity through aesthetic categories, and an awakening to the mediacy of the task in that the task has "yet to come" and yet its noncoming can only ever again be enacted.

·•· ·•· ·•· ·•· ·•·

Heidegger confines immediacy to the perceptible. This allows him to define the work of the work of art. However, the hermeneutic circle he constructs for the work of art relies on the immediate relation between art and politics. It is precisely this latter sense of immediacy that reproducibility seeks to repudiate. It does so by pointing out that such an immediate relation produces a compact mass that is manipulable—a mass that has lost a sense of the political for itself. To retain a link between art and politics entails for Benjamin inscribing in both of them the messianic temporality of the "yet to come." And this is only possible if the two are not collapsed into each other. Such a collapse requires the sacrifice of the human—its logic is a being toward death. Conversely, the potentiality that the "yet to come" indicates relies on a proliferation of relations. This is an affirmation of the living—a being in life. Thus, the artwork's relation to immediacy leads to the construction of two radically different political ontologies in Heidegger and Benjamin. For Heidegger such an ontology delineates the emergence of a new being—the new gods of the newly founded state. For Benjamin it is a repudiation of novelty as a way of opposing all forms of exceptionality that lead to dictatorial regimes and as a way of leaving open the possibilities contained in the political relations.

Notes

The author would like to thank Jeffrey Barash for his invaluable help.
1. For the relevance of immediacy to the political, see chapter 1 of my *Sovereignty and its Other* (New York: Fordham University Press, 2013).
2. A similar preoccupation with immediacy as the site of interaction between ontology and aesthetics can be found in Theodor Adorno. See, for example, his *Negative Dialectics*, trans. E. B. Ashton (London: Routledge, 1990) and *Aesthetic Theory*, trans. Robert Hullot-Kentor (London: Continuum, 2004).
3. It would detract from the main argument to analyze here in detail the importance of Greek philosophy for Heidegger or of the Romantics for Benjamin. The most important references in relation to their respective reflections on art are, for Heidegger, his meditations on *Antigone* in *Introduction to Metaphysics*, trans. Gregory Fried and Richard Polt (New Haven, CT: Yale University Press, 2000), which were originally lectures presented at Freiburg University in the summer of 1935—that is, just months before he delivered the "Origin" essay as a series of public lectures, in November of the same year. Cf. Clare Pearson Geiman, "Heidegger's Antigones," in Richard Polt and Gregory Fried, *A Companion to Heidegger's Introduction to Metaphysics* (New Haven, CT: Yale University Press, 2001), 161–182. Benjamin's most important work on Jena Romanticism is his doctoral dissertation, translated in the first volume of the *Selected Writings*. See also the essays collected in Beatrice Hanssen and Andrew Benjamin (eds.), *Walter Benjamin and Romanticism* (London: Continuum, 2002).
4. The link between distraction and the epic that Benjamin draws in this essay is also influenced by Brecht. For a collection of Benjamin's most important material on Brecht, see *Understanding Brecht*, trans. Anna Bostock (London: Verso, 1998).
5. All these conceptions of the thing are defined with reference to Greek terms. Specifically, the first in relation to *symbebekota*, the second in relation to *aesthesis*, and the final one in terms of *morphe* and *hyle*.

6. I am using here the second version of the "Reproducibility" essay, because it is more developed than the first one, and less edited than the third one. For an analysis of the "Reproducibility" essay that compares different versions, see Howard Caygill, *Walter Benjamin: The Colour of Experience* (London: Routledge, 1998).
7. Cf. George Markus, "Benjamin's Critique of Aesthetic Autonomy," in eds. Andrew Benjamin and Charles Rice, *Walter Benjamin and the Architecture of Modernity* (Melbourne: re.press, 2009), 111–127.
8. For a series of reflections on the relation between appearance and politics in Benjamin that resonate with the argument here on the relation between immediacy and the political, see the first part of Andrew Benjamin, *Style and Time: Essays on the Politics of Appearance* (Evanston, IL: Northwestern University Press, 2006).
9. Novalis, *Fichte Studies*, trans. Jane Kneller (Cambridge: Cambridge University Press, 2003), 14–15.
10. This is one possibility. In his dissertation, Benjamin argues that the concept of "criticizability" in Jena Romanticism avoids this problem precisely because the Romantic concept of criticism relies on mediation. In the "Reproducibility" essay, Benjamin articulates the transition from Goethe to Hegel in a footnote: "Hegel's statement that art strips away the 'semblance and deception of this false, transient world' from the 'true content of phenomena' . . . already diverges from the traditional experiential basis of this doctrine. By contrast, Goethe's work is still entirely imbued with beautiful semblance as an auratic reality" (*SW* 3: 127/ *GS* 7.1: 368).
11. See Hegel, *Aesthetics: Lectures on Fine Art*, trans. T. M. Knox (Oxford: Clarendon Press, 1998), vol. 1, and the first section of the *Phenomenology*.
12. For the most important book on the work aspect of Heidegger's theory of the work of art, see Krzysztof Ziarek, *The Force of Art* (Stanford, CA: Stanford University Press, 2004).
13. In fact, Heidegger assumed that this, the second and best preserved temple to Hera, was a temple to Poseidon, as it was commonly held at the time. See Joseph J. Kockelmans, *Heidegger on Art and Works* (Dordrecht: Martinus Nijhoff, 1985), 141–142 and Jeff Malpas, "Heidegger's Topology of Being," in eds. Steven Galt Crowell and Jeff. Malpas, *Transcendental Heidegger* (Stanford, CA: Stanford University Press, 2007), 119. This mistake was because Paestum means Poseidonia, the city dedicated to Poseidon. As Joseph Rykwert notes, Heidegger's description is not faithful—for example, the temple is not built on a rock, as Heidegger says. See Rykwert, *The Dancing Column: On Order in Architecture* (Cambridge, MA: MIT, 1998), 379–380. The other example

that Heidegger famously used in the first section of the "Origin" essay is Van Gogh's depiction of a pair of peasant shoes. The most important discussion of this related example can be found in Derrida's *The Truth in Painting*, trans. Geoff Bennington and Ian McLeod (Chicago: University of Chicago Press, 1987).

14. Heidegger co-taught the course with Erik Wolf, who was dean of the faculty of law at Freiburg University. The course has often been cited to discuss Heidegger's Nazism, usually in polemical terms that reside on personal relations, such as with the Nazi jurist Wolf, or in relation to contextual, historical information. See, for instance, Emmanuel Faye, *Heidegger: The Introduction of Nazism into Philosophy in Light of the Unpublished Seminars of 1933–1935*, trans. Michael B. Smith (New Haven, CT: Yale University Press, 2009). This negative publicity, as well as the fact that the notes of the "Hegel" course are not in Heidegger's own hand, may be the reasons why the course has not been chosen for publication in Heidegger's *Gesamtausgabe*. A more measured assessment of the course can be found in Jeffrey Andrew Barash, *Martin Heidegger and the Problem of Historical Meaning* (New York: Fordham University Press, 2003), 224–225. For a series of assessment on Heidegger's involvement with national socialism, see vol. 5 of the Heidegger-Jahrbuch, *Heidegger und der Nationalsozialismus II*, ed. Alfred Denker und Holger Zaborowski (Freiburg, München: Karl Alber, 2009).

15. For a discussion of Schmitt's argument on the autonomy of the political, see William Rasch, *Sovereignty and Its Discontents: On the Primacy of the Conflict and the Structure of the Political* (London: Birkbeck Law Press, 2004).

16. Carl Schmitt, *Political Theology: Four Chapters on the Concept of Sovereignty*, trans. George D. Schwab (Cambridge, MA: MIT, 1985), 5.

17. Sigrifried Bröse, who provided corrections and additions to Hallwachs' transcript, adds here the following sentence: "Vgl. dazu das Freund-Feind Verhältnis als das Politische von Carl Schmitt."

18. "Für die Bestimmung des Wesens des Politischen ist der Rückgang auf das Wesen des *Staates* das Allererste. Was heißt πόλις? . . . Was πόλις ist Erfahren wir schon aus Homer, Odyss. VI. Buch, Vers 9 ff. 'Um die πόλις herum zag er (fuhr er) mit einer Mauer, und baute Häuser und Tempel der Götter und teilte aus das Ackerland.' Πόλις ist so die eigentliche Mitte des Daseinsbereiches. . . . Πόλις ist die eigentlich bestimmende Mitte des geschichtlichen Daseins eines Volkes . . . Das Wesentliche des Daseins ist Selbstbehauptung. Mauer, Haus, Land, Götter. Von hier aus ist das Wesen des Politischen zu begreifen. Neuerdings ist das *Freund-Feindverhältnis* aufgetaucht als Wesen des Politischen. Es setzt die *Selbstbehauptung voraus*, ist also nur Wesens*folge* des Politischen.

Freund und Feind gibt es nur, wo Selbstbehauptung ist. Selbstbehauptung in diesem Sinn verlangt eine bestimmte Auffassung des geschichtlichen Seins des Volkes und des Staates selbst. Weil der Staat diese Selbstbehauptung des geschichtlichen Seins eines Volkes ist *und* weil man Staat = πόλις nennen kann, zeigt sich demzufolge das Politische als Freund-Feindverhältnis; aber nicht ist dieses Verhältnis = das Politische." Martin Heidegger and Erik Wolf, "Hegel, über den Staat," Freiburg University, Winter Semester 1934–1935, transcription Wilhelm Hallwachs. Heidegger Estate. Deutsches Literaturarchiv, Marbach, 50.

19. Cf. Derrida's critique of Carl Schmitt in *Politics of Friendship*, trans. George Collins (London: Verso, 1997).

20. Stuart Elden draws a similar conclusion on the distinction between Heidegger's notion of strife and Schmitt's enmity. After acknowledging that there are some similarities, Elden notes: "But the key contrast with Schmitt . . . is that the enemy is not named. Heidegger is not, seemingly, against anything in particular, but argues for a reading of politics as *polemos*. Unlike Schmitt, his *polemos* is not against a *polemios*, there is not an enemy. It is more a reading of politics as struggle, as *Auseinandersetzung*, as confrontation." Stuart Elden, *Speaking Against Number: Heidegger, Language, and the Politics of Calculation* (Edinburgh: Edinburgh University Press, 2006), 85.

21. As Gregory Fried explains, Schmitt himself had sent a copy of *The Concept of the Political* to Heidegger in 1933. Heidegger replied in a cordial letter to thank Schmitt and congratulate him on his interpretation of Heraclitus' Fragment 53 on "polemos basileus." Heidegger adds: "I have had such an interpretation with respect to the concept of truth set down for years" (quoted in Fried, *Heidegger's Polemos: From Being to Politics* [New Haven, CT: Yale University Press, 2000], 28). Maybe Heidegger refrained from naming his interlocutor in the "Origin" essay because of this cordial personal exchange as well as due to Schmitt's powerful position within the university system and the state at the time.

22. For the importance of the history of the medium in order to highlight the way that the medium determines history, see Sigrid Weigel, "Detail, Photographische under Kinematographische Bilder," in *Walter Benjamin: Die Kreatur, das Heilige, die Bilder* (Frankfurt am Main: Fischer, 2008), 297–332.

23. Peter Fenves makes a similar argument about the relation between the aestheticizing of politics and the politicizing of art in "Is there an Answer to the Aestheticizing the Political?" in ed. Andrew Benjamin, *Walter Benjamin and Art* (London: Continuum, 2005), 60–72.

24. The Heidegger interview can be downloaded from the Spiegel Archiv: http://wissen.spiegel.de/wissen/dokument/dokument-druck.html?id=9273095&top=SPIEGEL
25. Cf. Thomas Pepper, *Singularities: Extremes of Theory in the Twentieth Century* (Cambridge: Cambridge University Press, 1997), 87.
26. I cannot take up here the ways in which Heidegger's thought developed this idea of novelty, especially in terms of the *Ereignis* that appears in his later writings. See Andrew Benjamin's compelling analysis in *The Plural Event: Descartes, Hegel, Heidegger* (London: Routledge, 1993).
27. For a comparison on Benjamin and Schmitt's use of the exception, see Samuel Weber, "Taking Exception to the Decision: Walter Benjamin and Carl Schmitt," *Diacritics* 22 (1992), 5–18.
28. Philippe Lacoue-Labarthe argues, similarly, that in the 1930s Heidegger makes an argument about "the hegemony of the spiritual and the philosophical over political hegemony"—or to rephrase using the terms of the present essay, the hegemony of art over the autonomy of the political. See *Heidegger, Art and Politics: The Fiction of the Political*, trans. Chris Tuner (Oxford: Basil Blackwell, 1990), 13.
29. In the addendum to the "Origin" essay, which was included for the first time in 1956, Heidegger recognizes this problems and seeks to present strife without recourse to the distinction between the private and the public. However, he still relies on the notion of the decision. See "Origin," *BW* 211/ *GA* 5: 73–74.
30. Guy Debord, *The Society of the Spectacle* (New York: Zone Books, 1994), 12, emphasis added.
31. For the concept of the "people" in Heidegger, see James Phillips, *Heidegger's Volk: Between National Socialism and Poetry* (Stanford, CA: Stanford University Press, 2005).
32. Karl Marx, *The Eighteenth Brumaire of Louis Bonaparte*, trans. Clemens Dutt, in *Collected Works*, vol. 11 (New York: International, 1976), 111–112.
33. Marx, *18th Brumaire*, 186–188.
34. For an analysis of national socialism that is influenced by Marx's critique of the rise of Bonaparte's dictatorship in the *18th Brumaire*, see Franz Neuman, *Behemoth: The Structure and Practice of National Socialism, 1933–1944* (Chicago: Ivan R. Dee, 2009).
35. Cf. the last chapter of my *Sovereignty and its Other*.

ELEVEN

POLITICS OF THE USELESS

The Work of Art in Benjamin and Heidegger

David Ferris

At the end of the introductory section to the "The Work of Art in the Age of its Technical Reproducibility," Benjamin describes the intended significance of this essay in the following terms:

> In what follows the concepts introduced into the theory of art differ from the more common concepts in that they are completely useless for the purposes of fascism. On the other hand, they are useful for the formulation of revolutionary demands in the politics of art. (*SW* 4: 252, Benjamin's emphasis)[1]

What is striking about this remark is Benjamin's confidence that the concepts he introduces are not simply useless but *completely* useless (*vollkommen unbrauchbar*) for the purposes of fascism. Since fascist politics, in Benjamin's account, is a politics that represents itself through concepts of art associated with traditional aesthetics (semblance, beauty, originality, authenticity—basically everything that can be gathered together in his notion of the aura), what Benjamin proposes here is the possibility of concepts of art no longer complicit with an era that stretches from Plato to Schiller, namely, the era in which the properties of aesthetic works have served as a means to define politics. In the passage just cited, Benjamin anticipates an understanding of art that resides outside this era, that is, outside the history in which the aesthetic has been called on by politics in order to secure its meaning. That art can possess a significance distinct from this history is the point of contact between Benjamin's work of art essay and the nearly contemporaneous interpretation of art in Heidegger's "The Origin of the Work of Art" in the 1930s.[2] Although starting from quite different positions (Heidegger from the critique of an aesthetic tradition imbued with western metaphysics; Benjamin from the instrumental appropriation of that tradition in fascism), both undertake a redefinition of art that rejects its restriction to a representational and purposive activity.[3] As argued in this chapter, crucial to this redefinition, will be how Benjamin and Heidegger respond to an act that both evoke in different ways as the origin of another history in which the meaning of politics and the political is at stake. In Benjamin's case, this act is buried in a footnote to the second version of his essay in the form of a *Schlag* or "blow," through which play (subsequently reproducibility) emerges from its subordination to aura and aesthetic semblance. This emergence establishes the conflictual history that will culminate in Benjamin's version of a Hegelian and Marxist *Umschlagung*, or turning around, which figures importantly in all three versions of his essay. In Heidegger's case, this act goes by the name of a *Geworfenheit* or "thrownness," from which historical existence begins as a separation not yet organized as a conflict. It is this difference that frames the treatment of uselessness that Heidegger and Benjamin initially invoke in their different accounts of art and its modern significance.

Heidegger's encounter with a uselessness occurs in the first section of "The Origin of the Work of Art," when he examines the serviceability or usefulness of equipment in relation to art in order to distinguish the thing character of art from its work aspect. This approach does not fulfill his initial intention. Heidegger remarks: "we still know nothing of what we first sought: the thing's thingly character. And we know nothing at all of what we really and solely seek: the work-character of the work in the sense of the work of art [*das Werkhafte des Werkes im Sinne des Kunstwerkes*]" (*PLT* 35/ *GA* 5: 20). The purpose of equipment, serviceability (*Dienlichkeit*), fails to provide a knowledge of work and thing, and is therefore no help in distinguishing the nature of the work that produces a work of art. Heidegger then poses the following question: "Or did we now learn something unwittingly, in passing so to speak, about the work-being of the work?" (*PLT* 35/ *GA* 5: 20). What was useless for developing an understanding of the work of art now seems to offer hope for such an understanding; uselessness, it seems, is not completely useless.

In contrast to Heidegger, Benjamin's demand for a complete uselessness could be seen as an effect of the explicit commitment to the politicization of art, which appears in the epilogue to his essay. Yet, this commitment does not fully explain away the different presence that the political has in relation to art in Heidegger's essay. In his remarks on the way in which the truth occurs in the work of art, Heidegger describes this occurrence as a founding that is also present in the political when it takes the form of the state. Although this remark is not developed toward a politics of art, it does admit a way of thinking about the political that can be accessed through art. While each has a different intention (Heidegger to address the existence of the political and Benjamin to account for art in terms of a specific political movement, communism), insisting on this difference would deflect the central question addressed by both, namely, where and how the meaningfulness of art is to be located once that meaning can no longer be attributed to aesthetic categories (such as the beautiful). Is art, as Benjamin contends, now only capable of claiming meaning by radically divorcing itself from how it has been understood so that it will be completely useless to that understanding? And consequent to that question, by what means is that divorce political? Or, as Heidegger contends, is the meaning of art, and also the political, only discernible from within the aesthetic tradition whose historical reach Benjamin would bring to a close with the decay of the aura? Between these two accounts of art, the foundation of a politics of art is posed as a question about the way in which uselessness can be a basis for a usefulness that no longer sustains the purposive understanding of art. In short, it is a question of a politics of the useless.[4]

In Benjamin, the question of such a foundation appears in the last sentence to section IV of the work of art essay when he writes: "*At the moment when the authenticity of the production of art breaks down, the whole social function of art is revolutionized* [umgewälzt]. *In the place of its foundation on ritual, its foundation steps* [tritt] *on another practice: namely, its foundation on politics*" (SW 4: 257/ GS1: 482; Benjamin's emphasis). These sentences provide one of the few explicit references to politics outside of the introduction and epilogue in the third version of this essay; they insist that art "steps" away from authenticity in order to step on to politics as its foundation (*tritt ihre Fundierung auf Politik*).[5] This new foundation lies at the very bottom of Benjamin's disassociation of art from not just authenticity embedded in the aura but also from the secularized "realm of 'beautiful semblance'" (SW 4: 261). This disassociation opens the door for Benjamin to insist, first, that the meaning of art *is* now politics, and second, that politics is no longer a function of appearance and semblance. But by what means does this change occur?

Benjamin's account of what drives the history in which this transformation develops is given in the second version of his essay in the form of a sudden blow that awakens play, the forerunner of reproducibility from its slumber within mimesis. The recourse to something that happens suddenly has its counterpart in Heidegger when he extricates himself from the impasse he experiences in his attempt to distinguish between work and the material elements through which art is produced. In response to his own question about whether something was learned unwittingly about the "work-being of the work" from this impasse, Heidegger responds:

> The equipmental-being of equipment was discovered. But how? Not by a description and explanation of a pair of shoes actually present; not by a report about the process of making shoes; and also not by the observation of the actual use of shoes occurring here and there; but only by bringing ourselves before Van Gogh's painting. This painting spoke. In the vicinity of the work we were suddenly [*jäh*] somewhere else [*anderswo*] than we usually tend to be. (*PLT* 35/ *GA* 5: 20)

The resistance of the material element throws Heidegger back to the work of art and does so as the effect of a sudden change. The role of this suddenness as the origin of a foundation is then the crucial issue to be addressed by Benjamin and Heidegger. For Benjamin it opens the possibility for a complete uselessness, for Heidegger it indicates that complete uselessness remains an appearance.

Benjamin introduces this sudden moment in a long footnote attached to a passage in which film is cited as the example of an art that has escaped from beautiful semblance. In the second version of the work of art essay, Benjamin identifies the origin of art in mimesis and claims that "in mimesis, there sleeps, tightly interfolded like cotyledons [*eng ineinandergefaltet wie Keimblätter*], the two sides of art: semblance and play" (*SW* 3: 127n22/ *GS* 7: 368n10).[6] Then, after declaring that attributing the origin of art to play and semblance "says nothing new" (because it is already familiar to traditional aesthetics), Benjamin goes on to announce that "this abruptly [*mit einem Schlage*] changes as soon as these latter concepts lose their indifference toward history" (*SW* 3: 127n22/ *GS* 7: 368n10). The loss of this slumbering indifference is the crucial step in Benjamin's move toward an historical concept of art that stands apart from the orientation of traditional aesthetics toward an ideal of the beautiful. Consequently, how this indifference is lost—and on what grounds—is of paramount importance. The sentence just cited describes the loss of this indifference as something that happens all at once as if the mimesis in which semblance and play slumber had suddenly been struck a blow—precisely the sense of the phrase, "*mit einem Schlage*" (translated above as "abruptly"). What causes such a change to occur with all the force of being struck with a blow is not clear from this passage. What is clear is the result this blow produces: semblance and play now participate in a history that takes the form of their irresolvable conflict. Benjamin states: "this role is determined through [*Und zwar ist diese Rolle bestimmtdurch*] the world-historical conflict between the first and second technologies" (*SW* 3: 127n22/ *GS* 7: 368n10). First and second technologies are historical categories that disappear from the third version of Benjamin's "Work of Art" essay yet, in the second version, they are called on to embody the historical conflict that allows play to separate itself from semblance and begin the development that will eventually lead to the emergence of the art in which auratic semblance is no longer present, the art of technical reproducibility.[7]

The difficulty Benjamin contends with when he turns to first and second technologies as the opposition that drives a "world-historical conflict" resurfaces when he describes the means by which the second technology emerges in opposition to the first. Benjamin writes: "The origin of the second technology is to be sought where human beings by an unconscious ruse [*mit unbewußter List*], first began to distance themselves from nature. It lies, in other words, in play" (*SW* 3: 107/ *GS* 7: 359). The origin of the second technology is an unconscious act that takes the form of a ruse. So defined, this origin is accounted for in terms of the act of a human-being rather than a state of nature. With this turn to an unconscious ruse, a fundamental difference to Heidegger occurs. Benjamin's account of the origin of play as the source of an historical conflict (also the dominant effect of the second technology) in an unconscious act. This is radically different from Heidegger whose account of origin as "presencing" or "appearing" evokes no language of consciousness or a subject as its cause. Instead, Heidegger turns to the word *Dasein* or "being-there" to designate that the human being is always already in a relation to the world, including nature—with the result that consciousness is the result of this moment and not something that is already latent in a state of nature. To locate the origin of this relation to world and nature within consciousness would be, for Heidegger, to distort how the human being exists in the world. In "The Origin of the Work of Art" essay, Heidegger, drawing on *Being and Time*, describes this existence as originating in a "thrownness" (*Geworfenheit*), a term Heidegger also refers to when explaining how the work of art is "the becoming and happening of truth" (*PLT* 71/ *GA*5: 58). This thrownness, as Heidegger explains in *Being and Time*, is not an account of where a being (Dasein) has come from nor where it is going. Heidegger writes: "This characteristic of Dasein's Being—this 'that it is'—is veiled in its whence and whither [*in seinem Woher und Wohin verhüllten*] . . . we call it the 'thrownness of this entity into its 'there'" (*BT* 174/ *GA* 2: 135). Although the origin and destination (or end) of this thrownness remains veiled from it, this does not mean that origin and end exist independently from such thrownness nor do they exist historically prior as if they are something that can be revealed by lifting a veil. Rather, origin and end come into existence with this thrownness as one of the possibilities that arise from the fact of existing in the world. What this means in relation to Benjamin is that, for Heidegger, there is no need to resort to an "unconscious ruse" to produce a separation from nature and the world. Such a separation is what already happens with the fact of existing; no preceding slumbering existence from which art or the human needs to be awakened is necessary.

By claiming that play is what acts unconsciously to establish a separation between human beings and nature, Benjamin introduces hidden potential or latency as a crucial element in the historical development he traces to this origin.[8] This latency is created through an unconscious ruse performed by play but only once play has already attained historical consciousness (hence why latency involves the ruse of being unconscious). This act allows Benjamin to locate as an origin the two things that will drive the historical development of art, play, and semblance, but without admitting the conflict that comes to the fore after the *Schlag* or blow arrives. Here, the "unconscious ruse" establishes the existence of play as an element that awaits the "blow" that causes it to enter into an historical dialectic with semblance or aura, that is, it accounts for the latency through which a demand justifies itself with a backward look.[9]

The crucial role of this latency for the transformation of play into exhibition-value is affirmed in the passage where Benjamin speaks of the presence of cult value and exhibition value within semblance and play as saying nothing new to traditional aesthetics. This is because, by remaining in their latency and by not taking on a role within the "world-historical conflict," play and exhibition-value have no effect on how art is conceived as an historical rather than as a temporal phenomenon. This latency is embodied in the verb *verpuppen*, which describes the process of pupation through which the butterfly emerges from its chrysalis: "cult value and exhibition vale are latent [*verpuppt*] in the other pair of concepts at issue here [semblance and play]" (*SW* 3: 127n22). This latency is far from the account of origin given by Heidegger who, in his essay on the work of art, admits no element that can be unfolded like the emergence of a butterfly in order to establish an historical conflict as the basis for the development of art. As Heidegger's account of the *Geworfenheit* or thrownness of the human-being or *Dasein* indicates, the play that Benjamin uses to separate the human being from nature is already in the world but not because of some latent or unconscious ruse it performs on its own behalf. Benjamin's recourse to latent causes and their absence in Heidegger is pronounced enough to raise the following question: To what extent is such latency the necessary, if not foundational, requirement within Benjamin's critical project for a politics of art as well as the history that unfolds in the interest of this politics?

The "unconscious ruse" and reference to pupation are not the only occasions when Benjamin turns to latency in his account of the dialectical development of art—and nor is this recourse specific to the second version.[10] In a sentence that remains unchanged across all versions of the essay, Benjamin evokes latency in his account of what enabled the development of film after photography: "Just as the illustrated newspaper virtually lay hidden within lithography, so sound film lay hidden in photography [*Wenn in der Lithographie virtuell die illustrierte Zeitung verborgen war, so in der Photographie der Tonfilm*]" (*SW* 4: 253/ *GS*1: 475). The sense of a medium hidden or concealed in another preceding form reiterates how much, in this essay, Benjamin's historical thinking demands that what has already appeared (sound film) is the hidden potential waiting in another medium (here photography). In photography and film, this latency manifests itself most completely when reproducibility determines what the work of art is ("a work designed for reproducibility" [*SW* 4: 256]). The historical passage from mimesis to reproducibility is then the embodiment as well as the cause of the polarity that has been present from the origin of art in antiquity. As a result what is at stake for Benjamin is to account for the moment of separation, the *Schlag*, as the moment that allows play to sustain such a history.

Benjamin's justification of this moment takes the form of a backward look that calls on an important term in the Marxist account of the step that initiates the possibility of revolutionary change.[11] This occurs in section V when Benjamin claims that the quantitative (the comparative increase in reproducibility) has become qualitative and does by recapturing the *Schlag* that freed play from semblance:

> With the different methods of technical reproduction of the artwork, its exhibition ability increased to such an enormous degree that the quantitative shift between its two poles turned [*umschlägt*], as in primitive times, into a qualitative transformation [*Veränderung*] of its nature. Just as in primitive times the work of art, through the absolute importance it placed on its cult value, became primarily an instrument of magic which only later came to be known as a work of art, so today, the work of art, through the absolute importance it places on its exhibition value, turns [*wird . . . zu*] into an entity [*Gebild*] with completely new functions [*ganz neuen Funktionen*] and amongst these functions the one we are conscious of as standing out, the artistic function, may subsequently be recognized as incidental [*beiläufige*]. (*SW* 4: 257/ *GS* 1: 484)

Here, Benjamin calls on a verb he uses only once in the whole of the essay, *umschlagen*, to describe the nature of the shift between the two poles of art.[12] This verb, which occurs with some frequence in Lukács *History and Class-Consciousness*, is also an important Hegelian term before being taken up by Marxist thought. In fact, Hegel considers the nature of the shift described by this verb as "one of the most important of determinations" of dialectical thought. More precisely, Hegel states, *umschlagen* is the movement whereby "the extreme [*das Äußerste*] of a state or action tends to abruptly turn around [*umzuschlagen*] into its opposite."[13] A passage from *The Origin of the German Tragic Drama* confirms the extent to which Benjamin understands the movement of *umschlagen* as an effect of extremity. There, Benjamin sets the symbolic apotheosis of beautiful semblance (which seeks to "merge with the divine in an unbroken whole") against the "dialectical apotheosis of the Baroque," which manifests itself in an overturning of extremes that preserves their separation: "it [apotheosis] takes place in the overturning of extremes [*vollzieht sich im Umschlagen von Extremen*]" (*PLT* 160/ *GS* 1: 337). In a letter to Gershom Scholem from May 29, 1926, Benjamin speaks of this overturning as the identity of the extremes. But, in distinction to Hegel's account of *umschlagen* as a moment of reciprocal inversion, Benjamin emphasizes an aspect of this overturning that Hegel does not; namely an unmediated identity. In the case of the two extremes he refers to in his letter to Scholem, religious and political observance, Benjamin asserts: "I do not concede [*gestehe ich nicht zu*] a difference between these two observances in their quintessential being. Just as little [do I concede] that mediation is possible [between them]" (*GB* 3: 158).[14] Despite being expressed as the negation of a concession, these remarks would firmly assert the necessity of two poles whose identity to each other resides in the fact that they occupy the position of extremes. As such, they do not produce the appearance of synthesis or unity (that is the task of beautiful semblance); in the phrase Benjamin uses in the second version, they embody and maintain the "world-historical conflict" into which art was awakened by the *Schlag* or blow. This *Schlag* or blow now returns in the form of an *Umschlagen*, which, in effect, affirms the purpose of the original *Schlag* as the event of art's introduction to historical dialectics. *Schlag* is now, *in nuce*, the *Um-Schlag* that regulates and maintains the extremes in their identity with one another.

The difficulty that haunts this appropriation can be discerned if we turn back to the last passage cited from the "Work of Art" essay. There, the extreme is present in the moment when exhibition ability achieves "absolute importance"—such an absolute being the extreme point beyond which no further increase in exhibition ability is possible. Why is such an extreme necessary? Because it is the point at which the form and the means of production of the work of art can be defined solely by exhibition ability rather than simply display an increasing tendency toward this value.[15] But, because this *Umschlag* polices polarity at its limit, art can never completely escape the world-historical conflict in which this polarity is embodied. The complete uselessness on which Benjamin's politics of art depends now emerges as an extreme encased within a polarity that has been latent from the origin of art in mimesis. Because of this polarity, art cannot escape what Benjamin defines as a condition of its existence, namely, an "oscillation" (between ritual, cult, and aura on one side, and, on the other, the play, exhibition ability, and reproducibility) that "can be demonstrated for every individual work of art" (SW 4: 273–74n15). What Benjamin describes as the "completely new functions" of art are then the effect of an historical process that is confined to an oscillation between two extremes, two poles, whose names, as the different versions of Benjamin's essay is witness to, may change even if their function does not. In this case, what is "completely new" (SW 4: 257/ GS 1: 484) is only comparatively so and therefore is only useless within the historical unfolding of this comparison—which means that even at its most extreme moment it is *incompletely useless* and precisely because of the inversion it produces in order to protect the history of art as a dialectical process. As a result, Benjamin, at the end of the passage in which he speaks of the *Umschlagen* of the poles of art, the concept of art that privileged the function of the human artist does not become completely useless (*unbrauchbar*) but instead, we are told, that it "may subsequently be recognized as incidental [*später als eine beiläufige erkennen mag*]."[16] As something incidental, this human artistic function still survives at the very extreme of its usefulness thereby indicating the extent to which the demand Benjamin's essay seeks to establish as the foundation of a politics of art cannot render semblance or the auratic completely useless because, *in extremis*, semblance shelters the latent possibility of such a demand: semblance is necessary in order to affirm one of the extreme points that permits the reversal of *umschlagen* to take place.

So configured, what Benjamin's politics of art demands is the repeated reenactment of the decay of the aura until this repetition renders the aura so incidental that it will be forgotten. Only by repeating this act of negation can Benjamin's politics of art claim to avoid the logic that governs the reversal of auratic art through which it appears: the eventuality that once the extreme of reproducibility is reached, then, the other pole of art, semblance, theauratic will redefine the function of art. Because of the logic of this *umschlagen*, no pure demand can emerge to counter art's historical movement between two constitutive poles. If this is the fate of Benjamin's politics, then, the usefulness of such a politics is restricted to a history whose significance lies in the recurrent experience of its limit as the prognosis of something other than this limit. In other words, what is at stake is that this limit is a prognosis, that it is the latent presence of something different. This leads Benjamin to conclude, in a remark whose messianic privileging of delay and deferment has not received due attention, that: "it has always been one of the primary tasks of art to create a demand [*Nachfrage*] whose hour of full satisfaction has still not come" (SW 4: 266).[17] Here, art is understood as what defers the demand for its complete uselessness and does so by accounting for that demand as the effect of a future that lies waiting within the past of art—a demand unfolded by Benjamin's own account of art proceeding from "unconscious ruse," to play, to exhibition ability, to photography, to film. The *Schlag* or blow that initiates art into this history, together with the two tendencies (semblance and play) that contain the seed of this history, is already an effect of the dialectical conflict that subsequently "discovers" its origin in this framing of history as a passage between *Schlag* and *Umschlag*. Benjamin's account of art makes sense within the dialectical conflict that emerges from this passage as long as its history remains incapable of fulfilling a purpose. This explains why the messianic becomes an essential part of this historical understanding and also why *umschlagen* is configured by Benjamin as the moment that keeps art historical by turning it away from an end in which the polarity that drives this history would be overcome in the possibility of an art totally without semblance. At the same time, to overcome this polarity would be the cessation of history, precisely the end that history cannot attain but only hope for, and, through that hope, sustain its meaning in an end that history can *only* formulate and repeat as demand.

It is at this point that the question posed by Heidegger's understanding of thrownness can be addressed. As with Benjamin's recourse to *Schlag*, thrownness provides an account of the way in which whatever exists in the world is in that world without knowledge of its "whence and whither" (*Woher and Wohin*). Additionally, Heidegger says, this "whence and whither" remains veiled (*verhüllten*). There seems to be a crossing of paths between Benjamin and Heidegger on this point because both call on an unexplained act as the origin of an historical existence. But it is here that their paths diverge most radically. In Benjamin, the *Schlag* brings a preexisting relation out of its hiding place and does so as part of a historical development that demands a qualitative change in that relation. In Heidegger, what accords with this "bringing out" in Benjamin, at least superficially, is what he calls *unconcealment* or *Unverborgenheit*. As stated in a passage cited earlier, unconcealment describes how truth occurs both in the work of art and the founding of a state. For Heidegger, this unconcealment is historical precisely because (i) it exists in the world but it does not found a particular history even though it makes such histories possible—otherwise it would already be a purposive truth; and (ii) because it does not presuppose some relation that precedes it and in which lies latent within it. Instead of being latent, which would mean perceptible through the veil, what precedes thrownness and the unconcealment it enacts remains completely veiled and inaccessible. This understanding of unconcealment in Heidegger also affects the relation of uselessness to usefulness, which is so central to Benjamin's attempt to formulate a politics resistant to the purposes of fascism. As we saw earlier, Heidegger does not make the uselessness of his examination of equipment become the index of another concealed end; for him, it is a question of origin and how it appears rather than the question of an end. Consequently, not only must uselessness and usefulness possess a different relation to one another but it is one whose existence does not require a sudden blow, or *Schlag*, to awaken them into world historical conflict. Indeed, the closest Heidegger could come to such a blow and its suddenness is the moment when he recognizes that pursuing the difference between work and thing in equipment in order to understand what work is in the work of art was not a dead end after all. However, in Heidegger, this suddenness remains temporal and does not become the attribute or metaphor for a physical act.[18]

Heidegger's account of unconcealment also contains a different relation to foundation. Rather than have art step onto another foundation, Heidegger speaks of art and politics as each being ways in which foundation happens. This recurs across the different versions of Heidegger's essay in a sentence that claims that the question of the origin of the work of art is also a question of the origin of the realm of the political, the state. In the third section of his essay, Heidegger states that "Another way in which truth occurs is the act that founds a state [*Ein eandere Weise, wie Wahrheit west, ist die staatgründende Tat*]" (*PLT* 62/ *GA* 4: 49]). In the last revised version of this essay published by Heidegger, this statement appears in the context of four other ways in which truth occurs: setting itself into the work, in the nearness of Being, in the essential sacrifice, and in the thinker's questioning. While this section of Heidegger's essay emphasizes the first of these ways, truth setting itself into the work, it is evident from the passage describing the different ways in which truth occurs that the happening of truth in the work of art is a foundation that is not exclusive to a particular historical form.

Why Heidegger takes up this question of foundation with respect to art can be understood from remarks he makes at the very end of his *Contributions to Philosophy* (1936–1938), a work that overlaps with the period in which "The Origin of the Work of Art" is written. In the *Contributions* Heidegger indicates that the question of the origin of the work of art—and therefore, by analogy, the question of the origin of the political in the form of the state—cannot be decided from within those aesthetic traditions that Benjamin had insisted on setting aside as useless, incidental. In the following remarks, Heidegger, like Benjamin, also emphasizes the hold that the aesthetic has had on not just the discourse on art but also a tradition of thinking:

> This question [of the origin of the work of art] stands in the closest connection to the task of overcoming [*Überwindung*] aesthetics and that

means simultaneously overcoming a certain understanding of beings as what is objectively representable. The overcoming of aesthetics again results necessarily from the historical encounter with metaphysics as such. This metaphysics comprises the basic Western position toward beings and thereby the ground for the essence of Western art and its works up to the present moment. (*CP* 354/ *GA* 65: 503–504)[19]

Heidegger equates the overcoming of aesthetics to the overcoming of an understanding that is defined by the possibility of objective representation. The project of this overcoming, to the extent that it is equally destructive of aesthetics as it is of metaphysics, finds, at first sight, its counterpart in the rendering useless the aura and its aesthetic undertaken by Benjamin. But, as Benjamin's essay is also witness to when he cites Brecht's remark about the return of aura, this destruction is no simple step because it involves the danger that art's ability to possess a function will be lost (see note 16). Yet, what is at stake in Benjamin is quite different from Heidegger. For Heidegger, the danger is that any such step will be no more than a renewal of metaphysics and thus of the return of the aesthetic as a mode of representative appearance or semblance. Instead, Heidegger pursues an overcoming of metaphysical aesthetics to such a point that art can no longer be defined in terms of a function, even an incidental one. The question Heidegger's pursuit poses is whether, after the loss of a function for art, it is still possible to speak of art in political terms.

Instead of function, Heidegger insists on art as an occurrence of truth. When Heidegger speaks of this occurrence as an overcoming he does not, however, envisage an act of stepping on to another foundation as Benjamin does. Nor is it a simple act of stepping outside of aesthetics or metaphysics, rather it involves what he calls an "historical encounter."[20] This encounter is quite different from the *Schlag* or blow that Benjamin turns to in order to awaken art into history from its mimetic slumber. As Heidegger's word for this encounter, *Auseinandersetzung*, indicates, a placing of one against another in a relation that does not invoke either polarity or a turning around (*umschlagen*) as Benjamin proposes. Furthermore, this encounter occurs because metaphysics—which Heidegger sees as standing for the "ground for the essence of western art"—is recognized as one determination of existence among others and therefore remains historical even as it lays claims to an an historical understanding. The shift Heidegger sees as the result of this encounter does not preserve metaphysics or the aesthetic as one pole in which another pole lies slumbering until awakened into the conflict that preserves this polarity. As a result, the overcoming of metaphysics and the aesthetic that became its sensible appearance is not something that supersedes either; rather, it is the uncovering of their original relation to historical existence. Here, the aesthetic and its metaphysical claims are preserved in a way that is very different from what occurs in Benjamin's politics of art. Where Benjamin regulates their difference in a dialectical polar relation that denies any future synthesis between semblance and reproducibility (this is how they possess a history that already demands what Adorno later proposes as a negative dialectic), Heidegger locates the origin of historical existence as a separation into which conflict and dialectic are subsequently introduced as a decision about the meaning of that separation. In this respect, Benjamin's "world historical conflict" is far from what Heidegger describes as "the historical encounter with metaphysics *as such*" (emphasis added).

Heidegger emphasizes that such an encounter not demand any rejection whether in the form of a complete uselessness or otherwise. The overcoming that occurs in this encounter, Heidegger states "is not the rejection of hitherto existing philosophy but rather the leap into its first beginning, without wanting to renew (*erneuern*) this first beginning—something that remains historically (*historisich*) unreal and historically (*geschichtlich*) impossible" (*CP* 354/ *GA* 65: 504). To leap into a first beginning is not a leap into origin as a preceding historical space; rather, it is the leap into the relation out of which existing philosophy also emerges. This leap is the preparation for what Heidegger refers to as the other beginning in which the history that characterizes western metaphysics is overcome. But there is no clear demarcation between the encounter with this first beginning and the other beginning. Although Heidegger defines the first beginning as a history that stretches from Anaximander to Nietzsche, it does not simply end with Nietzsche:

> With the raising of preparedness for the crossing over from the end of the first beginning into the other beginning, it is not that man steps [*tritt*] into a "period" that still does not yet exist, rather he enters into a totally different domain of history. The end of the first beginning will for a long time still encroach into the crossing over, even into the other beginning. (*CP* 161/ *GA* 65: 227)

Here, in Heidegger's thought, is probably the moment that comes closest, linguistically, to Benjamin's demand that art "steps" onto the foundation of politics. Both use the same verb *treten* to describe the crossing out of the mode of appearance that links western metaphysics and western aesthetics. Yet, where Benjamin subsequently evokes a polarity within which this mode of appearance could be renewed, Heidegger, despite admitting that such appearance and metaphysical foundation persists beyond its end, as if it had become incidental, denies that its renewal can be considered within either of the versions of history that figure prominently in his thought: *historisch* or *geschichtlich*.²¹ According to the first, *historisch*, this renewal is "unreal," and, according to the second, *geschichtlich*, it is "impossible." In this case, Heidegger, more than Benjamin, posits the possibility of a passing out of the kind of aesthetics and metaphysics that no longer retains its categories in their incidental forms. And emphatically Heidegger does not see this other beginning as bearing the kind of polar relation that Benjamin retains. In the sections of the *Beiträge* that deal with first and other beginning, Heidegger states: "the other beginning is not counter-directed [*Gegenrichtung*] to the first. Rather, *as other* it stands outside this countering [*Gegen*] and outside immediate comparability [*Vergleichbarkeit*]" (*CP* 131/ *GA* 65: 187). It is on account of standing outside of comparability that Heidegger's other beginning does not take place within the kind of history invoked by Benjamin and which relies on a comparatively greater quantitative shift as the beginning of the qualitative shift that marks the history of art as it goes through the abrupt turn or *umschlagen* that separates aura from reproducibility while irrevocably tying one to the other. What is at stake here between Heidegger and Benjamin is precisely this relation and whether it is itself political or whether it only founds the possibility of the political as one way in which that relation exists historically.

In a section of the *Beiträge* just before the one last cited, Heidegger speaks of this relation in terms of a crossing-over (*Übergang*) that "implements a separation (*Scheidung*)" and then adds, "what is separated is so decisively separated that no common area of differentiation [*Unterschiedung*] can prevail at all" (*CP* 124/ *GA* 65: 177). This decisive separation entails a more fundamental account than the one Benjamin holds to when he invokes the two extremes that provide the frame within which the overturning movement of *umschlagen* takes place. Heidegger also refuses mediation when he speaks of the other beginning as "outside immediate [*unmittelbar*] comparability," nevertheless, because the other beginning is not separated from the first beginning by the kind of separation that makes one comparable to the other (as if they shared the same "quintessential being" as Benjamin claims). In Heidegger, the difference that separates these two beginnings does not permit their mingling or confine their history to one of substitution for the other. This is why Heidegger does not speak of the other beginning as a second beginning, as if this were a matter of the kind of separation that defines two cotyledons or two technologies in a polar relation. What Heidegger describes here is not a simple separation between two things that are bound to one another through this separation. The separation Heidegger presents here does not take place within a frame that makes one equal to the other in either function or historical meaning. What Heidegger presents is a relation that has already moved away from separation as the means through which an identity, unmediated or not in an

Umschlagung, is to be grasped. As Heidegger insists, the separation of the other beginning stands outside both the "countering" and the "immediate comparability" that structures the *umschlagen* at the core of Benjamin's account of the history of art. Such an *umschlagen* would, in Heidegger's terms, conceal and forget the founding separation that possesses "no common area of differentiation" precisely because it insists on a relation that semblance and play, aura and reproducibility have in common even if this relation remains a repeatedly interrupted synthesis. As a result, what Benjamin proposes is only a radical differentiation whose political force arises from a negative relation, namely, that western metaphysics and its aesthetics will find it completely useless. In other words, Benjamin founds a difference within that aesthetics, but a difference that requires constant reiteration because it remains bound to the terms and the means through which it is given historical existence: the conflict and polarity that maintain difference within a dialectical framing that defines history as the overturning of one by the other.

The dialectical overturning that gives a political turn to Benjamin's account of art is addressed by Heidegger in the section on Nietzsche's overturning of Platonism, again in the *Beiträge*. In the following remark, Heidegger speaks of the limitation of such overturning as well as its consequences: "every overturning [*Umkehrung*] is all the more a return to and an entanglement in the opposite . . . even though Nietzsche senses that this opposite too must lose its meaning" (*CP* 127/ *GA* 65: 182). The sense that this opposite "must lose its meaning" is identified by Heidegger as the response to an overcoming that is in fact no more than a turning over or inversion that defines the limits of the history he assigns to the first beginning (the history of philosophy that begins with Plato and ends with Nietzsche). Overturning, in this case, affirms historical development as a development that takes place within a polarity. But, as Heidegger notes, Nietzsche sensed that opposites "must also lose their meaning" in this overturning. To retain these opposites as the extremes through which the *Umschlagung* occurs is only possible if, in Benjamin's phrase, there is no difference in the "quintessential being" of these extremes. Here, Benjamin's work of art essay differs from Heidegger because of the former's hesitation to push the logic of his historical thought to the point where the extreme itself loses its meaning as a defining limit. The purpose of the extreme in Benjamin is to preserve the qualitative difference that allows the past to be seen as the error of an aesthetic ideology (against which the present stands as political truth). The differentiation or separation that enables the leap into the other beginning, Heidegger claims, has nothing to do with the assignment of error. Overturning, or overcoming, Heidegger states, "can never have the sense of proving that the history of the guiding-question and thus 'metaphysics' up to the present are an 'error'" (*CP* 131/ *GA* 65: 188). To reduce metaphysics or even aesthetic semblance to the status of an error is to consign both to a history whose defining characteristic is its uselessness in the present—precisely the task Benjamin's essay announces from its beginning. To see fascism as only an error, aberration, or distortion is then precisely the ground on which its return is already prepared since error already binds this extremity to its opposite, a truth that cannot disentangle itself from error (hence Benjamin's chiasmatic conclusion whereby the aestheticizing of politics is matched by the politicizing of art [*SW* 4: 270]). This is a danger that Benjamin's politics of art must also face if the decision about its usefulness for revolutionary demands depends on whether fascism finds its concepts completely useless or not. Like error and truth, usefulness and uselessness are here extremes that need and demand each other. What is at issue here, between Benjamin and Heidegger, is whether art, as a way of existing in the world, can itself be political and therefore answer to a demand, or whether the political can only exist alongside art in a way that refuses politics as the sole measure of human significance since politics is not itself the foundation for something else but a manner of existing in which the act of founding is also preserved.

In "The Origin of the Work of Art," Heidegger addresses this question when he takes up the happening of truth in art as a movement of concealment and unconcealment. Heidegger speaks of concealment in terms of a sheltering that belongs to the earth, and unconcealment in terms of a self-opening that belongs to the world:

> The world, in resting upon the earth, strives to surmount it. As self-opening, it cannot endure anything closed. The earth however, as sheltering and concealing tends always to draw the world into itself and keep it there. (*PLT* 49)

Heidegger emphasizes that this relation of sheltering and opening (unlike the aura) "does not wither away (*verkümmert*) into the empty unity of opposites" (*PLT* 49). Instead, this relation is a "striving" in which, Heidegger remarks, "each opponent carries the other beyond itself" (*PLT* 49). There is no question here of letting go, there is no question of something falling into mere uselessness or of the opponents turning into their opposite. Nor is it a question of separating the auratic from its function so that this function can survive incidentally after the aura loses its meaning.

While the paths of Benjamin and Heidegger differ markedly, that difference is nowhere more pronounced in how the positions taken up by each locate the place and role of shock, that is, what Heidegger calls *Erschütterung* and also *Erschecken* and what Benjamin calls simply *Chockwirkung*. Shock, for Benjamin, actualizes the political meaning of cinema through its interruption of the concepts associated with auratic aesthetics, in particular, contemplation. Heidegger contends that this agitation of received concepts is beside the point: "The shaking [Erschütterung] of this accustomed formulation [aesthetics] is not the essential point" (*PLT* 39). Instead, what is essential for Heidegger is "a first opening of sight [*erste Öffnung des Blickes*] to the fact that what is workly in the work, equipmental in equipment, and thingly in the thing comes closer to us only when we think the Being of beings" (*PLT* 39). What is central here is that the shock of this *Erschütterung* should not be restricted to what he calls "accustomed formulations." Present in these formulations, Heidegger contends, is an abandonment of Being that takes the form of "what is most familiar and therefore most unknown" (*CP* 11/ *GA* 65: 15). Rather than polarize the familiar and the unknown, Heidegger emphasizes that "what has been familiar for so long proves to be estranging and confining" (*CP* 11/ *GA* 65: 15). In the terms of Benjamin's argument, this is tantamount to saying that it is the aura itself and not reproducibility that brings about the recognition that makes the aura lose its familiarity and become known in its limitation. It is this recognition that Heidegger describes as occurring in a state of "startled dismay" or *Erschrecken* (*CP* 11/ *GA* 65: 15). While shock and startled dismay are the experience of the abandonment that occurs within "accustomed formulations," they are not to be dismissed for that reason because, Heidegger continues, they are also preparation for the way in which each opposing force can carry another beyond itself. What is then at stake for Heidegger in shock is the role it plays in preparing the crossing over into the "other beginning," that is, the crossing over which signals that founding is a separation without a common area and, as such, is not something that can be "stepped" on.

This difference between Heidegger and Benjamin, which turns on the matter of this step, is also what explains their different recourse to and deployment of shock. In Benjamin, shock is the effect of a medium that interrupts the contemplation of aesthetic semblance and does so as the defining index of an art no longer defined by aura. Benjamin writes, "The train of associations in the person contemplating these images is immediately interrupted by new images. This constitutes the shock effect of film, which, like all shock effects, will be absorbed/ cushioned (*aufgefangen*) through an agitated presence of mind" (*SW* 4: 267/ *GS* 1: 503). And even, more pointedly, in "Some Motifs in Baudelaire": "In a film, perception conditioned by shock was established as a formal principle. What determines the rhythm of production on a conveyor belt is the same thing that underlies the rhythm of reception in film" (*SW* 4: 328). The shock of this relentless assault on contemplative reception is how Benjamin conceives of the politics of art. Although this founding has to be repeated continuously, this repetition derives its significance from a constant overturning of aesthetic semblance, from a constant rendering of semblance as what is uselessness. But, it is a uselessness in constant need of reassertion. Accordingly, it is haunted by the return of aura. Consequently, if Benjamin's foundation is to fulfill the demands of the politics made in its name, the separation it enacts has to be known in terms of a history in which uselessness will be unequivocally aligned with the past as the site of error. It is here that the most divergent decision takes place between Benjamin and Heidegger. Where Benjamin articulates a politics based on the rendering useless of a past, Heidegger would interpret such uselessness as what prepares the step toward another beginning. In this respect, what Benjamin indicates as politics in "The Work of Art in the Age of its Reproducibility" would have, for Heidegger, all the character of a first beginning. In Heidegger's terms, the separation that founds politics in Benjamin would be the sign of an abandonment, a decision to refuse a separation that is in no way a polarity. To the extent that this separation is preserved in founding, as understood by Heidegger, then Benjamin's politics would be nothing other than the abandonment of the act that enframes the political in the founding of a state. To reproduce this abandonment is to see this separation as knowable only in what it separates rather than as the effect of separation in which not even difference can be recovered as something in common. To experience this separation as a difference held in common (what Benjamin presents as the experience of shock in collectivity) is the demand of his politics. It is perhaps the deficit of such a common area that is most useless of all. But, since this separation makes no demand on difference as the mark of something in common, it would be a mistake to define it as useless. Only when this separation is made to answer to a demand for either use or uselessness can it become useless. This is the demand in which the possibility of art as politics is founded by Benjamin—hence the need to account for art as a reproducibility in which that demand is made over and over again. In contrast, for Heidegger, such a demand sustains a common area of differentiation as the critical moment of a history that takes aesthetic semblance and the aura to its limit before turning back. Instead of preparing a crossing over to the "other beginning," this limit remains bound to the first beginning since it draws its meaning from a dialectic that can do no more than repeatedly overturn that beginning—the demand of the shock performed by film. In this case, Benjamin's positioning of shock as the mark of that limit risks abandoning the separation that Heidegger presents as a founding act that would include *both* aura and reproducibility within its reach, as well as fascism and what Benjamin proposes as an alternative, the politicization of aesthetics under the name of communism.

Notes

This chapter extends a paper presented at the Universidad Diego Portales, Santiago de Chile, October 2010. A version of that paper, under the title "Entre los fines del fascismo y las exigencias revolucionarias: la teología de arte en 'La obra de arte en la época de su reproductibilidad técnica' de Walter Benjamin" is published in *Esperanza, pero no para nosotros. Capitalismo, técnica y estética en W. Benjamin*, ed. Horst Nitschack and Miguel Vatter (Santiago de Chile: LOM ediciones S.A., 2014). Many of the quotations in English have been modified. Rather than note these each time, such modifications are flagged by the insertion within square brackets of the German word or phrase into the passage cited.

1. This chapter refers to each of the three versions of Benjamin's "The Work of Art in the Age of its Technological Reproducibility." Unless otherwise stated all references are to the third version. On occasion, when it is important to indicate the consistency of Benjamin's thought across each of the versions, this is indicated by the insertion of "all versions" in the parenthetical reference.
2. In the case of both Heidegger and Benjamin, their essays on the work of art exist in several versions as they are developed and revised in the 1930s. Heidegger first delivers his lecture on the origin of the work of art in Freiburg in November 1935, repeats this lecture in Zurich in January 1936, and then expands it into a set of three lectures given in Frankfurt in November and December 1936. The lectures given on this last occasion subsequently became the basis for the publication in 1950 of the final version of this. Benjamin first produces a version of his essay in late 1935, a second version in 1936, and then a third version in 1939. Suggestive as this coincidence of dates may be, no evidence has come to light to confirm that Benjamin knew of Heidegger's lectures on the work of art in Freiburg and Zurich in 1935 and 1936.
3. Here, Kant's aesthetics may also be invoked, specifically his understanding of the aesthetic in terms of a "purposiveness without purpose." Although Kant will rightly restrict the explicit presence of purpose to those judgments that are not aesthetic, Kant cannot remove some form of purpose from aesthetic judgments if they are to remain judgments whose significance is more than the mere fact of their utterance. It is for this reason that Kant will retain purpose if only in a form that has the appearance of a purpose.
4. Peter Fenves, in his essay, "Is There an Answer to the Aestheticizing of the Political?" (in *Walter Benjamin and Art*, ed. Andrew Benjamin [London: Continuum, 2005], 60–72), examines the role of antinomy as fundamental to Benjamin's task oriented thinking. Here, the incompatibility of the concepts

Benjamin seeks to develop can also be seen as the effect of defining the task of art.

5. Between the Introduction and the Epilogue, there are only three significant, direct references to the political in the text of the essay: the one just cited; the reference to Atget's photographs as constituting a "hidden political significance" (*SW* 4: 258); and a footnote concerning the parallel between the transportability of the image of the actor and a change in the manner of the public presentation of leaders (*SW* 4: 277n27). One other use of the word political in section X simply refers to different kinds of journals. The Epilogue contains five references, four of which reiterate fascism's aestheticization of politics and, a fifth that links this aestheticization to war (*SW* 4: 269–270).

6. Benjamin insists on the identity of art as this polarity on several occasions and in all versions of the "Work of Art" essay. In the first version: "Es wäre möglich, die Kunstgeschichte als Auseinandersetzung zweier Polaritäten im Kunstwerk selbst darzustellen und die Geschichte ihres Verlaufes in den wechselnden Verschiebungen des Schwergewichts vom einen Pol des Kunstwerks zum anderen zu erblicken. Diese beiden Pole sind sein Kultwert und sein Ausstellungswert" [It would be possible to demonstrate that the history of art is the setting apart from one another of two poles as well as see the history of their development in the alternating movement of emphasis from one pole to another] (*GS* 1: 443; trans. mine); in a fragment to the second version, "This polarity must find a place in the definition of art" [In der Definition der Kunst muß diese Polarität Platzfinden] (*SW* 3: 137/ *GS* 7: 667) and also in this version, mimesis, informed by polarity, is referred to "as the primal phenomenon of all artistic activity" [als dem Urphänomen aller künstlerischen Betätigung] (*SW* 3: 127n22/ *GS* 7: 369n10); and in the third version, the sentence quoted from the first sentence becomes the following: "Moreover, a certain oscillation between these two polar modes of reception can be demonstrated for each work of art" [Demungeachtet läßt sich ein gewisses Oszillieren zwischen jenen beiden polaren Rezeptionsarten prinzipiell für jedes einzelne Kunstwerk aufweisen] (*SW* 4: 273n15/*GS* 1: 483n11).

7. Although Benjamin drops all references to first and second technologies as well as the notion of play in the third version of the essay (*Schein* or semblance/appearance remains as an attribute of aura—as in the famous definition of aura as "the unique appearance of a distance"), how they relate to one another does not change. Of note here, and to be discussed later, is that the moment in the second version of the essay when Benjamin evokes first and second technologies, is displaced, in the third version, into a footnote that

addresses the incidental status of the artistic function in relation to the work of art. This footnote is discussed later.

8. In an earlier text that is also concerned with the work of art, Benjamin emphasizes the role of the unconscious as an originating force for both Fichte and the early romantics: "It will prove important for the relation between the Fichtean and early Romantic theories of knowledge that the formation of the 'not-I' in the 'I' rests on an unconscious function of the latter" (*The Concept of Art in Early German Romanticism*, SW 1: 124).

9. As Benjamin notes in the fragment "The Significance of Beautiful Semblance," it is a matter of a look back in order to recover what the history of "beautiful semblance" and its "offshoots" have obscured: "This [the offshoots of beautiful appearance] should not deter the onlooker from turning his gaze back to the origin, if only to encounter there the polar concept which hitherto has been obscured by that of semblance but which is now brought clearly into the light" (*SW* 3: 137).

10. The appearance of unconscious ruse at this origin prefigures the role repeated in all three versions of the essay when distraction is invoked as the means by which film teaches the newly formed mass audience "the new tasks of apperception" that belong to Benjamin's politics of art (*SW* 4: 268).

11. The following passage from Lukács is significant given what is at stake in Benjamin's dialectical account of art's development: "The transformation of quantity into quality is not only a particular aspect of the dialectical process of development, as Hegel represents it in his philosophy of nature and, following him, Engels in the *Anti-Dühring*. But going beyond that, as we have just shown with the aid of Hegel's *Logic*, it means the emergence of the truly objective form of existence and the destruction of those confusing categories of reflection which had deformed true objectivity into a posture of merely immediate, passive, contemplation" (*History and Class-Consciousness* [Cambridge: MIT Press, 1971], 166; trans. modified).

12. This verb occurs in the same sentence throughout all the versions of the essay. Only the first version has an additional occurrence when the nominal form is used (see *GS* 1.457).

13. Hegel, *Encyclopedia der philosophischen Wissenschaften I, Logik*, §133, §81 Zusatz 1. In *Werke in Zwanzig Bänden*, ed. Eva Moldenhauer and Karl Markus Miche (Frankfurt a/ Main: Suhrkamp, 1970); translation mine.

14. After refusing the possibility of mediation between these two kinds of observation, Benjamin goes on to state that they possess an identity that "alone shows itself in the paradoxical overturning [*paradoxen Umschlagen des einem*

in das andere] of one form of observance into the other (regardless of which direction)." Rainer Nägele, in "Dialectical Materialism between Brecht and the Frankfurt School" (*The Cambridge Companion to Walter Benjamin*, ed. David Ferris [Cambridge: Cambridge University Press, 2004], 156–157), discusses both this letter and the reference to *Umschlagen* in the *Origin of the German Tragic Drama* as a paradoxical event, which occurs (in his translation of the crucial sentence from the *Origin*) as "an inversion of the extremes into one another." By relating inversion and another sense of *Umschlag*—its meaning as an envelope—to Benjamin's account of the children's game in which a sock when rolled up has the appearance of a purse containing a dowry but which when unrolled reveals that it contains nothing (see "On the Image of Proust" [*SW* 2: 239–240]), Nägele argues that the result of the inversion is to produce a third form, "a readable surface." Here, the equivalent result for such an inversion would be a "politics of art."

15. At issue here is the identity of an exhibitionability that would be different from the one that Benjamin describes as a principle of auratic art in section I of the essay. Benjamin provides several examples of this principle in section V as he compares the portability of different forms of art. As both these sections indicate, Benjamin understands the historical development of art as a movement toward ever greater portability for the work of art, a movement that makes art gravitate from one pole to the other. However, in the case of the examples cited in these sections, the significance of this movement remains comparative and quantitative.

16. In a footnote to this use of the word "incidental," Benjamin refers to "analogous reflections" undertaken by Brecht. In one of these reflections, cited by Benjamin, Brecht addresses the auratic concept of art and its reliance on the artist when he warns that "we must omit [*weglassen*] this concept with due caution but without fear, lest we liquidate the function of the very thing as well" (*SW* 4: 274n16/ *GS* 1: 484n12). But, when Brecht states, after admitting the old concept may be taken up again, "and it will be; why not?" he recognizes that the aura is to be repeatedly pushed back. For Brecht a well as Benjamin, it is a matter of neither history nor logic but the incomplete fulfillment of a demand that places art on another foundation such as politics.

17. In a long footnote to this sentence (*SW* 4: 280n39), Benjamin reiterates the claim that the work of art is always the fulfillment of a past form striving for the effects that only a future work can achieve. In this model of historical development, the work of art is always anticipatory of a form that remains concealed within it. The form of art is, in this case, the model of the kind of demand that Benjamin calls on for a politics of art. But, for this model to be

actualized, for a politics that is not just a politics represented by art, such a demand must produce more than an historically quantitative series of forms of art. Here, the demand sheltered within art would have to be more than just a demand hence Benjamin's attempt to locate, to the extent possible, a demand within film that is not just its form even if this demand can only be attributed to its form (see the fragment, "The Dialectical Structure of Film" [*SW* 3: 94–95], in which Benjamin speaks of film's form as a dialectical structure). For such a demand to be more than an internal and formal aspect in which the history of art is made manifest, then a specific form has to be capable of arresting its moment in history (a demand Benjamin will concentrate into the dialectical image). Here, a fundamental and unresolved antinomy arises in the "Work of Art" essay since it requires a demand that can only be fulfilled by the arrest of the demand to which art owes the history of its forms.

18. Heidegger does not use the word *Schlag* at all to indicate suddenness in "The Origin of the Work of Art." However, *umschlagen* is used significantly once but it is devoid of either its Hegelian or Marxist determinations. And, rather than maintain the poles between which it operates in Benjamin, *umschlagen* describes a destruction rather than a preservation: "The earth thus shatters every attempt to penetrate into it. It causes every merely calculating importunity upon it to turn into destruction. [*Die Erde läßt so jedes Eindringen in sie an ihr selbst zerschellen. Sie läßt jede nur rechnerische Zudringlichkeit in eine Zerstörung umschlagen*]" (*PLT* 47: *GA* 33).

19. Given this remark, it is difficult to agree with Christopher P. Long's assertion that Heidegger reinvigorates the aura. See Long, "Art's Fateful Hour: Benjamin, Heidegger, Art and Politics," *New German Critique* 83 (2003), 89–115.

20. This step is complicated enough in Heidegger to have later required a change in terminology, from *Überwindung* to *Verwindung*, in order to avoid any sense that what is overcome can simply be set aside and ignored. Even without such a change in terminology, such complexity is already apparent at this stage of Heidegger's thinking and it has a direct bearing on the understanding of the political in its relation to the aesthetic.

21. On the distinction of these two words for the historical in Heidegger, compare his remarks in *The Principle of Reason* where he insists that *Geschichte* refers to a history that is not turned toward the past for its meaning but toward the present because of a "fate" (*Geschick*) that "endures and motivates us today" (Bloomington, IN: Indiana University Press). The awareness of this fate, which Heidegger names the forgetting of the question of Being, is what allows this question to be asked within a history (*Geschichte*) that does not submit to this forgetting and become a history restricted to objective representation.

BIOGRAPHICAL NOTES

ANDREW BENJAMIN is Professor at Monash University, Australia, and Kingston University London. His publications include the books *Working with Walter Benjamin: Recovering a Political Philosophy* (2013), *Of Jews and Animals* (2010), *Place, Commonality and Judgment: Continental Philosophy and the Ancient Greeks* (2010), *Style and Time: Essays on the Politics of Appearance* (2006), *Disclosing Spaces: On Painting* (2004), *Present Hope: Philosophy, Architecture, Judaism* (1997), *The Plural Event* (1993), *Art, Mimesis and the Avant-Garde* (1991). He has also published several essays on Walter Benjamin and edited *Problems of Modernity. Adorno and Benjamin* (1989), *Walter Benjamin's Philosophy. Destruction and Experience* (1993), *Walter Benjamin and Art* (2005), *Walter Benjamin and History* (2005), and *Walter Benjamin and the Architecture of Modernity* (2009).

ANTONIA EGEL teaches German Literature at Albert-Ludwigs-Universität Freiburg. Her publications include the monograph *"Musik ist Schöpfung": Rilkes musikalische Poetik* (Würzburg: Ergon, 2014) as well as several articles and book chapters.

PETER FENVES is the Joan and Serapta Harrison Professor of German, Comparative Literary Studies, and Jewish Studies at Northwestern University. He is the author of several books, most recently *Late Kant: Towards Another Law of the Earth* (2003) and *The Messianic Reduction: Walter Benjamin and the Shape of Time* (2011).

ILIT FERBER is Assistant Professor of Philosophy at Tel Aviv University. She is the author of *Philosophy and Melancholy: Benjamin's Early Reflections on Theater and*

Language (Stanford University Press, 2013) and co-editor of *Philosophy's Moods: The Affective Grounds of Thinking* (Springer, 2011) and *Lament in Jewish Thought* (De Gruyter, 2014). Ferber has published articles on Leibniz, Herder, Freud, Benjamin and Scholem, and her current research focuses on the role of pain in theories of language in the writings of Rousseau, Herder, Benjamin, and Wittgenstein.

DAVID FERRIS is Professor of Humanities and Comparative Literature and Director of the Humanities Program at the University of Colorado at Boulder. He is the editor of two volumes of essays on Walter Benjamin. His publications include a number of essays on Walter Benjamin as well as the *Cambridge Introduction to Walter Benjamin*. The essay published here is part of a book entitled *Politics After Aesthetics*.

JOANNA HODGE studied for her doctorate on Heidegger and truth, at the University of Oxford, England, and in Heidelberg and Berlin. She has taught at Oxford Brookes University, the University of York, and Manchester Metropolitan University, United Kingdom, where she is currently Professor of Philosophy. She has been President of the British Society for Phenomenology, and Chair of the Society for European Philosophy (United Kingdom). Her principal monographs are *Heidegger and Ethics* (London: Routledge, Taylor and Francis 1995) and *Derrida on Time* (London: Routledge, Taylor and Francis 2007). She is currently working on two projects: *The Politics of Excription: Reading Jean-Luc Nancy*, and *Retrieving Sexual Difference: On Generative Futurity*.

A. KIARINA KORDELA is Professor of German at Macalester College, and honorary adjunct professor at the University of Western Sydney, Australia. She is the author of *$urplus: Spinoza, Lacan* (State University of New York Press, 2007), *Being, Time, Bios: Capitalism and Ontology* (State University of New York Press, 2013), and co-editor, with Dimitris Vardoulakis, of *Freedom and Confinement in Modernity: Kafka's Cages* (Palgrave-Macmillan, 2011). She has published on a wide range of topics in several collections and journals, including *Angelaki, Cultural Critique, Differences, Political Theory, Parallax, Rethinking Marxism*, and *Umbr(a)*.

GERHARD RICHTER is Professor of German Studies and Comparative Literature at Brown University, where he also is Chair of the Department of German Studies. He is the author of *Afterness: Figures of Following in Modern Thought and Aesthetics* (Columbia University Press, 2011); *Thought-Images: Frankfurt School Writers' Reflections from Damaged Life* (Stanford University Press, 2007); *Ästhetik des Ereignisses. Sprache—Geschichte—Medium* (Wilhelm Fink Verlag, 2005);

and *Walter Benjamin and the Corpus of Autobiography* (Wayne State University Press, 2000, 2nd ed., 2002). He also is the editor of *Benjamins Grenzgänge—Benjamin's Frontiers*, with Karl Solibakke and Bernd Witte (Königshausen & Neumann, 2013); Jacques Derrida, *Copy, Archive, Signature: A Conversation on Photography* (Stanford University Press, 2010); *Language without Soil: Adorno and Late Philosophical Modernity* (Fordham University Press, 2010); *Sound Figures of Modernity: German Music and Philosophy*, with Jost Hermand (University of Wisconsin Press, 2006); *Literary Paternity, Literary Friendship* (University of North Carolina Press, 2002); and *Benjamin's Ghosts: Interventions in Contemporary Literary and Cultural Theory* (Stanford University Press, 2002).

PAULA SCHWEBEL is Assistant Professor of Philosophy at Ryerson University. She is the co-editor (with Ilit Ferber) of *Lament in Jewish Thought: Philosophical, Theological and Literary Perspectives* (De Gruyter, 2014). She has also published articles and chapters on Walter Benjamin, Gershom Scholem, and Franz Rosenzweig. She is currently working on a monograph on Walter Benjamin and Leibniz, provisionally entitled *Walter Benjamin's Monadology: Expression, Finitude, and Historical Time*.

DIMITRIS VARDOULAKIS is the Chair of the Philosophy Research Initiative at the University of Western Sydney. He is the author of *The Doppelgänger* (Fordham University Press, 2010) and *Sovereignty and its Other* (Fordham University Press, 2013) and the editor of *Spinoza Now* (University of Minnesota Press, 2011).

KRZYSZTOF ZIAREK is Professor and Chair of Comparative Literature at the State University of New York at Buffalo. He is the author of *Inflected Language: Toward a Hermeneutics of Nearness* (State University of New York Press), *The Historicity of Experience: Modernity, the Avant-Garde, and the Event* (Northwestern University Press), *The Force of Art* (Stanford University Press), and *Language After Heidegger* (Indiana University Press). He has published essays on Clark Coolidge, Susan Howe, Myung Mi Kim, Stein, Stevens, Heidegger, Levinas, Adorno, Irigaray, and Benjamin, and co-edited two collection of essays, *Future Crossings: Literature Between Philosophy and Cultural Studies* (Northwestern University Press) and *Adorno and Heidegger: Philosophical Questions* (Stanford University Press). He is also the author of two books of poetry in Polish, *Zaimejlowane z Polski* and *Sąd dostateczny*.

INDEX

Adorno, Theodor, xi, 21–22, 55, 112, 191–92, 204, 213n3, 240, 253n2, 271
Aeschylus, 200
Agamben, Giorgio, 57, 73, 88, 89n13, 220
Albertinus, Aegidius, 80
Anaximander, 271
Andreas-Salomé, Lou, 54
Aquinas, Thomas, 12, 89n8
Aragon, Louis, 35
Arendt, Hannah, xi–xii, 29, 31, 57n4, 191–92, 195, 214n3
Aristotle, 3–4, 6, 23, 80, 87, 89n8, 92
Arjakovsky, Phillipe, 235–36n11
Atget, Eugène, 278n5
Augustine, 89

Baudelaire, Charles, 36, 97, 102, 106, 148, 192, 206, 214n3, 275
Baumgarten, Alexander, 46
Beethoven, Ludwig van, 49
Benjamin, Andrew, 62–63n46, 106, 114–15n40, 173n6, 222, 224–25
Benjamin, Walter
   "According to the Theory of Dun Scotus," 92n36
   The Arcades Project, xii–xiii, 34–36, 56, 93n41, 109, 131–32, 137–39, 143n22, 148–50, 155, 157–59, 161–63, 166–68, 170–71, 172nn2–3, 174n16, 197–98, 251–52

"Berlin Childhood around 1900," 59n16
"Berlin Chronicle," 36, 149, 161
"Calderón's *El Mayor Monstruo, Los Celos* and Hebbel's *Herades und Mariamne*," 85
"Central Park," 110
The Concept of Criticism in German Romanticism, xiii, 34, 37, 116n67, 142n16, 191, 240, 253n3, 254n10, 279n8
"Critique of Violence," 14, 22, 219–24
Curriculum Vitae, 133, 142n15
"The Dialectical Structure of Film," 280–81n17
Dostoevsky's *The Idiot,* 206
"Eduard Fuchs, Collector and Historian," 109
Goethe's *Elective Affinities,* 31–32, 35–36, 192, 205, 211
"Karl Krauss," 110
"The Life of Students," 10–11, 31
"A Little History of Photography," 138
"The Metaphysics of Youth," 8, 25n8
"On Language as Such and on the Language of Man," 102, 194
"On the Concept of History," 123, 132, 139–40, 157, 173n9, 247
"On the Image of Proust," 280n14
"On the Program of the Coming Philosophy," 69–71, 87, 89n10

"On Some Motifs in Baudelaire," 97, 148, 275
One-Way Street, 35, 59n18, 101
The Origin of the German Tragic Drama, 39–40, 79–84, 91n30, 92nn33–35, 93n39, 101, 105, 115n42, 117n67, 123–25, 132–39, 148, 192, 238, 266, 279–80n14
"The Return of the *Flâneur*," 37
"The Rigorous Study of Art," 30
"The Role of Language in *Trauerspiel* and Tragedy," 194–95
"The Significance of Beautiful Semblance," 279n9
"Socrates," 8
"Stages of Intention," 92n36
"The Task of the Critic," 31
"The Task of the Translator," 3, 103, 189–90, 192, 194
"Theory of Knowledge," 135–36
"Tragedy and *Trauerspiel*," 104
"Two Poems by Friedrich Hölderlin: 'The Poet's Courage' and 'Timidity,'" 178–80, 184–87, 190, 192, 194, 204, 208–09
"Word and Concept," 12
"The Work of Art in the Age of its Technological Reproducibility," 17, 30, 96, 111, 237–41, 244–46, 250–51, 254n6, 254n10, 259, 261–67, 273–76, 277n1, 278nn5–6, 278n7, 279n10, 280–81n17

Bergson, Henri, 7, 13
Berliner, Arnold, 19
Biemel, Walter, 47
Binswanger, Ludwig, 88–89n5
Bissier, Julius, 183
Blochmann, Elisabeth, 9
Bohr, Niels, 18
Bonaparte, Louis, 252, 255, 257n34
Borges, Jorge Luis, 23
Boyarin, Jonathon, 234n3
Brecht, Bertolt, xiii, 32, 67, 192, 198, 253n4, 270, 280n16
Brentano, Franz, 70, 89n8
Bröse, Sigrifried, 255n17

Carnap, Rudolf, 58n7
Cassirer, Ernst, 26n16
Caygill, Howard, 30, 88n1, 95, 103–05, 107, 111–12
Celan, Paul, 29, 57
Cohen, Hermann, 6, 132
Comay, Rebecca, 95–97, 100–03, 109–10, 114n30, 173n7
Cornelius, Hans, 21

Dallmayr, Fred, 46, 236n13
Debord, Guy, 249, 251
Derrida, Jacques, 56–57, 62n45, 114–15n40, 220, 254–55n13
Descartes, René, 55, 69, 138, 144n28, 146, 167
Dreyfus, Hubert, 61–62n38
Duns Scotus, John, 12, 81, 88n1, 92n36, 197
Dürer, Albrecht, 40, 59n24

Eckhart, Meister, 52
Eddington, Arthur Stanley, 17
Einstein, Albert, 4, 17–18, 20, 24
Elden, Stuart, 256n20
Engels, Friedrich, 279n11
Erfurt, Thomas of, 197

Faulkner, William, 201
Faye, Emmanuel, 228, 235–36n11, 236n13
Fédier, François, 235–36n11
Fenves, Peter, 124, 142n9, 256n23, 277–78n4
Fichte, Johann, 33, 240, 279n8
Ficino, Marsilio, 80, 87
Figal, Günter, 187n5
Foucault, Michel, 55–56, 215n13, 227, 245
Freud, Sigmund, 49, 80, 84, 92n32, 114n50, 143n27, 169, 191, 196, 209
Fried, Gregory, 256n21

Gasché, Rodolphe, 45, 60n32, 96, 222
George, Stefan, 181
Goethe, Johann Wolfgang von, 37, 192, 205, 254n10
Grimme, Hubert, 30

Hamacher, Werner, 68, 92–93n36, 234nn2–3
Hamburger, Michael, 193–94, 202, 206–08
Hansen, Jim, 99–100
Hanssen, Beatrice, 91n30, 190, 192–93, 204, 206–10
Haverkamp, Anselm, 234nn2–3
Hegel, Georg Wilhelm Friedrich, 23, 38–42, 107, 117n67, 146, 161, 202, 228, 237, 240, 242, 247, 254n10, 260, 265–66, 279n11, 281n18
Heidegger, Martin
  "As on the Day of Celebration," 193, 202–03
  Basic Principles of Thinking, 141n2
  The Basic Problems of Phenomenology, 69
  Basic Questions of Philosophy: Selected "Problems" of "Logic," 77
  Being and Time, xi, 5–6, 13–14, 42–43, 47, 52, 69, 71, 73–78, 90n22, 90n24, 105, 107–08, 123, 130–31, 148, 152–53, 263
  Being and Truth, 199
  "Black Notebooks," 235–36n11
  "Building, Dwelling, Thinking," 47, 50
  "The Concept of Time in Historical Scholarship," 10–11
  Contributions to Philosophy (From Enowning), 229–30, 235n11, 269–73, 275
  Das Ereignis, 230
  Die Geschichte des Seyns, 219, 225–26, 230, 232–33
  "Die Kehre," 113n3
  Duns Scotus" Doctrine of Meaning and Categories, 12, 92n36, 197
  "Elucidations of Hölderlin's Poetry," 214n6, 215n14, 238
  "European Nihilism," 21
  "The End of Philosophy and the Task of Thinking," 43–44
  "The Essence of Power," 225–28
  The Fundamental Concepts of Metaphysics: World, Finitude, Solitude, 73–74, 77, 86, 90n22
  "Hegel, über den Staat," 242, 247, 255n14, 255–56n18
  "Hölderlin and the Essence of Composing," 197
  Hölderlin's Hymn "The Ister," 193, 199, 203, 207
  "Homecoming / To Kindred Ones," 178, 180–86
  "Introduction to Metaphysics," 15–16, 199, 202–03, 226, 253n3
  "Letter on 'Humanism,'" 41
  The Metaphysical Foundations of Logic, 123–31, 141n2, 141n8
  Mindfulness, 229–31
  "The Nature of Language," 173
  "New Research into Logic," 12
  "Nietzsche as Thinker of the Completion of Metaphysics," 21
  "Nietzsche's Doctrine of the Will to Power as Knowledge," 21–22
  Nietzsche, 141n2, 151–52, 156
  "On the Way to Language," 154
  "Only a God can save us now," 192, 247
  "The Origin of the Work of Art," 47, 49–50, 184, 237–9, 241–4, 247–9, 253n3, 254–55n13, 256n21, 257n29, 260, 262–63, 269, 274–75, 277n2, 281n18
  Phenomenology of Intuition and Expression, 13
  "Poetically Man Dwells . . . ," 50
  Poetry, Language, Thought, 181, 184, 260, 262–63, 269, 274–75, 281n18
  The Principle of Reason, 281
  "The Question Concerning Technology," 50, 113n4
  "Remembrance," 192, 199, 208, 214n6
  Schelling's Treatise on the Essence of Human Freedom, xiii, 238
  "The Thing," 31, 47, 50–53
  "Time and Being," 148, 154, 155–57, 169, 172n2
  Towards the Definition of Philosophy, 13
  "Über die Sixtina," 30
  "What is a Thing?" 31, 45–48

Heidegger (*continued*)
  "What is Called Thinking?" 50
  "What is Metaphysics?" 78, 86, 91n26
  "Who is Nietzsche's Zarathustra?" 53
  Zollikon Seminars, 68, 71, 76, 88n5
Heinle, Friedrich, 5, 178
Hellingrath, Norbert von, 181
Herbertz, Richard, 143n27
Herder, Johann, 33
Héring, Jean, 133
Hessel, Franz, 35, 37
Hitler, Adolf, 180, 193, 197, 199, 208
Hoeller, Keith, 188n7, 188n11
Hölderlin, Friedrich, xiii, 29–30, 49, 53, 177–83, 185–87, 187n3, 188n11, 189–213, 215n13, 238
Horkheimer, Max, 55, 131–32, 162, 192, 240
Husserl, Edmund, xi, 12, 31, 41, 70–71, 77, 81, 87, 89n9, 90n24, 92n36, 124–29, 132–34, 141n4, 141n9, 142n17, 191–92, 197

Jung, Carl, 150
Jünger, Ernst, 235n11

Kafka, Franz, 19, 23, 35,
Kant, Immanuel, xii, 3, 6, 19, 27–28, 30–34, 42, 44–50, 52, 54–57, 69–71, 81, 87, 89n10, 95, 99, 103, 112, 117n67, 189–90, 199, 213n2, 277n3
Kimmich, Dorothea, 58n15
Kisiel, Theodore, 24n4
Klages, Ludwig, 143n27
Klee, Paul, 183
Krauss, Karl, 102

Lacan, Jacques, xii, 49, 60n36, 95, 105, 107, 109, 196–97
Lacoue-Labarthe, Philippe, 190, 193, 207–08, 211–12, 257n28,
Lang, Berel, 29
Laplanche, Jean, 215n13
Lask, Emil, 6, 24n4
Leibniz, Gottfried, xiii, 46, 123–28, 134–40, 141n2, 143n23, 143n25, 143n27, 144n28, 144nn3-31, 163–65

Levinas, Emmanuel, 100
Lingis, Alphonso, 54
Lohenstein, Daniel Caspar von, 93n39
Long, Christopher P., 281n19
Ludz, Ursula, 57
Lukács, György, 265, 279n11

Macquarrie, John, 90n18
Man, Paul de, 99–100, 117n67
Marcuse, Herbert, 41
Marion, Jean-Luc, 69, 74
Marx, Karl, xii-iii, 16, 30, 41–42, 55–56, 95–101, 109, 114n30, 250–52, 260, 265, 281n18
Menninghaus, Winifried, 116–18n67
Montag, Warren, 114–15n40
Moore, Gerald, 119n80
Müller, Anton, 5
Musil, Robert, 25n11

Nägele, Rainer, 279–80n14
Natorp, Paul, 132
Nietzsche, Friedrich, 7, 21–22, 53, 85, 131, 141n2, 151–52, 190, 192–95, 198–99, 208, 210, 212, 227, 271, 273
Novalis (von Hardenberg, Friedrich), 34, 97, 240

Pensky, Max, 93n38
Peter, Klaus, 116–18n67
Pindar, 198, 206
Plato, 43, 50, 79, 110, 132, 137–38, 259, 273
Podolsky, Boris, 18, 20
Pope Pius X, 12
Proust, Marcel, 35, 206

Quine, Willard Van Orman, 58n7

Ranke, Leopold von, 161
Reichenbach, Hans, 18
Reijen, Willem van, 62–63n46
Rickert, Heinrich, xii, 3, 5–16, 21, 24nn3-5, 25nn6-7, 25n11, 26n14, 26n16, 197
Rilke, Rainer Maria, 53–54
Robinson, Edward, 90n18
Rodin, Auguste, 54

Rosen, Nathan, 18, 20
Rush, Fred, 115n42, 116–18n67

Sallis, John, 54
Sauer, Joseph, 12
Saussure, Ferdinand de, 97–98
Schelling, Friedrich Wilhelm Joseph von, xiii, 113n10, 116–18n67, 199, 238
Schiller, Johann Christoph Friedrich von, 192
Schlegel, Friedrich, 32–34, 97, 118n67
Schlemmer, Oskar, 183
Schmitt, Carl, xiii, 242–47, 255n15, 256n19–21, 257n27
Scholem, Gershom, xii–xiii, 4, 12–13, 24n4, 29, 32, 67, 131, 148, 192, 197, 198, 214n3, 266
Schrödinger, Erwin, 4, 18–20, 23
Scott, Charles E., 60–61n37
Seligson, Carla, 8–9, 25n11
Seligson, Rika, 178
Sophocles, 189, 194, 196, 198–200, 202, 206, 213

Spitzer, Leo, 72
Steinbock, Anthony, 141n4
Steiner, Uwe, 58n10
Swoyer, Chris, 144n30

Urbino, Raffaello Sanzio da, 30

Van Gogh, Vincent, 49

Walser, Robert, 35
Weber, Samuel, 37, 82, 88n1, 189–90, 199, 207
Weller, Shane, 187n3
Wigan, Willard, 54
Windelband, Wilhelm, 21
Wohlfarth, Irving, 101
Wolf, Erik, 255n14
Wyneken, Gustav, 5, 8–9

Zimmer, Ernst, 191

www.ingramcontent.com/pod-product-compliance
Ingram Content Group UK Ltd.
Pitfield, Milton Keynes, MK11 3LW, UK
UKHW041854111225
465990UK00015B/75